Deep Reinforcement Learning Hands-On

Apply modern RL methods, with deep Q-networks, value iteration, policy gradients, TRPO, AlphaGo Zero and more

Maxim Lapan

BIRMINGHAM - MUMBAI

Deep Reinforcement Learning Hands-On

Acquisition Editors: Frank Pohlmann, Suresh Jain
Project Editor: Kishor Rit
Technical Editor: Nidhisha Shetty
Proofreader: Tom Jacob
Indexer: Tejal Daruwale Soni
Graphics: Sandip Tadge
Production Coordinator: Shantanu Zagade

First published: June 2018

Production reference: 1150618

Published by Packt Publishing Ltd.
Livery Place
35 Livery Street
Birmingham B3 2PB, UK.

ISBN 978-1-78883-424-7

www.packtpub.com

`mapt.io`

Mapt is an online digital library that gives you full access to over 5,000 books and videos, as well as industry leading tools to help you plan your personal development and advance your career. For more information, please visit our website.

Why subscribe?

- Spend less time learning and more time coding with practical eBooks and Videos from over 4,000 industry professionals

- Learn better with Skill Plans built especially for you

- Get a free eBook or video every month

- Mapt is fully searchable

- Copy and paste, print, and bookmark content

PacktPub.com

Did you know that Packt offers eBook versions of every book published, with PDF and ePub files available? You can upgrade to the eBook version at `www.PacktPub.com` and as a print book customer, you are entitled to a discount on the eBook copy. Get in touch with us at `service@packtpub.com` for more details.

At `www.PacktPub.com`, you can also read a collection of free technical articles, sign up for a range of free newsletters, and receive exclusive discounts and offers on Packt books and eBooks.

Contributors

About the author

Maxim Lapan is a deep learning enthusiast and independent researcher. His background and 15 years' work expertise as a software developer and a systems architect lays from low-level Linux kernel driver development to performance optimization and design of distributed applications working on thousands of servers. With vast work experiences in big data, Machine Learning, and large parallel distributed HPC and nonHPC systems, he has a talent to explain a gist of complicated things in simple words and vivid examples. His current areas of interest lie in practical applications of Deep Learning, such as Deep Natural Language Processing and Deep Reinforcement Learning.

Maxim lives in Moscow, Russian Federation, with his family, and he works for an Israeli start-up as a Senior NLP developer.

I'd like to thank my family: wife Olga and kids Ksenia, Julia, and Fedor, for patience and support. It was a challenging time, writing this book and it wouldn't be possible without you, thanks! Julia and Fedor did a great job gathering samples for MiniWoB (Chapter 13, *Web Navigation*) and testing ConnectFour agent's playing skills (Chapter 18, *AlphaGo Zero*).

I also want to thank the technical reviewers, Oleg Vasilev and Mikhail Yurushkin, for their valuable comments and suggestions about the book contents.

About the reviewers

Basem O. F. Alijla received his Ph.D. degree in intelligent systems from USM, Malaysia, in 2015. He is currently an assistant professor with Software Development Department, IUG in Palestine. He has authored number of technical papers published in journals and international conferences. His current research interest include, Optimization, Machine Learning, and Data mining.

Oleg Vasilev is a professional with a background in Computer Science and Data Engineering. His university program is Applied Mathematics and Informatics in NRU HSE, Moscow, with a major in Distributed Systems. He is a staff member on a Git-course, Practical_RL and Practical_DL, taught on-campus in HSE and YSDA. Oleg's previous work experience includes working in Dialog Systems Group, Yandex, as Data Scientist. He currently holds a position of Vice President of Infrastructure Management in GoTo Lab, an educational corporation, and he works for Digital Contact as a software engineer.

> I'd like to thank Alexander Panin (`@justheuristic`), my mentor, for opening the world of Machine Learning to me. I am deeply grateful to other Russian researchers who helped me in mastering Computer Science: *Pavel Shvechikov, Alexander Grishin, Valery Kharitonov, Alexander Fritzler, Pavel Ostyakov, Michail Konobeev, Dmitrii Vetrov*, and *Alena Ilyna*. I also want to thank my friends and family for their kind support.

Mikhail Yurushkin holds a PhD in Applied Mathematics. His areas of research are high performance computing and optimizing compilers development. He was involved in the development of a state-of-the-art optimizing parallelizing compiler system. Mikhail is a senior lecturer at SFEDU university, Rostov on Don, Russia. He teaches advanced DL courses, namely Computer Vision and NLP. Mikhail has worked for over 7 years in cross-platform native C++ development, machine learning, and deep learning. Now he works as an individual consultant in ML/DL fields.

Packt is Searching for Authors Like You

If you're interested in becoming an author for Packt, please visit `authors.packtpub.com` and apply today. We have worked with thousands of developers and tech professionals, just like you, to help them share their insight with the global tech community. You can make a general application, apply for a specific hot topic that we are recruiting an author for, or submit your own idea.

Table of Contents

Preface

The topic of this book is Reinforcement Learning—which is a subfield of Machine Learning—focusing on the general and challenging problem of learning optimal behavior in complex environment. The learning process is driven only by reward value and observations obtained from the environment. This model is very general and can be applied to many practical situations from playing games to optimizing complex manufacture processes.

Due to flexibility and generality, the field of Reinforcement Learning is developing very quickly and attracts lots of attention both from researchers trying to improve existing or create new methods, as well as from practitioners interested in solving their problems in the most efficient way.

This book was written as an attempt to fill the obvious lack of practical and structured information about Reinforcement Learning methods and approaches. On one hand, there are lots of research activity all around the world, new research papers are being published almost every day, and a large portion of Deep Learning conferences such as NIPS or ICLR is dedicated to RL methods. There are several large research groups focusing on RL methods application in Robotics, Medicine, multi-agent systems, and others. The information about the recent research is widely available, but is too specialized and abstract to be understandable without serious efforts. Even worse is the situation with the practical aspect of RL application, as it is not always obvious how to make a step from the abstract method described in the mathematical-heavy form in a research paper to a working implementation solving actual problem. This makes it hard for somebody interested in the field to get an intuitive understanding of methods and ideas behind papers and conference talks. There are some very good blog posts about various RL aspects illustrated with working examples, but the limited format of a blog post allows the author to describe only one or two methods without building a complete structured picture and showing how different methods are related to each other. This book is my attempt to address this issue.

Another aspect of the book is its orientation to practice. Every method is implemented for various environments, from very trivial to quite complex. I've tried to make examples clean and easy to understand, which was made possible by the expressiveness and power of PyTorch. On the other hand, complexity and requirements of examples are oriented to RL hobbyists without access to very large computational resources, such as clusters of GPUs or very powerful workstations. This, I believe, will make the fun-filled and exciting RL domain accessible for a much wider audience than just research groups or large AI companies. However, it is still **Deep** Reinforcement Learning, so, having access to a GPU is highly recommended. Approximately, half of the examples in the book will benefit from running them on GPU. In addition to traditional medium-sized examples of environments used in RL, such as Atari games or continuous control problems, the book contains three chapters (8, 12, and 13) that contain larger projects, illustrating how RL methods could be applied to more complicated environments and tasks. These examples are still not full-sized real-life projects (otherwise they'll occupy a separate book on their own), but just larger problems illustrating how the RL paradigm can be applied to domains beyond well-established benchmarks.

Another thing to note about examples in the first three parts of the book is that I've tried to make examples self-contained and the source code was shown in full. Sometimes this led to repetition of code pieces (for example, training loop is very similar in most of the methods), but I believe that giving you the freedom to jump directly into the method you want to learn is more important than avoiding few repetitions. All examples in the book is available on Github: `https://github.com/PacktPublishing/Deep-Reinforcement-Learning-Hands-On`, and you're welcome to fork them, experiment, and contribute.

Who this book is for

The main target audience are people who have some knowledge in Machine Learning, but interested to get a practical understanding of the Reinforcement Learning domain. A reader should be familiar with Python and the basics of deep learning and machine learning. Understanding of statistics and probability will be a plus, but is not absolutely essential for understanding most of the book's material.

What this book covers

Chapter 1, What is Reinforcement Learning?, contains introduction to RL ideas and main formal models.

Chapter 2, OpenAI Gym, introduces the reader to the practical aspect of RL, using open-source library gym.

Chapter 3, Deep Learning with PyTorch, gives a quick overview of the PyTorch library.

Chapter 4, The Cross-Entropy Method, introduces you to one of the simplest methods of RL to give you the feeling of RL methods and problems.

Chapter 5, Tabular Learning and the Bellman Equation, gives an introduction to the Value-based family of RL methods.

Chapter 6, Deep Q-Networks, describes DQN, the extension of basic Value-based methods, allowing to solve complicated environment.

Chapter 7, DQN Extensions, gives a detailed overview of modern extension to the DQN method, to improve its stability and convergence in complex environments.

Chapter 8, Stocks Trading Using RL, is the first practical project, applying the DQN method to stock trading.

Chapter 9, Policy Gradients – An Alternative, introduces another family of RL methods, based on policy learning.

Chapter 10, The Actor-Critic Method, describes one of the most widely used method in RL.

Chapter 11, Asynchronous Advantage Actor-Critic, extends Actor-Critic with parallel environment communication, to improve stability and convergence.

Chapter 12, Chatbots Training with RL, is the second project, showing how to apply RL methods to NLP problems.

Chapter 13, Web Navigation, is another long project, applying RL to web page navigation, using MiniWoB set of tasks.

Chapter 14, Continuous Action Space, describes the specifics of environments, using continuous action spaces and various methods.

Chapter 15, Trust Regions – TRPO, PPO, and ACKTR, is yet another chapter about continuous action spaces describing "Trust region" set of methods.

Chapter 16, Black-Box Optimization in RL, shows another set of methods that don't use gradients in explicit form.

Chapter 17, Beyond Model-Free – Imagination, introduces model-based approach to RL, using recent research results about imagination in RL.

Chapter 18, AlphaGo Zero, describes the AlphaGo Zero method applied to game Connect Four.

To get the most out of this book

All chapters in the book describing RL methods have the same structure: in the beginning we discuss the motivation of the method, its theoretical foundation, and intuition behind it. Then, we follow several examples of the method applied to different environment with full source code. So, you can use the book in different ways:

1. To quickly become familiar with some method of methods you can read only introductory part of the relevant chapter or chapter's section.

2. To get deeper understanding of the way method is implemented you can read the code and the comments around.

3. To gain deep familiarity with the method (the best way to learn, I believe) you should try to reimplement the method and make it working, using provided source code as a reference point.

In any case, I hope the book will be useful for you!

Download the example code files

You can download the example code files for this book from your account at http://www.packtpub.com. If you purchased this book elsewhere, you can visit http://www.packtpub.com/support and register to have the files emailed directly to you.

You can download the code files by following these steps:

1. Log in or register at http://www.packtpub.com.

2. Select the **SUPPORT** tab.

3. Click on **Code Downloads & Errata**.

4. Enter the name of the book in the **Search** box and follow the on-screen instructions.

Once the file is downloaded, please make sure that you unzip or extract the folder using the latest version of:

- WinRAR / 7-Zip for Windows
- Zipeg / iZip / UnRarX for Mac
- 7-Zip / PeaZip for Linux

The code bundle for the book is also hosted on GitHub at `https://github.com/PacktPublishing/Deep-Reinforcement-Learning-Hands-On`. We also have other code bundles from our rich catalog of books and videos available at `https://github.com/PacktPublishing/`. Check them out!

Download the color images

We also provide a PDF file that has color images of the screenshots/diagrams used in this book. You can download it here: `https://www.packtpub.com/sites/default/files/downloads/DeepReinforcementLearningHandsOn_ColorImages.pdf`.

Conventions used

There are a number of text conventions used throughout this book.

`CodeInText`: Indicates code words in text, database table names, folder names, filenames, file extensions, pathnames, dummy URLs, user input, and Twitter handles. For example; "The method `get_observation()` is supposed to return to the agent the current environment's observation."

A block of code is set as follows:

```
def get_actions(self):
    return [0, 1]
```

When we wish to draw your attention to a particular part of a code block, the relevant lines or items are set in bold:

```
def get_actions(self):
    return [0, 1]
```

Any command-line input or output is written as follows:

```
$ xvfb-run -s "-screen 0 640x480x24" python 04_cartpole_random_monitor.py
```

Bold: Indicates a new term, an important word, or words that you see on the screen, for example, in menus or dialog boxes, also appear in the text like this. For example: "In practice it's some piece of code, which implements some **policy**."

Get in touch

Feedback from our readers is always welcome.

General feedback: Email feedback@packtpub.com, and mention the book's title in the subject of your message. If you have questions about any aspect of this book, please email us at questions@packtpub.com.

Errata: Although we have taken every care to ensure the accuracy of our content, mistakes do happen. If you have found a mistake in this book we would be grateful if you would report this to us. Please visit, http://www.packtpub.com/submit-errata, selecting your book, clicking on the Errata Submission Form link, and entering the details.

Piracy: If you come across any illegal copies of our works in any form on the Internet, we would be grateful if you would provide us with the location address or website name. Please contact us at copyright@packtpub.com with a link to the material.

If you are interested in becoming an author: If there is a topic that you have expertise in and you are interested in either writing or contributing to a book, please visit http://authors.packtpub.com.

Reviews

Please leave a review. Once you have read and used this book, why not leave a review on the site that you purchased it from? Potential readers can then see and use your unbiased opinion to make purchase decisions, we at Packt can understand what you think about our products, and our authors can see your feedback on their book. Thank you!

For more information about Packt, please visit packtpub.com.

1
What is Reinforcement Learning?

Reinforcement Learning is a subfield of machine learning which addresses the problem of automatic learning of optimal decisions over time. This is a general and common problem studied in many scientific and engineering fields.

In our changing world, even problems which look like static input-output problems become dynamic in a larger perspective. For example, consider that you're solving the simple supervised learning problem of pet image classification with two target classes—dog and cat. You've gathered the training dataset and implemented the classifier using your favorite deep learning toolkit, and after a while, the model that has converged demonstrates excellent performance. Good? Definitely! You've deployed it and left it running for a while. Then, after a vacation on some seaside resort, you discover that dog haircut fashions have changed, and a significant portion of your queries are now misclassified, so you need to update your training images and repeat the process again. Good? Definitely not!

The preceding example is intended to show that even simple **Machine Learning (ML)** problems have a hidden time dimension, which is frequently overlooked, but it might become an issue in a production system.

Reinforcement Learning (RL) is an approach that natively incorporates this extra dimension (which is usually time, but not necessarily) into learning equations, which puts it much close to the human perception of artificial intelligence. In this chapter, we will become familiar with the following:

- How RL is related to and differs from other ML disciplines: supervised and unsupervised learning
- What the main RL formalisms are and how they are related to each other
- Theoretical foundations of RL: the Markov decision processes

Learning – supervised, unsupervised, and reinforcement

You may be familiar with the notion of supervised learning, which is the most studied and well-known machine learning problem. Its basic question is: how do you automatically build a function that maps some input into some output, when given a set of example pairs? It sounds simple in those terms, but the problem includes many tricky questions that computers have only recently started to deal with some success. There are lots of examples of supervised learning problems, including the following:

- **Text classification**: Is this email message spam or not?
- **Image classification and object location**: Does this image contain a picture of a cat, dog, or something else?
- **Regression problems**: Given the information from weather sensors, what will be the weather tomorrow?
- **Sentiment analysis**: What's the customer satisfaction level of this review?

These questions can look different, but they share the same idea: we have many examples of the input and desired output, and we want to learn how to generate the output for some future, currently unseen inputs. The name, *supervised* comes from the fact that we learn from the known answers, which were obtained from some supervisor who has provided us with those labeled examples.

At the other extreme, we have the so-called unsupervised learning, which assumes no supervision that has no known labels assigned to our data. The main objective is to learn some hidden structure of the dataset at hand. One common example of such an approach to learning is the clustering of data. This happens when our algorithm tries to combine data items into a set of clusters, which can reveal relationships in data.

Another unsupervised learning method that is becoming more and more popular is, **Generative Adversarial Networks (GANs)**. When we have two competing neural networks, the first of them is trying to generate *fake data* to fool the second network, while the other is trying to discriminate artificially generated data from data sampled from our dataset. Over time, both of them are becoming more and more skillful in their tasks by capturing subtle specific patterns of your dataset.

RL is the third camp and lays somewhere in between full supervision and a complete lack of predefined labels. On the one hand, it uses many well-established methods of supervised learning such as deep neural networks for function approximation, stochastic gradient descent, and backpropagation, to learn data representation. On the other hand, it usually applies them in a different way.

In the next two sections of the chapter, we'll have the chance to explore specific details of the RL approach including its assumptions and abstractions in its strict mathematical form. For now, to compare RL to supervised and unsupervised learning, we'll take a less formal, but more intuitive description.

Imagine you have an agent that needs to take actions in some environment. A robot mouse in a maze is a good example, but we can also imagine an automatic helicopter trying to make a roll, or a chess program learning how to beat a grandmaster. Let's go with the robot mouse for simplicity.

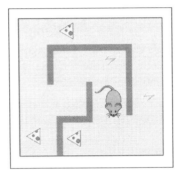

Figure 1: Robot mouse maze world

Its environment is a maze with food at some points and electricity at others. The robot mouse can take actions such as turn left/right and move forward. Finally, at every moment it can observe the full state of the maze to make a decision about the actions it may take. It is trying to find as much food as possible, while avoiding an electric shock whenever possible. These food and electricity signals stand as a reward given to the agent by the environment as additional feedback about the agent's actions. The reward is a very important concept in RL, and we'll talk about it later in the chapter. For now, it will be enough to understand that the final goal of the agent is to get as much total reward as possible. In our particular example, the mouse could suffer a bit of an electric shock to get to the place with plenty of food—this will be a better result for the mouse than just standing still and gaining nothing.

We don't want to hard-code knowledge about the environment and the best actions to take in every specific situation into the robot—it will take too much effort and may become useless even with a slight maze change. What we want to do is to have some magic set of methods that will allow our robot to learn on its own how to avoid electricity and gather as much food as possible.

Reinforcement Learning is exactly this magic toolbox, which plays differently from supervised and unsupervised learning methods. It doesn't work with predefined labels as supervised learning does. Nobody labels all the images the robot sees as *good* or *bad* or gives it the best direction to turn in.

However, we're not completely blind as in an unsupervised learning setup—we have a reward system. Rewards can be positive from gathering the food, negative from electric shocks, or neutral when nothing special happens. By observing such a reward and relating it to the actions we've taken, our agent learns how to perform an action better, gather more food, and get fewer electric shocks.

Of course, RL generality and flexibility comes with a price. RL is considered to be a much more challenging area than supervised and unsupervised learning. Let's quickly discuss what makes Reinforcement Learning tricky.

The first thing to note is that observation in RL depends on an agent's behavior and to some extent, it is the *result* of their behavior. If your agent decides to do inefficient things, then the observations will tell you nothing about what they have done wrong and what should be done to improve the outcome (the agent will just get negative feedback all the time). If the agent is stubborn and keeps making mistakes, then the observations can make the false impression that there is no way to get a larger reward—*life is suffering*—which could be totally wrong. In machine learning terms, it can be rephrased as *having non-i.i.d data*. The abbreviation **i.i.d** stands for **independent and identically distributed**, a requirement for most supervised learning methods.

The second thing that complicates our agent's life is that they need to not only **exploit** the policy they have learned, but to actively **explore** the environment, because, who knows, maybe by doing things differently we can significantly improve the outcome we get. The problem is that too much exploration may also seriously decrease the reward (not to mention that the agent can actually *forget* what they have learned before), so, we need to find a balance between these two activities somehow. This exploration/exploitation dilemma is one of the open fundamental questions in RL.

People face this choice all the time: should I go to an already known place for dinner or try this new fancy restaurant? How frequently should you change jobs? Should you study a new field or keep working in your area? There are no universal answers to these questions.

The third complication factor lays in the fact that reward can be seriously delayed from actions. In cases of chess, it can be one single strong move in the middle of the game that has shifted the balance. During learning, we need to discover such casualties, which can be tricky to do over the flow of time and our actions.

However, despite all these obstacles and complications, RL has made huge improvements over recent years and is becoming more and more active as a field of research and practical application.

Interested? Let's get to the details and look at RL formalisms and play rules.

RL formalisms and relations

Every scientific and engineering field has its own assumptions and limitations. In the previous section, we discussed supervised learning, in which such assumptions are the knowledge of input-output pairs. No labels for your data? Sorry, you need to figure out how to obtain labels or try to use some other theory. It doesn't make supervised learning *good* or *bad*, it just makes it inapplicable to your problem. It's important to know and understand those *play rules* for various methods, as it can save you tons of time in advance. However, we know there are many examples of practical and theoretical breakthroughs, when somebody tried to challenge the rules in a creative way. To do this you should first of all know the limitations.

Of course, such formalisms exist for RL, and now it is the right time to introduce them, as we'll spend the rest of the book analyzing them from various angles. You can see the following diagram showing two major RL entities: **Agent** and **Environment** and their communication channels: **Actions**, **Reward**, and **Observations**:

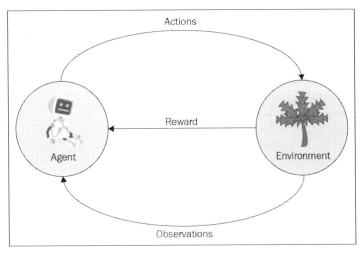

Figure 2: RL entities and their communications

Reward

The first thing to discuss is a notion of reward. In RL, it's just a scalar value we obtain periodically from the environment. It can be positive or negative, large or small, but it's just a number. The purpose of reward is to tell our agent how well they have behaved. We don't define how frequently the agent receives this reward; it can be every second or once in a lifetime, although it's common practice to receive a reward every fixed timestamp or every environment interaction, just for convenience. In the case of once-in-a-lifetime reward systems, all rewards except the last one will be zero.

As I mentioned, the purpose of a reward is to give an agent feedback about its success, and it's an important central thing in RL. Basically, the term *reinforcement* comes from the fact that a reward obtained by an agent should reinforce its behavior in a positive or negative way. Reward is *local*, meaning, it reflects the success of the agent's recent activity, not all the successes achieved by the agent so far. Of course, getting a large reward for some action doesn't mean that a second later you won't face dramatic consequences from your previous decisions. It's like robbing a bank: it could look like a good idea until you think about the consequences.

What an agent is trying to achieve is the largest *accumulated* reward over its sequence of actions. To give you a more intuitive understanding of reward, let's list some concrete examples with their rewards:

- **Financial trading**: An amount of profit is a reward for a trader buying and selling stocks.

- **Chess**: Here, reward is obtained at the end of the game, as a win, lose, or draw. Of course, it's up to interpretation. For me, for example, having a draw in a match against a chess master would be a huge reward. In practice, we need to explicitly specify the exact reward value, but it could be a fairly complicated expression. For instance, in case of chess, the reward could be proportional to the opponent's strength.

- **Dopamine system in a brain**: There is a part in the brain (limbic system) that produces dopamine every time it needs to send a positive signal to the rest of the brain. Higher concentrations of dopamine lead to a sense of pleasure, which reinforces activities considered by this system as *good*. Unfortunately, the limbic system is *ancient* in terms of things it considers good: food, reproduction, and dominance, but this is a totally different story.

- **Computer games**: They usually give obvious feedback to the player, which is either the number of enemies killed or a score gathered. Note in this example that reward is already accumulated, so the RL reward for arcade games should be the derivative of the score, that is, +1 every time a new enemy is killed and 0 at all other time steps.

- **Web navigation**: There is a set of problems with high practical value, which is to be able to automatically extract information present on the web. Search engines are trying to solve this task in general, but sometimes, to get to the data you're looking for you need to fill some forms or navigate through series of links, or complete captchas, which can be difficult for search engines to do. There is an RL-based approach to those tasks, in which the reward is the information or the outcome you need to get.

- **Neural network architecture search**: RL has been successfully applied to the domain of NN architecture optimization, where the aim is to get the best performance metric on some dataset by tweaking the number of layers or their parameters, adding extra bypass connections, or making other changes to the neural network architecture. The reward in this case is the performance (accuracy or another measure showing how accurate the NN predictions are).

- **Dog training**: If you have ever tried to train a dog, you know that you need to give it something tasty (but too not much) every time it does the thing you've asked. It's also common to punish your pet a bit (negative reward) when it doesn't follow your orders, although recent studies have shown this isn't as effective as positive rewards.

- **School marks**: We all have experience here! School marks are a reward system to give pupils feedback about their studying.

As you can see from the preceding examples, the notion of reward is a very general indication of the agent's performance, and it can be found or artificially injected into lots of practical problems around us.

The agent

An agent is somebody or something who/which interacts with the environment by executing certain actions, taking observations, and receiving eventual rewards for this. In most practical RL scenarios, it's our piece of software that is supposed to solve some problem in a more-or-less efficient way. For our initial set of six examples, the agents will be one of these:

- **Financial trading**: A trading system or a trader making decisions about order execution

- **Chess**: A player or a computer program

- **Dopamine system**: The brain itself, according to sensory data, decides if it was a good experience or bad

- **Computer games**: The player who enjoys the game or the computer program (*Andrey Karpathy* once stated in his tweet, "We were supposed to make AI do all the work and we play games but we do all the work and the AI is playing games!")

- **Web navigation**: The software that tells the browser which links to click on, where to move the mouse, or which text to enter

- **Neural network architecture search**: The software that controls the concrete architecture of the neural network being evaluated
- **Dog training**: Your beloved pet
- **School**: Student/pupil

The environment

The environment is everything outside of an agent. In the most general sense, it's the rest of the universe, but this goes slightly overboard and exceeds the capacity of even tomorrow's computers, so we usually follow the general sense here.

The environment is external to an agent, and its communication with the environment is limited by rewards (obtained from the environment), actions (executed by the agent and given to the environment), and observations (some information besides the rewards that the agent receives from the environment). We discussed rewards already, so let's talk about actions and observations.

Actions

Actions are things that an agent can do in the environment. Actions can be moves allowed by the rules of play (if it's some game), or it can be doing homework (in the case of school). They can be simple such as *move pawn one space forward*, or complicated such as *fill the tax form in for tomorrow morning*.

In RL, we distinguish between two types of actions: discrete or continuous. Discrete actions form the finite set of mutually exclusive things an agent could do, such as move left or right. Continuous actions have some value attached to the action, such as a car's action *steer the wheel* having an angle and direction of steering. Different angles could lead to a different scenario a second later, so just saying *steer the wheel* is definitely not enough.

Observations

Observations of the environment is the second information channel for an agent, with the first being a reward. You may be wondering, why do we need a separate data source? The answer is convenience. Observations are pieces of information that the environment provides the agent with, which say what's going on around them. It may be relevant to the upcoming reward (such as seeing a bank notification saying, *You have been paid*) or not. Observations even can include reward information in some vague or obfuscated form, such as score numbers on a computer game's screen. Score numbers are just pixels, but potentially we can convert them into reward values; it's not a big deal with modern deep learning at hand.

On the other hand, reward shouldn't be seen as a secondary or unimportant thing: the reward is the main force that drives the agent's learning process. If the reward is made wrong, noisy, or just slightly off-course of the primary objective, then there is a chance that training will go in a wrong way.

It's also important to distinguish between an environment's state and observations. The state of an environment potentially includes every atom in the universe, which makes it impossible to measure everything about the environment. Even if we limit the environment's state to be small enough, most of the time it's either still not possible to get full information or our measurements will contain noise. This is completely fine though, and RL was created to support such cases natively. Once again, let's support our intuition with our set of examples to capture the difference:

- **Financial trading**: Here the environment is the whole financial market and everything that influences it. This is a huge list of things such as the latest news, economic and political conditions, weather, food supplies, and Twitter trends. Even your decision to stay home today can potentially indirectly influence the world financial system. However, our observations are limited to stock prices, news, and so on. We don't have access to most of the environment's state, which makes trading such a nontrivial thing.

- **Chess**: The environment here is your board *plus* your opponent, which includes their chess skills, mood, brain state, chosen tactics, and so on. Observation is what you see (your current chess position), but, I guess, at some levels of play mastery, the knowledge of psychology and ability to read an opponent's mood could increase your chances.

- **Dopamine system**: The environment here is your brain PLUS nervous system and organ's states PLUS the whole world you can perceive. Observations are the inner brain state and signals coming from your senses.

- **Computer game**: Here, the environment is your computer's state, including all memory and disk data. For networked games, you need to include other computers PLUS all internet infrastructure between them and your machine. Observations are a screen's pixels and sound, that's it. A screen's pixels is not a tiny amount of information (somebody calculated that the total number of possible moderate-size images 1024 × 768 is significantly larger than the number of atoms in our galaxy), but the whole environment state is definitely larger.

- **Web navigation**: The environment here is the internet, including all the network infrastructure between the computer our agent works and the web server, which is a really huge system that includes millions and millions of different components. Observation is normally the web page that is loaded at the current navigation step.

- **Neural network architecture search**: In this example, the environment is fairly simple and includes the NN toolkit that performs the particular neural network evaluation and the dataset that is used to obtain the performance metric. In comparison to the internet, this looks like a tiny toy environment. Observations might be different and include some information about the testing, such as loss convergence dynamics or other metrics obtained from the evaluation step.

- **Dog training**: Here the environment is your dog (including its hardly observable inner reactions, mood, and life experiences) and everything around it, including other dogs and a cat hiding in a bush. Observations are signals from your senses and memory.

- **School**: The environment here is the school itself, the education system of the country, society, and the cultural legacy. Observations are the same as for the dog training: the student's senses and memory.

This is our mise en scène and we'll play around with it in the rest of the book. I think you've already noticed that the RL model is extremely flexible, general, and could be applied to a variety of scenarios. Let's look at how RL is related to other disciplines, before diving into the details of RL's model.

There are many other areas that contribute or relate to RL. The most significant are shown in the following diagram (taken from *David Silver's* RL course http://www0.cs.ucl.ac.uk/staff/d.silver/web/Teaching.html), which includes six large domains heavily overlapping each other on the methods and specific topics related to decision making (shown inside the inner gray circle). In the intersection of all those related, but still different scientific areas, sits RL, which is so general and flexible that it can take the best from these varying domains:

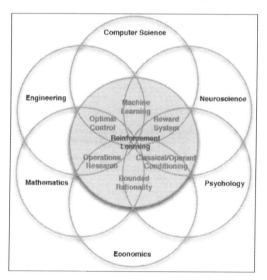

Figure 3: Various domains in RL

- **Machine learning (ML)**: RL, being a subfield of ML, borrows lots of its machinery, tricks, and techniques from ML. Basically, the goal of RL is to learn how an agent should behave when it is given imperfect observational data.

- **Engineering (especially optimal control)**: This helps in taking a sequence of optimal actions to get the best result.

- **Neuroscience**: We saw the dopamine system as our example, and it has been shown that the human brain acts closely to the RL model.

- **Psychology**: This studies behavior in various conditions, such as how people react and adapt, which is close to the RL topic.

- **Economics**: One of the important topics is how to maximize reward in terms of imperfect knowledge and the changing conditions of the real world.

- **Mathematics**: This works with idealized systems, and also devotes significant attention to finding and reaching the optimal conditions in the field of operations research.

Markov decision processes

In this part of the chapter, we'll get familiar with the theoretical foundation of RL, which makes it possible to start moving toward the methods used to solve the RL problem. This section is important to understand the rest of the book and will ensure that you familiarize yourself with RL. First, we introduce you to the mathematical representation and notation of formalisms (reward, agent, actions, observations, and environment) we just discussed. Second, using this basis, we introduce you to the second-order notions of the *RL language* including state, episode, history, value, and gain, which will be used repeatedly to describe different methods later in the book. Finally, our description of Markov decision processes is built like a Russian matryoshka doll: we start from the simplest case of a **Markov Process** (**MP**) (also known as a Markov chain), then extend it with rewards, which will turn it into a Markov reward processes. Then we'll put this idea into one other extra envelope by adding actions, which will lead us to **Markov Decision Processes** (**MDPs**).

Markov processes and Markov decision processes are widely used in computer science and other engineering fields. So reading this chapter will be useful for you not only in RL contexts but also for a much wider range of topics.

If you're already familiar with MDPs, then you can quickly skim this chapter, paying attention only to the terminology definitions, as we'll use them later on.

Markov process

Let's start with the simplest child of the Markov family: the **Markov process**, also known as a **Markov chain**. Imagine that you have some system in front of you that you can only observe. What you observe is called **states**, and the system can switch between states according to some laws of dynamics. Again, you cannot influence the system, but only watch the states changing.

All possible states for a system form a set called *state space*. In Markov processes, we require this set of states to be finite (but it can be extremely large to compensate this limitation). Your observations form a sequence of states or a *chain* (that's why Markov processes are also called Markov chains). For example, looking at the simplest model of the weather in some city, we can observe the current day as *sunny* or *rainy*, which is our state space. A sequence of observations over time forms a chain of states, such as [*sunny, sunny, rainy, sunny, …*], and is called **history**.

To call such a system a MP, it needs to fulfil the **Markov property**, which means that the future system dynamics from any state have to depend on this state only. The main point of the Markov property is to make every observable state self-contained to describe the future of the system. In other words, the Markov property requires the states of the system to be distinguishable from each other and unique. In this case, only one state is required to model the future dynamics of the system, not the whole history or, say, the last N states.

In the case of our *toy weather* example, the Markov property limits our model to represent only the cases when a sunny day can be followed by a rainy one, with the same probability, regardless of the amount of sunny days we've seen in the past. It's not a very realistic model, as from common sense we know that the chance of rain tomorrow depends not only on the current condition, but on a large number of other factors, such as the season, our latitude, and the presence of mountains and sea nearby. It was recently proven that even solar activity has a major influence on weather. So, our example is really naïve, but it's important to understand the limitations and make conscious decisions about them.

Of course, if we want to make our model more complex, we can always do this by extending our state space, which will allow us to capture more dependencies in the model at the cost of a larger state space. For example, if you want to capture separately the probability of rainy days during summer and winter, then you can include the season in your state. In this case, your state space will be [*sunny+summer, sunny+winter, rainy+summer, rainy+winter*] and so on.

As your system model complies with the Markov property, you can capture transition probabilities with a **transition matrix**, which is a square matrix of the size $N \times N$, where N is the number of states in our model. Every cell in a row i and a column j in the matrix contains the probability of the system to transition from the state i to state j.

For example, in our sunny/rainy example the transition matrix could be as follows:

	sunny	rainy
sunny	0.8	0.2
rainy	0.1	0.9

In this case, if we have a sunny day, then there is an 80% chance that the next day will be sunny and a 20% chance that the next day will be rainy. If we observe a rainy day, then there is a 10% probability that the weather will become better and a 90% probability of the next day being rainy.

So, that's it. The formal definition of Markov process is as follows:

- A set of states (S) that a system can be in
- A transition matrix (T), with transition probabilities, which defines the system dynamics

The useful visual representation of MP is a graph with nodes corresponding to system states and edges, labeled with probabilities representing a possible transition from state to state. If the probability of transition is 0, we don't draw an edge (there is no way to go from one state to another). This kind of representation is also widely used in *finite state machine* representation, which is studied in the automata theory. For our sunny/rainy weather model the graph is as shown here:

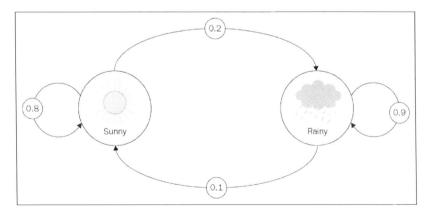

Figure 4: Sunny/Rainy weather model

Again, now we're talking about observation only. There is no way for us to influence the weather, so we just observe and record our observations.

To give you a more complicated example, we'll consider another model of *Office Worker* (Dilbert, the main character in Scott Adams' famous cartoons, is a good example). His state space in our example has the following states:

- **Home**: He's not at the office
- **Computer**: He's working on his computer at the office
- **Coffee**: He's drinking coffee at the office
- **Chatting**: He's discussing something with colleagues at the office

The state transition graph looks like this:

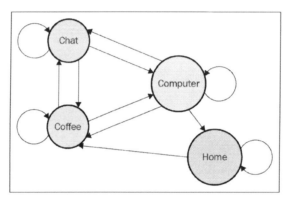

Figure 5: State transition graph

We expect that his work day usually starts from the **Home** state and that he always starts his work day with **Coffee**, without exception (no **Home** → **Computer** edge and no **Home** → **Chatting** edge). The preceding diagram also shows that work days always end (that is, the going to the **Home** state) from the **Computer** state. The transition matrix for the preceding diagram is as follows:

	Home	Coffee	Chat	Computer
Home	60%	40%	0%	0%
Coffee	0%	10%	70%	20%
Chat	0%	20%	50%	30%
Computer	20%	20%	10%	50%

The transition probabilities could be placed directly on the state transition graph, as shown here:

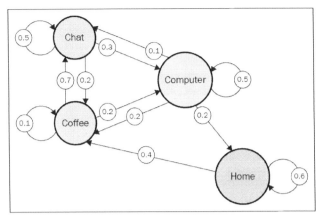

Figure 6: State transition graph with transition probabilities

In practice, we rarely have the luxury of knowing the exact transition matrix. A much more real-world situation is when we have only observations of our systems' states, which are also called *episodes*:

- home → coffee → coffee → chat → chat → coffee → computer → computer → home

- computer → computer → chat → chat → coffee → computer → computer → computer

- home → home → coffee → chat → computer → coffee → coffee

It's not complicated to estimate the transition matrix by our observation; we just count all the transitions from every state and normalize them to a sum of 1. The more observation data we have, the closer our estimation will be to the true underlying model.

It's also worth noting that the Markov property implies stationarity (that is, the underlying transition distribution for any state does not change over time). Nonstationarity means that there is some hidden factor that influences our system dynamics, and this factor is not included in observations. However, this contradicts the Markov property, which requires the underlying probability distribution to be the same for the same state regardless of the transition history. It's important to understand the difference between the actual transitions observed in an episode and the underlying distribution given in the transition matrix. Concrete episodes that we observe are randomly sampled from the distribution of the model, so they can differ from episode to episode. However, the probability of concrete transition to be sampled remains the same. If this is not the case, Markov chain formalism becomes nonapplicable.

Now we can go further and extend the Markov process model to make it closer to our RL problems. Let's add rewards to the picture!

Markov reward process

To introduce rewards, we need to extend our Markov process model a bit. First, we need to add value to our transition from state to state. We already have probability, but probability is being used to capture the dynamics of the system, so now we have an extra scalar number without an extra burden.

Reward can be represented in various forms. The most general way is to have another square matrix similar to the transition matrix with rewards for transitioning from state i to state j residing in row i and column j. Rewards can be positive or negative, large or small—it's just a number. In some cases, this representation is redundant and can be simplified. For example, if the reward is given for reaching the state regardless of the previous state, we can keep only state → reward pairs, which is a more compact representation. However, this is applicable only if the reward value depends only on the target state, which is not always the case.

The second thing we're adding to the model is discount factor γ (gamma), a single number from 0 to 1 (inclusive). The meaning will be explained later, after we define the extra characteristics of our Markov reward process.

As you remember, we observe a chain of state transitions in a Markov process. This is still the case for a Markov reward process, but for every transition, we have our extra quantity—reward. So now, all our observations have a reward value attached to every transition of the system.

For every episode, we define **return** at the time t as this quantity:

$$G_t = R_{t+1} + \gamma R_{t+2} + \ldots = \sum_{k=0}^{\infty} \gamma^k R_{t+k+1}$$

Let's try to understand what this means. For every time point, we calculate **return** as a sum of subsequent rewards, but more distant rewards are multiplied by the discount factor raised to the power of the number of steps we are away from the starting point at time t. The discount factor stands for the foresightedness of an agent. If gamma equals to 1, then return G_t just equals a sum of all subsequent rewards and corresponds to the agent with perfect visibility of any subsequent rewards. If gamma equals 0, our return G_t will be just immediate reward without any subsequent state and correspond to absolute *short-sightedness*.

These extreme values are not useful, and usually gamma is set to something in between, such as 0.9 or 0.99. In this case, we will look into future rewards, but not too far.

This gamma parameter is important in RL, and we'll meet it a lot in the subsequent chapters. For now, think about it as a measure of how far into the future we look to estimate the future return: the closer to 1, the more steps ahead of us we take into account.

This **return** quantity is not very useful in practice, as it was defined for every specific chain we observed from our Markov reward process, so it can vary widely even for the same state. However, if we go to the extremes and calculate the mathematical expectation of return for any state (by averaging large amount of chains), we'll get a much more useful quantity, called a **value of state**:

$$V(s) = \mathbb{E}[G|S_t = s]$$

This interpretation is simple: for every state s, the value $V(s)$ is the average (or expected) return we get by following the Markov reward process.

To show how this theoretical stuff is related to practice, let's extend our Dilbert process with rewards and turn it into a **Dilbert Reward Process (DRP)**. Our reward values will be as follows:

- home → home: 1 (as it's good to be home)
- home → coffee: 1
- computer → computer: 5 (working hard is a good thing)
- computer → chat: -3 (it's not good to be distracted)
- chat → computer: 2
- computer → coffee: 1
- coffee → computer: 3
- coffee → coffee: 1
- coffee → chat: 2
- chat → coffee: 1
- chat → chat: -1 (long conversation becomes boring)

A diagram with rewards is shown here:

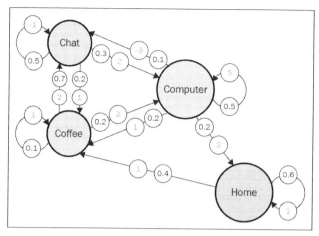

Figure 7: State transition graph with transition probabilities (dark) and rewards (light)

Let's return to our gamma parameter and think about the values of states with different values of gamma. We will start with a simple case: gamma = 0. How do you calculate the values of states here?

To answer this question, let's fix our state to **Chat**. What could the subsequent transition be? The answer is: *It depends on chance*. According to our transition matrix for the Dilbert process, there is a 50% probability that the next state will be **Chat** again, 20% that it will be **Coffee**, and in 30% of cases, we return to the **Computer** state. When gamma = 0, our return is equal only to a value of the next immediate state. So, if we want to calculate the value of the **Chat** state, then we need to sum all transition values, and multiply it by their probabilities:

$V(chat) = -1 * 0.5 + 2 * 0.3 + 1 * 0.2 = 0.3$

$V(coffee) = 2 * 0.7 + 1 * 0.1 + 3 * 0.2 = 2.1$

$V(home) = 1 * 0.6 + 1 * 0.4 = 1.0$

$V(computer) = 5 * 0.5 + (-3) * 0.1 + 1 * 0.2 + 2 * 0.2 = 2.8$

So, **Computer** is the most valuable state to be in (if we care only about immediate reward), which is not surprising as **Computer** → **Computer** is frequent, has a large reward, and the ratio of interruptions is not too high.

Now a trickier question: what's the value when gamma = 1? Think about this carefully.

The answer is: the value is infinite for all states. Our diagram doesn't contain *sink* states (states without outgoing transitions), and when our discount equals 1, we care about a potentially infinite amount of transitions in the future. As we've seen in the case of gamma = 0, all our values are positive in the short term, so the sum of the infinite amount of positive values will give us an infinite value, regardless of the starting state.

This infinite result shows us one of the reasons to introduce gamma into a Markov reward process, instead of just summing all future rewards. In most cases, the process can have an infinite (or large) amount of transitions. As it is not very practical to deal with infinite values, we would like to limit the horizon we calculate values for. Gamma with a value less than 1 provides such a limitation, and we'll discuss this later in chapters about the value iteration methods family. On the other hand, if you're dealing with finite-horizon environments (for example, the TicTacToe game which is limited by at most 9 steps), then it will be fine to use gamma = 1. As another example, there is an important class of environments with only one step called *Multi-Armed Bandit MDP*. This means that on every step you need to make a selection of one alternative action, which provides you with some reward and the episode ends.

As I already said about the Markov reward process definition, gamma is usually set to a value between 0 and 1 (commonly used values for gamma are 0.9 and 0.99); however, with such values it becomes almost impossible to calculate accurately the values by hand, even for MRPs as small as our Dilbert example, because it will require summing of hundreds of values. Computers are good at tedious tasks such as summing thousands of numbers, and there are several simple methods which can quickly calculate values for MRPs, given transition and reward matrices. We'll see and even implement one such method in *Chapter 5, Tabular Learning and the Bellman Equation*, when we'll start looking at Q-learning methods.

For now, let's put another layer of complexity around our Markov reward processes and introduce the final missing piece: actions.

Markov decision process

You may already have ideas about how to extend our MRP to include actions into the picture. First, we must add a set of actions (A), which has to be finite. This is our agent's *action space*.

Then, we need to condition our transition matrix with action, which basically means our matrix needs an extra *action* dimension, which turns it into a cube. If you remember, in the case of MPs and MRPs, the transition matrix had a square form, with source state in rows and target state in columns. So, every row *i* contained a list of probabilities to jump to every state:

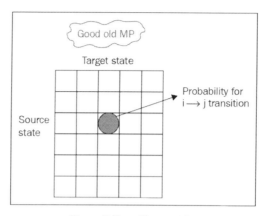

Figure 8: Transition matrix

Now the agent no longer passively observes state transitions, but can actively choose an action to take **at every time**. So, for every state, we don't have a list of numbers, but a matrix, where the *depth dimension* contains actions that the agent can take, and the other dimension is that the target state system will jump to after this action is performed by the agent. The following diagram shows our new transition table that became a cube with source state as the height dimension (indexed by **i**), target state as width (**j**), and action the agent can choose from is depth (**k**) of the transition table:

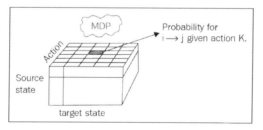

Figure 9: Transition probabilities for MDP

So, in general, by choosing an action, the agent can affect the probabilities of target states, which is a useful ability.

To give you an idea of why we need so many complications, let's imagine a small robot which lives in a 3 × 3 grid and can execute the actions *turn left, turn right*, and *go forward*. The state of the world is the robot's position plus orientation (up, down, left, and right), which gives us 3 × 3 × 4 = 36 states (the robot can be at any location in any orientation).

Also, imagine that the robot has imperfect motors (which is frequently the case in the real world), and when it executes *turn left* or *turn right*, there is a 90% chance that the desired turn happens, but sometimes, with 10% probability, the wheel slips and the robot's position stays the same. The same happens with *go forward*: in 90% of cases it works, but for the rest (10%) the robot stays at the same position.

In the following illustration, a small part of a transition diagram is shown, displaying the possible transitions from the state (1, 1, up), when the robot is in the center of the grid and facing up. If it tries to move forward, there is a 90% chance that it will end up in the state (0, 1, up), but there is a 10% probability that the wheels will slip and the target position will remain (1, 1, up).

To properly capture all these details about the environment and possible reactions on the agent's actions, the general MDP has a 3D transition matrix with dimensions (source state, action, and target state).

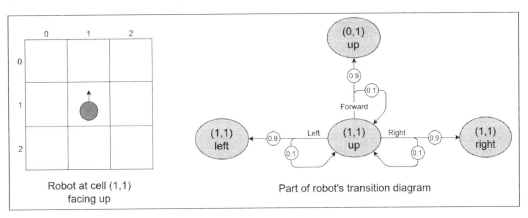

Figure 10: Grid world environment

Finally, to turn our MRP into an MDP, we need to add actions to our reward matrix in the same way we did with the transition matrix: our reward matrix will depend not only on state but also on action. In other words, it means that the reward the agent obtains now depends not only on the state it ends up in but also on the action that leads to this state. It's similar as when putting effort into something, you're usually gaining skills and knowledge, even if the result of your efforts wasn't too successful. So, the reward could be better if you're doing something, rather than not doing something, even if the final result is the same.

Now, with a formally defined MDP, we're finally ready to introduce the most important central thing for MDPs and RL: **policy**.

The intuitive definition of policy is that it is some set of rules that controls the agent's behavior. Even for fairly simple environments, we can have a variety of policies. For example, in the preceding example with the robot in the grid world, the agent can have different policies, which will lead to different sets of visited states. For example, this robot can perform the following actions:

- Blindly move forward regardless of anything
- Try to go around obstacles by checking whether that previous *forward* action failed
- Funnily spin around to entertain its creator
- Choose an action randomly modelling a *drunk robot in the grid world* scenario, and so on …

You may remember that the main objective of the agent in RL is to gather as much return (which was defined as discounted cumulative reward) as possible. So, again, intuitively, different policies can give us different return, which makes it important to find a good policy. This is why the notion of policy is important, and it's the central thing we're looking for.

Formally, policy is defined as the probability distribution over actions for every possible state:

$$\pi(a|s) = P[A_t = a | S_t = s]$$

This is defined as probability, not as a concrete action, to introduce randomness into an agent's behavior. We'll talk later why this is important and useful. Finally, deterministic policy is a special case of probabilistics with needed action having 1 as its probability.

Another useful notion is that if our policy is **fixed** and not changing, then our MDP becomes an MRP, as we can reduce transition and reward matrices with a policy's probabilities and get rid of action dimensions.

So, my congratulations on getting to this stage! This chapter was challenging, but it was important for subsequent practical material. After two more introductory chapters about OpenAI gym and deep learning, we can finally start tackling the question: how do I teach agents to solve practical tasks?

Summary

In this chapter, we started our journey into the RL world by learning what makes RL special and how it relates to the supervised and unsupervised learning paradigm. We then learned about the basic RL formalisms and how they interact with each other, after which we defined Markov process, Markov reward process, and Markov decision process.

In the next chapter, we'll move away from the formal theory into the practice of RL. We'll cover the setup required, libraries, and write our first agent.

2
OpenAI Gym

After talking so much about the theoretical concepts of **RL**, let's start doing something practical. In this chapter, we'll learn the basics of the OpenAI Gym API and write our first randomly behaving agent to make ourselves familiar with all the concepts.

The anatomy of the agent

As we saw in the previous chapter, there are several entities in RL's view of the world:

- **Agent**: A person or a thing that takes an active role. In practice, it's some piece of code, which implements some **policy**. Basically, this policy must decide what action is needed at every time step, given our observations.

- **Environment**: Some model of the world, which is external to the agent and has the responsibility of providing us with observations and giving us rewards. It changes its state based on our actions.

Let's show how both of them can be implemented in Python for a simplistic situation. We will define an environment that gives the agent random rewards for a limited number of steps, regardless of the agent's actions. This scenario is not very useful, but will allow us to focus on specific methods in both the environment and the agent classes. Let's start with the environment:

```
class Environment:
    def __init__(self):
        self.steps_left = 10
```

In the preceding code, we allow the environment to initialize its internal state. In our case, the state is just a counter that limits the number of time steps the agent is allowed to take to interact with the environment:

```
def get_observation(self):
    return [0.0, 0.0, 0.0]
```

The `get_observation()` method is supposed to return the current environment's observation to the agent. It is usually implemented as some function of the internal state of the environment. In our example, the observation vector is always zero, as the environment basically has no internal state:

```
def get_actions(self):
    return [0, 1]
```

The `get_actions()` method allows the agent to query the set of actions it can execute. Normally, the set of actions that the agent can execute does not change over time, but some actions can become impossible in different states (for example, not every move is possible in any position of the TicTacToe game). In our simplistic example, there are only two actions that the agent can carry out, encoded with the integers 0 and 1:

```
def is_done(self):
    return self.steps_left == 0
```

The preceding method signals the end of the episode to the agent. As we saw in *Chapter 1, What is Reinforcement Learning?,* the series of environment — the agent interactions is divided into a sequence of steps called episodes. Episodes can be finite, like in a game of chess, or infinite like the Voyager 2 mission (which is a famous space probe launched over 40 years ago that has travelled beyond our Solar System). To cover both scenarios, the environment provides us with a way to detect when an episode is over and there is no way to communicate with it anymore:

```
def action(self, action):
    if self.is_done():
        raise Exception("Game is over")
    self.steps_left -= 1
    return random.random()
```

The `action()` method is the central piece in the environment's functionality. It does two things: handles the agent's action and returns the reward for this action. In our example, the reward is random and its action is discarded. Additionally, we update the count of steps and refuse to continue the episodes which are over.

Now when looking at the agent's part, it is much simpler and includes only two methods: the constructor and the method that performs one step in the environment:

```
class Agent:
    def __init__(self):
        self.total_reward = 0.0
```

In the constructor, we initialize the counter that will keep the total reward accumulated by the agent during the episode:

```
def step(self, env):
    current_obs = env.get_observation()
    actions = env.get_actions()
    reward = env.action(random.choice(actions))
    self.total_reward += reward
```

The step function accepts the environment instance as an argument and allows the agent to perform the following actions:

- Observe the environment
- Make a decision about the action to take based on the observations
- Submit the action to the environment
- Get the reward for the current step

For our example, the agent is dull and ignores observations obtained during the decision process about which action to take. Instead, every action is selected randomly. The final piece is the glue code, which creates both classes and runs one episode:

```
if __name__ == "__main__":
    env = Environment()
    agent = Agent()

    while not env.is_done():
        agent.step(env)

    print("Total reward got: %.4f" % agent.total_reward)
```

You can find the preceding code in this book's Git repository at https://github.com/PacktPublishing/Deep-Reinforcement-Learning-Hands-On in the Chapter02/01_agent_anatomy.py directory. It has no external dependencies and should work with any more-or-less modern Python version. By running it several times, you'll get different amounts of reward gathered by the agent.

The simplicity of the preceding code allows us to illustrate important basic concepts that come from the RL model. The environment could be an extremely complicated physics model, and an agent could easily be a large neural network implementing the latest RL algorithm, but the basic pattern stays the same: on every step, an agent takes some observations from the environment, does its calculations, and selects the action to issue. The result of this action is a reward and new observation.

You may wonder, if the pattern is the same, why do we need to write it from scratch? Perhaps it is already implemented by somebody and could be used as a library? Of course, such frameworks exist, but before we spend some time discussing them, let's prepare your development environment.

Hardware and software requirements

The examples in this book were implemented and tested using Python version 3.6. I assume that you're already familiar with the language and common concepts such as virtual environments, so I won't cover in detail how to install the package and how to do this in an isolated way. The external libraries we'll use in this book are open source software, including the following:

- **NumPy**: This is a library for scientific computing and implementing matrix operations and common functions.

- **OpenCV Python bindings**: This is a computer vision library, which provides many functions for image processing.

- **Gym**: This is a RL framework developed and maintained by OpenAI with various environments that can be communicated with, in a unified way.

- **PyTorch**: This is a flexible and expressive **Deep Learning (DL)** library. A short essential crash course on it will be given in the next chapter.

- **Ptan** (https://github.com/Shmuma/ptan): This is an open source extension to Gym created by the author to support the modern deep RL methods and building blocks. All used classes will be described in detail together with the source code.

A significant portion of this book (parts two, three, and four) is focused on the modern deep RL methods that have been developed over the past few years. The word "deep" in this context means deep learning is heavily used and you may be aware that DL methods are computationally hungry. One modern GPU can be 10- to 100-times faster than even the fastest multiCPU systems. In practice, this means that the same code that takes one hour to train on a system with a GPU, could take from half a day to one week even on the fastest CPU system. It doesn't mean that you can't try the examples from this book without having access to a GPU, but it will take longer. To experiment with the code on your own (the most useful way to learn anything), it would be better get access to a machine with a GPU. This can be done in various ways:

- Buying a modern GPU suitable for CUDA
- Using cloud instances: Both Amazon AWS and Google Cloud can provide you with GPU-powered instances

The instructions on how to set up the system are beyond the scope of the book, but there are plenty of manuals available on the internet. In terms of OS, you should use Linux or macOS, as both PyTorch and most of Gym's environments don't support Windows (at least at the time of writing).

To give you the exact versions of the external dependencies that we'll use throughout the book, here is an output of the `pip freeze` command (it could be useful for the potential troubleshooting of examples in the book, as open source software and DL toolkits are evolving extremely quickly):

```
numpy==1.14.2
atari-py==0.1.1
gym==0.10.4
ptan==0.3
opencv-python==3.4.0.12
scipy==1.0.1
torch==0.4.0
torchvision==0.2.1
tensorboard-pytorch==0.7.1
tensorflow==1.7.0
tensorboard==1.7.0
```

All the examples in the book were written and tested with PyTorch 0.4, which can be installed with the `pip install pytorch==0.4.0` command.

Now, let's go to the details of the OpenAI Gym API, which are not complicated, but provide us with tons of environments, from trivial to challenging ones.

OpenAI Gym API

The Python library called `Gym` was developed and has been maintained by OpenAI (`www.openai.com`). The main goal of Gym is to provide a rich collection of environments for RL experiments using a unified interface. So, it's not surprising that the central class in the library is an environment, which is called `Env`. It exposes several methods and fields that provide the required information about an environment's capabilities. From high level, every environment provides you with these pieces of information and functionality:

- A set of actions that are allowed to be executed in an environment. Gym supports both discrete and continuous actions, as well as their combination.
- The shape and boundaries of the observations that an environment provides the agent with.
- A method called `step` to execute an action, which returns the current observation, reward, and indication that the episode is over.
- A method called `reset` to return the environment to its initial state and to obtain the first observation.

Let's talk about those components of the environment in detail.

Action space

As you may remember, the actions that an agent can execute can be discrete, continuous, or a combination of both. Discrete actions are a fixed set of things that an agent could do, for example, directions in a grid like left, right, up, or down. Another example is a push button, which could be either pressed or released. Both states are mutually exclusive, because a main characteristic of a discrete action space is that only one action from the action space is possible.

A continuous action has a value attached to it, for instance, a steering wheel, which can be turned at a specific angle, or an accelerator pedal, which can be pressed with different levels of force. A description of a continuous action includes the boundaries of the value that the action could have. In the case of a steering wheel, it could be from −720 degrees to 720 degrees. For an accelerator pedal, it's usually from 0 to 1.

Of course, we're not limited to a single action to perform, and the environment could have multiple actions, such as pushing multiple buttons simultaneously or steering the wheel and pressing two pedals (brake and accelerator). To support such cases, Gym defines a special container class that allows the nesting of several action spaces into one unified action.

Observation space

Observations are pieces of information that an environment provides the agent with, on every timestamp, besides the reward. Observations can be as simple as a bunch of numbers or as complex as several multidimensional tensors containing color images from several cameras. An observation can even be discrete, much like action spaces. An example of such a discrete observation space could be a light bulb, which could be in two states: on or off, given to us as a Boolean value.

So, you can see the similarity between actions and observations and how they have found their representation in Gym's classes. Let's look at a class diagram:

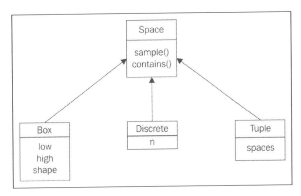

Figure 1: The hierarchy of the Space classes in Gym

The basic abstract class Space includes two methods relevant to us:

- sample(): This returns a random sample from the space
- contains(x): This checks if the argument x belongs to the space's domain

Both of these methods are abstract and reimplemented in the child classes Space class':

- The Discrete class represents a mutually-exclusive set of items, numbered from 0 to n−1. Its only field *n* is a count of the items it describes. For example, Discrete(n=4) can be used for an action space of four directions to move [left, right, up, or down].

- The `Box` class represents an n-dimensional tensor of rational numbers with intervals [low, high]. For instance, an accelerator pedal with one single value between 0.0 and 1.0 could be encoded by `Box(low=0.0, high=1.0, shape=(1,), dtype=np.float32)` (the `shape` argument is assigned a tuple of length 1 with a single value of 1, which gives us a one-dimensional tensor with a single value). The `dtype` parameter specifies the space's value type and here we specify it as a NumPy `32-bit float`. Another example of `Box` could be an Atari screen observation (we'll see lots of Atari environments later), which is an RGB image of size 210 × 160: `Box(low=0, high=255, shape=(210, 160, 3), dtype=np.uint8)`. In this case, the `shape` argument is a tuple of three elements: the first dimension is the height of the image, the second is the width, and the third equals 3, which all correspond to three color planes for red, green, and blue, respectively. So, in total, every observation is a 3D tensor with 100,800 bytes.

- The final child of `Space` we want to mention here is a `Tuple` class, which allows us to combine several `Space` class instances together. This enables us to create action and observation spaces of any complexity that we want. For example, imagine we want to create an action space specification for a car. The car has several controls that could be changed at every timestamp, including the steering wheel angle, brake pedal position, and accelerator pedal position. These three controls could be specified by three float values in one single `Box` instance. Besides these essential controls, the car has extra discrete controls, like a turn signal (which could be "off," "right," or "left'"), horn ("on" or "off"), and others. To combine all this into one action space specification class, we can create `Tuple(spaces=(Box(low=-1.0, high=1.0, shape=(3,), dtype=np.float32), Discrete(n=3), Discrete(n=2)))`. This flexibility is rarely used, for example, in this book we'll see only the `Box` and `Discrete` actions and observation spaces, but the `Tuple` class could be useful in some cases.

There are other `Space` subclasses defined in Gym, but the preceding three are the most useful ones we'll deal with. All subclasses implement the `sample()` and `contains()` methods. The `sample()` function performs a random sample corresponding to the `Space` class and parameters. This is mostly useful for action spaces, when we need to choose the random action. The `contains()` method verifies that the given arguments comply with `Space` parameters, and it is used in the internals of Gym to check an agent's actions for sanity. For example, `Discrete.sample()` returns a random element from a discrete range, and `Box.sample()` will be a random tensor with proper dimensions and values lying inside the given range.

Every environment has two members of type `Space`, called `action_space` and `observation_space`. This allows you to create generic code, which could work with any environment. Of course, dealing with pixels of the screen is different from handling discrete observations (as in the former case, you may want to preprocess images with convolutional layers or with other methods from the computer vision toolbox); so, most of the time, we will optimize our code for a particular environment or group of environments, but Gym doesn't prevent you from writing generic code.

The environment

The environment is represented in Gym by the `Env` class, which has the following members:

- `action_space`: This is the field of the `Space` class, providing a specification for allowed actions in the environment.
- `observation_space`: This field has the same `Space` class, but specifies the observations provided by the environment.
- `reset()`: This resets the environment to its initial state, returning the initial observation vector
- `step()`: This method allows the agent to give the action and returns the information about the outcome of the action: the next observation, local reward, and end-of-episode flag. This method is a bit complicated and we'll look at it in detail later in this section.

There are extra utility methods in the `Env` class, such as `render()`, which allows you to obtain the observation in a human-friendly form, but we won't use them. You can find the full list in Gym's documentation, but let's now focus on the core `Env` methods: `reset()` and `step()`.

So far we've seen how our code can get information about an environment's actions and observations, so now it's time to get familiar with actioning itself. Communications with the environment are performed via two methods of the `Env` class: `step` and `reset`.

As reset is much simpler, we'll start with it. The `reset()` method has no arguments, and it instructs an environment to reset into its initial state and obtain the initial observation. Note that you have to call `reset()` after the creation of the environment. As you may remember from *Chapter 1, What is Reinforcement Learning?*, the agent's communication with the environment could have an end (like a "Game Over" screen). Such sessions are called **episodes**, and after the end of the episode, an agent needs to start over. The value returned by this method is the first observation of the environment.

The `step()` method is the central piece in the environment's functionality, which does several things in one call, which are as follows:

1. Telling the environment which action we'll execute on the next step
2. Getting the new observation from the environment after this action
3. Getting the reward the agent gained with this step
4. Getting the indication that the episode is over

The first item (action) is passed as the only argument to this method, and the rest is returned by function. Precisely, it's a tuple (Python tuple, not the `Tuple` class we discussed in the previous section) of four elements (observation, reward, done, and extra_info). They have these types and meanings:

- **observation**: This is a NumPy vector or a matrix with observation data.
- **reward**: This is the float value of the reward.
- **done**: This is a Boolean indicator, which is `True` when the episode is over.
- **extra_info**: This could be anything environment-specific with extra information about the environment. The usual practice is to ignore this value in general RL methods (not taking into account the specific details of the particular environment).

So, you may have already got the idea of environment usage in an agent's code: in a loop, call the `step()` method with an action to perform until this method's done flag becomes `True`. Then we can call `reset()` to start over. There is only one piece missing: how we create `Env` objects in the first place.

Creation of the environment

Every environment has a unique name of the `EnvironmentName-vN` form, where `N` is the number used to distinguish between different versions of the same environment (when, for example, some bugs get fixed in an environment or some other major changes are performed). To create the environment, the `Gym` package provides the `make(env_name)` function with the only argument of the environment's name in the string form.

At the time of writing, Gym version 0.9.3 contains 777 environments with different names. Of course, all of those are not unique environments, as this list includes all versions of an environment. Additionally, the same environment can have different variations in the settings and observations spaces. For example, the Atari game Breakout has these environment names:

- **Breakout-v0, Breakout-v4**: The original breakout with a random initial position and direction of the ball

- **BreakoutDeterministic-v0**, **BreakoutDeterministic-v4**: Breakout with the same initial placement and speed vector of the ball

- **BreakoutNoFrameskip-v0**, **BreakoutNoFrameskip-v4**: Breakout with every frame displayed to the agent

- **Breakout-ram-v0**, **Breakout-ram-v4**: Breakout with observation of full Atari emulation memory (128 bytes) instead of screen pixels.

- Breakout-ramDeterministic-v0, Breakout-ramDeterministic-v4

- Breakout-ramNoFrameskip-v0, Breakout-ramNoFrameskip-v4

In total, there are 12 environments for good old Breakout. In case you've never seen it before, here is a screenshot of its gameplay:

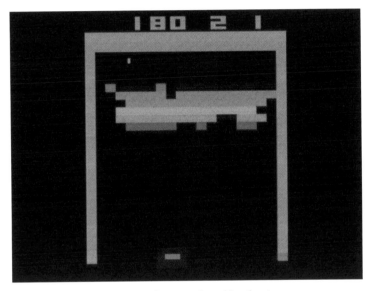

Figure 2: The gameplay of Breakout

Even after the removal of such duplicates, Gym 0.9.3 comes with an impressive list of 116 unique environments, which can be divided into several groups:

- **Classic control problems**: These are toy tasks that are used in optimal control theory and RL papers as benchmarks or demonstrations. They are usually simple, with a low-dimension observation and action spaces, but they are useful as quick checks when implementing algorithms. Think about them as the "MNIST for RL" (in case you haven't heard about MNIST, it is a handwriting digit recognition dataset from *Yann LeCun*).

- **Atari 2600**: These are games from the classic game platform from the 1970s. There are 63 unique games.

- **Algorithmic**: These are problems that aim to perform small computation tasks, such as copying the observed sequence or adding numbers.

- **Board games**: These are the games of Go and Hex.

- **Box2D**: These are environments that use the Box2D physics simulator to learn walking or car control.

- **MuJoCo**: This is another physics simulator used for several continuous control problems.

- **Parameter tuning**: This is RL being used to optimize neural network parameters.

- **Toy text**: These are simple grid-world text environments.

- **PyGame**: These are several environments implemented using the PyGame engine.

- **Doom**: These are nine mini-games implemented on top of ViZdoom.

The full list of environments can be found at `https://gym.openai.com/envs` or on the wiki page in the project's GitHub repository. An even larger set of environments is available in the OpenAI Universe, which provides general connectors to virtual machines, while running Flash and native games, web browsers, and other real-world applications. OpenAI Universe extends the Gym API, but follows the same design principles and paradigm. You can check it out at `https://github.com/openai/universe`.

Enough theorization, let's now look at a Python session working with one of Gym's environments.

The CartPole session

```
$ python
Python 3.6.5 |Anaconda, Inc.| (default, Mar 29 2018, 18:21:58)
[GCC 7.2.0] on linux
Type "help", "copyright", "credits" or "license" for more information.
>>> import gym
>>> e = gym.make('CartPole-v0')
WARN: gym.spaces.Box autodetected dtype as <class 'numpy.float32'>.
Please provide explicit dtype.
```

Here we will import the `Gym` package and create an environment called `CartPole`. This environment is from the "classic control" group and its gist is to control the platform with a stick attached by its bottom part (see the following figure). The trickiness is that this stick tends to fall right or left and you need to balance it by moving the platform to the right or left on every step. The warning message we see is not our fault, but a small inconsistency inside Gym, which doesn't affect the result.

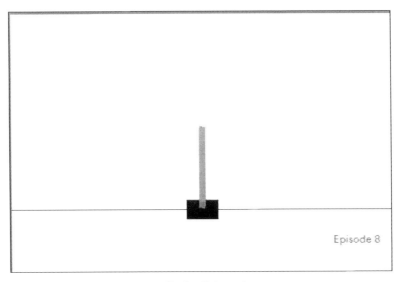

Figure 3: The CartPole environment

The observation of this environment is four float numbers containing information about the *x* coordinate of the stick's center of mass, its speed, its angle to the platform, and its angular speed. Of course, by applying some math and physics knowledge, it won't be complicated to convert these numbers into actions when we need to balance the stick, but our problem is much trickier: how do we learn to balance this system **without knowing** the exact meaning of the observed numbers and only by getting the reward? The reward in this environment is 1 given on every time step. The episode continues until the stick falls; so to get a more accumulated reward, we need to balance the platform in a way to avoid the stick falling.

This problem may look difficult, but in just two chapters we'll write the algorithm that will easily solve this CartPole in minutes, without any idea about what the observed numbers mean. We will do it only by trial-and-error and a bit of RL magic.

However, let's continue to play with our session:

```
>>> obs = e.reset()
>>> obs
array([-0.04937814, -0.0266909 , -0.03681807, -0.00468688])
```

Here we reset the environment and obtain the first observation (we always need to reset the newly created environment). As I've just said, the observation is four numbers, so let's check how we can know this in advance:

```
>>> e.action_space
Discrete(2)
>>> e.observation_space
Box(4,)
```

The `action_space` field is of the `Discrete` type, so our actions will be just 0 or 1, where 0 means pushing the platform to the left and 1 means to the right. The observation space is of `Box(4,)` which means a vector of size four with values inside the `[-inf, inf]` interval:

```
>>> e.step(0)
(array([-0.04991196, -0.22126602, -0.03691181,  0.27615592]), 1.0,
False, {})
```

Here we pushed our platform to the left by executing the action `0` and got the tuple of four elements:

- A new observation that is a new vector of four numbers
- A reward of `1.0`
- The `done flag` = `False`, which means that the episode is not over yet and we're more or less okay
- Extra information about the environment that is an empty dictionary

```
>>> e.action_space.sample()
0
>>> e.action_space.sample()
1
>>> e.observation_space.sample()
array([  2.06581792e+00,   6.99371255e+37,   3.76012475e-02,
        -5.19578481e+37])
>>> e.observation_space.sample()
array([4.6860966e-01, 1.4645028e+38, 8.6090848e-02,
3.0545910e+37],
      dtype=float32)
```

Here we used the `sample()` method of the `Space` class on `action_space` and `observation_space`. This method returns a random sample from the underlying space, which in the case of our `Discrete` action space means a random number of 0 or 1 and for the observation space is a random vector of four numbers. The random sample of the observation space may not look useful, and this is true, but the sample from the action space could be used when we're not sure how to perform an action. This feature is especially handy for us, as we don't know any RL methods yet, but still want to play around with the Gym environment. Now we know enough to implement our first random-behaving agent for CartPole, so let's do it.

The random CartPole agent

Although the environment is much more complex than our first example in
The anatomy of the agent section, the code of the agent is much shorter. This is
the power of reusability, abstractions, and third-party libraries!

So, here is the code (you can find it in Chapter02/02_cartpole_random.py):

```
import gym

if __name__ == "__main__":
    env = gym.make("CartPole-v0")
    total_reward = 0.0
    total_steps = 0
    obs = env.reset()
```

Here, we create the environment and initialize the counter of steps and the reward
accumulator. On the last line, we reset the environment to obtain the first observation
(which we'll not use, as our agent is stochastic):

```
    while True:
        action = env.action_space.sample()
        obs, reward, done, _ = env.step(action)
        total_reward += reward
        total_steps += 1
        if done:
            break

    print("Episode done in %d steps, total reward %.2f" %
(total_steps, total_reward))
```

In this loop, we sample a random action, then ask the environment to execute it and
return to us the next observation(obs), the reward, and the done flag. If the episode
is over, we stop the loop and show how many steps we've done and how much
reward has been accumulated. If you start this example, you'll see something like
this (not exactly, due to the agent's randomness):

```
rl_book_samples/Chapter02$ python 02_cartpole_random.py
WARN: gym.spaces.Box autodetected dtype as <class
'numpy.float32'>. Please provide explicit dtype.
Episode done in 12 steps, total reward 12.00
```

As with the interactive session, the warning is not related to our code, but to Gym's internals. On average, our random agent makes 12–15 steps before the pole falls and the episode ends. Most of the environments in Gym have a "reward boundary," which is the average reward that the agent should gain during 100 consecutive episodes to "solve" the environment. For CartPole, this boundary is 195, which means that on average, the agent must hold the stick during 195-time steps or longer. Using this perspective, our random agent's performance looks poor. However, don't be disappointed too early, because we are just at the beginning, and soon we will solve CartPole and many other much more interesting and challenging environments.

The extra Gym functionality – wrappers and monitors

What we discussed so far covers two-thirds of the Gym core API and the essential functions required to start writing agents. The rest of the API you can live without, but it will make your life easier and your code cleaner. So, let's look at a quick overview of the rest of the API.

Wrappers

Very frequently, you will want to extend the environment's functionality in some generic way. For example, an environment gives you some observations, but you want to accumulate them in some buffer and provide to the agent the *N* last observations, which is a common scenario for dynamic computer games, when one single frame is just not enough to get the full information about the game state. Another example is when you want to be able to crop or preprocess an image's pixels to make it more convenient for the agent to digest or if you want to normalize reward scores somehow. There are many such situations that have the same structure: you'd like to "wrap" the existing environment and add some extra logic doing something. Gym provides you with a convenient framework for these situations, called the `Wrapper` class. The class structure is shown in the following diagram.

The `Wrapper` class inherits the `Env` class. Its constructor accepts the only argument: the instance of the `Env` class to be "wrapped." To add extra functionality, you need to redefine the methods you want to extend such as `step()` or `reset()`. The only requirement is to call the original method of the superclass.

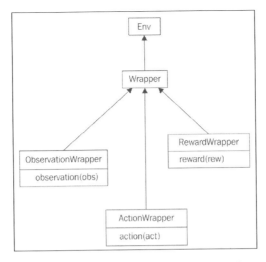

Figure 4: The hierarchy of `Wrapper` classes in Gym

To handle more specific requirements, such as a `Wrapper` class that wants to process only observations from the environment or only actions, there are subclasses of `Wrapper` that allow filtering of only a specific portion of information.

They are as follows:

- `ObservationWrapper`: You need to redefine `observation(obs)` method of the parent. The `obs` argument is an observation from the wrapped environment, and this method should return the observation that will be given to the agent.

- `RewardWrapper`: This exposes the `reward(rew)` method, which could modify the reward value given to the agent.

- `ActionWrapper`: You need to override the `action(act)` method, which could tweak the action passed to the wrapped environment to the agent.

To make it slightly more practical, let's imagine a situation where we want to intervene in the stream of actions sent by the agent and, with a probability of 10%, replace the current action with a random one. It might look like an unwise thing to do, but this simple trick is one of the most practical and powerful methods to solving the "exploration/exploitation problem" I mentioned briefly in *Chapter 1, What is Reinforcement Learning?*. By issuing the random actions, we make our agent explore the environment and from time to time drift away from the beaten track of its policy. This is an easy thing to do, using the `ActionWrapper` class (full example, `Chapter02/03_random_action_wrapper.py`).

```
import gym
import random
```

```
class RandomActionWrapper(gym.ActionWrapper):
    def __init__(self, env, epsilon=0.1):
        super(RandomActionWrapper, self).__init__(env)
        self.epsilon = epsilon
```

Here we initialize our wrapper by calling a parent's `__init__` method and saving epsilon (a probability of a random action):

```
def action(self, action):
    if random.random() < self.epsilon:
        print("Random!")
        return self.env.action_space.sample()
    return action
```

This is a method that we need to override from a parent's class to tweak the agent's actions. Every time we roll the die and with the probability of epsilon, we sample a random action from the action space and return it instead of the action the agent has sent to us. Note that using `action_space` and wrapper abstractions, we were able to write abstract code, which will work with *any* environment from the Gym. Additionally, we print the message every time we replace the action, just to verify that our wrapper is working. In the production code, of course, this won't be necessary:

```
if __name__ == "__main__":
    env = RandomActionWrapper(gym.make("CartPole-v0"))
```

Now it's time to apply our wrapper. We will create a normal CartPole environment and pass it to our wrapper constructor. From here on, we use our wrapper as a normal `Env` instance, instead of the original CartPole. As the `Wrapper` class inherits the `Env` class and exposes the same interface, we can nest our wrappers in any combination we want. This is a powerful, elegant, and generic solution:

```
obs = env.reset()
total_reward = 0.0

while True:
    obs, reward, done, _ = env.step(0)
    total_reward += reward
    if done:
        break

print("Reward got: %.2f" % total_reward)
```

Here is almost the same code, except that every time we issue the same action: 0. Our agent is dull and always does the same thing. By running the code, you should see that the wrapper is indeed working:

```
rl_book_samples/Chapter02$ python 03_random_actionwrapper.py
WARN: gym.spaces.Box autodetected dtype as <class
'numpy.float32'>. Please provide explicit dtype.
Random!
Random!
Random!
Random!
Reward got: 12.00
```

If you want, you can play with the epsilon parameter on the wrapper's creation and verify that randomness improves the agent's score on average. We should move on and look at another interesting gem hidden inside Gym: `Monitor`.

Monitor

Another class you should be aware of is `Monitor`. It is implemented like `Wrapper` and can write information about your agent's performance in a file with an optional video recording of your agent in action. Some time ago, it was possible to upload the result of the `Monitor` class' recording to the `https://gym.openai.com` website and see your agent's position in comparison to other people's results (see thee following screenshot), but, unfortunately, at the end of August 2017, OpenAI decided to shut down this upload functionality and froze all the results. There are several activities to implement an alternative to the original website, but they are not ready yet. I hope this situation will be resolved soon, but at the time of writing it's not possible to check your result against those of others.

Just to give you an idea of how the Gym web interface looked, here is the CartPole environment leaderboard:

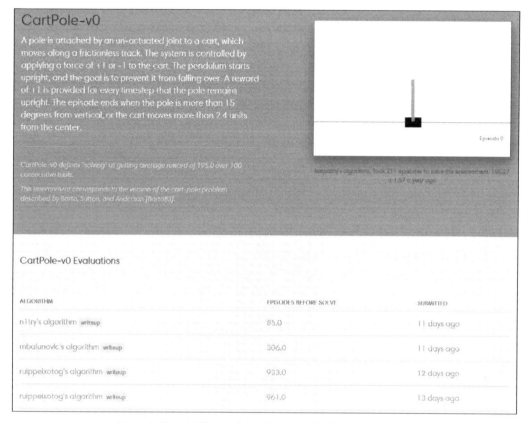

Figure 5: OpenAI Gym web interface with CartPole submissions

Every submission in the web interface had details about training dynamics.
For example, the following is the author's solution for one of Doom's mini-games:

Figure 6: Submission dynamics on the DoomDefendLine environment

Despite this, `Monitor` is still useful, as you can take a look at your agent's life inside the environment. So, here is how we add `Monitor` to our random CartPole agent, which is the only difference (the entire code is in `Chapter02/04_cartpole_random_monitor.py`):

```
if __name__ == "__main__":
    env = gym.make("CartPole-v0")
    env = gym.wrappers.Monitor(env, "recording")
```

The second argument that we pass to `Monitor` is the name of the directory it will write the results to. This directory shouldn't exist, otherwise your program will fail with an exception (to overcome this, you could either remove the existing directory or pass the `force=True` argument to the `Monitor` class' constructor).

The `Monitor` class requires the `FFmpeg` utility to be present on the system, which is used to convert captured observations into an output video file. This utility must be available, otherwise `Monitor` will raise an exception. The easiest way to install `FFmpeg` is using your system's package manager, which is OS distribution-specific.

To start this example, one of these three extra prerequisites should be met:

- The code should be run in an X11 session with the OpenGL extension (GLX)
- The code should be started in an `Xvfb` virtual display
- You can use X11 forwarding in ssh connection

The cause of this is video recording, which is done by taking screenshots of the window drawn by the environment. Some of the environment uses OpenGL to draw its picture, so the graphical mode with OpenGL needs to be present. This could be a problem for a virtual machine in the cloud, which physically doesn't have a monitor and graphical interface running. To overcome this, there is a special "virtual" graphical display, called **Xvfb (X11 virtual framebuffer)**, which basically starts a virtual graphical display on the server and forces the program to draw inside it. This would be enough to make Monitor happily create the desired videos.

To start your program in the Xvbf environment, you need to have it installed on your machine (it usually requires installing the xvfb package) and run the special script, xvfb-run:

```
$ xvfb-run -s "-screen 0 640x480x24" python 04_cartpole_random_monitor.py
[2017-09-22 12:22:23,446] Making new env: CartPole-v0
[2017-09-22 12:22:23,451] Creating monitor directory recording
[2017-09-22 12:22:23,570] Starting new video recorder writing to
recording/openaigym.video.0.31179.video000000.mp4
Episode done in 14 steps, total reward 14.00
[2017-09-22 12:22:26,290] Finished writing results. You can upload
them to the scoreboard via gym.upload('recording')
```

As you may see from the preceding log, the video has been written successfully, so you can peek inside one of your agent's sections by playing it.

Another way to record your agent's actions is to use ssh X11 forwarding, which uses the ssh ability to tunnel X11 communications between the X11 client (Python code which wants to display some graphical information) and X11 server (software which knows how to display this information and has access to your physical display). In X11 architecture, the client and the server are separated and can work on different machines. To use this approach, you need the following:

1. An X11 server running on your local machine. Linux comes with X11 server as a standard component (all desktop environments are using X11). On a Windows machine, you can set up third-party X11 implementations such as open source VcXsrv (available in https://sourceforge.net/projects/vcxsrv/).

2. The ability to log in to your remote machine via ssh, passing the -X command-line option: ssh -X servername. This enables X11 tunneling and allows all processes started in this session to use your local display for graphics output.

Then you can start a program that uses the Monitor class and it will display the agent's actions, capturing the images into a video file.

Summary

My congratulations! You have started to learn the practical side of RL! In this chapter, we installed OpenAI Gym with tons of environments to play with, studied its basic API and created a randomly behaving agent. You also learned how to extend the functionality of existing environments in a modular way and got familiar with a way to record our agent's activity using the `Monitor` wrapper.

In the next chapter, we will do a quick DL recap using PyTorch, which is a favorite library among DL researchers. Stay tuned.

3
Deep Learning with PyTorch

In the previous chapter, we became familiar with open source libraries, which provided us with a collection of RL environments. However, recent developments in RL, especially its combination with **deep learning** (**DL**), now make it possible to solve much more complex and challenging problems than before. This is partly due to the development of DL methods and tools.

This chapter is dedicated to one such tool, which makes it possible to implement complex DL models in just a bunch of lines of Python code. The chapter doesn't pretend to be a complete DL manual, as the field is very wide and dynamic. The goal is to make you familiar with the PyTorch library specifics and implementation details, assuming that you're already familiar with DL fundamentals.

Compatibility note: All of the examples in this chapter were updated for the latest PyTorch 0.4.0, which has a number of changes compared with the previous 0.3.1 release. If you're using the old PyTorch, consider upgrading. Throughout this chapter, we will discuss the differences seen in the latest version.

Tensors

A tensor is the fundamental building block of all DL toolkits. The name sounds cool and mystic, but the underlying idea is that a tensor is a multi-dimensional array. One single number is like a point, which is zero-dimensional, while a vector is one-dimensional like a line segment, and a matrix is a two-dimensional object. Three-dimensional number collections can be represented by a parallelepiped of numbers, but don't have a separate name in the same way as *matrix*. We can keep this term for collections of higher dimensions, which are named multi-dimensional matrices or tensors.

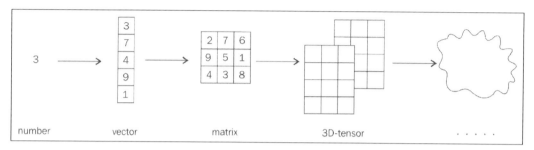

Figure 1: Going from a single number to an n-dimension tensor

Creation of tensors

If you're familiar with the NumPy library (and you should be), then you already know that its central purpose is the handling of multi-dimensional arrays in a generic way. In NumPy, such arrays aren't called tensors, but, in fact, they are tensors. Tensors are used very widely in scientific computations, as generic storage for data. For example, a color image could be encoded as a 3D tensor with dimensions of width, height, and color plane.

Apart from dimensions, a tensor is characterized by the type of its elements. There are eight types supported by PyTorch: three float types (16-bit, 32-bit, and 64-bit) and five integer types (8-bit signed, 8-bit unsigned, 16-bit, 32-bit, and 64-bit). Tensors of different types are represented by different classes, with the most commonly used being `torch.FloatTensor` (corresponding to a 32-bit float), `torch.ByteTensor` (an 8-bit unsigned integer), and `torch.LongTensor` (a 64-bit signed integer). The rest can be found in the documentation.

There are three ways to create a tensor in PyTorch:

1. By calling a constructor of the required type.
2. By converting a NumPy array or a Python list into a tensor. In this case, the type will be taken from the array's type.

3. By asking PyTorch to create a tensor with specific data for you. For example, you can use the `torch.zeros()` function to create a tensor filled with zero values.

To give you examples of these methods, let's look at a simple session:

```
>>> import torch
>>> import numpy as np
>>> a = torch.FloatTensor(3, 2)
>>> a
tensor([[ 4.1521e+09,   4.5796e-41],
        [ 1.9949e-20,   3.0774e-41],
        [ 4.4842e-44,   0.0000e+00]])
```

Here, we imported both PyTorch and NumPy and created an uninitialized tensor of size 3 × 2. By default, PyTorch allocates memory for the tensor, but doesn't initialize it with anything. To clear the tensor's content, we need to use its operation:

```
>>> a.zero_()
tensor([[ 0.,   0.],
        [ 0.,   0.],
        [ 0.,   0.]])
```

There are two types of operation for tensors: inplace and functional. Inplace operations have an underscore appended to their name and operate on the tensor's content. After this, the object itself is returned. The functional equivalent creates a *copy* of the tensor with the performed modification, leaving the original tensor untouched. Inplace operations are usually more efficient from a performance and memory point of view.

Another way to create a tensor by its constructor is to provide a Python iterable (for example, a list or tuple), which will be used as the contents of the newly created tensor:

```
>>> torch.FloatTensor([[1,2,3],[3,2,1]])
tensor([[ 1.,   2.,   3.],
        [ 3.,   2.,   1.]])
```

Here we are creating the same zero object using NumPy:

```
>>> n = np.zeros(shape=(3, 2))
>>> n
array([[ 0.,   0.],
       [ 0.,   0.],
       [ 0.,   0.]])
>>> b = torch.tensor(n)
>>> b
```

```
tensor([[ 0.,   0.],
        [ 0.,   0.],
        [ 0.,   0.]], dtype=torch.float64)
```

The `torch.tensor` method accepts the NumPy array as an argument and creates a tensor of appropriate shape from it. In the preceding example, we created a NumPy array initialized by zeros, which created a double (64-bit float) array by default. So, the resulting tensor has the `DoubleTensor` type (which is shown in the preceding example with the `dtype` value). Usually, in DL, double precision is not required and it adds an extra memory and performance overhead. The common practice is to use the 32-bit float type, or even the 16-bit float type, which is more than enough. To create such a tensor, you need to specify explicitly the type of NumPy array:

```
>>> n = np.zeros(shape=(3, 2), dtype=np.float32)
>>> torch.tensor(n)
tensor([[ 0.,   0.],
        [ 0.,   0.],
        [ 0.,   0.]])
```

As an option, the type of the desired tensor could be provided to the `torch.tensor` function in the `dtype` argument. However, be careful, since this argument expects to get a PyTorch type specification, not the NumPy one. PyTorch types are kept in the `torch` package, for example, `torch.float32`, `torch.uint8`.

```
>>> n = np.zeros(shape=(3,2))
>>> torch.tensor(n, dtype=torch.float32)
tensor([[ 0.,   0.],
        [ 0.,   0.],
        [ 0.,   0.]])
```

Compatibility note: The `torch.tensor()` method and explicit PyTorch type specification were added in the 0.4.0 release, and this is a step toward simplification of tensor creation. In previous versions, the `torch.from_numpy()` function was a recommended way to convert NumPy arrays, but it had issues with handling the combination of the Python list and NumPy arrays. This `from_numpy()` function is still present for backward compatibility, but it is deprecated in favor of the more flexible `torch.tensor()` method.

Scalar tensors

Since the 0.4.0 release, PyTorch supports zero-dimensional tensors that correspond to scalar values (on the left of *Figure 1*). Such tensors can be a result of some operations, such as summing all values in a tensor. Earlier, such cases were handled by the creation of a one-dimension (vector) tensor with single dimension equal to one. This solution worked, but wasn't very simple, as extra indexation was needed to access the value.

Now zero-dimension tensors are natively supported and returned by the appropriate functions and can be created by the `torch.tensor()` function. To access the actual Python value of such a tensor, they have the special `item()` method:

```
>>> a = torch.tensor([1,2,3])
>>> a
tensor([ 1,   2,   3])
>>> s = a.sum()
>>> s
tensor(6)
>>> s.item()
6
>>> torch.tensor(1)
tensor(1)
```

Tensor operations

There are lots of operations that you can perform on tensors, and there are too many to list them all. Usually, it's enough to search in the PyTorch documentation at `http://pytorch.org/docs/`. Here we need to mention that besides the inplace and functional variants we already discussed (that is, with and without underscore, like `zero()` and `zero_()`), there are two places to look for operations: the `torch` package and the tensor class. In the first case, the function usually accepts the tensor as an argument. In the second, it operates on the called tensor.

Most of the time, tensor operations are trying to correspond to their NumPy equivalent, so if there is some not-very-specialized function in NumPy, then there is a good chance that PyTorch will also have it. Examples are `torch.stack()`, `torch.transpose()`, and `torch.cat()`.

GPU tensors

PyTorch transparently supports CUDA GPUs, which means that all operations have two versions—CPU and GPU—which are automatically selected. The decision is made based on the type of tensors that you are operating on. Every tensor type that we mentioned is for CPU and has its GPU equivalent. The only difference is that GPU tensors reside in the `torch.cuda` package, instead of just `torch`. For example, `torch.FloatTensor` is a 32-bit float tensor which resides in CPU memory, but `torch.cuda.FloatTensor` is its GPU counterpart. To convert from CPU to GPU, there is a tensor method, `to(device)`, which creates a copy of the tensor to a specified device (which could be CPU or GPU). If the tensor is already on the device, nothing happens and the original tensor will be returned. Device type can be specified in different ways. First of all, you can just pass a string name of the device, which is "cpu" for CPU memory or "cuda" for GPU. A GPU device could have an optional device index specified after the colon, for example, the second GPU card in the system could be addressed by "cuda:1" (index is zero-based).

Another slightly more efficient way to specify a device in the `to()` method is using the `torch.device` class, which accepts the device name and optional index. For accessing the device that your tensor is currently residing in, it has a `device` property.

```
>>> a = torch.FloatTensor([2,3])
>>> a
tensor([ 2.,   3.])
>>> ca = a.cuda(); ca
tensor([ 2.,   3.], device='cuda:0')
```

Here, we created a tensor on CPU, then copied it to GPU memory. Both copies could be used in computations and all GPU-specific machinery is transparent to the user:

```
>>> a + 1
tensor([ 3.,   4.])
>>> ca + 1
tensor([ 3.,   4.], device='cuda:0')
>>> ca.device
device(type='cuda', index=0)
```

Compatibility note: The `to()` method and `torch.device` class were introduced in 0.4.0. In previous versions, copying between CPU and GPU was performed by separate tensor methods, `cpu()` and `cuda()`, respectively, which required adding the extra lines of code to explicitly convert tensors into their CUDA versions. In the latest version, you can create a desired `torch.device` object in the beginning of the program and use `to(device)` on every tensor you're creating. The old methods, `cpu()` and `cuda()` in the tensor are still present, but deprecated.

Gradients

Even with transparent GPU support, all of this dancing with tensors isn't worth bothering with, without one "killer feature": the automatic computation of gradients. This functionality was originally implemented in the Caffe toolkit and then became the de-facto standard in DL libraries. Computing gradients manually was extremely painful to implement and debug, even for the simplest **neural network (NN)**. You had to calculate derivatives for all your functions, apply the chain rule, and then implement the result of the calculations, praying that everything was done right. This could be a very useful exercise for understanding the nuts and bolts of DL, but it's not something that you wanted to repeat over and over again by experimenting with different NN architectures.

Luckily, those days have gone now, much like programming your hardware using a soldering iron and vacuum tubes! Now defining an NN of hundreds of layers requires nothing more than assembling it from predefined building blocks or, in the extreme case of you doing something fancy, defining the transformation expression manually. All gradients will be carefully calculated for you, backpropagated, and applied to the network. To be able to achieve this, you need to define your network architecture in terms of the DL library used, which can be different in details, but in general, must be the same: you define the order in which your network will transform inputs to outputs.

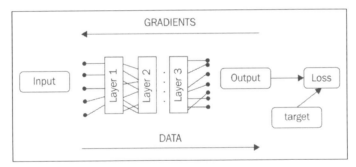

Figure 2: Data and gradients flow through the neural network

What can make the fundamental difference is *how* your gradients will be calculated. There are two approaches:

1. **Static graph**: In this method, you need to define your calculations in advance and it won't be possible to change them later. The graph gets processed and optimized by the DL library before any computation can be made. This model is implemented in TensorFlow, Theano, and many other DL toolkits.

2. **Dynamic graph**: You don't need to define your graph in advance exactly as it will be executed. You just execute operations that you want to use for data transformation on your actual data. During this, the library records the order of operations performed, and when you ask it to calculate gradients, it unrolls its history of operations, accumulating the gradients of network parameters. This method is also called **notebook gradients** and is implemented in PyTorch, Chainer, and some others.

Both methods have their strengths and weaknesses. For example, static graph is usually faster, as all computations can be moved to the GPU, minimizing the data transfer overhead. Additionally, in static graph, the library has much more freedom in optimizing the order that computations are performed in or even removing parts of the graph. On the other hand, dynamic graph has a higher computation overhead, but gives a developer much more freedom. For example, they can say, "For this piece of data, I can apply this network two times, and for this piece of data, I'll use a completely different model with gradients clipped by the batch mean." Another very appealing strength of the dynamic graph model is that it allows you to express your transformation more naturally, in a more "Pythonic" way. In the end, it's just a Python library with bunch of functions, so just call them and let the library do the magic.

Tensors and gradients

PyTorch tensors have a built-in gradient calculation and tracking machinery, so all you need to do is to convert the data into tensors and perform computations using the tensor's methods and functions provided by `torch`. Of course, if you need to access underlying low-level details, you always can, but most of the time, PyTorch does what you're expecting.

There are several attributes related to gradients that every tensor has:

* `grad`: A property which holds a tensor of the same shape containing computed gradients.

* `is_leaf`: `True`, if this tensor was constructed by the user and `False`, if the object is a result of function transformation.

* `requires_grad`: `True` if this tensor requires gradients to be calculated. This property is inherited from leaf tensors, which get this value from the tensor construction step (`torch.zeros()` or `torch.tensor()` and so on). By default, the constructor has `requires_grad=False`, so if you want gradients to be calculated for your tensor, then you need to explicitly say so.

To make all of this gradient-leaf machinery clearer, let's consider this session:

```
>>> v1 = torch.tensor([1.0, 1.0], requires_grad=True)
>>> v2 = torch.tensor([2.0, 2.0])
```

In the preceding code, we created two tensors. The first requires gradients to be calculated and the second doesn't:

```
>>> v_sum = v1 + v2
>>> v_res = (v_sum*2).sum()
>>> v_res
tensor(12.)
```

So now we've added both vectors element-wise (which is vector [3, 3]), doubled every element, and summed them together. The result is a zero-dimension tensor with the value 12. Okay, so this is simple math so far. Now let's look at the underlying graph that our expressions created:

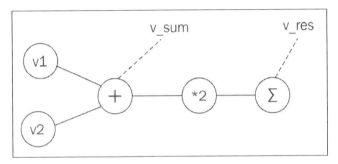

Figure 3: Graph representation of the expression

If we check the attributes of our tensors, then we find that **v1** and **v2** are the only leaf nodes and every variable except **v2** requires gradients to be calculated:

```
>>> v1.is_leaf, v2.is_leaf
(True, True)
>>> v_sum.is_leaf, v_res.is_leaf
(False, False)
>>> v1.requires_grad
True
>>> v2.requires_grad
False
>>> v_sum.requires_grad
True
>>> v_res.requires_grad
True
```

Now, let's tell PyTorch to calculate the gradients of our graph:

```
>>> v_res.backward()
>>> v1.grad
tensor([ 2.,  2.])
```

By calling the `backward` function, we asked PyTorch to calculate the numerical derivative of the v_res variable, with respect to any variable that our graph has. In other words, what influence do small changes to the v_res variable have on the rest of the graph? In our particular example, the value of 2 in v1's gradients means that by increasing every element of v1 by one, the resulting value of v_res will grow by two.

As mentioned, PyTorch calculates gradients only for leaf tensors with `requires_grad=True`. Indeed, if we try to check the gradients of v2 we get nothing:

```
>>> v2.grad
```

The reason for that is efficiency in terms of computations and memory: in real life, our network can have millions of optimized parameters, with hundreds of intermediate operations performed on them. During gradient descent optimization, we're not interested in gradients of any intermediate matrix multiplication; the only thing we want to adjust in the model is gradients of loss with respect to model parameters (weights). Of course, if you want to calculate the gradients of input data (it could be useful if you want to generate some adversarial examples to fool the existing NN or adjust pretrained word embeddings), then you can easily do so, by passing `requires_grad=True` on tensor creation.

Basically, you now have everything needed to implement your own NN optimizer. The rest of this chapter is about extra convenient functions, which will provide you with higher-level building blocks of NN architectures, popular optimization algorithms and common loss functions. However, don't forget that you can easily reimplement all of these bells and whistles in any way that you like. This is why PyTorch is so popular among DL researchers: for its elegance and flexibility.

Compatibility note: Support of gradients calculation in tensors is one of the major changes in PyTorch 0.4.0. In previous versions, graph tracking and gradients accumulation were done in a separate, very thin class `Variable`, which worked as a wrapper around the tensor and automatically performed saving of the history of computations in order to be able to backpropagate. This class is still present in 0.4.0, but it is deprecated and will go away soon, so new code should avoid using it. From my perspective, this change is great, as the `Variable` logic was really thin, but still required extra code and the developer's attention to wrap and unwrap tensors. Now gradients are a built-in tensor property, which makes the API much cleaner.

NN building blocks

In the `torch.nn` package, you'll find tons of predefined classes providing you with the basic functionality blocks. All of them are designed with practice in mind (for example, they support minibatches, have sane default values, and the weights are properly initialized). All modules follow the convention of *callable*, which means that the instance of any class can act as a function when applied to its arguments. For example, the `Linear` class implements a feed-forward layer with optional bias:

```
>>> import torch.nn as nn
>>> l = nn.Linear(2, 5)
>>> v = torch.FloatTensor([1, 2])
>>> l(v)
tensor([ 0.1975,  0.1639,  1.1130, -0.2376, -0.7873])
```

Here, we created a randomly initialized feed-forward layer, with two inputs and five outputs, and applied it to our float tensor. All classes in the `torch.nn` packages inherit from the `nn.Module` base class, which you can use to implement your own higher-level NN blocks. We'll see how you can do this in the next section, but, for now, let's look at useful methods that all `nn.Module` children provide. They are as follows:

- `parameters()`: A function that returns iterator of all variables which require gradient computation (that is, module weights)
- `zero_grad()`: This function initializes all gradients of all parameters to zero
- `to(device)`: This moves all module parameters to a given device (CPU or GPU)
- `state_dict()`: This returns the dictionary with all module parameters and is useful for model serialization
- `load_state_dict()`: This initializes the module with the state dictionary

The whole list of available classes can be found in the documentation at `http://pytorch.org/docs`.

Now we should mention one very convenient class that allows you to combine other layers into the pipe: `Sequential`. The best way to demonstrate `Sequential` is through an example:

```
>>> s = nn.Sequential(
... nn.Linear(2, 5),
... nn.ReLU(),
... nn.Linear(5, 20),
... nn.ReLU(),
... nn.Linear(20, 10),
```

```
...   nn.Dropout(p=0.3),
...   nn.Softmax(dim=1))
>>> s
Sequential (
    (0): Linear (2 -> 5)
    (1): ReLU ()
    (2): Linear (5 -> 20)
    (3): ReLU ()
    (4): Linear (20 -> 10)
    (5): Dropout (p = 0.3)
    (6): Softmax ()
)
```

Here, we defined a three-layer NN with softmax on output, applied along dimension 1 (dimension 0 is batch samples), ReLU nonlinearities and dropout. Let's push something through it:

```
>>> s(torch.FloatTensor([[1,2]]))
tensor([[ 0.1410,   0.1380,   0.0591,   0.1091,   0.1395,   0.0635,
0.0607,
             0.1033,   0.1397,   0.0460]])
```

So, our minibatch is one example successfully traversed through the network!

Custom layers

In the previous section, we briefly mentioned the nn.Module class as a base parent for all NN building blocks exposed by PyTorch. It's not only a unifying parent for the existing layers—it's much more than that. By subclassing the nn.Module class, you can create your own building blocks which can be stacked together, reused later, and integrated into the PyTorch framework flawlessly.

At its core, nn.Module provides quite rich functionality to its children:

- It tracks all submodules that the current module includes. For example, your building block can have two feed-forward layers used somehow to perform the block's transformation.

- It provides functions to deal with all parameters of the registered submodules. You can obtain a full list of the module's parameters (parameters() method), zero its gradients (zero_grads() method), move to CPU or GPU (to(device) method), serialize and deserialize the module (state_dict() and load_state_dict()), and even perform generic transformations using your own callable (apply() method).

- It establishes the convention of module application to data. Every module needs to perform its data transformation in the `forward()` method by overriding it.
- There are some more functions, such as the ability to register a hook function to tweak module transformation or gradients flow, but it's more for advanced use cases.

These functionalities allow us to nest our submodels into higher-level models in a unified way, which is extremely useful when dealing with complexity. It could be a simple one-layer linear transformation or a 1001-layer ResNet monster, but if they follow the conventions of `nn.Module`, then both of them could be handled in the same way. This is very handy for code simplicity and reusability.

To make our life simpler, when following the preceding convention, PyTorch authors simplified the creation of modules by careful design and a good dose of Python magic. So, to create a custom module, we usually have to do only two things: register submodules and implement the `forward()` method. Let's look at how this can be done for our `Sequential` example from the previous section, but in a more generic and reusable way (full sample is `Chapter03/01_modules.py`):

```python
class OurModule(nn.Module):
    def __init__(self, num_inputs, num_classes, dropout_prob=0.3):
        super(OurModule, self).__init__()
        self.pipe = nn.Sequential(
            nn.Linear(num_inputs, 5),
            nn.ReLU(),
            nn.Linear(5, 20),
            nn.ReLU(),
            nn.Linear(20, num_classes),
            nn.Dropout(p=dropout_prob),
            nn.Softmax()
        )
```

This is our module class that inherits `nn.Module`. In the constructor, we pass three parameters: the size of input, size of output, and optional dropout probability. The first thing we need to do is to call the parent's constructor to let it initialize itself. In the second step, we create an already familiar `nn.Sequential` with a bunch of layers and assign it to our class field named `pipe`. By assigning a `Sequential` instance to our field, we automatically register this module (`nn.Sequential` inherits from `nn.Module` as does everything in the `nn` package). To register, we don't need to call anything, we just assign our submodules to fields. After the constructor finishes, all those fields will be registered automatically (if you really want to, there is a function in `nn.Module` to register submodules):

```python
    def forward(self, x):
        return self.pipe(x)
```

Here, we override the forward function with our implementation of data transformation. As our module is a very simple wrapper around other layers, we just need to ask them to transform the data. Note that to apply a module to the data, you need to call the module as callable (that is, pretend that the module instance is a function and call it with the arguments) and *not* use the `forward()` function of the `nn.Module` class. This is because `nn.Module` overrides the `__call__()` method, which is being used when we treat an instance as callable. This method does some `nn.Module` magic stuff and calls your `forward()` method. If you call `forward()` directly, you'll intervene with the `nn.Module` duty, which can give you wrong results.

So, that's what we need to do to define our own module. Now, let's use it:

```
if __name__ == "__main__":
    net = OurModule(num_inputs=2, num_classes=3)
    v = torch.FloatTensor([[2, 3]])
    out = net(v)
    print(net)
    print(out)
```

We create our module, providing it with the desired number of inputs and outputs, then we create a tensor, wrapped into the `Variable` and ask our module to transform it, following the same convention of using it as callable. Then we print our network's structure (`nn.Module` overrides `__str__()` and `__repr__()`) to represent the inner structure in a nice way. The last thing we show is the result of the network's transformation.

The output of our code should look like this:

```
rl_book_samples/Chapter03$ python 01_modules.py
OurModule(
  (pipe): Sequential(
    (0): Linear(in_features=2, out_features=5, bias=True)
    (1): ReLU()
    (2): Linear(in_features=5, out_features=20, bias=True)
    (3): ReLU()
    (4): Linear(in_features=20, out_features=3, bias=True)
    (5): Dropout(p=0.3)
    (6): Softmax()
  )
)
tensor([[ 0.3672,  0.3469,  0.2859]])
```

Of course, everything that was said about the dynamic nature of PyTorch is still true. Your `forward()` method will get control for every batch of data, so if you want to do some complex transformations based on the data you need to process, like hierarchical softmax or a random choice of net to apply, then nothing can stop you from doing so. The count of arguments to your module is also not limited by one parameter. So, if you want, you can write a module with multiple required parameters and dozens of optional arguments, and it will be fine.

Now we need to get familiar with two important pieces of the PyTorch library, which will simplify our lives: loss functions and optimizers.

Final glue – loss functions and optimizers

The network which transforms input data into output is not enough to start training it. We need to define our learning objective, which is to have a function that accepts two arguments: the network's output and the desired output. Its responsibility is to return to us a single number: how close the network's prediction is from the desired result. This function is called the **loss function**, and its output is the **loss value**. Using the loss value, we calculate gradients of network parameters and adjust them to decrease this loss value, which pushes our model to better results in the future. Both of those pieces — the loss function and the method of tweaking a network's parameters by gradients — are so common and exist in so many forms that both of them form a significant part of the PyTorch library. Let's start with loss functions.

Loss functions

Loss functions reside in the nn package and are implemented as an `nn.Module` subclass. Usually, they accept two arguments: output from the network (prediction), and desired output (ground-truth data which is also called the label of the data sample). At the time of writing, PyTorch 0.4 contains 17 different loss functions. The most commonly used are:

- `nn.MSELoss`: The mean square error between arguments, which is the standard loss for regression problems

- `nn.BCELoss` and `nn.BCEWithLogits`: Binary cross-entropy loss. The first version expects a single probability value (usually it's the output of the `Sigmoid` layer), while the second version assumes raw scores as input and applies `Sigmoid` itself. The second way is usually more numerically stable and efficient. These losses (as their names suggest) are frequently used in binary classification problems.

- nn.CrossEntropyLoss and nn.NLLLoss: Famous "maximum likelihood" criteria, which is used in multi-class classification problems. The first version expects raw scores for each class and applies LogSoftmax internally, while the second expects to have log probabilities as the input.

There are other loss functions available and you are always free to write your own Module subclass to compare output and target. Now let's look at the second piece of the optimization process.

Optimizers

The responsibility of the basic optimizer is to take gradients of model parameters and change these parameters, in order to decrease loss value. By decreasing loss value, we're pushing our model towards desired outputs, which can give us hope of better model performance in the future. "Change parameters" may sound simple, but there are lots of details here and the optimizer procedure is still a hot research topic. In the torch.optim package, PyTorch provides lots of popular optimizer implementations and the most widely known are as follows:

- SGD: A vanilla stochastic gradient descent algorithm with optional momentum extension
- RMSprop: An optimizer, proposed by G. Hinton
- Adagrad: An adaptive gradients optimizer

All optimizers expose the unified interface, which makes it easy to experiment with different optimization methods (sometimes the optimization method can really make a difference in convergence dynamics and final result). On construction, you need to pass an iterable of Variables, which will be modified during the optimization process. The usual practice is to pass the result of the params() call of the upper-level nn.Module instance, which will return an iterable of all leaf Variables with gradients.

Now, let's discuss the common blueprint of a training loop:

```
for batch_samples, batch_labels in iterate_batches(data,
batch_size=32):                                             # 1
    batch_samples_t = torch.tensor(batch_samples))          # 2
    batch_labels_t = torch.tensor(batch_labels))            # 3
    out_t = net(batch_samples_t)                            # 4
    loss_t = loss_function(out_t, batch_labels_t)           # 5
    loss_t.backward()                                       # 6
    optimizer.step()                                        # 7
    optimizer.zero_grad()                                   # 8
```

Usually, you iterate over your data over and over again (one iteration over a full set of examples is called an *epoch*). Data is usually too large to fit into CPU or GPU memory at once, so it is split into batches of equal size. Every batch includes data samples and target labels, and both of them have to be tensors (lines 2 and 3). You pass data samples to your network (line 4) and feed its output and target labels to the loss function (line 5). The result of the loss function shows the "badness" of the network result relative to the target labels. As input to the network and the network's weights are tensors, all transformations of your network are nothing more than a graph of operations with intermediate tensor instances. The same is true for the loss function: its result is also a tensor of one single loss value. Every tensor in this computation graph remembers its parent, so to calculate gradients for the whole network, all you need to do is to call the `backward()` function on a loss function result (line 6).

The result of this call will be the unrolling of the graph of the performed computations and the calculating of gradients for every leaf tensor with `require_grad=True`. Usually, such tensors are our model's parameters, such as weights and biases of feed-forward networks, and convolution filters. Every time a gradient is calculated, it is accumulated in the `tensor.grad` field, so one tensor can participate in a transformation multiple times and its gradients will be properly summed up together. For example, one single **RNN** (which stands for **recurrent neural networks** and we'll talk about them in *Chapter 12, Chatbots Training with RL*) cell could be applied to multiple input items.

After the `loss.backward()` call is finished, we have the gradients accumulated, and now it's time for the optimizer to do its job: it takes all gradients from the parameters we've passed to it on construction and applies them. All this is done with the method `step()` (line 7).

The last, but not least, piece of the training loop is our responsibility to zero gradients of parameters. It can be done by calling `zero_grad()` on our network, but, for our convenience, optimizer also exposes such a call, which does the same thing (line 8). Sometimes `zero_grad()` is placed at the beginning of the training loop, but it doesn't matter much.

The preceding scheme is a very flexible way to perform optimization and can fulfill the requirements even in sophisticated research. For example, you can have two optimizers tweaking the options of different models on the same data (and this is a real-life scenario from GAN training).

So, we are done with the essential functionality of PyTorch required to train NNs. This chapter ends with a practical medium-size example to demonstrate all the concepts we've learned, but before we go to it, we need to discuss one important topic which is essential for a NN practitioner: the monitoring of the learning process.

Monitoring with TensorBoard

If you have ever tried to train a NN on your own, then you may know how painful and uncertain it can be. I'm not talking about following the existing tutorials and demos, when all hyperparameters are already tuned for you, but about taking some data and creating something from scratch. Even with modern DL high-level toolkits, where all best practices such as proper weights initialization and optimizers' betas, gammas, and other options are set to sane defaults, and tons of other stuff is hidden under the hood, there are still lots of decisions that you can make, hence lots of things could go wrong. As a result, your network almost never works from the first run and this is something that you should get used to.

Of course, with practice and experience, you'll develop a strong intuition about the possible causes of problems, but intuition needs input data about what's going on inside your network. So you need to be able to peek inside your training process somehow and observe its dynamics. Even small networks (such as tiny MNIST tutorial networks) could have hundreds of thousands of parameters with quite nonlinear training dynamics. DL practitioners have developed a list of things that you should observe during your training, which usually includes the following:

- Loss value, which normally consists of several components like base loss and regularization losses. You should monitor both total loss and individual components over time.

- Results of validation on training and test sets.

- Statistics about gradients and weights.

- Learning rates and other hyperparameters, if they are adjusted over time.

The list could be much longer and include domain-specific metrics, such as word embeddings' projections, audio samples, and images generated by GAN. You also may want to monitor values related to training speed, like how long an epoch takes, to see the effect of your optimizations or problems with hardware.

To make a long story short, you need a generic solution to track lots of values over time and represent them for analysis, preferably developed specially for DL (just imagine looking at such statistics in an Excel spreadsheet). Luckily, such tools exist.

TensorBoard 101

In fact, at the time of writing, there are not many alternatives to choose from, especially open source and generic ones. From the first public version, TensorFlow included a special tool called TensorBoard, developed to solve the problem we are talking about: how to observe and analyze various NN characteristics over training. TensorBoard is a powerful, generic solution with a large community and it looks quite pretty:

Figure 4: The TensorBoard web interface

From the architecture point of view, TensorBoard is a Python web service which you can start on your computer, passing it the directory where your training process will save values to be analyzed. Then you point your browser to TensorBoard's port (usually `6006`), and it shows you an interactive web interface with values updated in real-time. It's nice and convenient, especially when your training is performed on a remote machine somewhere in the cloud.

Originally, TensorBoard was deployed as a part of TensorFlow, but recently, it has been moved to a separate project (it's still being maintained by Google) and has its own package name. However, TensorBoard still uses the TensorFlow data format, so to be able to write training statistics from PyTorch optimization, you'll need both the `tensorflow` and `tensorflow-tensorboard` packages installed. As TensorFlow depends on TensorBoard, to install both, you need to run `pip install tensorflow` in your virtual environment.

In theory, this is all you need to start monitoring your networks, as the `tensorflow` package provides you with classes to write the data that TensorBoard will be able to read. However, it's not very practical, as those classes are very low level. To overcome this, there are several third-party open-source libraries that provide a convenient high-level interface. One of my favorites, which is used in this book, is `tensorboard-pytorch` (`https://github.com/lanpa/tensorboard-pytorch`). It can be installed with `pip install tensorboard-pytorch`.

Plotting stuff

To give you an impression of how simple `tensorboard-pytorch` is, let's consider a small example that is not related to NNs, but is just about writing stuff into TensorBoard (the full example code is in `Chapter03/02_tensorboard.py`).

```
import math
from tensorboardX import SummaryWriter

if __name__ == "__main__":
    writer = SummaryWriter()

    funcs = {"sin": math.sin, "cos": math.cos, "tan": math.tan}
```

We import the required packages, create a writer of data, and define functions that we're going to visualize. By default, `SummaryWriter` will create a unique directory under the `runs` directory for every launch, to be able to compare different launches of training. Names of the new directory include the current date and time, and hostname. To override this, you can pass the `log_dir` argument to `SummaryWriter`. You also can add a suffix to the name of the directory by passing a comment option, for example to capture different experiments' semantics, such as `dropout=0.3` or `strong_regularisation`

```
    for angle in range(-360, 360):
        angle_rad = angle * math.pi / 180
        for name, fun in funcs.items():
            val = fun(angle_rad)
            writer.add_scalar(name, val, angle)
    writer.close()
```

Here, we loop over angle ranges in degrees, convert them into radians, and calculate our functions' values. Every value is being added to the writer using the `add_scalar` function, which takes three arguments: the name of the parameter, its value, and the current iteration (which has to be an integer).

The last thing we need to do after the loop is to close the writer. Note that the writer does a periodical flush (by default, every two minutes), so even in the case of a lengthy optimization process, you still will see your values.

The result of running this will be zero output on the console, but you will see a new directory created inside the `runs` directory with a single file. To look at the result, we need to start TensorBoard:

```
rl_book_samples/Chapter03$ tensorboard --logdir runs --host localhost
TensorBoard 0.1.7 at http://localhost:6006 (Press CTRL+C to
quit)
```

Now you can open `http://localhost:6006` in your browser to see something like this:

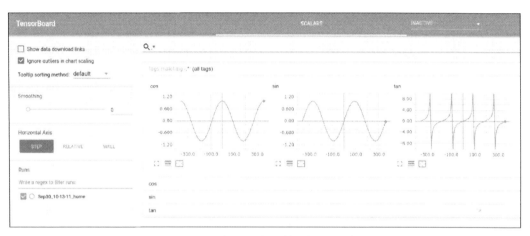

Figure 5: Plots produced by the example

The graphs are interactive, so you can hover over them with your mouse to see the actual values and select regions to zoom into details. To zoom out, double-click inside the graph. If you run your program several times, then you will see several items in the "runs" list on the left, which can be enabled and disabled in any combinations, allowing you to compare the dynamics of several optimizations. TensorBoard allows you to analyze not only scalar values but also images, audio, text data, and embeddings, and it can even show you the structure of your network. Refer to the documentation of `tensorboard-pytorch` and `tensorboard` for all those features.

Now it's time to unite everything you learned in this chapter and look at a real NN optimization problem using PyTorch.

Example – GAN on Atari images

Almost every book about DL uses the MNIST dataset to show you the power of DL, which, over the years, has made this dataset extremely boring, like a fruit fly for genetic researchers. To break this tradition, and add a bit more fun to the book, I've tried to avoid well-beaten paths and illustrate PyTorch using something different. You may have heard about **generative adversarial networks (GANs)**, which were invented and popularized by *Ian Goodfellow*. In this example, we'll train a GAN to generate screenshots of various Atari games.

The simplest GAN architecture is this: we have two networks and the first works as a "cheater" (it is also called generator), and the other is a "detective" (another name is discriminator). Both networks compete with each other: the generator tries to generate fake data, which will be hard for the discriminator to distinguish from your dataset, and the discriminator tries to detect the generated data samples. Over time, both networks improve their skills: the generator produces more and more realistic data samples, and the discriminator invents more sophisticated ways to distinguish the fake items. Practical usage of GANs includes image quality improvement, realistic image generation, and feature learning. In our example, practical usefulness is almost zero, but it will be a good example of how clean and short PyTorch code can be for quite complex models.

So, let's get started. The whole example code is in the file Chapter03/03_atari_gan.py. Here we'll look at only significant pieces of code, without the import section and constants declaration:

```python
class InputWrapper(gym.ObservationWrapper):
    def __init__(self, *args):
        super(InputWrapper, self).__init__(*args)
        assert isinstance(self.observation_space, gym.spaces.Box)
        old_space = self.observation_space
        self.observation_space =
gym.spaces.Box(self.observation(old_space.low),
self.observation(old_space.high), dtype=np.float32)

    def observation(self, observation):
        # resize image
        new_obs = cv2.resize(observation, (IMAGE_SIZE,
IMAGE_SIZE))
        # transform (210, 160, 3) -> (3, 210, 160)
        new_obs = np.moveaxis(new_obs, 2, 0)
        return new_obs.astype(np.float32) / 255.0
```

This class is a wrapper around a Gym game, which includes several transformations:

- Resize input image from 210 × 160 (standard Atari resolution) to a square size 64 × 64

- Move color plane of the image from the last position to the first, to meet the PyTorch convention of convolution layers that input a tensor with the shape of channels, height, and width

- Cast the image from bytes to float and rescale its values to a 0..1 range

Then we define two `nn.Module` classes: `Discriminator` and `Generator`. The first takes our scaled color image as input and, by applying five layers of convolutions, converts it into a single number, passed through a sigmoid nonlinearity. The output from `Sigmoid` is interpreted as the probability that `Discriminator` thinks our input image is from the real dataset.

`Generator` takes as input a vector of random numbers (latent vector) and using the "transposed convolution" operation (it is also known as **deconvolution**), converts this vector into a color image of the original resolution. We will not look at those classes here as they are lengthy and not very relevant to our example. You can find them in the complete example file.

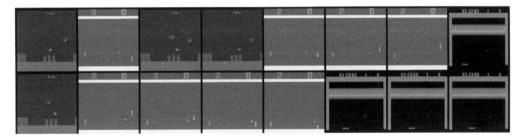

Figure 6: A sample screenshot from three Atari games

As input, we'll use screenshots from several Atari games played simultaneously by a random agent. *Figure 6* is an example of what the input data looks like and it is generated by the following function:

```
def iterate_batches(envs, batch_size=BATCH_SIZE):
    batch = [e.reset() for e in envs]
    env_gen = iter(lambda: random.choice(envs), None)

    while True:
        e = next(env_gen)
        obs, reward, is_done, _ = e.step(e.action_space.sample())
        if np.mean(obs) > 0.01:
            batch.append(obs)
```

```
        if len(batch) == batch_size:
            yield torch.FloatTensor(batch)
            batch.clear()
        if is_done:
            e.reset()
```

This infinitely samples the environment from the provided array, issues random actions and remembers observations in the `batch` list. When the batch becomes of the required size, we convert it to a tensor and `yield` from the generator. The check for the nonzero mean of the observation is required due to a bug in one of the games to prevent the flickering of an image.

Now let's look at our main function, which prepares models and runs the training loop:

```
if __name__ == "__main__":
    parser = argparse.ArgumentParser()
    parser.add_argument("--cuda", default=False,
action='store_true')
    args = parser.parse_args()
    device = torch.device("cuda" if args.cuda else "cpu")

    env_names = ('Breakout-v0', 'AirRaid-v0', 'Pong-v0')
    envs = [InputWrapper(gym.make(name)) for name in env_names]
    input_shape = envs[0].observation_space.shape
```

Here, we process the command-line arguments (which could be only one optional argument, `--cuda`, enabling GPU computation mode) and create our environment pool with a wrapper applied. This environment array will be passed to the `iterate_batches` function to generate training data:

```
    Writer = SummaryWriter()
    net_discr = Discriminator(input_shape=input_shape).to(device)
    net_gener = Generator(output_shape=input_shape).to(device)

    objective = nn.BCELoss()
    gen_optimizer = optim.Adam(params=net_gener.parameters(),
lr=LEARNING_RATE)
    dis_optimizer = optim.Adam(params=net_discr.parameters(),
lr=LEARNING_RATE)
```

In this piece, we create our classes: a summary writer, both networks, a loss function, and two optimizers. Why two? It's because that's the way that GANs get trained: to train the discriminator, we need to show it both real and fake data samples with appropriate labels (1 for real, 0 for fake). During this pass, we update only the discriminator's parameters.

After that, we pass both real and fake samples through the discriminator again, but this time the labels are 1s for all samples, and now we update only the generator's weights. The second pass teaches the generator how to fool the discriminator and confuse real samples with the generated ones:

```
gen_losses = []
dis_losses = []
iter_no = 0

true_labels_v = torch.ones(BATCH_SIZE, dtype=torch.float32,
device=device)
    fake_labels_v = torch.zeros(BATCH_SIZE, dtype=torch.float32,
device=device)
```

Here, we define arrays, which will be used to accumulate losses, iterator counters, and variables with the `True` and `Fake` labels.

```
for batch_v in iterate_batches(envs):
        # generate extra fake samples, input is 4D: batch,
filters, x, y
        gen_input_v = torch.FloatTensor(BATCH_SIZE,
LATENT_VECTOR_SIZE, 1, 1).normal_(0, 1).to(device)
        batch_v = batch_v.to(device)
        gen_output_v = net_gener(gen_input_v)
```

At the beginning of the training loop, we generate a random vector and pass it to the `Generator` network.

```
        dis_optimizer.zero_grad()
        dis_output_true_v = net_discr(batch_v)
        dis_output_fake_v = net_discr(gen_output_v.detach())
        dis_loss = objective(dis_output_true_v, true_labels_v) +
objective(dis_output_fake_v, fake_labels_v)
        dis_loss.backward()
        dis_optimizer.step()
        dis_losses.append(dis_loss.item())
```

At first, we train the discriminator by applying it two times: to the true data samples in our batch and to the generated ones. We need to call the `detach()` function on the generator's output to prevent gradients of this training pass from flowing into the generator (`detach()` is a method of tensor, which makes a copy of it without connection to the parent's operation).

```
        gen_optimizer.zero_grad()
        dis_output_v = net_discr(gen_output_v)
        gen_loss_v = objective(dis_output_v, true_labels_v)
        gen_loss_v.backward()
        gen_optimizer.step()
        gen_losses.append(gen_loss_v.item())
```

Now it's the generator's training time. We pass the generator's output to the discriminator, but now we don't stop the gradients. Instead, we apply the objective function with `True` labels. It will push our generator in the direction where the samples that it generates make the discriminator confuse them with the real data.

That's all real training, and the next couple of lines report losses and feed image samples to TensorBoard:

```
iter_no += 1
if iter_no % REPORT_EVERY_ITER == 0:
        log.info("Iter %d: gen_loss=%.3e, dis_loss=%.3e",
iter_no, np.mean(gen_losses), np.mean(dis_losses))
        writer.add_scalar("gen_loss", np.mean(gen_losses),
iter_no)
        writer.add_scalar("dis_loss", np.mean(dis_losses),
iter_no)
        gen_losses = []
        dis_losses = []
    if iter_no % SAVE_IMAGE_EVERY_ITER == 0:
        writer.add_image("fake",
vutils.make_grid(gen_output_v.data[:64]), iter_no)
        writer.add_image("real",
vutils.make_grid(batch_v.data[:64]), iter_no)
```

The training of this example is quite a lengthy process. On a GTX 1080 GPU, 100 iterations take about 40 seconds. At the beginning, the generated images are completely random noise, but after 10k-20k iterations, the generator becomes more and more proficient at its job and the generated images become more and more similar to the real game screenshots.

My experiments gave the following images after 40k-50k of training iterations (several hours on a GPU):

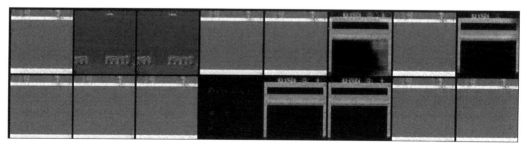

Figure 7: Sample images produced by the generator network

Summary

In this chapter, we saw a quick overview of PyTorch functionality and features. We talked about basic fundamental pieces such as tensor and gradients, saw how an NN can be made from the basic building blocks, and learned how to implement those blocks ourselves. We discussed loss functions and optimizers, as well as the monitoring of training dynamics. The goal of the chapter was to give a very quick introduction to PyTorch, which will be used later in the book.

For the next chapter, we're ready to start dealing with the main subject of this book: RL methods.

4
The Cross-Entropy Method

In this chapter, we will wrap up the part one of the book and get familiar with one of the RL methods — cross-entropy. Despite the fact that it is much less famous than other tools in the RL practitioner's toolbox, such as **deep Q-network (DQN)** or Advantage Actor-Critic, this method has its own strengths. The most important are as follows:

- **Simplicity**: The cross-entropy method is really simple, which makes it an intuitive method to follow. For example, its implementation on PyTorch is less than 100 lines of code.

- **Good convergence**: In simple environments that don't require complex, multistep policies to be learned and discovered and have short episodes with frequent rewards, cross-entropy usually works very well. Of course, lots of practical problems don't fall into this category, but sometimes they do. In such cases, cross-entropy (on its own or as a part of a larger system) can be the perfect fit.

In the following sections, we will start from the practical side of cross-entropy, and then look at how it works in two environments in Gym (the familiar CartPole and the "grid world" of FrozenLake). Then, at the end of the chapter, we will take a look at the theoretical background of the method. This section is optional and requires a bit more knowledge of probability and statistics, but if you want to understand why the method works then you can delve into it.

Taxonomy of RL methods

The cross-entropy method falls into the *model-free* and *policy-based* category of methods. These notions are new, so let's spend some time exploring them. All methods in RL can be classified into various aspects:

- Model-free or model-based
- Value-based or policy-based
- On-policy or off-policy

There are other ways that you can taxonomize RL methods, but for now we're interested in the preceding three. Let's define them, as your problem specifics can influence your decision on a particular method.

The term **model-free** means that the method doesn't build a model of the environment or reward; it just directly connects observations to actions (or values that are related to actions). In other words, the agent takes current observations and does some computations on them, and the result is the action that it should take. In contrast, **model-based** methods try to predict what the next observation and/ or reward will be. Based on this prediction, the agent is trying to choose the best possible action to take, very often making such predictions multiple times to look more and more steps into the future.

Both classes of methods have strong and weak sides, but usually pure model-based methods are used in deterministic environments, such as board games with strict rules. On the other hand, model-free methods are usually easier to train as it's hard to build good models of complex environments with rich observations. All of the methods described in this book are from the model-free category, as those methods have been the most active area of research for the past few years. Only recently have researchers started to mix the benefits from both worlds (for example, refer to DeepMind's papers on imagination in agents. This approach will be described in *Chapter 17, Beyond Model-Free – Imagination*).

By looking from an other angle, **policy-based** methods are directly approximating the policy of the agent, that is, what actions the agent should carry out at every step. Policy is usually represented by probability distribution over the available actions. In contrast, the method could be **value-based**. In this case, instead of the probability of actions, the agent calculates the value of every possible action and chooses the action with the best value. Both of those families of methods are equally popular and we'll discuss value-based methods in the next part of the book. Policy methods will be the topic of part three.

The third important classification of methods is **on-policy** versus **off-policy**. We'll discuss this distinction more in parts two and three of the book, but for now, it will be enough to explain off-policy as the ability of the method to learn on old historical data (obtained by a previous version of the agent or recorded by human demonstration or just seen by the same agent several episodes ago).

So, our cross-entropy method is model-free, policy-based, and on-policy, which means the following:

- It doesn't build any model of the environment; it just says to the agent what to do at every step
- It approximates the policy of the agent
- It requires fresh data obtained from the environment

Practical cross-entropy

The cross-entropy method description is split into two unequal parts: practical and theoretical. The practical part is intuitive in its nature, while the theoretical explanation of *why* cross-entropy works, and what's happening is more sophisticated.

You may remember that the central, trickiest thing in RL is the agent, which is trying to accumulate as much total reward as possible by communicating with the environment. In practice, we follow a common ML approach and replace all of the complications of the agent with some kind of nonlinear trainable function, which maps the agent's input (observations from the environment) to some output. The details of the output that this function produces may depend on a particular method or a family of methods, as described in the previous section (such as value-based versus policy-based methods). As our cross-entropy method is policy-based, our nonlinear function (neural network) produces *policy*, which basically says for every observation which action the agent should take.

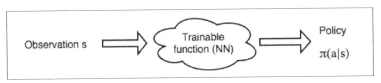

Figure 1: A high-level approach to RL

In practice, policy is usually represented as probability distribution over actions, which makes it very similar to a classification problem, with the amount of classes being equal to amount of actions we can carry out. This abstraction makes our agent very simple: it needs to pass an observation from the environment to the network, get probability distribution over actions, and perform random sampling using probability distribution to get an action to carry out. This random sampling adds randomness to our agent, which is a good thing, as at the beginning of the training when our weights are random, the agent behaves randomly. After the agent gets an action to issue, it fires the action to the environment and obtains the next observation and reward for the last action. Then the loop continues.

During the agent's lifetime, its experience is present as episodes. Every episode is a sequence of observations that the agent has got from the environment, actions it has issued, and rewards for these actions. Imagine that our agent has played several such episodes. For every episode, we can calculate the total reward that the agent has claimed. It can be discounted or not discounted, but for simplicity, let's assume a discount factor of gamma = 1, which means just a sum of all local rewards for every episode. This total reward shows how good this episode was for the agent. Let's illustrate this with a diagram, which contains four episodes (note that different episodes have different values for o_i, a_i, and r_i):

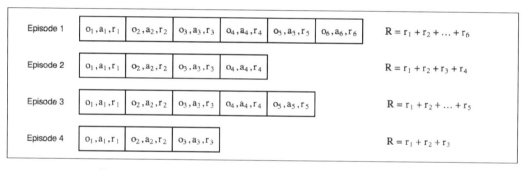

Figure 2: Sample episodes with their observations, actions, and rewards

Every cell represents the agent's step in the episode. Due to randomness in the environment and the way that the agent selects actions to take, some episodes will be better than others. The core of the cross-entropy method is to throw away bad episodes and train on better ones. So, the steps of the method are as follows:

1. Play *N* number of episodes using our current model and environment.

2. Calculate the total reward for every episode and decide on a reward boundary. Usually, we use some percentile of all rewards, such as 50th or 70th.

3. Throw away all episodes with a reward below the boundary.

4. Train on the remaining "elite" episodes using observations as the input and issued actions as the desired output.

5. Repeat from step 1 until we become satisfied with the result.

So, that's all about the cross-entropy method description. With the preceding procedure, our neural network learns how to repeat actions, which leads to a larger reward, constantly moving the boundary higher and higher. Despite the simplicity of this method, it works well in simple environments, it's easy to implement, and it's quite robust to hyperparameters changing, which makes it an ideal baseline method to try. Let's now apply it to our CartPole environment.

Cross-entropy on CartPole

The whole code for this example is in `Chapter04/01_cartpole.py`, but the following are the most important parts. Our model's core is a one-hidden-layer neural network, with ReLU and 128 hidden neurons (which is absolutely arbitrary). Other hyperparameters are also set almost randomly and aren't tuned, as the method is robust and converges very quickly.

```
HIDDEN_SIZE = 128
BATCH_SIZE = 16
PERCENTILE = 70
```

We define constants at the top of the file and they include the count of neurons in the hidden layer, the count of episodes we play on every iteration (16), and the percentile of episodes' total rewards that we use for elite episode filtering. We'll take the 70th percentile, which means that we'll leave the top 30% of episodes sorted by reward:

```
class Net(nn.Module):
    def __init__(self, obs_size, hidden_size, n_actions):
        super(Net, self).__init__()
        self.net = nn.Sequential(
            nn.Linear(obs_size, hidden_size),
            nn.ReLU(),
            nn.Linear(hidden_size, n_actions)
        )
```

```
def forward(self, x):
    return self.net(x)
```

There is nothing special about our network; it takes a single observation from the environment as an input vector and outputs a number for every action we can perform. The output from the network is a probability distribution over actions, so a straightforward way to proceed would be to include softmax nonlinearity after the last layer. However, in the preceding network we don't apply softmax to increase the numerical stability of the training process. Rather than calculating softmax (which uses exponentiation) and then calculating cross-entropy loss (which uses logarithm of probabilities), we'll use the PyTorch class, nn.CrossEntropyLoss, which combines both softmax and cross-entropy in a single, more numerically stable expression. CrossEntropyLoss requires raw, unnormalized values from the network (also called logits), and the downside of this is that we need to remember to apply softmax every time we need to get probabilities from our network's output.

```
Episode = namedtuple('Episode', field_names=['reward', 'steps'])
EpisodeStep = namedtuple('EpisodeStep', field_names=['observation',
'action'])
```

Here we will define two helper classes that are named tuples from the collections package in the standard library:

- EpisodeStep: This will be used to represent one single step that our agent made in the episode, and it stores the observation from the environment and what action the agent completed. We'll use episode steps from elite episodes as training data.

- Episode: This is a single episode stored as total undiscounted reward and a collection of EpisodeStep.

Let's look at a function that generates batches with episodes:

```
def iterate_batches(env, net, batch_size):
    batch = []
    episode_reward = 0.0
    episode_steps = []
    obs = env.reset()
    sm = nn.Softmax(dim=1)
```

The preceding function accepts the environment (the `Env` class instance from the Gym library), our neural network, and the count of episodes it should generate on every iteration. The `batch` variable will be used to accumulate our batch (which is a list of the `Episode` instances). We also declare a reward counter for the current episode and its list of steps (the `EpisodeStep` objects). Then we reset our environment to obtain the first observation and create a softmax layer, which will be used to convert the network's output to a probability distribution of actions. That's all about our preparations; so we're ready to start the environment loop:

```
while True:
    obs_v = torch.FloatTensor([obs])
    act_probs_v = sm(net(obs_v))
    act_probs = act_probs_v.data.numpy()[0]
```

At every iteration, we convert our current observation to a PyTorch tensor and pass it to the network to obtain action probabilities. There are several things to note here:

- All `nn.Module` instances in PyTorch expect a batch of data items and the same is true for our network, so we convert our observation (which is a vector of four numbers in CartPole) into a tensor of size 1 × 4 (to achieve this we pass an observation in a single-element list).

- As we haven't used nonlinearity at the output of our network, it outputs raw action scores, which we need to feed through the softmax function.

- Both our network and the softmax layer return tensors which track gradients, so we need to unpack this by accessing the `tensor.data` field and then converting the tensor into a NumPy array. This array will have the same two-dimensional structure as the input, with the batch dimension on axis 0, so we need to get the first batch element to obtain a one-dimensional vector of action probabilities:

```
        action = np.random.choice(len(act_probs),
p=act_probs)
        next_obs, reward, is_done, _ = env.step(action)
```

Now that we have the probability distribution of actions, we can use this distribution to obtain the actual action for the current step by sampling this distribution using NumPy's function, `random.choice()`. After this, we will pass this action to the environment to get our next observation, our reward, and the indication of the episode ending:

```
        episode_reward += reward
        episode_steps.append(EpisodeStep(observation=obs,
    action=action))
```

Reward is added to the current episode's total reward, and our list of episode steps is also extended with an (observation, action) pair. Note that we save the observation that was used to choose the action, but not the observation returned by the environment as a result of the action. These are the tiny but important details that you need to keep in mind.

```
if is_done:
        batch.append(Episode(reward=episode_reward,
steps=episode_steps))
        episode_reward = 0.0
        episode_steps = []
        next_obs = env.reset()
        if len(batch) == batch_size:
            yield batch
            batch = []
```

This is how we handle the situation when the current episode is over (in the case of CartPole, the episode ends when the stick has fallen down despite our efforts). We append the finalized episode to the batch, saving the total reward (as the episode has been completed and we've accumulated all reward) and steps we've taken. Then we reset our total reward accumulator and clean the list of steps. After that, we reset our environment to start over.

In case our batch has reached the desired count of episodes, we return it to the caller for processing, using `yield`. Our function is a generator, so every time the `yield` operator is executed, the control is transferred to the outer iteration loop and then continues after the `yield` line. If you're not familiar with Python's generator functions, refer to the Python documentation. After processing, we will clean up the batch:

```
obs = next_obs
```

The last, but very important, step in our loop is to assign an observation obtained from the environment to our current observation variable. After that, everything repeats infinitely: we pass the observation to the net, sample the action to perform, ask the environment to process the action, and remember the result of this processing.

One very important fact to understand in this function logic is that the training of our network and the generation of our episodes are performed *at the same time*. They are not completely in parallel, but every time our loop accumulates enough episodes (16), it passes control to this function caller, which is supposed to train the network using the gradient descent. So, when `yield` is returned, the network will have different, slightly better (we hope) behavior.

We don't need to explore proper synchronization, as our training and data gathering activities are performed at the same thread of execution, but you need to understand those constant jumps from network training to its utilization.

Okay, now we need to define yet another function and we'll be ready to switch to the training loop:

```
def filter_batch(batch, percentile):
    rewards = list(map(lambda s: s.reward, batch))
    reward_bound = np.percentile(rewards, percentile)
    reward_mean = float(np.mean(rewards))
```

This function is at the core of the cross-entropy method: from the given batch of episodes and percentile value, it calculates a boundary reward, which is used to filter elite episodes to train on. To obtain the boundary reward, we're using NumPy's percentile function, which from the list of values and the desired percentile, calculates the percentile's value. Then we will calculate mean reward, which is used only for monitoring.

```
    train_obs = []
    train_act = []
    for example in batch:
        if example.reward < reward_bound:
            continue
        train_obs.extend(map(lambda step: step.observation,
example.steps))
        train_act.extend(map(lambda step: step.action,
example.steps))
```

Next, we will filter off our episodes. For every episode in the batch, we will check that the episode has a higher total reward than our boundary and if it has, we will populate lists of observations and actions that we will train on.

```
    train_obs_v = torch.FloatTensor(train_obs)
    train_act_v = torch.LongTensor(train_act)
    return train_obs_v, train_act_v, reward_bound, reward_mean
```

As the final step of the function, we will convert our observations and actions from elite episodes into tensors, and return a tuple of four: observations, actions, the boundary of reward, and the mean reward. The last two values will be used only to write them into TensorBoard to check the performance of our agent.

Now, the final chunk of code that glues everything together and mostly consists of the training loop is as follows:

```
if __name__ == "__main__":
    env = gym.make("CartPole-v0")
    # env = gym.wrappers.Monitor(env, directory="mon", force=True)
    obs_size = env.observation_space.shape[0]
    n_actions = env.action_space.n

    net = Net(obs_size, HIDDEN_SIZE, n_actions)
    objective = nn.CrossEntropyLoss()
    optimizer = optim.Adam(params=net.parameters(), lr=0.01)
    writer = SummaryWriter()
```

In the beginning, we will create all the required objects: the environment, our neural network, the objective function, the optimizer, and the summary writer for TensorBoard. The commented line creates a monitor to write videos of your agent's performance.

```
    for iter_no, batch in enumerate(iterate_batches(env, net,
BATCH_SIZE)):
        obs_v, acts_v, reward_b, reward_m = filter_batch(batch,
PERCENTILE)
        optimizer.zero_grad()
        action_scores_v = net(obs_v)
        loss_v = objective(action_scores_v, acts_v)
        loss_v.backward()
        optimizer.step()
```

In the training loop, we will iterate our batches (which are a list of `Episode` objects), then we perform filtering of the elite episodes using the `filter_batch` function. The result is variables of observations and taken actions, the reward boundary used for filtering and the mean reward. After that, we zero gradients of our network and pass observations to the network, obtaining its action scores. These scores are passed to the objective function, which calculates cross-entropy between the network output and the actions that the agent took. The idea of this is to reinforce our network to carry out those "elite" actions which have led to good rewards. Then, we will calculate gradients on the loss and ask the optimizer to adjust our network.

```
        print("%d: loss=%.3f, reward_mean=%.1f, reward_bound=%.1f" % (
            iter_no, loss_v.item(), reward_m, reward_b))
        writer.add_scalar("loss", loss_v.item(), iter_no)
        writer.add_scalar("reward_bound", reward_b, iter_no)
        writer.add_scalar("reward_mean", reward_m, iter_no)
```

The rest of the loop is mostly the monitoring of progress. On the console, we show iteration number, loss, the mean reward of the batch, and the reward boundary. We also write the same values to TensorBoard, to get a nice chart of the agent's learning performance.

```
        if reward_m > 199:
            print("Solved!")
            break
    writer.close()
```

The last check in the loop is the comparison of the mean rewards of our batch episodes. When this becomes greater than 199, we stop our training. Why 199? In Gym, the CartPole environment is considered to be solved when the mean reward for last 100 episodes is greater than 195, but our method converges so quickly that 100 episodes are usually what we need. The properly trained agent can balance the stick infinitely long (obtaining any amount of score), but the length of the episode in CartPole is limited to 200 steps (if you look at the environment variable of CartPole, you may notice the TimeLimit wrapper, which stops the episode after 200 steps). With all this in mind, we will stop training after the mean reward in the batch is greater than 199, which is a good indication that our agent knows how to balance the stick as a pro.

That's it. So let's start our first RL training!

```
rl_book_samples/Chapter04$ ./01_cartpole.py
[2017-10-04 12:44:39,319] Making new env: CartPole-v0
0: loss=0.701, reward_mean=18.0, reward_bound=21.0
1: loss=0.682, reward_mean=22.6, reward_bound=23.5
2: loss=0.688, reward_mean=23.6, reward_bound=25.5
3: loss=0.675, reward_mean=22.8, reward_bound=22.0
4: loss=0.658, reward_mean=31.9, reward_bound=34.0
.........
36: loss=0.527, reward_mean=135.9, reward_bound=168.5
37: loss=0.527, reward_mean=147.4, reward_bound=160.5
38: loss=0.528, reward_mean=179.8, reward_bound=200.0
39: loss=0.530, reward_mean=178.7, reward_bound=200.0
40: loss=0.532, reward_mean=192.1, reward_bound=200.0
41: loss=0.523, reward_mean=196.8, reward_bound=200.0
42: loss=0.540, reward_mean=200.0, reward_bound=200.0
Solved!
```

It usually doesn't take the agent more than 50 batches to solve the environment. My experiments show something from 25 to 45 episodes, which is a really good learning performance (remember, we need to play only 16 episodes for every batch). TensorBoard shows our agent consistently making progress, pushing the upper boundary at almost every batch (there are some periods of rolling down, but most of the time it improves).

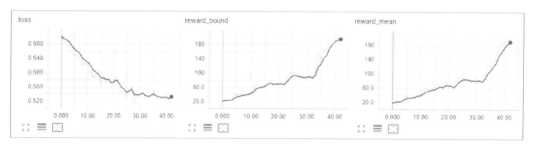

Figure 3: Loss, reward boundary, and reward during the training

To check our agent in action, you can enable `Monitor` by uncommenting the next line after the environment creation. After restarting (possibly with `xvfb-run` to provide a virtual X11 display), our program will create a `mon` directory with videos recorded at different training steps:

```
rl_book_samples/Chapter04$ xvfb-run -s "-screen 0 640x480x24" ./01_
cartpole.py
[2017-10-04 13:52:23,806] Making new env: CartPole-v0
[2017-10-04 13:52:23,814] Creating monitor directory mon
[2017-10-04 13:52:23,920] Starting new video recorder writing to mon/
openaigym.video.0.4430.video000000.mp4
[2017-10-04 13:52:25,229] Starting new video recorder writing to mon/
openaigym.video.0.4430.video000001.mp4
[2017-10-04 13:52:25,771] Starting new video recorder writing to mon/
openaigym.video.0.4430.video000008.mp4
0: loss=0.682, reward_mean=18.9, reward_bound=20.5
[2017-10-04 13:52:26,297] Starting new video recorder writing to mon/
openaigym.video.0.4430.video000027.mp4
1: loss=0.687, reward_mean=16.6, reward_bound=19.0
2: loss=0.677, reward_mean=21.1, reward_bound=21.0
[2017-10-04 13:52:26,964] Starting new video recorder writing to mon/
openaigym.video.0.4430.video000064.mp4
3: loss=0.653, reward_mean=33.2, reward_bound=48.5
4: loss=0.642, reward_mean=37.4, reward_bound=42.5
.........
29: loss=0.561, reward_mean=111.6, reward_bound=122.0
30: loss=0.540, reward_mean=135.1, reward_bound=166.0
```

```
[2017-10-04 13:52:40,176] Starting new video recorder writing to mon/
openaigym.video.0.4430.video000512.mp4
31: loss=0.546, reward_mean=147.5, reward_bound=179.5
32: loss=0.559, reward_mean=140.0, reward_bound=171.5
33: loss=0.558, reward_mean=160.4, reward_bound=200.0
34: loss=0.547, reward_mean=167.6, reward_bound=195.5
35: loss=0.550, reward_mean=179.5, reward_bound=200.0
36: loss=0.563, reward_mean=173.9, reward_bound=200.0
37: loss=0.542, reward_mean=162.9, reward_bound=200.0
38: loss=0.552, reward_mean=159.1, reward_bound=200.0
39: loss=0.548, reward_mean=189.6, reward_bound=200.0
40: loss=0.546, reward_mean=191.1, reward_bound=200.0
41: loss=0.548, reward_mean=199.1, reward_bound=200.0
Solved!
```

As you can see from the output, it turns a periodical recording of the agent's activity into separate video files, which can give you an idea of what your agent's sessions look like.

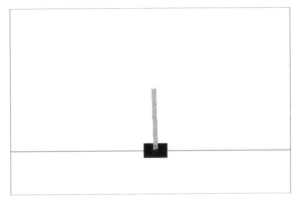

Figure 4: Visualization of the CartPole state

Let's now pause a bit and think about what's just happened. Our neural network has learned how to play the environment purely from observations and rewards, without any one word interpretation of observed values. The environment could easily be not a cart with a stick but, say, a warehouse model with product quantities as an observation and money earned as a reward. Our implementation doesn't depend on environment details. This is the beauty of the RL model, and in the next section, we'll look at how exactly the same method can be applied to a different environment from the Gym collection.

Cross-entropy on FrozenLake

The next environment we'll try to solve using the cross-entropy method is FrozenLake. Its world is from the so-called "grid world" category, when your agent lives in a grid of size 4 × 4 and can move in four directions: up, down, left, and right. The agent always starts at a top-left position, and its goal is to reach the bottom-right cell of the grid. There are holes in the fixed cells of the grid and if you get into those holes, the episode ends and your reward is zero. If the agent reaches the destination cell, then it obtains the reward 1.0 and the episode ends.

To make life more complicated, the world is slippery (it's a frozen lake after all), so the agent's actions do not always turn out as expected: there is a 33% chance that it will slip to the right or to the left. You want the agent to move left, for example, but there is a 33% probability that it will indeed move left, a 33% chance that it will end up in the cell above, and a 33% chance that it will end up in the cell below. As we'll see at the end of the section, this makes progress difficult.

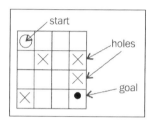

Figure 5: The FrozenLake environment

Let's look how this environment is represented in Gym:

```
>>> e = gym.make("FrozenLake-v0")
[2017-10-05 12:39:35,827] Making new env: FrozenLake-v0
>>> e.observation_space
Discrete(16)
>>> e.action_space
Discrete(4)
>>> e.reset()
0
>>> e.render()

SFFF
FHFH
FFFH
HFFG
```

Our observation space is discrete, which means that it's just a number from zero to 15 inclusive. Obviously, this number is our current position in the grid. The action space is also discrete, but can be from zero to three. Our network from the CartPole example expects a vector of numbers. To get this, we can apply the traditional "one-hot encoding" of discrete inputs, which means that input to our network will have 16 float numbers and zero everywhere, except the index that we'll encode. To minimize changes in our code, we can use the `ObservationWrapper` class from Gym and implement our `DiscreteOneHotWrapper` class:

```
class DiscreteOneHotWrapper(gym.ObservationWrapper):
    def __init__(self, env):
        super(DiscreteOneHotWrapper, self).__init__(env)
        assert isinstance(env.observation_space,
gym.spaces.Discrete)
        self.observation_space = gym.spaces.Box(0.0, 1.0,
(env.observation_space.n, ), dtype=np.float32)

    def observation(self, observation):
        res = np.copy(self.observation_space.low)
        res[observation] = 1.0
        return res
```

With that wrapper applied to the environment, both the observation space and action space are 100% compatible with our CartPole solution (source code `Chapter04/02_ frozenlake_naive.py`). However, by launching it, we can see that this doesn't improve the score over time.

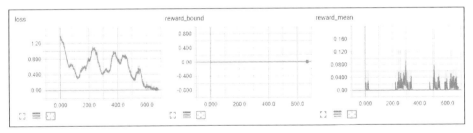

Figure 6: Lack of convergence of the original cross-entropy code in the FrozenLake environment

To understand what's going on, we need to look deeper at the reward structure of both environments. In CartPole, every step of the environment gives us the reward 1.0, until the moment that the pole falls. So, the longer our agent balanced the pole, the more reward it obtained. Due to randomness in our agent's behavior, different episodes were of different lengths, which gave us a pretty normal distribution of the episodes' rewards. After choosing a reward boundary, we rejected less successful episodes and learned how to repeat better ones (by training on successful episodes' data).

This is shown in the following diagram:

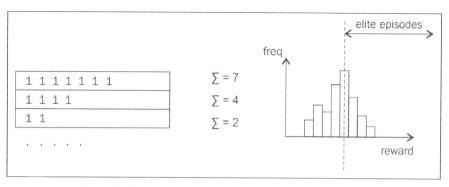

Figure 7: Distribution of reward in the CartPole environment

In the FrozenLake environment, episodes and their reward look different. We get the reward of 1.0 only when we reach the goal, and this reward says nothing about how good each episode was. Was it quick and efficient or did we make four rounds on the lake before we randomly stepped into the final cell? We don't know, it's just 1.0 reward and that's it. The distribution of rewards for our episodes are also problematic. There are only two kinds of episodes possible, with zero reward (failed) and one reward (successful), and failed episodes will obviously dominate in the beginning of the training. So, our percentile selection of "elite" episodes is totally wrong and gives us bad examples to train on. This is the reason for our training failure.

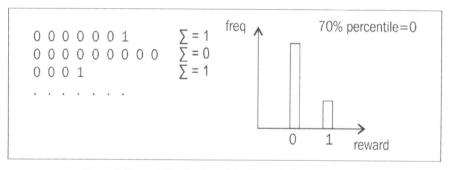

Figure 8: Reward distribution of the FrozenLake environment

This example shows us the limitations of the cross-entropy method:

- For training, our episodes have to be finite and, preferably, short
- The total reward for the episodes should have enough variability to separate good episodes from bad ones
- There is no intermediate indication about whether the agent has succeeded or failed

Later in the book, we'll become familiar with other methods, which address these limitations. For now, if you're curious about how FrozenLake can be solved using cross-entropy, here is a list of tweaks of the code that you need to make (the full example is in Chapter04/03_frozenlake_tweaked.py):

- **Larger batches of played episodes**: In CartPole, it was enough to have 16 episodes on every iteration, but FrozenLake requires at least 100 just to get some successful episodes.

- **Discount factor applied to reward**: To make the total reward for the episode depend on episode length, and add variety in episodes, we can use a discounted total reward with the discount factor 0.9 or 0.95. In this case, the reward for shorter episodes will be higher than the reward for longer ones.

- **Keeping "elite" episodes for a longer time**: In the CartPole training, we sampled episodes from the environment, trained on the best ones, and threw them away. In FrozenLake, a successful episode is a much rarer animal, so we need to keep them for several iterations to train on them.

- **Decrease learning rate**: This will give our network time to average more training samples.

- **Much longer training time**: Due to the sparsity of successful episodes, and the random outcome of our actions, it's much harder for our network to get an idea of the best behavior to perform in any particular situation. To reach 50% successful episodes, about 5k training iterations are required.

To incorporate all these into our code, we need to change the filter_batch function to calculate discounted reward and return "elite" episodes for us to keep:

```
def filter_batch(batch, percentile):
    disc_rewards = list(map(lambda s: s.reward * (GAMMA **
len(s.steps)), batch))
    reward_bound = np.percentile(disc_rewards, percentile)
    train_obs = []
    train_act = []
    elite_batch = []
    for example, discounted_reward in zip(batch, disc_rewards):
        if discounted_reward > reward_bound:
            train_obs.extend(map(lambda step: step.observation,
example.steps))
            train_act.extend(map(lambda step: step.action,
example.steps))
            elite_batch.append(example)
    return elite_batch, train_obs, train_act, reward_bound
```

Then, in the training loop, we will store previous "elite" episodes to pass them to the preceding function on the next training iteration.

```
full_batch = []
for iter_no, batch in enumerate(iterate_batches(env, net,
BATCH_SIZE)):
    reward_mean = float(np.mean(list(map(lambda s: s.reward,
batch))))
    full_batch, obs, acts, reward_bound = filter_batch(full_batch
+ batch, PERCENTILE)
    if not full_batch:
        continue
    obs_v = torch.FloatTensor(obs)
    acts_v = torch.LongTensor(acts)
    full_batch = full_batch[-500:]
```

The rest of the code is the same, except that the learning rate decreased 10 times and the BATCH_SIZE was set to 100. After a period of patient waiting (the new version takes about one and a half hours to finish 10k iterations), we can see that the training of the model stopped improving around 55% of solved episodes. There are ways to address this (by applying entropy loss regularization, for example), but those techniques will be discussed in the upcoming chapters.

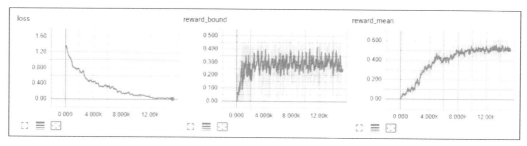

Figure 9: Convergence of FrozenLake with tweaked cross-entropy implementation

The final point to note here is the effect of "slipperiness" in the FrozenLake environment. Each of our actions with 33% probability is replaced with the 90° rotated one (the "up" action, for instance, will succeed with 0.33 probability and with 0.33 chance that it will be replaced with the "left" action and 0.33 with the "right" action).

The nonslippery version is in `Chapter04/04_frozenlake_nonslippery.py`, and the only difference is in the environment creation (we need to peek into the core of Gym to create the instance of the environment with tweaked arguments):

```
env =
gym.envs.toy_text.frozen_lake.FrozenLakeEnv(is_slippery=False)
    env = gym.wrappers.TimeLimit(env, max_episode_steps=100)
    env = DiscreteOneHotWrapper(env)
```

The effect is dramatic! The nonslippery version of the environment can be solved in 120-140 batch iterations, which is 100 times faster than the noisy environment:

```
rl_book_samples/Chapter04$ ./04_frozenlake_nonslippery.py
0: loss=1.379, reward_mean=0.010, reward_bound=0.000, batch=1
1: loss=1.375, reward_mean=0.010, reward_bound=0.000, batch=2
2: loss=1.359, reward_mean=0.010, reward_bound=0.000, batch=3
3: loss=1.361, reward_mean=0.010, reward_bound=0.000, batch=4
4: loss=1.355, reward_mean=0.000, reward_bound=0.000, batch=4
5: loss=1.342, reward_mean=0.010, reward_bound=0.000, batch=5
6: loss=1.353, reward_mean=0.020, reward_bound=0.000, batch=7
7: loss=1.351, reward_mean=0.040, reward_bound=0.000, batch=11
......
124: loss=0.484, reward_mean=0.680, reward_bound=0.000, batch=68
125: loss=0.373, reward_mean=0.710, reward_bound=0.430, batch=114
126: loss=0.305, reward_mean=0.690, reward_bound=0.478, batch=133
128: loss=0.413, reward_mean=0.790, reward_bound=0.478, batch=73
129: loss=0.297, reward_mean=0.810, reward_bound=0.478, batch=108
Solved!
```

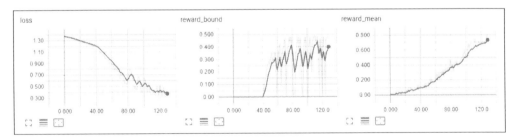

Figure 10: Convergence of the nonslippery version of FrozenLake

Theoretical background of the cross-entropy method

This section is optional and included for readers who are interested in why the method works. If you wish, you can refer to the original paper on cross-entropy, which will be given at the end of the section.

The basis of the cross-entropy method lies in the importance sampling theorem, which states this:

$$\mathbb{E}_{x \sim p(x)}[H(x)] = \int_x p(x) H(x) dx = \int_x q(x) \frac{p(x)}{q(x)} H(x) dx = \mathbb{E}_{x \sim q(x)}[\frac{p(x)}{q(x)} H(x)]$$

In our RL case, H(x) is a reward value obtained by some policy x and p(x) is a distribution of all possible policies. We don't want to maximize our reward by searching all possible policies, instead we want to find a way to approximate p(x)H(x) by q(x), iteratively minimizing the distance between them. The distance between two probability distributions is calculated by **Kullback-Leibler (KL)** divergence which is as follows:

$$KL(p_1(x)\|p_2(x)) = \mathbb{E}_{x \sim p_1(x)} \log \frac{p_1(x)}{p_2(x)} = \mathbb{E}_{x \sim p_1(x)}[\log p_1(x)] - \mathbb{E}_{x \sim p_1(x)}[\log p_2(x)]$$

The first term in KL is called **entropy** and doesn't depend on that, so could be omitted during the minimization. The second term is called **cross-entropy** and is a very common optimization objective in DL.

Combining both formulas, we can get an iterative algorithm, which starts with $q_0(x) = p(x)$ and on every step improves. This is an approximation of p(x)H(x) with an update:

$$q_{i+1}(x) = \underset{q_{i+1}(x)}{\arg\min} - \mathbb{E}_{x \sim q_i(x)} \frac{p(x)}{q_i(x)} H(x) \log q_{i+1}(x)$$

This is a generic cross-entropy method, which can be significantly simplified in our RL case. Firstly, we replace our H(x) with an indicator function, which is 1 when the reward for the episode is above the threshold and 0 if the reward is below. Our policy update will look like this:

$$\pi_{i+1}(a|s) = \underset{\pi_{i+1}}{\arg\min} - \mathbb{E}_{z \sim \pi_i(a|s)}[R(z) \geq \psi_i] \log \pi_{i+1}(a|s)$$

.

Strictly speaking, the preceding formula misses the normalization term, but it still works in practice without it. So, the method is quite clear: we sample episodes using our current policy (starting with some random initial policy) and minimize the negative log likelihood of the most successful samples and our policy.

There is a whole book dedicated to this method, written by *Dirk P. Kroese*. A shorter description can be found in the *Cross-Entropy Method* paper by *Dirk P.Kroese* (https://people.smp.uq.edu.au/DirkKroese/ps/eormsCE.pdf).

Summary

In this chapter, we became familiar with the first RL method cross-entropy, which is simple but quite powerful, despite its limitations. We applied it to a CartPole environment (with huge success) and to FrozenLake (with much more modest success). This chapter ends the introductory part of the book.

In the upcoming chapters, we will explore more complex, but more powerful tools of deep RL.

5
Tabular Learning and the Bellman Equation

In the previous chapter, we got acquainted with our first **Reinforcement Learning (RL)** method, cross-entropy, and saw its strengths and weaknesses. In this new part of the book, we'll look at another group of methods, called Q-learning, which have much more flexibility and power.

This chapter will establish the required background shared by those methods. We'll also revisit the FrozenLake environment and show how new concepts will fit with this environment and help us to address the issues of the environment's uncertainty.

Value, state, and optimality

You may remember our definition of the value of the state in *Chapter 1, What is Reinforcement Learning?*. This is a very important notion and the time has come to explore it further. This whole part of the book is built around the value and how to approximate it. We defined value as an expected total reward that is obtainable from the state. In a formal way, the value of the state is: $V(s) = \mathbb{E}[\sum_{t=0}^{\infty} r_t \gamma^t]$, where r_t is the local reward obtained at the step t of the episode.

The total reward could be discounted or not; it's up to us how to define it. Value is always calculated in the respect of some policy that our agent follows. To illustrate, let's consider a very simple environment with three states:

1. The agent's initial state.
2. The final state that the agent is in after executing action "left" from the initial state. The reward obtained from this is 1.

3. The final state that the agent is in after action "down". The reward obtained from this is 2:

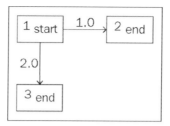

Figure 1: An example of an environment's states transition with rewards

The environment is always deterministic: every action succeeds and we always start from state **1**. Once we reach either state **2** or state **3**, the episode ends. Now, the question is, what's the value of state **1**? This question is meaningless without information about our agent's behavior or, in other words, its policy. Even in such a simple environment, our agent can have an infinite amount of behaviors, each of which will have its own value for state **1**. Consider this example:

- Agent always goes left
- Agent always goes down
- Agent goes left with a probability of 0.5 and down with a probability of 0.5
- Agent goes left in 10% of cases and in 90% of cases executes the "down" action

To demonstrate how the value is calculated, let's do it for all the preceding policies:

- The value of state **1** in the case of the "always left" agent is **1.0** (every time it goes left, it obtains 1 and the episode ends)
- For the "always down" agent, the value of state **1** is **2.0**
- For the 50% left/50% down agent, the value will be $1.0*0.5 + 2.0*0.5 = $ **1.5**
- In the last case, the value will be $1.0*0.1 + 2.0*0.9 = $ **1.9**

Now, another question: what's the optimal policy for this agent? The goal of RL is to get as much total reward as possible. For this one-step environment, the total reward is equal to the value of state **1**, which, obviously, is at the maximum at policy 2 (always down).

Unfortunately, such simple environments with an obvious optimal policy are not that interesting in practice. For interesting environments, the optimal policy is much harder to formulate and it's even harder to prove their optimality. However, don't worry, we're moving toward the point when we'll be able to make computers learn the optimal behavior on their own.

From the preceding example, you may have a false impression that we should always take the action with the highest reward. In general, it's not that simple. To demonstrate this, let's extend our preceding environment with yet another state that is reachable from state **3**. State **3** is no longer a terminal state, but a transition to state **4**, with a bad reward of **-20**. Once we've chosen the "down" action in state **1**, this bad reward is unavoidable, as from state **3** we have only one exit. So, it's a trap for the agent who has decided that "being greedy" is a good strategy.

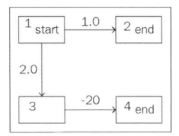

Figure 2: The same environment, with an extra state added

With that addition, our values for state **1** will be calculated this way:

- "Always left" agent is the same: **1.0**
- "Always down" agent gets: *2.0 + (-20) =* **-18**
- "50%/50% agent": *0.5*1.0 + 0.5*(20 + (-20)) =* **-8.5**
- "10%/90% agent": *0.1*1.0 + 0.9*(2.0 + (-20)) =* **-8**

So, the best policy for this new environment is now policy number one: always go left.

We spent some time discussing naïve and trivial environments so that you realize the complexity of this optimality problem and can appreciate the results of *Richard Bellman* better. Richard was an American mathematician, who formulated and proved his famous "Bellman equation". We'll talk about it in the next section.

The Bellman equation of optimality

To explain the Bellman equation, it's better to go a bit abstract. Don't be afraid, I'll provide the concrete examples later to support your intuition! Let's start with a deterministic case, when all our actions have a 100% guaranteed outcome. Imagine that our agent observes state s_0 and has **N** available actions. Every action leads to another state, $s_1 \ldots s_N$, with a respective reward, $r_1 \ldots r_N$. Also assume that we know the values, V_i, of all states connected to the state s_0. What will be the best course of action that the agent can take in such a state?

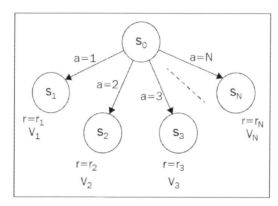

Figure 3: An abstract environment with N states reachable from the initial state

If we choose the concrete action a_i, and calculate the value given to this action, then the value will be $V_0(a = a_i) = r_i + V_i$. So, to choose the best possible action, the agent needs to calculate the resulting values for every action and choose the maximum possible outcome. In other words: $V_0 = \max_{a \in 1 \ldots N}(r_a + V_a)$. If we're using discount factor γ, we need to multiply the value of the next state by gamma: $V_0 = \max_{a \in 1 \ldots N}(r_a + \gamma V_a)$.

This may look very similar to our greedy example from the previous section, and, in fact, it is. However, there is one difference: when we act greedily, we do not only look at the immediate reward for the action, but at the immediate reward plus the long-term value of the state. *Richard Bellman* proved that with that extension, our behavior will get the best possible outcome. In other words, it will be optimal. So, the preceding equation is called the **Bellman equation** of value (for a deterministic case):

It's not very complicated to extend this idea for a stochastic case, when our actions have the chance to end up in different states. What we need to do is to calculate the expected value for every action, instead of just taking the value of the next state. To illustrate this, let's consider one single action available from state s_0, with three possible outcomes.

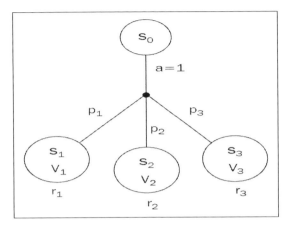

Figure 4: An example of the transition from the state in a stochastic case

Here we have one action, which can lead to three different states with different probabilities: with probability p_1 it can end up in state s_1, p_2 in state s_2, and p_3 in state s_3 ($p_1 + p_2 + p_3 = 1$, of course). Every target state has its own reward (r_1, r_2, or r_3). To calculate the expected value after issuing action 1, we need to sum all values, multiplied by their probabilities:

$$V_0(a = 1) = p_1(r_1 + \gamma V_1) + p_2(r_2 + \gamma V_2) + p_3(r_3 + \gamma V_3)$$

or more formally,

$$V_0(a) = \mathbb{E}_{s \sim S}[r_{s,a} + \gamma V_s] = \sum_{s \in S} p_{a,0 \to s}(r_{s,a} + \gamma V_s)$$

By combining the Bellman equation, for a deterministic case, with a value for stochastic actions, we get the Bellman optimality equation for a general case:

$$V_0 = \max_{a \in A} \mathbb{E}_{s \sim S}[r_{s,a} + \gamma V_s] = \max_{a \in A} \sum_{s \in S} p_{a,0 \to s}(r_{s,a} + \gamma V_s)$$

(Note that $p_{a,i \to j}$ means the probability of action a, issued in state i, to end up in state j.)

The interpretation is still the same: the optimal value of the state is equal to the action, which gives us the maximum possible expected immediate reward, plus discounted long-term reward for the next state. You may also notice that this definition is recursive: the value of the state is defined via the values of immediate reachable states.

This recursion may look like cheating: we define some value, pretending that we already know it. However, this is a very powerful and common technique in computer science and even in math in general (proof by induction is based on the same trick). This Bellman equation is a foundation not only in RL but also in much more general dynamic programming, which is a widely used method for solving practical optimization problems.

These values not only give us the best reward that we can obtain, but they basically give us the optimal policy to obtain that reward: if our agent knows the value for every state, then it automatically knows how to gather all this reward. Thanks to Bellman's optimality proof, at every state the agent ends up in, it needs to select the action with the maximum expected reward for the action, which is a sum of the immediate reward and the one-step discounted long-term reward. That's it. So, those values are really useful stuff to know. Before we get familiar with a practical way to calculate them, we need to introduce one more mathematical notation. It's not as fundamental as value, but we need it for our convenience.

Value of action

To make our life slightly easier, we can define different quantities in addition to the value of state V_s: value of action $Q_{s,a}$. Basically, it equals the total reward we can get by executing action a in state s and can be defined via V_s. Being a much less fundamental entity than V_s, this quantity gave a name to the whole family of methods called "Q-learning", because it is slightly more convenient in practice. In these methods, our primary objective is to get values of Q for every pair of state and action.

$$Q_{s,a} = \mathbb{E}_{s' \sim S}[r_{s,a} + \gamma V_{s'}] = \sum_{s' \in S} p_{a,s \to s'}(r_{s,a} + \gamma V_{s'})$$

Q for this state s and action a equals the expected immediate reward and the discounted long-term reward of the destination state. We also can define V_s via $Q_{s,a}$:

$$V_s = \max_{a \in A} Q_{s,a}$$

This just means that the value of some state equals to the value of the maximum action we can execute from this state. It may look very close to the value of state, but there is still a difference, which is important to understand. Finally, we can express $Q(s, a)$ via itself, which will be used in the next chapter's topic of Q-learning:

$$Q(s, a) = r_{s,a} + \gamma \max_{a' \in A} Q(s', a')$$

To give you a concrete example, let's consider an environment which is similar to FrozenLake, but has a much simpler structure: we have one initial state s_0 surrounded by four target states, s_1, s_2, s_3, s_4, with different rewards.

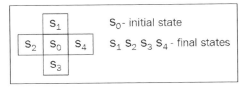

Figure 5: A simplified grid-like environment

Every action is probabilistic in the same way as in FrozenLake: with a 33% chance that our action will be executed without modifications, but with a 33% chance we will slip to the left, relatively, of our target cell and a 33% chance we will slip to the right. For simplicity, we use discount factor gamma=1.

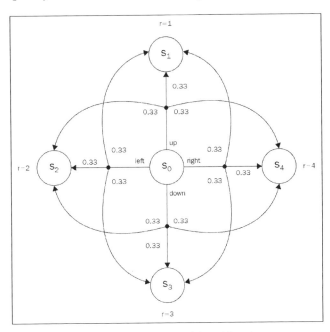

Figure 6: A transition diagram of the grid environment

Let's calculate the values of actions to begin with. Terminal states $s_1 \ldots s_4$ have no outbound connections, so Q for those states is zero for all actions. Due to this, the values of the Terminal states are equal to their immediate reward (once we get there, our episode ends without any subsequent states): $V_1 = 1, V_2 = 2, V_3 = 3, V_4 = 4$.

The values of actions for state 0 are a bit more complicated. Let's start with the "up" action. Its value, according to the definition, is equal to the expected sum of the immediate reward plus long-term value for subsequent steps. We have no subsequent steps for any possible transition for the "up" action, so

$$Q(s_0, up) = 0.33 \cdot V_1 + 0.33 \cdot V_2 + 0.33 \cdot V_4 = 0.33 \cdot 1 + 0.33 \cdot 2 + 0.33 \cdot 4 = 2.31$$.

Repeating this for the rest of s_0 actions results in the following:

$$Q(s_0, left) = 0.33 \cdot V_1 + 0.33 \cdot V_2 + 0.33 \cdot V_3 = 1.98$$
$$Q(s_0, right) = 0.33 \cdot V_4 + 0.33 \cdot V_1 + 0.33 \cdot V_3 = 2.64$$
$$Q(s_0, down) = 0.33 \cdot V_3 + 0.33 \cdot V_2 + 0.33 \cdot V_4 = 2.97$$

The final value for state s_0 is the maximum of those actions' values, which is 2.97.

Q values are much more convenient in practice, as for the agent it's much simpler to make decisions about actions based on Q than based on V. In the case of Q, to choose the action based on the state, the agent just needs to calculate Q for all available actions, using the current state and choose the action with the largest value of Q. To do the same using values of states, the agent needs to know not only values, but also probabilities for transitions. In practice, we rarely know them in advance, so the agent needs to estimate transition probabilities for every action and state pair. Later in this chapter, we'll see this in practice by solving the FrozenLake environment both ways. However, to be able to do this, we have one important thing still missing: a general way to calculate those Vs and Qs.

The value iteration method

In the simplistic example we just saw, to calculate the values of states and actions, we have exploited the structure of the environment: we had no loops in transitions, so we could start from terminal states, calculate their values and then proceed to the central state. However, just one loop in the environment builds an obstacle in our approach. Let's consider such an environment with two states:

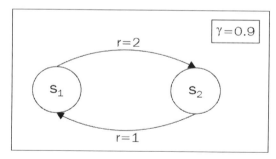

Figure 7: A sample environment with a loop in the transition diagram

We start from state s_1, and the only action we can take leads us to state s_2. We get reward **r=1**,and the only transition from s_2 is an action, which brings us back to the s_1. So, the life of our agent is an infinite sequence of states $[s_1, s_2, s_1, s_2, s_1, s_2, s_1, s_2, \ldots]$. To deal with this infinity loop, we can use a discount factor $\gamma = 0.9$. Now, the question is, what are the values for both the states?

The answer is not very complicated, though. Every transition from s_1 to s_2 gives us a reward of 1 and every back transition gives us 2. So, our sequence of rewards will be [1, 2, 1, 2, 1, 2, 1, 2, ...]. As there is only one action available in every state, our agent has no choice, so we can omit the max operation in formulas (there is only one alternative). The value for every state will be equal to the infinite sum:

$$V(s_1) = 1 + \gamma(2 + \gamma(1 + \gamma(2 + \ldots))) = \sum_{i=0}^{\infty} 1\gamma^{2i} + 2\gamma^{2i+1}$$

$$V(s_2) = 2 + \gamma(1 + \gamma(2 + \gamma(1 + \ldots))) = \sum_{i=0}^{\infty} 2\gamma^{2i} + 1\gamma^{2i+1}$$

Strictly speaking, we cannot calculate the exact values for our states, but with $\gamma = 0.9$, the contribution of every transition quickly decreases over time. For example, after 10 steps, $\gamma^{10} = 0.910 = 0.349$, but after 100 steps it becomes just 0.0000266. Due to this, we can stop after 50 iterations and still get quite a precise estimation.

```
>>> sum([0.9**(2*i) + 2*(0.9**(2*i+1)) for i in range(50)])
14.736450674121663
>>> sum([2*(0.9**(2*i)) + 0.9**(2*i+1) for i in range(50)])
15.262752483911719
```

The preceding example could be used to get a gist of a more general procedure, called the "value iteration algorithm" which allows us to numerically calculate the values of states and values of actions of MDPs with known transition probabilities and rewards. The procedure (for values of states) includes the following steps:

1. Initialize values of all states V_i to some initial value (usually zero)
2. For every state s in the MDP, perform the Bellman update:
    $V_s \leftarrow \max_a \sum_{s'} p_{a,s \to s'}(r_{s,a} + \gamma V_{s'})$
3. Repeat step 2 for some large number of steps or until changes become too small

In the case of action values (that is Q), only minor modifications to the preceding procedure are required:

1. Initialize all $Q_{s,a}$ to zero
2. For every state s and every action a in this state, perform update:
   $Q_{s,a} \leftarrow \sum_{s'} p_{a,s \rightarrow s'}(r_{s,a} + \gamma \max_{a'} Q_{s',a'})$
3. Repeat step 2

Okay, so that's the theory. What about the practice? In practice, this method has several obvious limitations. First of all, our state space should be discrete and small enough to perform multiple iterations over all states. This is not an issue for FrozenLake-4x4 and even for FrozenLake-8x8 (it exists in Gym as a more challenging version), but for CartPole it's not totally clear what to do. Our observation for CartPole is four float values, which represent some physical characteristics of the system. Even a small difference in those values could have an influence on the state's value. A potential solution for that could be discretization of our observation's values, for example, we can split the observation space of the CartPole into bins and treat every bin as an individual discrete state in space. However, this will create lots of practical problems, such as how large bin intervals should be and how much data from the environment we'll need to estimate our values. We'll address this issue in subsequent chapters, when we get to the usage of neural networks in Q-learning.

The second practical problem arises from the fact that we rarely know the transition probability for the actions and rewards matrix. Remember what interface provides Gym to the agent's writer: we observe the state, decide on an action and only then do we get the next observation and reward for the transition. We don't know (without peeking into Gym's environment code) what the probability is to get into state s_1 from state s_0 by issuing action a_0. What we do have is just the history from the agent's interaction with the environment. However, in Bellman's update, we need both a reward for every transition and the probability of this transition. So, the obvious answer to this issue is to use our agent's experience as an estimation for both unknowns. Rewards could be used as they are. We just need to remember what reward we've got on transition from s_0 to s_1, using action a, but to estimate probabilities we need to maintain counters for every tuple (s_0, s_1, a) and normalize them.

Okay, now let's look at how the value iteration method will work for FrozenLake.

Value iteration in practice

The complete example is in `Chapter05/01_frozenlake_v_learning.py`. The central data structures in this example are as follows:

- **Reward table**: A dictionary with the composite key "source state" + "action" + "target state". The value is obtained from the immediate reward.

- **Transitions table**: A dictionary keeping counters of the experienced transitions. The key is the composite "state" + "action" and the value is another dictionary that maps the target state into a count of times that we've seen it. For example, if in state 0 we execute action 1 ten times, after three times it leads us to state 4 and after seven times to state 5. Entry with the key (0, 1) in this table will be a dict {4: 3, 5: 7}. We use this table to estimate the probabilities of our transitions.

- **Value table**: A dictionary that maps a state into the calculated value of this state.

The overall logic of our code is simple: in the loop, we play 100 random steps from the environment, populating the reward and transition tables. After those 100 steps, we perform a value iteration loop over all states, updating our value table. Then we play several full episodes to check our improvements using the updated value table. If the average reward for those test episodes is above the 0.8 boundary, then we stop training. During test episodes, we also update our reward and transition tables to use all data from the environment.

Okay, so let's come to the code. In the beginning, we import used packages and define constants:

```
import gym
import collections
from tensorboardX import SummaryWriter

ENV_NAME = "FrozenLake-v0"
GAMMA = 0.9
TEST_EPISODES = 20
```

Then we define the `Agent` class, which will keep our tables and contain functions we'll be using in the training loop:

```
class Agent:
    def __init__(self):
        self.env = gym.make(ENV_NAME)
        self.state = self.env.reset()
        self.rewards = collections.defaultdict(float)
        self.transits = collections.defaultdict(collections.Counter)
        self.values = collections.defaultdict(float)
```

In the `class` constructor, we create the environment we'll be using for data samples, obtain our first observation, and define tables for rewards, transitions, and values.

```
def play_n_random_steps(self, count):
    for _ in range(count):
        action = self.env.action_space.sample()
        new_state, reward, is_done, _ = self.env.step(action)
        self.rewards[(self.state, action, new_state)] = reward
        self.transits[(self.state, action)][new_state] += 1
        self.state = self.env.reset() if is_done else new_state
```

This function is used to gather random experience from the environment and update reward and transition tables. Note that we don't need to wait for the end of the episode to start learning; we just perform N steps and remember their outcomes. This is one of the differences between Value iteration and Cross-entropy, which can learn only on full episodes.

The next function calculates the value of the action from the state, using our transition, reward and values tables. We will use it for two purposes: to select the best action to perform from the state and to calculate the new value of the state on value iteration. Its logic is illustrated in the following diagram and we do the following:

1. We extract transition counters for the given state and action from the transition table. Counters in this table have a form of dict, with target states as key and a count of experienced transitions as value. We sum all counters to obtain the total count of times we've executed the action from the state. We will use this total value later to go from an individual counter to probability.

2. Then we iterate every target state that our action has landed on and calculate its contribution into the total action value using the Bellman equation. This contribution equals to immediate reward plus discounted value for the target state. We multiply this sum to the probability of this transition and add the result to the final action value.

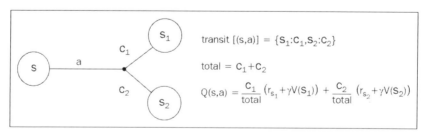

Figure 8: The calculation of the state's value

In our diagram, we have an illustration of a calculation of value for state s and action a. Imagine that during our experience, we have executed this action several times (c_1+c_2) and it ends up in one of two states, s_1 or s_2. How many times we have switched to each of these states is stored in our transition table as dict $\{s_1:c_1, s_2:c_2\}$. Then, the approximate value for the state and action $Q(s, a)$ will be equal to the probability of every state, multiplied to the value of the state. From the Bellman equation, this equals to the sum of the immediate reward and the discounted long-term state value.

```
def calc_action_value(self, state, action):
    target_counts = self.transits[(state, action)]
    total = sum(target_counts.values())
    action_value = 0.0
    for tgt_state, count in target_counts.items():
        reward = self.rewards[(state, action, tgt_state)]
        action_value += (count / total) * (reward + GAMMA *
self.values[tgt_state])
    return action_value
```

The next function uses the function we just described to make a decision about the best action to take from the given state. It iterates over all possible actions in the environment and calculates value for every action. The action with the largest value wins and is returned as the action to take. This action selection process is deterministic, as the `play_n_random_steps()` function introduces enough exploration. So, our agent will behave greedily in regard to our value approximation.

```
def select_action(self, state):
    best_action, best_value = None, None
    for action in range(self.env.action_space.n):
        action_value = self.calc_action_value(state, action)
        if best_value is None or best_value < action_value:
            best_value = action_value
            best_action = action
    return best_action
```

The `play_episode` function uses `select_action` to find the best action to take and plays one full episode using the provided environment. This function is used to play test episodes, during which we don't want to mess up with the current state of the main environment used to gather random data. So, we're using the second environment passed as an argument. The logic is very simple and should be already familiar to you: we just loop over states accumulating reward for one episode:

```
def play_episode(self, env):
    total_reward = 0.0
    state = env.reset()
```

```
    while True:
        action = self.select_action(state)
        new_state, reward, is_done, _ = env.step(action)
        self.rewards[(state, action, new_state)] = reward
        self.transits[(state, action)][new_state] += 1
        total_reward += reward
        if is_done:
            break
        state = new_state
    return total_reward
```

The final method of the `Agent` class is our value iteration implementation and it
is surprisingly simple, thanks to the preceding functions. What we do is just loop
over all states in the environment, then for every state we calculate the values for
the states reachable from it, obtaining candidates for the value of the state. Then we
update the value of our current state with the maximum value of the action available
from the state:

```
def value_iteration(self):
    for state in range(self.env.observation_space.n):
        state_values = [self.calc_action_value(state, action)
                            for action in range(self.env.action_
space.n)]
        self.values[state] = max(state_values)
```

That's all our agent's methods, and the final piece is a training loop and the
monitoring of the code:

```
if __name__ == "__main__":
    test_env = gym.make(ENV_NAME)
    agent = Agent()
    writer = SummaryWriter(comment="-v-learning")
```

We create the environment we'll be using for testing, the `Agent` class instance and the
summary writer for TensorBoard:

```
    iter_no = 0
    best_reward = 0.0
    while True:
        iter_no += 1
        agent.play_n_random_steps(100)
        agent.value_iteration()
```

The two lines in the preceding code snippet are the key piece in the training loop. First, we perform 100 random steps to fill our reward and transition tables with fresh data and then we run value iteration over all states. The rest of the code plays test episodes using the value table as our policy, then writes data into TensorBoard, tracks the best average reward, and checks for the training loop stop condition.

```
reward = 0.0
for _ in range(TEST_EPISODES):
    reward += agent.play_episode(test_env)
reward /= TEST_EPISODES
writer.add_scalar("reward", reward, iter_no)
if reward > best_reward:
    print("Best reward updated %.3f -> %.3f" %
(best_reward, reward))
    best_reward = reward
if reward > 0.80:
    print("Solved in %d iterations!" % iter_no)
    break
writer.close()
```

Okay, let's run our program:

```
rl_book_samples/Chapter05$ ./01_frozenlake_v_learning.py
[2017-10-13 11:39:37,778] Making new env: FrozenLake-v0
[2017-10-13 11:39:37,988] Making new env: FrozenLake-v0
Best reward updated 0.000 -> 0.150
Best reward updated 0.150 -> 0.500
Best reward updated 0.500 -> 0.550
Best reward updated 0.550 -> 0.650
Best reward updated 0.650 -> 0.800
Best reward updated 0.800 -> 0.850
Solved in 36 iterations!
```

Our solution is stochastic, and my experiments usually required from 12 to 100 iterations to reach a solution, but in all cases, it took less than a second to find a good policy that could solve the environment in 80% of runs. If you remember how many hours were required to achieve a 60% success ratio using Cross-entropy, then you can understand that this is a major improvement. There are several reasons for that.

First of all, the stochastic outcome of our actions, plus the length of the episodes (6-10 steps on average), makes it hard for the Cross-entropy method to understand what was done right in the episode and which step was a mistake. The value iteration works with individual values of state (or action) and incorporates the probabilistic outcome of actions naturally, by estimating probability and calculating the expected value. So, it's much simpler for the value iteration and requires much less data from the environment (which is called **sample efficiency** in RL).

The second reason is the fact that the value iteration doesn't need full episodes to start learning. In an extreme case, we can start updating our values just from the single example. However, for FrozenLake, due to the reward structure (we get 1 only after successfully reaching the target state), we still need to have at least one successful episode to start learning from a useful value table, which may be challenging to achieve in more complex environments. For example, you can try switching existing code to a larger version of FrozenLake, which has the name **FrozenLake8x8-v0**. The larger version of FrozenLake can take from 50 to 400 iterations to solve, and, according to TensorBoard charts, most of the time it waits for the first successful episode, then very quickly reaches convergence. The following is a chart with two lines. Orange corresponds to the reward during the training of **FrozenLake-v0 (4x4)** and blue is the reward of **FrozenLake8x8-v0.**:

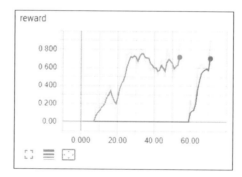

Figure 9: The convergence of FrozenLake 4x4 and 8x8

Now it's time to compare the code that learns the values of states, as we just discussed, to the code that learns the values of actions.

Q-learning for FrozenLake

The whole example is in the `Chapter05/02_frozenlake_q_learning.py` file, and the difference is really minor. The most obvious change is to our value table. In the previous example, we kept the value of the state, so the key in the dictionary was just a state. Now we need to store values of the Q-function, which has two parameters: state and action, so the key in the value table is now a composite.

The second difference is in our `calc_action_value` function. We just don't need it anymore, as our action values are stored in the value table. Finally, the most important change in the code is in the agent's `value_iteration` method. Before, it was just a wrapper around the `calc_action_value` call, which did the job of Bellman approximation. Now, as this function has gone and was replaced by a value table, we need to do this approximation in the `value_iteration` method.

Let's look at the code. As it's almost the same, I'll jump directly to the most interesting `value_iteration` function:

```
def value_iteration(self):
    for state in range(self.env.observation_space.n):
        for action in range(self.env.action_space.n):
            action_value = 0.0
            target_counts = self.transits[(state, action)]
            total = sum(target_counts.values())
            for tgt_state, count in target_counts.items():
                reward = self.rewards[(state, action,
tgt_state)]
                best_action = self.select_action(tgt_state)
                action_value += (count / total) * (reward +
GAMMA * self.values[(tgt_state, best_action)])
            self.values[(state, action)] = action_value
```

The code is very similar to `calc_action_value` in the previous example and in fact it does almost the same thing. For the given state and action, it needs to calculate the value of this action using statistics about target states that we've reached with the action. To calculate this value, we use the Bellman equation and our counters, which allow us to approximate the probability of the target state. However, in Bellman's equation we have the value of the state and now we need to calculate it differently. Before, we had it stored in the value table (as we approximated the value of states), so we just took it from this table. We can't do this anymore, so we have to call the `select_action` method, which will choose for us the action with the largest Q-value, and then we take this Q-value as the value of the target state. Of course, we can implement another function which could calculate for us this value of state, but `select_action` does almost everything we need, so we will reuse it here.

There is another piece of this example that I'd like to emphasize here. Let's look at our `select_action` method:

```
def select_action(self, state):
    best_action, best_value = None, None
    for action in range(self.env.action_space.n):
        action_value = self.values[(state, action)]
        if best_value is None or best_value < action_value:
```

```
                best_value = action_value
                best_action = action
        return best_action
```

As I said, we don't have the `calc_action_value` method anymore, so, to select action, we just iterate over the actions and look up their values in our values table. It could look like a minor improvement, but if you think about the data that we used in `calc_action_value`, it may become obvious why the learning of the Q-function is much more popular in RL than the learning of the V-function.

Our `calc_action_value` function uses both information about reward and probabilities. It's not a huge problem for the value iteration method, which relies on this information during training. However, in the next chapter, we'll learn about the value iteration method extension, which doesn't require probability approximation, but just takes it from the environment samples. For such methods, this dependency on probability adds an extra burden for the agent. In the case of Q-learning, what the agent needs to make the decision is just Q-values.

I don't want to say that V-functions are completely useless, because they are an essential part of Actor-Critic method which we'll talk about in part three of this book. However, in the area of value learning, Q-functions is the definite favorite. With regard to convergence speed, both our versions are almost identical (but the Q-learning version requires four times more memory for the value table).

```
rl_book_samples/Chapter05$ ./02_frozenlake_q_learning.py
[2017-10-13 12:38:56,658] Making new env: FrozenLake-v0
[2017-10-13 12:38:56,863] Making new env: FrozenLake-v0
Best reward updated 0.000 -> 0.050
Best reward updated 0.050 -> 0.200
Best reward updated 0.200 -> 0.350
Best reward updated 0.350 -> 0.700
Best reward updated 0.700 -> 0.750
Best reward updated 0.750 -> 0.850
Solved in 22 iterations!
```

Summary

My congratulations, you've made another step towards understanding modern, state-of-the-art RL methods! We learned about some very important concepts that are widely used in deep RL: the value of state, the value of actions, and the Bellman equation in various forms. We saw the value iteration method, which is a very important building block in the area of Q-learning. Finally, we got to know how value iteration can improve our FrozenLake solution.

In the next chapter, we'll learn about deep Q-networks, which started the deep RL revolution in 2013, by beating humans on lots of Atari 2600 games.

6
Deep Q-Networks

In the previous chapter, we became familiar with the Bellman equation and the practical method of its application called Value iteration. This approach allowed us to significantly improve our speed and convergence in the FrozenLake environment, which is promising, but can we go further?

In this chapter, we'll try to apply the same theory to problems of much greater complexity: arcade games from the Atari 2600 platform, which are the de-facto benchmark of the RL research community. To deal with this new and more challenging goal, we'll talk about problems with the Value iteration method and introduce its variation, called Q-learning. In particular, we'll look at the application of Q-learning to so-called "grid world" environments, which is called tabular Q-learning, and then we'll discuss Q-learning in conjunction with neural networks. This combination has the name DQN. At the end of the chapter, we'll reimplement a DQN algorithm from the famous paper, *Playing Atari with Deep Reinforcement Learning* by *V. Mnih and others*, published in 2013, which started a new era in RL development.

Real-life value iteration

The improvements we got in the FrozenLake environment by switching from Cross-Entropy to the Value iteration method are quite encouraging, so it's tempting to apply the value iteration method to more challenging problems. However, let's first look at the assumptions and limitations that our Value iteration method has.

We will start with a quick recap of the method. The Value iteration method on every step does a loop on all states, and for every state, it performs an update of its value with a Bellman approximation. The variation of the same method for Q-values (values for actions) is almost the same, but we approximate and store values for every state and action. So, what's wrong with this process?

The first obvious problem is the count of environment states and our ability to iterate over them. In the Value iteration, we assume that we know all states in our environment in advance, can iterate over them and can store value approximation associated with the state. It's definitely true for the simple "grid world" environment of FrozenLake, but what about other tasks? First, let's try to understand how scalable the Value iteration approach is, or, in other words, how many states we can easily iterate over in every loop. Even a moderate-sized computer can keep several billion float values in memory (8.5 billion in 32 GB of RAM), so the memory required for value tables doesn't look like a huge constraint. Iteration over billions of states and actions will be more memory intensive, but not an insurmountable problem.

Nowadays, we have multicore systems that are mostly idle. The real problem is the number of samples required to get good approximations for state transition dynamics. Imagine that you have some environment with, say, a billion states (this corresponds approximately to a FrozenLake of size 31600 × 31600). To calculate even a rough approximation for every state of this environment, we'll need hundreds of billions of transitions evenly distributed over our states, which is not practical.

To give you an example of an environment with a much larger number of potential states, let's consider the Atari 2600 game console again. This was very popular in the 1980s and many arcade-style games were available for it. The Atari console is archaic by today's gaming standards, but its games give an excellent set of RL problems that humans can master fairly quickly, but still are challenging for computers. Not surprisingly, this platform (using an emulator, of course) is a very popular benchmark among RL researches.

Let's calculate the state space for the Atari platform. The resolution of the screen is 210 x 160 pixels, and every pixel has one of 128 colors. So, every frame of the screen has $210 \times 160 = 33600$ pixels and the total amount of different screens possible is 128^{33600}, which is slightly more than 10^{70802}. If we decide to just enumerate all possible states of Atari once, it will take billions of billions of years even for the fastest supercomputer. Also, 99(.9)% of this job will be a waste of time, as most of the combinations will never be shown during even long gameplay, so we'll never have samples of those states. However, the value iteration method wants to iterate over them *just in case*.

Another problem with the value iteration approach is that it limits us to discrete action spaces. Indeed, both $Q(s, a)$ and $V(s)$ approximations assume that our actions are a mutually exclusive discrete set, which is not true for continuous control problems where actions can represent continuous variables, such as the angle of a steering wheel, the force on an actuator, or the temperature of a heater. This issue is much more challenging than the first, and we'll talk about it in the last part of the book, in chapters dedicated to continuous action space problems. For now, let's assume that we have a discrete count of actions and this count is not very large (orders of tens). How should we handle the state space size issue?

Tabular Q-learning

First of all, do we really need to iterate over every state in the state space? We have an environment that can be used as a source of real-life samples of states. If some state in the state space is not shown to us by the environment, why should we care about its value? We can use states obtained from the environment to update values of states, which can save us lots of work.

This modification of the Value iteration method is known as Q-learning, as mentioned earlier, and for cases with explicit state-to-value mappings, has the following steps:

1. Start with an empty table, mapping states to values of actions.

2. By interacting with the environment, obtain the tuple s, a, r, s' (state, action, reward, and the new state). In this step, we need to decide which action to take, and there is no single proper way to make this decision. We discussed this problem as *exploration versus exploitation* and will talk a lot about this.

3. Update the Q(s, a) value using the Bellman approximation:
$$Q_{s,a} \leftarrow r + \gamma \max_{a' \in A} Q_{s',a'}$$

4. Repeat from step 2.

As in Value iteration, the end condition could be some threshold of the update or we can perform test episodes to estimate the expected reward from the policy. Another thing to note here is how to update the Q-values. As we take samples from the environment, it's generally a bad idea to just assign new values on top of existing values, as training can become unstable. What is usually done in practice is to update the Q(s, a) with approximations using a "blending" technique, which is just averaging between old and new values of Q using learning rate α with a value from 0 to 1:

$$Q_{s,a} \leftarrow (1 - \alpha)Q_{s,a} + \alpha(r + \gamma \max_{a' \in A} Q_{s',a'})$$

This allows values of Q to converge smoothly, even if our environment is noisy. The final version of the algorithm is here:

1. Start with an empty table for Q(s, a).

2. Obtain (s, a, r, s') from the environment.

3. Make a Bellman update:
$$Q_{s,a} \leftarrow (1 - \alpha)Q_{s,a} + \alpha(r + \gamma \max_{a' \in A} Q_{s',a'}).$$

4. Check convergence conditions. If not met, repeat from step 2.

As mentioned earlier, this method is called **tabular Q-learning**, as we keep a table of states with their Q-values. Let's try it on our FrozenLake environment. The whole example code is in Chapter06/01_frozenlake_q_learning.py.

```
import gym
import collections
from tensorboardX import SummaryWriter

ENV_NAME = "FrozenLake-v0"
GAMMA = 0.9
ALPHA = 0.2
TEST_EPISODES = 20

class Agent:
    def __init__(self):
        self.env = gym.make(ENV_NAME)
        self.state = self.env.reset()
        self.values = collections.defaultdict(float)
```

In the beginning, we import packages and define constants. The new thing here is the value of α, which will be used as the learning rate in the value update. The initialization of our Agent class is simpler now, as we don't need to track the history of rewards and transition counters, just our value table. This will make our memory footprint smaller, which is not a big issue for FrozenLake, but can be critical for larger environments.

```
    def sample_env(self):
        action = self.env.action_space.sample()
        old_state = self.state
        new_state, reward, is_done, _ = self.env.step(action)
        self.state = self.env.reset() if is_done else new_state
        return (old_state, action, reward, new_state)
```

The preceding method is used to obtain the next transition from the environment. We sample a random action from the action space and return the tuple of the old state, action taken, reward obtained, and the new state. The tuple will be used in the training loop later.

```
    def best_value_and_action(self, state):
        best_value, best_action = None, None
        for action in range(self.env.action_space.n):
            action_value = self.values.get[(state, action)]
            if best_value is None or best_value < action_value:
                best_value = action_value
                best_action = action
        return best_value, best_action
```

The next method receives the state of the environment and finds the best action to take from this state by taking the action with the largest value that we have in the table. If we don't have the value associated with the state and action pair, then we take it as zero. This method will be used two times: first, in the test method that plays one episode using our current values table (to evaluate our policy quality), and the second, in the method that performs the value update to get the value of the next state.

```
def value_update(self, s, a, r, next_s):
    best_v, _ = self.best_value_and_action(next_s)
    new_val = r + GAMMA * best_v
    old_val = self.values[(s, a)]
    self.values[(s, a)] = old_val * (1-ALPHA) + new_val * ALPHA
```

Here we update our values table using one step from the environment. To do this, we're calculating the Bellman approximation for our state *s* and action *a* by summing the immediate reward with the discounted value of the next state. Then we obtain the previous value of the state and action pair, and blend these values together using the learning rate. The result is the new approximation for the value of state *s* and action *a*, which is stored in our table.

```
def play_episode(self, env):
    total_reward = 0.0
    state = env.reset()
    while True:
        _, action = self.best_value_and_action(state)
        new_state, reward, is_done, _ = env.step(action)
        total_reward += reward
        if is_done:
            break
        state = new_state
    return total_reward
```

The last method in our `Agent` class plays one full episode using the provided test environment. The action on every step is taken using our current value table of Q-values. This method is used to evaluate our current policy to check the progress of learning. Note that this method doesn't alter our value table: it only uses it to find the best action to take.

The rest of the example is the training loop, which is very similar to examples from the previous chapter: we create a test environment, agent, and summary writer, then in the loop, we do one step in the environment and perform a value update using the obtained data. Then we test our current policy by playing several test episodes. If a good reward is obtained, then we stop training.

```python
if __name__ == "__main__":
    test_env = gym.make(ENV_NAME)
    agent = Agent()
    writer = SummaryWriter(comment="-q-learning")

    iter_no = 0
    best_reward = 0.0
    while True:
        iter_no += 1
        s, a, r, next_s = agent.sample_env()
        agent.value_update(s, a, r, next_s)

        reward = 0.0
        for _ in range(TEST_EPISODES):
            reward += agent.play_episode(test_env)
        reward /= TEST_EPISODES
        writer.add_scalar("reward", reward, iter_no)
        if reward > best_reward:
            print("Best reward updated %.3f -> %.3f" %
(best_reward, reward))
            best_reward = reward
        if reward > 0.80:
            print("Solved in %d iterations!" % iter_no)
            break
    writer.close()
```

The result of the example is shown here:

```
rl_book_samples/Chapter06$ ./01_frozenlake_q_learning.py
[2017-10-20 14:21:23,459] Making new env: FrozenLake-v0
[2017-10-20 14:21:23,682] Making new env: FrozenLake-v0
Best reward updated 0.000 -> 0.200
Best reward updated 0.200 -> 0.250
Best reward updated 0.250 -> 0.350
Best reward updated 0.350 -> 0.400
Best reward updated 0.400 -> 0.500
Best reward updated 0.500 -> 0.750
```

```
Best reward updated 0.750 -> 0.800
Best reward updated 0.800 -> 0.850
Solved in 1860 iterations!
```

You may have noticed that this version used more iterations to solve the problem compared to the value iteration method from the previous chapter. The reason for that is that we're no longer using the experience obtained during testing. (In `Chapter05/02_frozenlake_q_iteration.py`, periodical tests cause an update of Q-table statistics. Here we don't touch Q-values during the test, which cause more iterations before the environment gets solved.) Overall, the total amount of samples required from the environment is almost the same. The reward chart in TensorBoard also shows good training dynamics, which are very similar to the value iteration method.

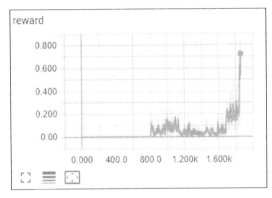

Figure 1: Reward dynamics of FrozenLake

Deep Q-learning

The Q-learning method that we've just seen solves the issue with iteration over the full set of states, but still can struggle with situations when the count of the observable set of states is very large. For example, Atari games can have a large variety of different screens, so if we decide to use raw pixels as individual states, we'll quickly realize that we have too many states to track and approximate values for.

In some environments, the count of different observable states could be almost infinite. For example, in CartPole the state given to us by the environment is four floating point numbers. The number of combinations of values is finite (they're represented as bits), but this number is extremely large. We could create some bins to discretize those values, but this often creates more problems than it solves: we would need to decide what ranges of parameters are important to distinguish as different states and what ranges could be clustered together.

In the case of Atari, one single pixel change doesn't make much difference, so it's efficient to treat both images as a single state. However, we still need to distinguish some of the states. The following image shows two different situations in a game of Pong. We're playing against the AI opponent by controlling a paddle (our paddle is on the right and has a green color, whereas our opponent's is light brown and on the left). The objective of the game is to get the bounding ball past our opponent's paddle, while preventing it from getting past our paddle. The two situations can be considered to be completely different: in the right-hand situation, the ball is close to the opponent, so we can relax and watch. However, the situation on the left is more demanding: assuming that the ball is moving from left to right, which means that the ball is moving toward our side, so we need to move our paddle quickly to avoid losing a point. The situations below are just two from the 10^{70802} possible situations, but we want our agent to act on them differently.

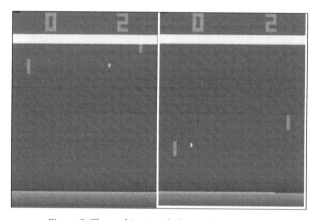

Figure 2: The ambiguity of observations in Pong

As a solution to this problem, we can use a nonlinear representation that maps both state and action onto a value. In machine learning this is called a "regression problem." The concrete way to represent and train such a representation can vary, but, as you may have already guessed from this section's title, using a deep neural network is one of the most popular options, especially when dealing with observations represented as screen images. With this in mind, let's make modifications to the Q-learning algorithm:

1. Initialize $Q(s, a)$ with some initial approximation
2. By interacting with the environment, obtain the tuple (s, a, r, s')
3. Calculate loss: $\mathcal{L} = (Q_{s,a} - r)^2$ if episode has ended or
   $\mathcal{L} = (Q_{s,a} - (r + \gamma \max_{a' \in A} Q_{s',a'}))^2$ otherwise
4. Update $Q(s, a)$ using the **stochastic gradient descent (SGD)** algorithm, by minimizing the loss with respect to the model parameters
5. Repeat from step 2 until converged

The preceding algorithm looks simple but, unfortunately, it won't work very well. Let's discuss what could go wrong.

Interaction with the environment

First of all, we need to interact with the environment somehow to receive data to train on. In simple environments, such as FrozenLake, we can act randomly, but is this the best strategy to use? Imagine the game of Pong. What's the probability of winning a single point by randomly moving the paddle? It's not zero but it's extremely small, which just means that we'll need to wait for a very long time for such a rare situation. As an alternative, we can use our Q function approximation as a source of behavior (as we did before in the value iteration method, when we remembered our experience during testing).

If our representation of Q is good, then the experience that we get from the environment will show the agent relevant data to train on. However, we're in trouble when our approximation is not perfect (at the beginning of the training, for example). In such a case, our agent can be stuck with bad actions for some states without ever trying to behave differently. This *exploration versus exploitation* dilemma was mentioned briefly in *Chapter 1, What is Reinforcement Learning?*. On the one hand, our agent needs to explore the environment to build a complete picture of transitions and action outcomes. On the other hand, we should use interaction with the environment efficiently: we shouldn't waste time by randomly trying actions we've already tried and have learned their outcomes. As you can see, random behavior is better at the beginning of the training when our Q approximation is bad, as it gives us more uniformly distributed information about the environment states. As our training progresses, random behavior becomes inefficient and we want to fall back to our Q approximation to decide how to act.

A method which performs such a mix of two extreme behaviors is known as an **epsilon-greedy** method, which just means switching between random and Q policy using the probability hyperparameter ϵ. By varying ϵ we can select the ratio of random actions. The usual practice is to start with $\epsilon = 1.0$ (100% random actions) and slowly decrease it to some small value such as 5% or 2% of random actions. Using an epsilon-greedy method helps both to explore the environment in the beginning and to stick to good policy at the end of the training. There are other solutions to the "exploration versus exploitation" problem, and we'll discuss some of them in part three of the book. This problem is one of the fundamental open questions in RL and an active area of research, which is not even close to being resolved completely.

SGD optimization

The core of our Q-learning procedure is borrowed from the supervised learning. Indeed, we are trying to approximate a complex, nonlinear function $Q(s, a)$ with a neural network. To do this, we calculate targets for this function using the Bellman equation and then pretend that we have a supervised learning problem at hand. That's okay, but one of the fundamental requirements for SGD optimization is that the training data is **independent and identically distributed** (frequently abbreviated as **i.i.d**).

In our case, data that we're going to use for the SGD update doesn't fulfill these criteria:

1. Our samples are not independent. Even if we accumulate a large batch of data samples, they all will be very close to each other, as they belong to the same episode.

2. Distribution of our training data won't be identical to samples provided by the optimal policy that we want to learn. Data that we have is a result of some other policy (our current policy, random, or both in the case of ϵ-greedy), but we don't want to learn how to play randomly: we want an optimal policy with the best reward.

To deal with this nuisance, we usually need to use a large buffer of our past experience and sample training data from it, instead of using our latest experience. This method is called **replay buffer**. The simplest implementation is a buffer of fixed size, with new data added to the end of the buffer so that it pushes the oldest experience out of it. Replay buffer allows us to train on more-or-less independent data, but data will still be fresh enough to train on samples generated by our recent policy.

Correlation between steps

Another practical issue with the default training procedure is also related to the lack of i.i.d in our data, but in a slightly different manner. The Bellman equation provides us with the value of $Q(s, a)$ via $Q(s', a')$ (which has the name of bootstrapping). However, both states s and s' have only one step between them. This makes them very similar and it's really hard for neural networks to distinguish between them. When we perform an update of our network's parameters, to make $Q(s, a)$ closer to the desired result, we indirectly can alter the value produced for $Q(s', a')$ and other states nearby. This can make our training really unstable, like chasing our own tail: when we update Q for state s, then on subsequent states we discover that $Q(s', a')$ becomes worse, but attempts to update it can spoil our $Q(s, a)$ approximation, and so on.

To make training more stable, there is a trick, called *target network*, when we keep a copy of our network and use it for the $Q(s', a')$ value in the Bellman equation. This network is synchronized with our main network only periodically, for example, once in N steps (where N is usually quite a large hyperparameter, such as 1k or 10k training iterations).

The Markov property

Our RL methods use MDP formalism as their basis, which assumes that the environment obeys the Markov property: observation from the environment is all that we need to act optimally (in other words, our observations allow us to distinguish states from one another). As we've seen on the preceding Pong's screenshot, one single image from the Atari game is not enough to capture all important information (using only one image we have no idea about the speed and direction of objects, like the ball and our opponent's paddle). This obviously violates the Markov property and moves our single-frame Pong environment into the area of **partially observable MDPs (POMDP)**. A POMDP is basically MDP without the Markov property and they are very important in practice. For example, for most card games where you don't see your opponents' cards, game observations are POMDPs, because current observation (your cards and cards on the table) could correspond to different cards in your opponents' hands.

We'll not discuss POMPDs in detail in this book, so, for now, we'll use a small technique to push our environment back into the MDP domain. The solution is maintaining several observations from the past and using them as a state. In the case of Atari games, we usually stack k subsequent frames together and use them as the observation at every state. This allows our agent to deduct the dynamics of the current state, for instance, to get the speed of the ball and its direction. The usual "classical" number of k for Atari is four. Of course, it's just a hack, as there can be longer dependencies in the environment, but for most of the games it works well.

The final form of DQN training

There are many more tips and tricks that researchers have discovered to make DQN training more stable and efficient, and we'll cover the best of them in the next chapter. However, ϵ-greedy, replay buffer, and target network form? the basis that allows DeepMind to successfully train a DQN on a set of 49 Atari games and demonstrate the efficiency of this approach applied to complicated environments.

The original paper (without target network) was published at the end of 2013 (*Playing Atari with Deep Reinforcement Learning* 1312.5602v1, *Mnih and others.*), and they used seven games for testing. Later, at the beginning of 2015, a revised version of the article, with 49 different games, was published in *Nature* (*Human-Level Control Through Deep Reinforcement Learning* doi:10.1038/nature14236, *Mnih and others.*)

The algorithm for DQN from the preceding papers has the following steps:

1. Initialize parameters for $Q(s, a)$ and $\hat{Q}(s, a)$ with random weights, $\epsilon \leftarrow 1.0$, and empty replay buffer

2. With probability ϵ, select a random action a, otherwise $a = \arg\max_a Q_{s,a}$

3. Execute action a in an emulator and observe reward r and the next state s'

4. Store transition (s, a, r, s') in the replay buffer

5. Sample a random minibatch of transitions from the replay buffer

6. For every transition in the buffer, calculate target $y = r$ if the episode has ended at this step or $y = r + \gamma \max_{a' \in A} \hat{Q}_{s',a'}$ otherwise

7. Calculate loss: $\mathcal{L} = (Q_{s,a} - y)^2$

8. Update $Q(s, a)$ using the SGD algorithm by minimizing the loss in respect to model parameters

9. Every N steps copy weights from Q to $\hat{Q}_t$

10. Repeat from step 2 until converged

Let's implement it now and try to beat some of the Atari games!

DQN on Pong

Before we jump into the code, some introduction is needed. Our examples are becoming increasingly challenging and complex, which is not surprising, as the complexity of problems we're trying to tackle is also growing. The examples are as simple and concise as possible, but some of the code may be difficult to understand at first.

Another thing to note is performance. Our previous examples for FrozenLake, or CartPole, were not demanding from a performance perspective, as observations were small, neural network parameters were tiny, and shaving off extra milliseconds in the training loop wasn't important. However, from now on, that's not the case anymore. One single observation from the Atari environment is 100k values, which has to be rescaled, converted to floats, and stored in the replay buffer. One extra copy of this data array can cost you training speed, which is not seconds and minutes anymore, but could be hours even on the fastest GPU available. The neural network training loop could also be a bottleneck. Of course, RL models are not such huge monsters as state-of-the-art ImageNet models, but even the DQN model from 2015 has more than 1.5M parameters, which is a lot for a GPU to crunch. So, to make a long story short: performance matters, especially when you're experimenting with hyperparameters and need to wait not for a single model to train, but for dozens of them.

PyTorch is quite expressive, so more-or-less efficient processing code could look much less cryptic than optimized TensorFlow graphs, but there is still lots of opportunity for doing things slowly and making mistakes. For example, a naive version of DQN loss computation, which loops over every batch sample, is about two times slower than a parallel version. However, a single extra copy of the data batch can make the speed of the same code 13 times slower, which is quite significant.

This example has been split into three modules due to its length, logical structure, and reusability. The modules are as follows:

- `Chapter06/lib/wrappers.py`: These are Atari environment wrappers mostly taken from the OpenAI Baselines project
- `Chapter06/lib/dqn_model.py`: This is the DQN neural net layer, with the same architecture as the DeepMind DQN from the *Nature* paper
- `Chapter06/02_dqn_pong.py`: This is the main module with the training loop, loss function calculation, and experience replay buffer

Wrappers

Tackling Atari games with RL is quite demanding from a resource perspective. To make things faster, several transformations are applied to the Atari platform interaction, which are described in DeepMind's paper. Some of these transformations influence only performance, but some address Atari platform features that make learning long and unstable. Transformations are usually implemented as OpenAI Gym wrappers of various kinds. The full list is quite lengthy and there are several implementations of the same wrappers in various sources. My personal favorite is in the OpenAI repository called **baselines**, which is a set of RL methods and algorithms implemented in TensorFlow and applied to popular benchmarks, to establish the common ground for comparing methods. The repository is available from `https://github.com/openai/baselines`, and wrappers are available in this file: `https://github.com/openai/baselines/blob/master/baselines/common/atari_wrappers.py`.

The full list of Atari transformations used by RL researchers includes:

- Converting individual lives in the game into separate episodes. In general, an episode contains all the steps from the beginning of the game until the "Game over" screen appears?, which can last for thousands of game steps (observations and actions). Usually, in arcade games, the player is given several lives, which provide several attempts in the game. This transformation splits a full episode into individual small episodes for every life that a player has. Not all games support this feature (for example, Pong doesn't), but for the supported environments, it usually helps to speed up convergence as our episodes become shorter.

- In the beginning of the game, performing a random amount (up to 30) of no-op actions. This should stabilize training, but there is no proper explanation why it is the case.

- Making an action decision every K steps, where K is usually 4 or 3. On intermediate frames, the chosen action is simply repeated. This allows training to speed up significantly, as processing every frame with a neural network is quite a demanding operation, but the difference between consequent frames is usually minor.

- Taking the maximum of every pixel in the last two frames and using it as an observation. Some Atari games have a flickering effect, which is due to the platform's limitation (Atari has a limited amount of sprites that can be shown on a single frame). For a human eye, such quick changes are not visible, but they can confuse neural networks.

- Pressing **FIRE** in the beginning of the game. Some games (including Pong and Breakout) require a user to press the **FIRE** button to start the game. In theory, it's possible for a neural network to learn to press **FIRE** itself, but it will require much more episodes to be played. So, we press **FIRE** in the wrapper.

- Scaling every frame down from 210 × 160, with three color frames, into a single-color 84 × 84 image. Different approaches are possible. For example, the DeepMind paper describes this transformation as taking the Y-color channel from the YCbCr color space and then rescaling the full image to an 84 × 84 resolution. Some other researchers do grayscale transformation, cropping non-relevant parts of the image and then scaling down. In the Baselines repository (and in the following example code), the latter approach is used.

- Stacking several (usually four) subsequent frames together to give the network the information about the dynamics of the game's objects.

- Clipping the reward to −1, 0, and 1 values. The obtained score can vary wildly among the games. For example, in Pong you get a score of 1 for every ball that your opponent passes behind you. However, in some games, like KungFu, you get a reward of 100 for every enemy killed. This spread in reward values makes our loss have completely different scales between the games, which makes it harder to find common hyperparameters for a set of games. To fix this, reward just gets clipped to the range [−1...1].

- Converting observations from `unsigned` bytes to `float32` values. The screen obtained from the emulator is encoded as a tensor of bytes with values from 0 to 255, which is not the best representation for a neural network. So, we need to convert the image into floats and rescale the values to the range [0.0...1.0].

In our example on Pong, we don't need some of the above wrappers, such as converting lives into separate episodes and reward clipping, so those wrappers aren't included in the example code. However, you should be aware of them, just in case you decide to experiment with other games. Sometimes, when the DQN is not converging, the problem is not in the code but in the wrongly wrapped environment. I've spend several days debugging convergence issues caused by missing the **FIRE** button press at the beginning of a game!

Let's take a look at the implementation of individual wrappers from `Chapter06/lib/wrappers.py`:

```
import cv2
import gym
```

```
import gym.spaces
import numpy as np
import collections

class FireResetEnv(gym.Wrapper):
    def __init__(self, env=None):
        super(FireResetEnv, self).__init__(env)
        assert env.unwrapped.get_action_meanings()[1] == 'FIRE'
        assert len(env.unwrapped.get_action_meanings()) >= 3

    def step(self, action):
        return self.env.step.action()

    def reset(self):
        self.env.reset()
        obs, _, done, _ = self.env.step(1)
        if done:
            self.env.reset()
        obs, _, done, _ = self.env.step(2)
        if done:
            self.env.reset()
        return obs
```

The preceding wrapper presses the **FIRE** button in environments that require them for the game to start. In addition to pressing **FIRE**, this wrapper checks for several corner cases that are present in some games.

```
class MaxAndSkipEnv(gym.Wrapper):
    def __init__(self, env=None, skip=4):
        """Return only every 'skip'-th frame"""
        super(MaxAndSkipEnv, self).__init__(env)
        # most recent raw observations (for max pooling across
time steps)
        self._obs_buffer = collections.deque(maxlen=2)
        self._skip = skip

    def step(self, action):
        total_reward = 0.0
        done = None
        for _ in range(self._skip):
            obs, reward, done, info = self.env.step(action)
            self._obs_buffer.append(obs)
            total_reward += reward
            if done:
```

```
                break
            max_frame = np.max(np.stack(self._obs_buffer), axis=0)
            return max_frame, total_reward, done, info

    def _reset(self):
        self._obs_buffer.clear()
        obs = self.env.reset()
        self._obs_buffer.append(obs)
        return obs
```

This wrapper combines the repetition of actions during K frames and pixels from two consecutive frames.

```
class ProcessFrame84(gym.ObservationWrapper):
    def __init__(self, env=None):
        super(ProcessFrame84, self).__init__(env)
        self.observation_space = gym.spaces.Box(low=0, high=255,
shape=(84, 84, 1), dtype=np.uint8)

    def observation(self, obs):
        return ProcessFrame84.process(obs)

    @staticmethod
    def process(frame):
        if frame.size == 210 * 160 * 3:
            img = np.reshape(frame, [210, 160,
3]).astype(np.float32)
        elif frame.size == 250 * 160 * 3:
            img = np.reshape(frame, [250, 160,
3]).astype(np.float32)
        else:
            assert False, "Unknown resolution."
        img = img[:, :, 0] * 0.299 + img[:, :, 1] * 0.587 + img[:,
:, 2] * 0.114
        resized_screen = cv2.resize(img, (84, 110),
interpolation=cv2.INTER_AREA)
        x_t = resized_screen[18:102, :]
        x_t = np.reshape(x_t, [84, 84, 1])
        return x_t.astype(np.uint8)
```

The goal of this wrapper is to convert input observations from the emulator, which normally has a resolution of 210 × 160 pixels with RGB color channels, to a grayscale 84 × 84 image. It does this using a colorimetric grayscale conversion (which is closer to human color perception than a simple averaging of color channels), resizing the image and cropping the top and bottom parts of the result.

```python
class BufferWrapper(gym.ObservationWrapper):
    def __init__(self, env, n_steps, dtype=np.float32):
        super(BufferWrapper, self).__init__(env)
        self.dtype = dtype
        old_space = env.observation_space
        self.observation_space =
gym.spaces.Box(old_space.low.repeat(n_steps, axis=0),
            old_space.high.repeat(n_steps, axis=0), dtype=dtype)

    def reset(self):
        self.buffer = np.zeros_like(self.observation_space.low,
dtype=self.dtype)
        return self.observation(self.env.reset())

    def observation(self, observation):
        self.buffer[:-1] = self.buffer[1:]
        self.buffer[-1] = observation
        return self.buffer
```

This class creates a stack of subsequent frames along the first dimension and returns them as an observation. The purpose is to give the network an idea about the dynamics of the objects, such as the speed and direction of the ball in Pong or how enemies are moving. This is very important information, which it is not possible to obtain from a single image.

```python
class ImageToPyTorch(gym.ObservationWrapper):
    def __init__(self, env):
        super(ImageToPyTorch, self).__init__(env)
        old_shape = self.observation_space.shape
        self.observation_space = gym.spaces.Box(low=0.0, high=1.0,
    shape=(old_shape[-1], old_shape[0], old_shape[1]),
dtype=np.float32)

    def observation(self, observation):
        return np.moveaxis(observation, 2, 0)
```

This simple wrapper changes the shape of the observation from HWC to the CHW format required by PyTorch. The input shape of the tensor has a color channel as the last dimension, but PyTorch's convolution layers assume the color channel to be the first dimension.

```
class ScaledFloatFrame(gym.ObservationWrapper):
    def observation(self, obs):
        return np.array(obs).astype(np.float32) / 255.0
```

The final wrapper we have in the library converts observation data from bytes to floats and scales every pixel's value to the range [*0.0...1.0*].

```
def make_env(env_name):
    env = gym.make(env_name)
    env = MaxAndSkipEnv(env)
    env = FireResetEnv(env)
    env = ProcessFrame84(env)
    env = ImageToPyTorch(env)
    env = BufferWrapper(env, 4)
    return ScaledFloatFrame(env)
```

At the end of the file is a simple function that creates an environment by its name and applies all the required wrappers to it. That's it for wrappers, so let's look at our model.

DQN model

The model published in *Nature* has three convolution layers followed by two fully connected layers. All layers are separated by ReLU nonlinearities. The output of the model is Q-values for every action available in the environment, without nonlinearity applied (as Q-values can have any value). The approach to have all Q-values calculated with one pass through the network helps us to increase speed significantly in comparison to treating $Q(s, a)$ literally and feeding observations and actions to the network to obtain the value of the action.

The code of the model is in Chapter06/lib/dqn_model.py:

```
import torch
import torch.nn as nn
import numpy as np


class DQN(nn.Module):
    def __init__(self, input_shape, n_actions):
        super(DQN, self).__init__()

        self.conv = nn.Sequential(
            nn.Conv2d(input_shape[0], 32, kernel_size=8,
stride=4),
            nn.ReLU(),
            nn.Conv2d(32, 64, kernel_size=4, stride=2),
```

```
        nn.ReLU(),
        nn.Conv2d(64, 64, kernel_size=3, stride=1),
        nn.ReLU()
    )

    conv_out_size = self._get_conv_out(input_shape)
    self.fc = nn.Sequential(
        nn.Linear(conv_out_size, 512),
        nn.ReLU(),
        nn.Linear(512, n_actions)
    )
```

To be able to write our network in the generic way, it was implemented in two parts: convolution and sequential. PyTorch doesn't have a 'flatter' layer which could transform a 3D tensor into a 1D vector of numbers, required to feed convolution output to the fully connected layer. This problem is solved in the `forward()` function, where we can reshape our batch of 3D tensors into a batch of 1D vectors.

Another small problem is that we don't know the exact number of values in the output from the convolution layer produced with input of the given shape. However, we need to pass this number to the first fully connected layer constructor. One possible solution would be to hard-code this number, which is a function of input shape (for 84 × 84 input, the output from the convolution layer will have 3136 values), but it's not the best way, as our code becomes less robust to input shape change. The better solution would be to have a simple function (`_get_conv_out()`) that accepts the input shape and applies the convolution layer to a fake tensor of such a shape. The result of the function will be equal to the number of parameters returned by this application. It will be fast, as this call will be done once on model creation but will allow us to have generic code:

```
    def _get_conv_out(self, shape):
        o = self.conv(torch.zeros(1, *shape))
        return int(np.prod(o.size()))

    def forward(self, x):
        conv_out = self.conv(x).view(x.size()[0], -1)
        return self.fc(conv_out)
```

The final piece of the model is the `forward()` function, which accepts the 4D input tensor (the first dimension is batch size, the second is the *color* channel, which is our stack of subsequent frames, while the third and fourth are image dimensions). The application of transformations is done in two steps: first we apply the convolution layer to the input and then we obtain a 4D tensor on output. This result is flattened to have two dimensions: a batch size and all the parameters returned by the convolution for this batch entry as one long vector of numbers. This is done by the `view()` function of the tensors, which lets one single dimension be a `-1` argument as a *wildcard* for the rest of the parameters. For example, if we have a tensor `T` of shape `(2, 3, 4)`, which is a 3D tensor of 24 elements, we can reshape it into a 2D tensor with six rows and four columns using `T.view(6, 4)`. This operation doesn't create a new memory object or move the data in memory, it just changes the higher-level shape of the tensor. The same result could be obtained by `T.view(-1, 4)` or `T.view(6, -1)`, which is very convenient when your tensor has a batch size in the first dimension. Finally, we pass this flattened 2D tensor to our fully connected layers to obtain Q-values for every batch input.

Training

The third module contains the experience replay buffer, the agent, the loss function calculation, and the training loop itself. Before going into the code, something needs to be said about the training hyperparameters. DeepMind's *Nature* paper contained a table with all the details about hyperparameters used to train its model on *all* 49 Atari games used for evaluation. DeepMind kept all those parameters the same for all games (but trained individual models for every game), and it was the team's intention to show that the method is robust enough to solve lots of games with varying complexity, action space, reward structure, and other details using one single model architecture and hyperparameters. However, our goal here is much more modest: we want to solve just the Pong game.

Pong is quite simple and straightforward in comparison to other games in the Atari test set, so the hyperparameters in the paper are overkill for our task. For example, to get the best result on all 49 games, DeepMind used a million-observations replay buffer, which requires approximately 20 GB of RAM to keep and lots of samples from the environment to populate. The epsilon decay schedule that was used is also not the best for a single Pong game. In the training, DeepMind linearly decayed epsilon from 1.0 to 0.1 during the first million frames obtained from the environment. However, my own experiments have shown that for Pong, it's enough to decay epsilon over the first 100k frames and then keep it stable. The replay buffer can also be much smaller: 10k transitions will be enough. In the following example, I've used my parameters. These differ from the parameters in the paper but allow us to solve Pong about ten times faster. On a GeForce GTX 1080 Ti, the following version converges to a mean score of 19.5 in one to two hours, but with DeepMind's hyperparameters it will require at least a day.

This speed up, of course, is fine-tuning for one particular environment and can break convergence on other games. You're free to play with the options and other games from the Atari set.

```
from lib import wrappers
from lib import dqn_model

import argparse
import time
import numpy as np
import collections

import torch
import torch.nn as nn
import torch.optim as optim

from tensorboardX import SummaryWriter
```

First, we import required modules and define hyperparameters.

```
DEFAULT_ENV_NAME = "PongNoFrameskip-v4"
MEAN_REWARD_BOUND = 19.5
```

These two values set the default environment to train on and the reward boundary for the last 100 episodes to stop training. They are just defaults; you can redefine them using the command line.

```
GAMMA = 0.99
BATCH_SIZE = 32
REPLAY_SIZE = 10000
REPLAY_START_SIZE = 10000
LEARNING_RATE = 1e-4
SYNC_TARGET_FRAMES = 1000
```

These parameters define the following:

- Our gamma value used for Bellman approximation
- The batch size sampled from the replay buffer (BATCH_SIZE)
- The maximum capacity of the buffer (REPLAY_SIZE)
- The count of frames we wait for before starting training to populate the replay buffer (REPLAY_START_SIZE)
- The learning rate used in the Adam optimizer, which is used in this example

- How frequently we sync model weights from the training model to the target model, which is used to get the value of the next state in the Bellman approximation.

```
EPSILON_DECAY_LAST_FRAME = 10**5
EPSILON_START = 1.0
EPSILON_FINAL = 0.02
```

The last batch of hyperparameters is related to the epsilon decay schedule. To achieve proper exploration, at early stages of training, we start with epsilon=1.0, which causes all actions to be selected randomly. Then, during first 100,000 frames, epsilon is linearly decayed to 0.02, which corresponds to the random action taken in 2% of steps. A similar scheme was used in the original DeepMind paper, but the duration of decay was 10 times longer (so, epsilon = 0.02 is reached after a million frames).

The next chunk of the code defines our experience replay buffer, the purpose of which is to keep the last transitions obtained from the environment (tuples of the observation, action, reward, done flag, and the next state). Each time we do a step in the environment, we push the transition into the buffer, keeping only a fixed number of steps, in our case 10k transitions. For training, we randomly sample the batch of transitions from the replay buffer, which allows us to break the correlation between subsequent steps in the environment.

```
Experience = collections.namedtuple('Experience',
    field_names=['state', 'action', 'reward', 'done', 'new_state'])


class ExperienceBuffer:
    def __init__(self, capacity):
        self.buffer = collections.deque(maxlen=capacity)

    def __len__(self):
        return len(self.buffer)

    def append(self, experience):
        self.buffer.append(experience)

    def sample(self, batch_size):
        indices = np.random.choice(len(self.buffer), batch_size,
replace=False)
        states, actions, rewards, dones, next_states =
zip(*[self.buffer[idx] for idx in indices])
        return np.array(states), np.array(actions),
np.array(rewards, dtype=np.float32), \
                np.array(dones, dtype=np.uint8),
np.array(next_states)
```

Most of the experience replay buffer code is quite straightforward: it basically exploits the capability of the `deque` class to maintain the given number of entries in the buffer. In the `sample()` method, we create a list of random indices and then repack the sampled entries into NumPy arrays for more convenient loss calculation.

The next class we need to have is an `Agent`, which interacts with the environment and saves the result of the interaction into the experience replay buffer that we've just seen:

```
class Agent:
    def __init__(self, env, exp_buffer):
        self.env = env
        self.exp_buffer = exp_buffer
        self._reset()

    def _reset(self):
        self.state = env.reset()
        self.total_reward = 0.0
```

During the agent's initialization, we need to store references to the environment and experience replay buffer, tracking the current observation and the total reward accumulated so far.

```
    def play_step(self, net, epsilon=0.0, device="cpu"):
        done_reward = None

        if np.random.random() < epsilon:
            action = env.action_space.sample()
        else:
            state_a = np.array([self.state], copy=False)
            state_v = torch.tensor(state_a).to(device)
            q_vals_v = net(state_v)
            _, act_v = torch.max(q_vals_v, dim=1)
            action = int(act_v.item())
```

The main method of the agent is to perform a step in the environment and store its result in the buffer. To do this, we need to select the action first. With the probability epsilon (passed as an argument) we take the random action, otherwise we use the past model to obtain the Q-values for all possible actions and choose the best.

```
        new_state, reward, is_done, _ = self.env.step(action)
        self.total_reward += reward
        new_state = new_state

        exp = Experience(self.state, action, reward, is_done,
new_state)
```

```
            self.exp_buffer.append(exp)
            self.state = new_state
            if is_done:
                done_reward = self.total_reward
                self._reset()
            return done_reward
```

As the action has been chosen, we pass it to the environment to get the next observation and reward, store the data in the experience buffer and the handle the end-of-episode situation. The result of the function is the total accumulated reward if we've reached the end of the episode with this step, or None if not.

Now it is time for the last function in the training module, which calculates the loss for the sampled batch. This function is written in a form to maximally exploit GPU parallelism by processing all batch samples with vector operations, which makes it harder to understand when compared with a naive loop over the batch. Yet this optimization pays off: the parallel version is more than two times faster than an explicit loop over the batch.

As a reminder, here is the loss expression we need to calculate:
$L = \left(Q_{s,a} - \left(r + \gamma \max_{a' \in A} Q_{s',a'}\right)\right)^2$ for steps which aren't at the end of the episode, or $L = \left(Q_{s,a} - r\right)^2$ for final steps.

```
    def calc_loss(batch, net, tgt_net, device="cpu"):
        states, actions, rewards, dones, next_states = batch
```

In arguments, we pass our batch as a tuple of arrays (repacked by the sample() method in the experience buffer), our network that we're training and the target network, which is periodically synced with the trained one. The first model (passed as the argument net) is used to calculate gradients, while the second model in the tgt_net argument is used to calculate values for the next states and this calculation shouldn't affect gradients. To achieve this, we're using the detach() function of the PyTorch tensor to prevent gradients from flowing into the target network's graph. This function was described in *Chapter 3, Deep Learning with PyTorch.*

```
        states_v = torch.tensor(states).to(device)
        next_states_v = torch.tensor(next_states).to(device)
        actions_v = torch.tensor(actions).to(device)
        rewards_v = torch.tensor(rewards).to(device)
        done_mask = torch.ByteTensor(dones).to(device)
```

The preceding code is simple and straightforward: we wrap individual NumPy arrays with batch data in PyTorch tensors and copy them to GPU if the CUDA device was specified in arguments.

```
state_action_values = net(states_v).gather(1,
    actions_v.unsqueeze(-1)).squeeze(-1)
```

In the line above, we pass observations to the first model and extract the specific Q-values for the taken actions using the `gather()` tensor operation. The first argument to the `gather()` call is a dimension index that we want to perform gathering on (in our case it is equal to 1, which corresponds to actions). The second argument is a tensor of indices of elements to be chosen. Extra `unsqueeze()` and `squeeze()` calls are required to fulfill the requirements of the `gather` functions to the index argument and to get rid of extra dimensions that we created (the index should have the same number of dimensions as the data we're processing). In the following image, you can see an illustration of what `gather` does on the example case, with a batch of six entries and four actions.

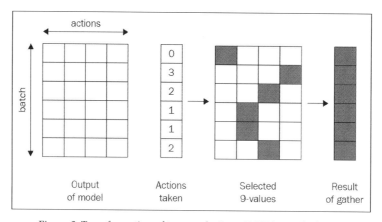

Figure 3: Transformation of tensors during a DQN loss calculation

Keep in mind that the result of `gather()` applied to tensors is a differentiable operation, which will keep all gradients with respect to the final loss value.

```
next_state_values = tgt_net(next_states_v).max(1)[0]
```

On in the above line, we apply the target network to our next state observations and calculate the maximum Q-value along the same *action* dimension 1. Function `max()` returns both maximum values and indices of those values (so it calculates both max and argmax), which is very convenient. However, in this case, we're interested only in values, so we take the first entry of the result.

```
next_state_values[done_mask] = 0.0
```

Here we make one simple, but very important, point: if transition in the batch is from the last step in the episode, then our value of the action doesn't have a discounted reward of the next state, as there is no next state to gather reward from. This may look minor, but this is very important in practice: without this, training will not converge.

```
next_state_values = next_state_value.detach()
```

In this line, we detach the value from its computation graph to prevent gradients from flowing into the neural network used to calculate Q approximation for next states. This is important, as without this our backpropagation of the loss will start to affect both predictions for the current state and the next state. However, we don't want to touch predictions for the next state, as they're used in the Bellman equation to calculate reference Q-values. To block gradients from flowing into this branch of the graph, we're using the `detach()` method of the tensor, which returns the tensor without connection to its calculation history. In previous versions of PyTorch, we used a volatile attribute of the `Variable` class, which was obsoleted with the 0.4.0 release. More information was provided in *Chapter 3, Deep Learning with PyTorch*.

```
    expected_state_action_values = next_state_values * GAMMA +
rewards_v
    return nn.MSELoss()(state_action_values,
expected_state_action_values)
```

Finally, we calculate the Bellman approximation value and the mean squared error loss. This ends our loss function calculation, and the rest of the code is our training loop.

```
if __name__ == "__main__":
    parser = argparse.ArgumentParser()
    parser.add_argument("--cuda", default=False,
action="store_true", help="Enable cuda")
    parser.add_argument("--env", default=DEFAULT_ENV_NAME,
                        help="Name of the environment, default=" +
DEFAULT_ENV_NAME)
    parser.add_argument("--reward", type=float,
default=MEAN_REWARD_BOUND,
                        help="Mean reward boundary for stop of
training, default=%.2f" % MEAN_REWARD_BOUND)
    args = parser.parse_args()
    device = torch.device("cuda" if args.cuda else "cpu")
```

To begin with, we create a parser of command-line arguments. Our script allows us to enable CUDA and train on environments that are different from the default.

```
    env = wrappers.make_env(args.env)
    net = dqn_model.DQN(env.observation_space.shape,
env.action_space.n).to(device)
```

```
    tgt_net = dqn_model.DQN(env.observation_space.shape,
env.action_space.n).to(device)
```

Here we create our environment with all required wrappers applied, the neural network we're going to train, and our target network with the same architecture. In the beginning, they'll be initialized with different random weights, but it doesn't matter much as we'll sync them every 1k frames, which roughly corresponds to one episode of Pong.

```
    writer = SummaryWriter(comment="-" + args.env)
    print(net)


    buffer = ExperienceBuffer(REPLAY_SIZE)
    agent = Agent(env, buffer)
    epsilon = EPSILON_START
```

Then we create our experience replay buffer of the required size and pass it to the agent. Epsilon is initially initialized to 1.0, but will be decreased every iteration.

```
    optimizer = optim.Adam(net.parameters(), lr=LEARNING_RATE)
    total_rewards = []
    frame_idx = 0
    ts_frame = 0
    ts = time.time()
    best_mean_reward = None
```

The last things we do before the training loop are to create an optimizer, a buffer for full episode rewards, a counter of frames and several variables to track our speed, and the best mean reward reached. Every time our mean reward beats the record, we'll save the model in the file.

```
    while True:
        frame_idx += 1
        epsilon = max(EPSILON_FINAL, EPSILON_START - frame_idx /
EPSILON_DECAY_LAST_FRAME)
```

At the beginning of the training loop, we count the number of iterations completed and decrease epsilon according to our schedule. Epsilon will drop linearly during the given number of frames (EPSILON_DECAY_LAST_FRAME=100k) and then will be kept on the same level of EPSILON_FINAL=0.02.

```
        reward = agent.play_step(net, epsilon, device=device)
        if reward is not None:
            total_rewards.append(reward)
            speed = (frame_idx - ts_frame) / (time.time() - ts)
            ts_frame = frame_idx
            ts = time.time()
```

```
            mean_reward = np.mean(total_rewards[-100:])
            print("%d: done %d games, mean reward %.3f, eps %.2f,
    speed %.2f f/s" % (
                frame_idx, len(total_rewards), mean_reward,
    epsilon,
                speed
            ))
            writer.add_scalar("epsilon", epsilon, frame_idx)
            writer.add_scalar("speed", speed, frame_idx)
            writer.add_scalar("reward_100", mean_reward,
    frame_idx)
            writer.add_scalar("reward", reward, frame_idx)
```

In this block of code, we ask our agent to make a single step in the environment (using our current network and value for epsilon). This function returns a non-None result only if this step is the final step in the episode. In that case, we report our progress. Specifically, we calculate and show, both in the console and in TensorBoard, these values:

- Speed as a count of frames processed per second
- Count of episodes played
- Mean reward for the last 100 episodes
- Current value for epsilon

```
            if best_mean_reward is None or best_mean_reward <
    mean_reward:
                torch.save(net.state_dict(), args.env + "-
    best.dat")
                if best_mean_reward is not None:
                    print("Best mean reward updated %.3f -> %.3f,
    model saved" % (best_mean_reward, mean_reward))
                best_mean_reward = mean_reward
            if mean_reward > args.reward:
                print("Solved in %d frames!" % frame_idx)
                break
```

Every time our mean reward for the last 100 episodes reaches a maximum, we report this and save the model parameters. If our mean reward exceeds the specified boundary, then we stop training. For Pong, the boundary is 19.5, which means winning more than 19 games from 21 possible games.

```
        if len(buffer) < REPLAY_START_SIZE:
            continue
```

```
if frame_idx % SYNC_TARGET_FRAMES == 0:
    tgt_net.load_state_dict(net.state_dict())
```

Here we check whether our buffer is large enough for training. In the beginning, we should wait for enough data to start, which in our case is 10k transitions. The next condition syncs parameters from our main network to the target net every SYNC_TARGET_FRAMES, which is 1k by default.

```
optimizer.zero_grad()
batch = buffer.sample(BATCH_SIZE)
loss_t = calc_loss(batch, net, tgt_net, device=device)
loss_t.backward()
optimizer.step()
```

The last piece of the training loop is very simple, but requires the most time to execute: we zero gradients, sample data batches from the experience replay buffer, calculate loss, and perform the optimization step to minimize the loss.

Running and performance

This example is demanding on resources. On Pong, it requires about 400k frames to reach a mean reward of 17 (which means winning more than 80% of games). A similar number of frames will be required to get from 17 to 19.5, as our learning progress saturates and it's hard for the model to improve the score. So, on average, a million frames are needed to train it fully. On the GTX 1080 Ti, I have a speed of about 150 frames per second, which is about two hours of training. On a CPU, the speed is much slower: about nine frames per second, which will take about a day and a half. Remember that this is for Pong, which is relatively easy to solve. Other games require hundreds of millions of frames and a 100 times larger experience replay buffer.

In the next chapter, we'll look at various approaches, found by researchers since 2015, which can help to increase both training speed and data efficiency. Nevertheless, for Atari you'll need resources and patience. The following image shows a TensorBoard screenshot with training dynamics:

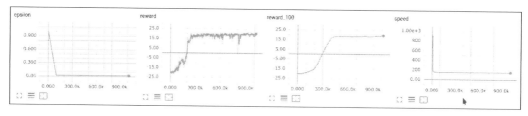

Figure 4: Characteristics of the training process (the X axis is the iteration number)

In the beginning of the training:

```
rl_book_samples/Chapter06$ ./02_dqn_pong.py --cuda
DQN (
  (conv): Sequential (
    (0): Conv2d(4, 32, kernel_size=(8, 8), stride=(4, 4))
    (1): ReLU ()
    (2): Conv2d(32, 64, kernel_size=(4, 4), stride=(2, 2))
    (3): ReLU ()
    (4): Conv2d(64, 64, kernel_size=(3, 3), stride=(1, 1))
    (5): ReLU ()
  )
  (fc): Sequential (
    (0): Linear (3136 -> 512)
    (1): ReLU ()
    (2): Linear (512 -> 6)
  )
)
```

```
1048: done 1 games, mean reward -19.000, eps 0.99, speed 83.45 f/s
1894: done 2 games, mean reward -20.000, eps 0.98, speed 913.37 f/s
2928: done 3 games, mean reward -20.000, eps 0.97, speed 932.16 f/s
3810: done 4 games, mean reward -20.250, eps 0.96, speed 923.60 f/s
4632: done 5 games, mean reward -20.400, eps 0.95, speed 921.52 f/s
5454: done 6 games, mean reward -20.500, eps 0.95, speed 918.04 f/s
6379: done 7 games, mean reward -20.429, eps 0.94, speed 906.64 f/s
7409: done 8 games, mean reward -20.500, eps 0.93, speed 903.51 f/s
8259: done 9 games, mean reward -20.556, eps 0.92, speed 905.94 f/s
9395: done 10 games, mean reward -20.500, eps 0.91, speed 898.05 f/s
10204: done 11 games, mean reward -20.545, eps 0.90, speed 374.76 f/s
10995: done 12 games, mean reward -20.583, eps 0.89, speed 160.55 f/s
11887: done 13 games, mean reward -20.538, eps 0.88, speed 160.44 f/s
12949: done 14 games, mean reward -20.571, eps 0.87, speed 160.67 f/s
```

Hundreds of games later, our DQN should start to figure out how to win one or two games out of 21. The speed has decreased due to epsilon drop: we need to use our model not only for training but also for the environment step.

```
101032: done 83 games, mean reward -19.506, eps 0.02, speed 143.06 f/s
103349: done 84 games, mean reward -19.488, eps 0.02, speed 142.99 f/s
```

```
106444: done 85 games, mean reward -19.424, eps 0.02, speed 143.15 f/s
108359: done 86 games, mean reward -19.395, eps 0.02, speed 143.18 f/s
110499: done 87 games, mean reward -19.379, eps 0.02, speed 143.01 f/s
113011: done 88 games, mean reward -19.352, eps 0.02, speed 142.98 f/s
115404: done 89 games, mean reward -19.326, eps 0.02, speed 143.07 f/s
117821: done 90 games, mean reward -19.300, eps 0.02, speed 143.03 f/s
121060: done 91 games, mean reward -19.220, eps 0.02, speed 143.10 f/s
```

Finally, after many more games, it can finally dominate and beat the (not very sophisticated) built-in Pong AI opponent:

```
982059: done 520 games, mean reward 19.500, eps 0.02, speed 145.14 f/s
984268: done 521 games, mean reward 19.420, eps 0.02, speed 145.39 f/s
986078: done 522 games, mean reward 19.440, eps 0.02, speed 145.24 f/s
987717: done 523 games, mean reward 19.460, eps 0.02, speed 145.06 f/s
989356: done 524 games, mean reward 19.470, eps 0.02, speed 145.07 f/s
991063: done 525 games, mean reward 19.510, eps 0.02, speed 145.31 f/s
Best mean reward updated 19.500 -> 19.510, model saved
Solved in 991063 frames!
```

Your model in action

Just to make your waiting a bit more fun, our code saves the best model's weights. In the `Chapter06/03_dqn_play.py` file, we have a program which can load this model file and play one episode, displaying the model's dynamics.

The code is very simple, but seeing how several matrices, with a million parameters, play Pong with superhuman accuracy, by observing only the pixels, can be like magic.

```
import gym
import time
import argparse
import numpy as np
import torch
```

```
from lib import wrappers
from lib import dqn_model

DEFAULT_ENV_NAME = "PongNoFrameskip-v4"
FPS = 25
```

In the beginning, we import the familiar PyTorch and Gym modules. The preceding
FPS parameter specifies the approximate speed of the shown frames.

```
If __name__ == "__main__":
    parser = argparse.ArgumentParser()
    parser.add_argument("-m", "--model", required=True, help="Model
file to load")
    parser.add_argument("-e", "--env", default=DEFAULT_ENV_NAME,
                        help="Environment name to use, default=" +
DEFAULT_ENV_NAME)
    parser.add_argument("-r", "--record", help="Directory to store
video recording")
    args = parser.parse_args()
```

The script accepts the filename of the saved model and allows the specification
of the Gym environment (of course, the model and environment have to match).
Additionally, you can pass option -r with the name of a non existent directory,
which will be used to save a video of your game (using the Monitor wrapper).
By default, the script just shows frames, but if you want to upload your model's
gameplay to YouTube, for example, -r could be handy.

```
    env = wrappers.make_env(args.env)
    if args.record:
        env = gym.wrappers.Monitor(env, args.record)
    net = dqn_model.DQN(env.observation_space.shape,
env.action_space.n)
    net.load_state_dict(torch.load(args.model))
```

The preceding code should be clear without comments: we create the environment
and our model, then we load weights from the file passed in the arguments.

```
    state = env.reset()
    total_reward = 0.0
    while True:
```

```
start_ts = time.time()
env.render()
state_v = torch.tensor(np.array([state], copy=False))
q_vals = net(state_v).data.numpy()[0]
action = np.argmax(q_vals)
```

This is almost an exact copy of `Agent` class' method `play_step()` from the training code, with the lack of epsilon-greedy action selection. We just pass our observation to the agent and select the action with maximum value. The only new thing here is the `render()` method in the environment, which is a standard way in Gym to display the current observation (you need to have a GUI for this).

```
state, reward, done, _ = env.step(action)
total_reward += reward
if done:
    break
delta = 1/FPS - (time.time() - start_ts)
if delta > 0:
    time.sleep(delta)
print("Total reward: %.2f" % total_reward)
```

The rest of the code is also simple. We pass the action to the environment, count the total reward, and stop our loop when the episode ends.

Things to try: If you're curious and want to experiment with this chapter's material on your own, then here is a short list of directions to explore. Be warned though: they can take lots of time and can cause you some moments of frustration during your experiments. However, these experiments are a very efficient way to really master the material from a practical point of view:

- Try to take some other games from the Atari set, such as Breakout or Atlantis or RiverRaid (my childhood favorite). This could require the tuning of hyperparameters.

- As an alternative to FrozenLake, there is another tabular environment, Taxi, which emulates a taxi driver who needs to pick up passengers and take them to a destination.

- Play with Pong hyperparameters. Is it possible to train faster? OpenAI claims that it can solve Pong in 30 minutes using the A3C method (which is a subject of part three of this book). Maybe it's possible with a DQN.

- Can you make the DQN training code faster? The OpenAI Baselines project has shown 350 frames per second using TensorFlow on GTX 1080 Ti. So, it looks like it's possible to optimize the PyTorch code.

- Can you get *The Ultimate Pong Dominator* model with a mean score of 21? It shouldn't be very hard: learning rate decay is the obvious method to try.

Summary

In this chapter, we introduced lots of new and complex material. We became familiar with the limitations of value iteration in complex environments with large observation spaces and discussed how to overcome them with Q-learning. We checked the Q-learning algorithm on the FrozenLake environment and discussed the approximation of Q-values with neural networks and the extra complications that arise from this approximation. We covered several tricks for DQNs to improve their training stability and convergence, such as experience replay buffer, target networks, and frame stacking. Finally, we combined those extensions in to one single implementation of DQN that solves the Pong environment from the Atari games suite.

In the next chapter, we'll look at a set of tricks that researchers have found, since 2015, to improve DQN convergence and quality, which (combined) can produce state-of-the-art results on most of the 54 Atari games. This set was published in 2017 and we'll analyze and reimplement all of the tricks.

7
DQN Extensions

In the previous chapter, we implemented the Deep Q-Network (DQN) model published by DeepMind in 2015. This paper had a significant effect on the Reinforcement Learning (RL) field by demonstrating that, despite common belief, it's possible to use nonlinear approximators in RL. This proof of concept stimulated large interest in the deep Q-learning field in particular and in deep RL in general.

Since then, many improvements have been proposed, along with tweaks to the basic architecture, which significantly improve convergence, stability and sample efficiency of the basic DQN invented by DeepMind. In this chapter, we'll take a deeper look at some of those ideas. Very conveniently, in October 2017, DeepMind published a paper called *Rainbow: Combining Improvements in Deep Reinforcement Learning* ([1] *Hessel and others*, 2017), which presented the seven most important improvements to DQN, some of which were invented in 2015, but some of which are very recent. In this paper, state-of-the-art results on the Atari Games suite were reached, just by combining all those seven methods together.

This chapter will go through all those methods. We will analyze the ideas behind them, alongside how they could be implemented and compared to the classic DQN performance. At the end, we'll check the combined system with all the methods.

The DQN extensions we'll become familiar with are as follows:

- **N-steps DQN**: How to improve convergence speed and stability with a simple unrolling of the Bellman equation and why it's not an ultimate solution
- **Double DQN**: How to deal with DQN overestimation of the values of actions
- **Noisy networks**: How to make exploration more efficient by adding noise to the network weights

- **Prioritized replay buffer**: Why uniform sampling of our experience is not the best way to train
- **Dueling DQN**: How to improve convergence speed by making our network's architecture closer represent the problem we're solving
- **Categorical DQN**: How to go beyond the single expected value of action and work with full distributions

First, we should simplify our experiments a bit by incorporating higher-level libraries in our DQN code.

The PyTorch Agent Net library

In *Chapter 6, Deep Q-Networks*, we implemented a DQN from scratch, using only PyTorch, OpenAI Gym, and `pytorch-tensorboard`. It suited our needs to demonstrate how things work, but now we're going to extend the basic DQN with extra tweaks. Some tweaks are quite simple and trivial, but some will require a major code modification. To be able to focus only on the significant parts, it would be useful to have as small and concise version of a DQN as possible, preferably with reusable code pieces. This will be extremely helpful when you're experimenting with some methods published in papers or your own ideas. In that case, you don't need to reimplement the same functionality again and again, fighting with the inevitable bugs.

With this in mind, some time ago I started to implement my own toolkit for the deep RL domain. I called it PTAN, which stands for PyTorch Agent Net, as it was inspired by another open-source library called AgentNet (`https://github.com/yandexdataschool/AgentNet`). The basic design principles I tried to follow in PTAN are as follows:

- Being as simple and clean as possible
- PyTorch-nativeness
- Containing small, reusable pieces of functionality
- Extensibility and flexibility

The library is available in GitHub: `https://github.com/Shmuma/ptan`. All the subsequent examples were implemented using version 0.3 of PTAN, which can be installed in your virtual environment by running the following:

```
pip install ptan==0.3
```

Let's look at the basic building blocks that PTAN provides.

Agent

The agent entity provides a unified way of bridging **observations** from the environment and the **actions** that we want to execute. So far, we've seen only a simple, stateless DQN agent that uses a neural net to obtain actions' values from the current observation and behaves greedily on those values. We've used epsilon-greedy behavior to explore the environment, but this doesn't change the picture much.

In the RL field, this could be more complicated. For example, instead of predicting the values of the actions, our agent can predict probability distribution over actions. Such agents are called policy agents and we'll talk about those methods in part three of the book. The other requirement could be some kind of memory in the agent. For example, very often one observation (or even k last observation) is not enough to make a decision about the action and we want to keep some memory in the agent to capture the necessary information. There is a whole subdomain of RL which tries to address this complication with Partially-Observable Markov Decision Process (POMDP) formalism. We'll briefly touch on this case in the last part of the book.

To capture all those variants and make the code flexible, the agent in the PTAN is implemented as an extensible hierarchy of classes with the `ptan.agent.BaseAgent` abstract class at the top. From the high level, the agent needs to accept the batch of observation (in the form of a NumPy array) and return the batch of actions that the agent wants to take. The batch is used to make the processing more efficient, as processing several observations in one pass in GPU is frequently much faster than processing them individually. The abstract base class doesn't define the type of input and output, which makes it very flexible and easy to extend. For example, in the continuous domain, our actions won't any longer be indices of discrete actions, but float values.

The agent that corresponds to our current DQN requirements is `ptan.agent.DQNAgent`, which uses the provided PyTorch `nn.Module` to convert a batch of observations into action values. To convert the network's output into actual actions to be taken, the `DQNAgent` class needs the second object to be passed on creation: action selector.

The purpose of action selector is to convert the output of the network (usually it's a vector of numbers) into some action. In a discrete action space case, the action will be one or several action indices to be taken. There are two action selectors in the PTAN that we'll need: `ptan.actions.ArgmaxActionSelector` and `ptan.actions.EpsilonGreedyActionSelector`. As you may guess from the names, the first one (`ArgmaxActionSelector`) applies argmax to the provided values, which corresponds to greedy actions over Q-values.

The second action selector supports epsilon-greedy behavior, by having epsilon as a parameter and with this probability taking the random action instead of the greedy selection. To combine all this together, to create the agent for CartPole, with epsilon-greedy action selection, we can write the following code:

```
import gym
import ptan
import numpy as np
import torch.nn as nn

env = gym.make("CartPole-v0")
net = nn.Sequential(
    nn.Linear(env.observation_space.shape[0], 256),
    nn.ReLU(),
    nn.Linear(256, env.action_space.n)
)


action_selector =
ptan.actions.EpsilonGreedyActionSelector(epsilon=0.1)
agent = ptan.agent.DQNAgent(net, action_selector)
```

Then, we can just pass the observation to the agent to ask it about the actions to take.

```
>>> obs = np.array([env.reset()], dtype=np.float32)
>>> agent(obs)
(array([0]), [None])
```

The first item in the resulting tuple is the batch of actions to take, while the second value is related to stateful agents and should be ignored. During the run, we can change the epsilon attribute in our action selector to change the random action probability during the training.

Agent's experience

The second important abstraction in PTAN is the so-called *experience source*. In our DQN example in the previous chapter, we worked with one-step experience pieces, which include four things:

- The observed state of the environment at some time step: s_t
- The action the agent has taken: a_t
- The reward the agent has obtained: r_t
- The observation of the next state: s_{t+1}

We used those values (s_t, a_t, r_t, s_{t+1}) to update our Q approximation using the Bellman equation. However, for a general case, we can be interested in longer chains of experience, including more time steps of the agent's interaction with the environment.

Bellman's equation also could be unrolled to longer experience chains.

$$Q(s_t, a_t) = \mathbb{E}[r_t + \gamma r_{t+1} + \gamma^2 r_{t+2} + \ldots + \gamma^k \max_a Q(s_{t+k,a})]$$

One of the methods to improve DQN stability and convergence, discussed in this chapter, does just this: by unrolling the Bellman's equation to k steps forward (when k is usually 2...5), we significantly improve the speed of our training convergence.

To support this situation in a generic way, in PTAN we have the `ptan.experience.ExperienceSourceFirstLast` class, which takes the environment and the agent and provides to us the stream of experience tuples: (s_t, a_t, R_t, s_{t+k}), where $R_t = r_t t + \gamma r_{t+1} + \gamma^2 r_{t+2} + \ldots + \gamma^{k-1} r_{t+k-1}$. When k = 1, R_t is just the r_t.

This class automatically handles end-of-episode situations, letting us know about them by setting the last tuple entry to None. In such cases, a reset of the environment is performed automatically. Class `ExperienceSourceFirstLast` exposes the iterator interface, generating on every iteration the tuple with experience. The example of this class is as follows:

```
>> exp_source = ptan.experience.ExperienceSourceFirstLast(env, agent,
gamma=0.99, steps_count=1)
>> it = iter(exp_source)
>> next(it)
ExperienceFirstLast(state=array([ 0.03937284, -0.01242409,
0.03980117,  0.02457287]), action=0, reward=1.0, last_state=array([
0.03912436, -0.20809355,  0.04029262,  0.32954308]))
```

Experience buffer

In case of a DQN, we rarely want to learn from the experience once we get it. We usually store it in some large buffer and perform a random sample from it to obtain the minibatch to train on. This scenario is supported by the `ptan.experience.ExperienceReplayBuffer` class, which is very similar to the implementation we've seen in the previous chapter. To construct it, we need to pass the experience source and size of the buffer. By calling the `populate(n)` method, we ask the buffer to pull n examples from the experience source and store them in the buffer. The `sample(batch_size)` method returns a random sample of the given size from the current buffer contents.

Gym env wrappers

To avoid implementing (or copy-pasting) common Atari wrappers over and over again, I put them in the `ptan.common.wrappers` module. They are mostly the same (with minor PyTorch-specific modifications) as wrappers available in the OpenAI Baselines project: `https://github.com/openai/baselines`. To wrap the Atari environment in one line, it's enough to call the `ptan.common.wrappers.wrap_dqn(env)` method. That's basically it! As I've said before, PTAN wasn't supposed to be *the ultimate RL framework*; it's just a collection of entities designed to be used together, but not to depend much on each other.

Basic DQN

By combining all the above, we can reimplement the same DQN agent in a much shorter, but still flexible, way, which will become handy later, when we'll start to modify and change various DQN parts to make the DQN better.

In the basic DQN implementation we have three modules:

- `Chapter07/lib/dqn_model.py`: The DQN neural network, which is the same as we've seen in the previous chapter

- `Chapter07/lib/common.py`: Common functions used in this chapter's examples, but too specialized to be moved to PTAN

- `Chapter07/01_dqn_basic.py`: The creation of all used pieces and the training loop

Let's start with the contents of `lib/common.py`. First of all, we have here hyperparameters for our Pong environment, that was introduced in the previous chapter. The hyperparameters are stored in the dict, with keys as the configuration name and values as a dict of parameters. This makes it easy to add another configuration set for more complicated Atari games.

```
HYPERPARAMS = {
    'pong': {
        'env_name':         "PongNoFrameskip-v4",
        'stop_reward':      18.0,
        'run_name':         'pong',
        'replay_size':      100000,
        'replay_initial':   10000,
        'target_net_sync':  1000,
        'epsilon_frames':   10**5,
        'epsilon_start':    1.0,
        'epsilon_final':    0.02,
```

```
        'learning_rate':    0.0001,
        'gamma':            0.99,
        'batch_size':       32
    },
}
```

In addition, common.py has a function that takes the batch of transitions and packs it into the set of NumPy arrays. Every transition from `ExperienceSourceFirstLast` has a type of `namedtuple` with the following fields:

- `state`: Observation from the environment.

- `action`: Integer action taken by the agent.

- `rewards`: If we've created `ExperienceSourceFirstLast` with attribute `steps_count=1`, it's just the immediate reward. For larger step counts, it contains the discounted sum of rewards for this number of steps.

- `last_state`: If the transition corresponds to the final step in the environment, then this field is `None`, otherwise it contains the last observation in the experience chain.

The code of `unpack_batch` is as follows:

```
def unpack_batch(batch):
    states, actions, rewards, dones, last_states = [], [], [], [], []
    for exp in batch:
        state = np.array(exp.state, copy=False)
        states.append(state)
        actions.append(exp.action)
        rewards.append(exp.reward)
        dones.append(exp.last_state is None)
        if exp.last_state is None:
            last_states.append(state)
        # the result will be masked anyway
        else:
            last_states.append(np.array(exp.last_state, copy=False))
    return np.array(states, copy=False), np.array(actions), \
np.array(rewards, dtype=np.float32), \
        np.array(dones, dtype=np.uint8), np.array(last_states, \
copy=False)
```

Note how we handle the final transitions in the batch. To avoid the special handling of such cases, for terminal transitions we store the initial state in the `last_states` array. To make our calculations of the Bellman update correct, we'll mask such batch entries during the loss calculation using the `dones` array. Another solution would be to calculate the value of last states only for non-terminal transitions, but it would make our loss function logic a bit more complicated.

The loss function is exactly the same as we had in the previous chapter. We calculate the values of actions taken from the first state, then calculate the values of the same actions using the Bellman equation. The resulting loss is a Mean Square Error between those two quantities:

```
def calc_loss_dqn(batch, net, tgt_net, gamma, device="cpu"):
    states, actions, rewards, dones, next_states = unpack_batch(batch)

    states_v = torch.tensor(states).to(device)
    next_states_v = torch.tensor(next_states).to(device)
    actions_v = torch.tensor(actions).to(device)
    rewards_v = torch.tensor(rewards).to(device)
    done_mask = torch.ByteTensor(dones).to(device)

    state_action_values = net(states_v).gather(1,
actions_v.unsqueeze(-1)).squeeze(-1)
    next_state_values = tgt_net(next_states_v).max(1)[0]
    next_state_values[done_mask] = 0.0

    expected_state_action_values = next_state_values.detach() *
gamma + rewards_v
    return nn.MSELoss()(state_action_values,
expected_state_action_values)
```

Also, in `common.py`, we have two utility classes to help us to simplify the training loop:

```
class EpsilonTracker:
    def __init__(self, epsilon_greedy_selector, params):
        self.epsilon_greedy_selector = epsilon_greedy_selector
        self.epsilon_start = params['epsilon_start']
        self.epsilon_final = params['epsilon_final']
        self.epsilon_frames = params['epsilon_frames']
        self.frame(0)

    def frame(self, frame):
        self.epsilon_greedy_selector.epsilon = \
            max(self.epsilon_final, self.epsilon_start - frame /
self.epsilon_frames)
```

The `EpsilonTracker` class takes the instance of `EpsilonGreedyActionSelector` and our hyperparams for a specific configuration. Also, in its only method `frame()`, it updates the value of epsilon according to the standard DQN epsilon decay schedule: linearly decreasing it for the first `epsilon_frames` steps and then keeping it constant.

The second class, `RewardTracker`, is supposed to be informed about the total reward at the end of every episode and track mean reward for the last episodes, report the current values in TensorBoard and console, and, finally, check that the game has been successfully solved. It also measures the speed in frames per second, which is useful to know, as performance is an important metric of the training.

```
class RewardTracker:
    def __init__(self, writer, stop_reward):
        self.writer = writer
        self.stop_reward = stop_reward

    def __enter__(self):
        self.ts = time.time()
        self.ts_frame = 0
        self.total_rewards = []
        return self

    def __exit__(self, *args):
        self.writer.close()
```

The class is implemented to be used as a context manager, automatically closing the TensorBoard writer on exit. The main logic is performed in the `reward()` method, which is being called every time an episode finishes. It's mostly the same code as the previous chapter training loop.

```
    def reward(self, reward, frame, epsilon=None):
        self.total_rewards.append(reward)
        speed = (frame - self.ts_frame) / (time.time() - self.ts)
        self.ts_frame = frame
        self.ts = time.time()
        mean_reward = np.mean(self.total_rewards[-100:])
        epsilon_str = "" if epsilon is None else ", eps %.2f" % epsilon
        print("%d: done %d games, mean reward %.3f, speed %.2f f/s%s" % (
            frame, len(self.total_rewards), mean_reward, speed,
            epsilon_str
        ))
        sys.stdout.flush()
        if epsilon is not None:
            self.writer.add_scalar("epsilon", epsilon, frame)
```

```
        self.writer.add_scalar("speed", speed, frame)
        self.writer.add_scalar("reward_100", mean_reward, frame)
        self.writer.add_scalar("reward", reward, frame)
        if mean_reward > self.stop_reward:
            print("Solved in %d frames!" % frame)
            return True
    return False
```

That's it for `common.py`. It has another function, which is not relevant yet and will be used in later examples. Now, let's take a look at `01_dqn_basic.py`, which contains only the creation of the needed classes and the training loop.

```
#!/usr/bin/env python3
import gym
import ptan
import argparse
import torch
import torch.optim as optim
from tensorboardX import SummaryWriter
from lib import dqn_model, common
```

First of all, we import the required modules.

```
if __name__ == "__main__":
    params = common.HYPERPARAMS['pong']
    parser = argparse.ArgumentParser()
    parser.add_argument("--cuda", default=False, action="store_true",
help="Enable cuda")
    args = parser.parse_args()
    device = torch.device("cuda" if args.cuda else "cpu")

    env = gym.make(params['env_name'])
    env = ptan.common.wrappers.wrap_dqn(env)
```

Then, we get our hyperparameters for the Pong game, parse the option for CUDA and create our environment. Next, we use DQN wrappers from PTAN, which applies the common set of preprocessing to the environment.

```
    writer = SummaryWriter(comment="-" + params['run_name'] +
"-basic")
    net = dqn_model.DQN(env.observation_space.shape, env.action_
space.n).to(device)
    tgt_net = ptan.agent.TargetNet(net)
```

Then we create a summary writer for TensorBoard and our DQN neural network (NN) using observations and actions' dimensionality. The `ptan.agent.TargetNet` class is an extremely simple wrapper around the network, which allows us to create a copy of our NN's weights and sync them periodically.

```
    selector = ptan.actions.EpsilonGreedyActionSelector(epsilon=params
['epsilon_start'])
    epsilon_tracker = common.EpsilonTracker(selector, params)
    agent = ptan.agent.DQNAgent(net, selector, device=device)
```

Here we create our agent, which needs a network to convert observations into the action values and an action selector to decide which action to take. For the action selector, we use epsilon-greedy policy with epsilon decayed according to our schedule defined by hyperparams.

```
    exp_source = ptan.experience.ExperienceSourceFirstLast(env, agent,
gamma=params['gamma'], steps_count=1)
    buffer = ptan.experience.ExperienceReplayBuffer(exp_source,
buffer_size=params['replay_size'])
```

The next element to define is our experience source, which is one-step `ExperienceSourceFirstLast` and experience replay buffer, which will store a fixed amount of transitions.

```
    optimizer = optim.Adam(net.parameters(), lr=params
['learning_rate'])
    frame_idx = 0
```

The last step needed before the training loop is an optimizer and frame counter.

```
    with common.RewardTracker(writer, params['stop_reward']) as
reward_tracker:
        while True:
            frame_idx += 1
            buffer.populate(1)
            epsilon_tracker.frame(frame_idx)
```

In the beginning of the training loop, we create the reward tracker, which will report mean reward for every episode completed, increment the frame counter and ask our experience replay buffer to pull one transition from the experience source. This call to `buffer.populate(1)` will start the following chain of actions inside the PTAN lib:

- `ExperienceReplayBuffer` will ask the experience source to get the next transition.

- The experience source will feed the current observation to the agent to obtain the action.

- The agent will apply the NN to the observation to calculate Q-values, then ask the action selector to choose the action to take.

- The action selector (which is an epsilon-greedy selector) will generate the random number to check how to act: greedily or randomly. In both cases, it will decide which action to take.

- The action will be returned to the experience source, which will feed it into the environment to obtain the reward and the next observation. All this data (the current observation, action, reward, and next observation) will be returned to the buffer.

- The buffer will store the transition, pushing out old observations to keep its length constant.

All the above may look complicated, but, basically, it's the same process that we completed before, just wrapped in a different way.

```
new_rewards = exp_source.pop_total_rewards()
if new_rewards:
    if reward_tracker.reward(new_rewards[0], frame_idx,
selector.epsilon):
        break
```

The above piece of the training loop asks the experience source for the list of the finished episodes' rewards (the total undiscounted reward) and passes it to the reward tracker for reporting and checking that training has been done. As we performed only the single step before, it could be only one or zero completed episodes. If the reward tracker returns True, then it's an indication that the mean reward has reached the score boundary and we can stop our training.

```
if len(buffer) < params['replay_initial']:
    continue
```

Here we check that the length of the buffer is large enough to start training. Otherwise, we just wait for more data to be gathered.

```
optimizer.zero_grad()
batch = buffer.sample(params['batch_size'])
loss_v = common.calc_loss_dqn(batch, net, tgt_net.target_
model, gamma=params['gamma'], device=device)
loss_v.backward()
optimizer.step()
```

This piece performs a standard Stochastic Gradient Descent (SGD) update. We zero gradients, sample the minibatch from the experience replay buffer, and calculate loss using the function we've already seen.

```
if frame_idx % params['target_net_sync'] == 0:
    tgt_net.sync()
```

The last piece of the training loop performs a periodical sync between our main model (being trained) and the target network we used to calculate action values in the Bellman update.

Okay, let's train the model and check its convergence.

```
rl_book_samples/Chapter07$ ./01_dqn_basic.py --cuda
865: done 1 games, mean reward -20.000, eps 0.99, speed 364.42 f/s
2147: done 2 games, mean reward -20.500, eps 0.98, speed 493.27 f/s
3061: done 3 games, mean reward -20.333, eps 0.97, speed 493.09 f/s
3974: done 4 games, mean reward -20.500, eps 0.96, speed 492.45 f/s
4810: done 5 games, mean reward -20.600, eps 0.95, speed 490.46 f/s
5836: done 6 games, mean reward -20.500, eps 0.94, speed 495.29 f/s
6942: done 7 games, mean reward -20.571, eps 0.93, speed 491.58 f/s
7953: done 8 games, mean reward -20.500, eps 0.92, speed 491.78 f/s
9109: done 9 games, mean reward -20.444, eps 0.91, speed 492.71 f/s
. . .
```

Every line in the output is written at the end of the next episode, showing the current frame counter, amount of completed episodes, average reward for the last 100 games, epsilon and computation speed. During the first 10k frames, speed is high, as we do no training, waiting for our replay buffer to be populated. For the basic DQN version, it usually takes about 1M frames to reach the mean reward of 17, so be patient. After the training, we can check the dynamics of the training process in TensorBoard, which shows charts for epsilon, raw reward values, average reward and speed.

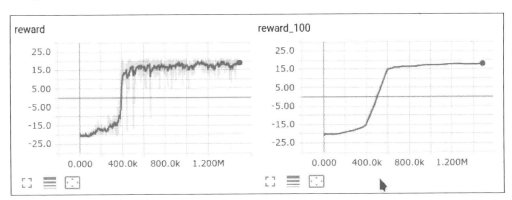

Figure 1: The convergence of a basic DQN implementation

N-step DQN

The first improvement that we'll implement and evaluate is quite an old one. It was first introduced in the paper by Richard Sutton ([2] Sutton, 1988). To get the idea, let's look at the Bellman update used in Q-learning once again.

$$Q(s_t, a_t) = r_t + \gamma \max_a Q(s_{t+1}, a_{t+1})$$

This equation is recursive, which means that we can express $Q(s_{t+1}, a_{t+1})$ in terms of itself, which gives us this result:

$$Q(s_t, a_t) = r_t + \gamma \max_a [r_{a,t+1} + \gamma \max_{a'} Q(s_{t+2}, a')]$$

Value $r_{a,t+1}$ means local reward at time *t+1*, after issuing action *a*. However, if we assume that our action a at the step *t+1* was chosen optimally, or close to optimally, we can omit *max_a* and operation and obtain this:

$$Q(s_t, a_t) = r_t + \gamma r_{t+1} + \gamma^2 \max_{a'} Q(s_{t+2}, a')$$

This value could be unrolled again and again any number of times. As you may guess, this unrolling can be easily applied to our DQN update by replacing one-step transition sampling with longer transition sequences of n-steps. To understand why this unrolling will help us to speed up training, let's consider the example illustrated below. Here we have a simple environment of four states, s_1, s_2, s_3, s_4, and the only action available at every state, except s_4, which is a terminal state.

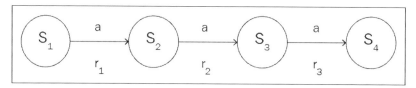

Figure 2: A transition diagram for a simple environment

So, what happens in a one-step case? We have three total updates possible (we don't use *max*, as there is only one action available):

1. $Q(s_1, a) \leftarrow r_1 + \gamma \, Q(s_2, a)$
2. $Q(s_2, a) \leftarrow r_2 + \gamma \, Q(s_3, a)$
3. $Q(s_3, a) \leftarrow r_3$

Let's imagine that, at the beginning of the training, we complete the updates above in this order. The first two updates will be useless, as our current $Q(s_2,a)$ and $Q(s_3,a)$ are incorrect and contain initial random data. The only useful update will be update three, which correctly assigns reward r_3 to the state s_3, prior to the terminal state. Now let's complete the updates above over and over again. On the second iteration, the correct value will be assigned to the $Q(s_2,a)$, but the update of $Q(s_1,a)$ will still be noisy. Only on the third iteration will we get the valid values for all Q. So, even in a one-step case, it takes three steps to *propagate* the correct values to all the states.

Now let's consider a two-step case. This situation again has three updates:

1. $Q(s_1,a) \leftarrow r_1 + \gamma r_2 + \gamma^2 Q(s_3,a)$
2. $Q(s_2,a) \leftarrow r_2 + \gamma r_3$
3. $Q(s_3,a) \leftarrow r_3$

In this case, on the first loop over the updates, the correct values will be assigned to both $Q(s_2,a)$ and $Q(s_3,a)$. On the second iteration, the value of $Q(s_1,a)$ will be also properly updated. So, multiple steps improve the propagation speed of values, which improves convergence. Okay, you may be thinking that if it's so helpful, let's unroll the Bellman equation, say, 100 steps ahead. Will it speed up our convergence 100 times? Unfortunately, the answer is no.

Despite our expectations, our DQN will fail to converge at all. To understand why, let's again return to our unrolling process, especially where we dropped the max_a. Was it correct? Strictly speaking, no. We've omitted the max operation at the intermediate step, assuming that our action selection during experience gathering (or our *policy*) was optimal. What if it wasn't, for example, in the beginning of the training, when our agent acted randomly? In that case, our calculated value for $Q(s_t,a_t)$ may be smaller than the optimal value of the state (as some steps we've taken randomly, but not following the most promising paths by maximizing the Q-value). The more steps that we unroll the Bellman equation on, the more incorrect our update could be.

Our large experience replay buffer will make the situation even worse, as it increases the chance of getting transitions obtained from the old bad policy (dictated by old bad approximations of Q). This will lead to a wrong update of the current Q approximation, so it can easily break our training progress. The above problem is a fundamental characteristic of RL methods, as was briefly mentioned in *Chapter 4, The Cross-Entropy Method*, when we talked about RL methods' taxonomy. There are two large classes: the **off-policy** and **on-policy** methods.

The first class of off-policy methods doesn't depend on "freshness of data". For example, a simple DQN is off-policy, which means that we can use very old data sampled from the environment several million steps ago, and this data will still be useful for learning. That's because we're just updating the value of the action $Q(s_t, a_t)$ with immediate reward, plus discounted current approximation of the best action's value. Even if the action at was sampled randomly, it doesn't matter because for this particular action a_t, in the state s_t, our update will be correct. That's why in off-policy methods, we can use a very large experience buffer to make our data closer to being **independent and identically distributed (i.i.d)**.

On the other hand, on-policy methods heavily depend on the training data to be sampled according to the current policy we're updating. That happens because on-policy methods are trying to improve the current policy indirectly (as in the n-step DQN above) or directly (the whole of part three of the book is devoted to such methods).

So, which class of methods is better? Well, it depends. Off-policy methods allow you to train on the previous large history of data or even on human demonstrations, but, usually, they are slower to converge. On-policy methods are usually faster, but require much more fresh data from the environment, which can be costly. Just imagine a self-driving car trained with the on-policy method. It will cost you lots of crashed cars before the system learns that walls and trees are things that it should avoid.

You may have a question: why are we talking about an n-step DQN if this "n-stepness" turns it into an on-policy method, which will make our large experience buffer useless? In practice, this is usually not black and white. You may still use an n-step DQN if it will help to speed up DQNs, but you need to be modest with the selection of n. Small values of two or three usually work well, because our trajectories in the experience buffer are not that different from one-step transitions. In such cases, convergence speed usually improves proportionally, but large values of n can break the training process. So, the number of steps should be tuned, but convergence speeding up usually makes it worth doing.

Implementation

As the `ExperienceSourceFirstLast` class already supports the multi-step Bellman unroll, our n-step version of a DQN is extremely simple. There are only two modifications that we need to make in the basic DQN to turn it into an n-step version:

- Pass the count of steps that we want to unroll on
  `ExperienceSourceFirstLast` creation in the `steps_count` parameter.

- Pass the correct gamma to the `calc_loss_dqn` function. This modification is really easy to overlook, but it can be harmful to convergence. As our Bellman is now n-steps, the discount coefficient for the last state in the experience chain will no longer be just γ, but γ^n.

You can find the whole example in `Chapter07/02_dqn_n_steps.py`, but below are the modified lines:

```
exp_source = ptan.experience.ExperienceSourceFirstLast(env, agent,
gamma=params['gamma'], steps_count=args.n)
```

The `args.n` value is count of steps passed in command-line arguments, default is to use 2 steps.

```
loss_v = common.calc_loss_dqn(batch, net, tgt_net.target_model,
                    gamma=params['gamma']**args.n, device=device)
```

The following are the charts for rewards and the mean 100 rewards for both a simple DQN (light line) and two-step DQN (dark line).

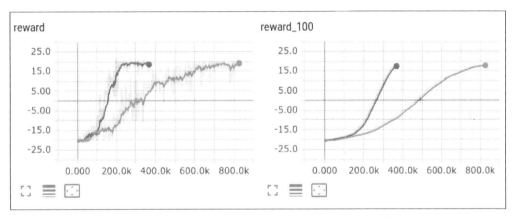

Figure 3: The convergence of a two-step DQN in comparison to a basic DQN

As you may see in the diagram, the two-step DQN converges more than two-times faster than the simple DQN, which is a nice improvement. So, what about a larger *n*? Below is a chart showing a two-step (dark) versus three-step DQN (light):

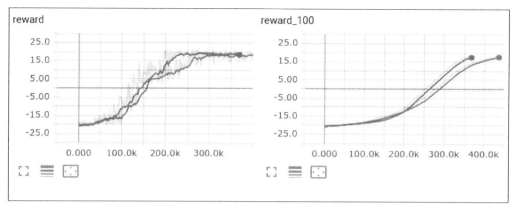

Figure 4: A comparison of a two-step DQN and three-step DQN

So, there is no improvement when compared to two-steps. The optimization process is stochastic, so your results may differ slightly.

Double DQN

The next fruitful idea on how to improve a basic DQN came from DeepMind researchers in a paper titled *Deep Reinforcement Learning with Double Q-Learning ([3] van Hasselt, Guez, and Silver, 2015)*. In the paper, the authors demonstrated that the basic DQN has a tendency to overestimate values for Q, which may be harmful to training performance and sometimes can lead to suboptimal policies. The root cause of this is the max operation in the Bellman equation, but the strict proof is too complicated to write down here. As a solution to this problem, the authors proposed modifying the Bellman update a bit.

In the basic DQN, our target value for Q looked like this:

$$Q(s_t, a_t) = r_t + \gamma \max_a Q'(s_{t+1}, a_{t+1})$$

$Q(s_{t+1}, a)$ was Q-values calculated using our target network, so we update with the trained network every n steps. The authors of the paper proposed choosing actions for the next state using the trained network but taking values of Q from the target net. So, the new expression for target Q-values will look like this:

$$Q(s_t, a_t) = r_t + \gamma \max_a Q'(s_{t+1}, \arg\max_a Q(s_{t+1}, a))$$

The authors proved that this simple tweak fixes overestimation completely and they called this new architecture **double DQN**.

Implementation

The core implementation is very simple. What we need to do is to slightly modify our loss function. Let's go a step further and compare action values produced by the basic DQN and double DQN. To do this, we store a random held-out set of states and periodically calculate the mean value of the best action for every state in the evaluation set.

The complete example is in Chapter07/03_dqn_double.py. Let's first take a look at the loss function.

```
def calc_loss(batch, net, tgt_net, gamma, device="cpu", double=True):
    states, actions, rewards, dones, next_states = common.unpack_
batch(batch)
```

The double extra argument turns on and off the double-DQN way of calculating actions to take.

```
states_v = torch.tensor(states).to(device)
next_states_v = torch.tensor(next_states).to(device)
actions_v = torch.tensor(actions).to(device)
rewards_v = torch.tensor(rewards).to(device)
done_mask = torch.ByteTensor(dones).to(device)
```

The above section is the same as before.

```
state_action_values = net(states_v).gather(1, actions_v.
unsqueeze(-1)).squeeze(-1)
    if double:
        next_state_actions = net(next_states_v).max(1)[1]
        next_state_values = tgt_net(next_states_v).gather
(1, next_state_actions.unsqueeze(-1)).squeeze(-1)
    else:
        next_state_values = tgt_net(next_states_v).max(1)[0]
```

Here is the difference compared to the basic DQN loss function. If double DQN is enabled, we calculate the best action to take in the next state using our main trained network, but values corresponding to this action come from the target network. Of course, this part could be implemented in a faster way, by combining `next_states_v` with `states_v` and calling our main network only once, but it will make the code less clear.

```
    next_state_values[done_mask] = 0.0
    expected_state_action_values = next_state_values.detach() *
gamma + rewards_v
    return nn.MSELoss()(state_action_values, expected_state_action_
values)
```

The rest of the function is the same: we mask completed episodes and compute Mean Squared Error (MSE) loss between Q-values predicted by the network and approximated Q-values. The last function that we consider calculates the values of our held-out state.

```
def calc_values_of_states(states, net, device="cpu"):
    mean_vals = []
    for batch in np.array_split(states, 64):
        states_v = torch.tensor(batch).to(device)
        action_values_v = net(states_v)
        best_action_values_v = action_values_v.max(1)[0]
        mean_vals.append(best_action_values_v.mean().item())
    return np.mean(mean_vals)
```

There is nothing too complicated here: we just split our held-out states array into equal chunks and pass every chunk to the network to obtain action values. From those values, we choose the action with the largest value and calculate the mean of such values. As our array with states is fixed for the whole training process, and this array is large enough (in the code we store 1000 states), we can compare the dynamics of this mean value in both DQN variants.

The rest of the `03_dqn_double.py` file is the training loop of our model, which is mostly the same as before.

```
if __name__ == "__main__":
    params = common.HYPERPARAMS['pong']
    parser = argparse.ArgumentParser()
    parser.add_argument("--cuda", default=False, action="store_true",
help="Enable cuda")
    parser.add_argument("--double", default=False, action=
"store_true", help="Enable double DQN")
    args = parser.parse_args()
    device = torch.device("cuda" if args.cuda else "cpu")
```

The program now has an extra command line option to switch on and off double DQN extension, to be able to compare action values during the training (note that you need to explicitly provide the option to enable double DQN behavior).

```
    env = gym.make(params['env_name'])
    env = ptan.common.wrappers.wrap_dqn(env)

    writer = SummaryWriter(comment="-" + params['run_name'] +
"-double=" + str(not args.no_double))
    net = dqn_model.DQN(env.observation_space.shape, env.action_
space.n).to(device)

    tgt_net = ptan.agent.TargetNet(net)
    selector = ptan.actions.EpsilonGreedyActionSelector(epsilon=params
['epsilon_start'])
    epsilon_tracker = common.EpsilonTracker(selector, params)
    agent = ptan.agent.DQNAgent(net, selector, device=device)

    exp_source = ptan.experience.ExperienceSourceFirstLast(env, agent,
gamma=params['gamma'], steps_count=1)
    buffer = ptan.experience.ExperienceReplayBuffer(exp_source,
buffer_size=params['replay_size'])
    optimizer = optim.Adam(net.parameters(), lr=params
['learning_rate'])

    frame_idx = 0
    eval_states = None
```

The preceding code has no differences from the basic DQN variant. The `eval_states` variable will be populated with our held-out states after the initial replay buffer fill.

```
    with common.RewardTracker(writer, params['stop_reward']) as
reward_tracker:
        while True:
            frame_idx += 1
            buffer.populate(1)
            epsilon_tracker.frame(frame_idx)

            new_rewards = exp_source.pop_total_rewards()
            if new_rewards:
                if reward_tracker.reward(new_rewards[0], frame_idx,
selector.epsilon):
                    break
```

```
        if len(buffer) < params['replay_initial']:
            continue
```

This part is also the same as before.

```
        if eval_states is None:
            eval_states = buffer.sample(STATES_TO_EVALUATE)
            eval_states = [np.array(transition.state, copy=False)
    for transition in eval_states]
            eval_states = np.array(eval_states, copy=False)
```

Here we perform the initial creation of our states to be evaluated during training. The STATES_TO_EVALUATE constant is defined in the beginning of the program and equals 1000, which is large enough to have a representative set of game states.

```
        optimizer.zero_grad()
        batch = buffer.sample(params['batch_size'])
        loss_v = calc_loss(batch, net, tgt_net.target_model,
    gamma=params['gamma'], device=device, double=args.double)
        loss_v.backward()
        optimizer.step()

        if frame_idx % params['target_net_sync'] == 0:
            tgt_net.sync()
```

This part also hasn't changed much, except for the flag that we're passing to the loss function, which enables or disables double DQN.

```
        if frame_idx % EVAL_EVERY_FRAME == 0:
            mean_val = calc_values_of_states(eval_states, net,
    device=device)
            writer.add_scalar("values_mean", mean_val, frame_idx)
```

Finally, for every 100 frames (defined in the EVAL_EVERY_FRAME constant), we calculate the mean value of our states and write it into TensorBoard.

Results

To train a double DQN, with extension enabled, pass the --double command-line argument:

```
rl_book_samples/Chapter07$ ./03_dqn_double.py --cuda --double
1041: done 1 games, mean reward -19.000, speed 272.36 f/s, eps 0.99
2056: done 2 games, mean reward -19.000, speed 396.04 f/s, eps 0.98
3098: done 3 games, mean reward -19.000, speed 462.68 f/s, eps 0.97
3918: done 4 games, mean reward -19.500, speed 569.58 f/s, eps 0.96
```

```
4819: done 5 games, mean reward -19.600, speed 563.84 f/s, eps 0.95
5697: done 6 games, mean reward -19.833, speed 565.74 f/s, eps 0.94
6596: done 7 games, mean reward -20.000, speed 563.71 f/s, eps 0.93
...
```

To compare the action values for a basic DQN, train it again without the `--double` option. Training will take some time, depending on your computing power. On GTX 1080Ti, 1M frames take about two hours. The reward chart is shown below and reveals that despite the similar dynamics in the beginning of the training, the double DQN has reached convergence faster.

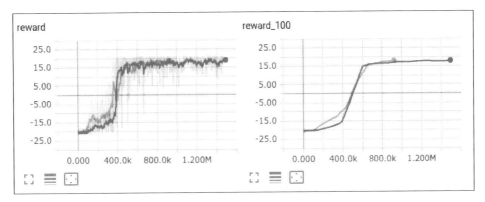

Figure 5: The comparison of double DQN (light) and basic DQN (dark)

At the same time, the chart with value shows that the classic DQN overestimates the values of the actions most of the time. At the end of training, the classic DQN is even required to decrease the value to reach the convergence.

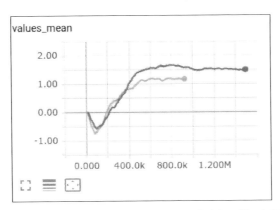

Figure 6: The mean value of actions in double DQN (light) and basic DQN (dark)

Noisy networks

The next improvement that we're going to check addresses another RL problem: exploration of the environment. The paper is called *Noisy Networks for Exploration* (*[4] Fortunato and others, 2017*) and has a very simple idea for learning exploration characteristics during training, instead of having a separate schedule related to the exploration.

Classical DQN achieves exploration by choosing random actions with specially defined hyperparameter epsilon, which is slowly decreased over time from 1.0 (fully random actions) to some small ratio of 0.1 or 0.02. This process works well for simple environments with short episodes, without much non-stationarity during the game, but even in such simple cases, it requires tuning to make training processes efficient.

In the above-mentioned paper, the authors propose a quite simple solution, which, nevertheless, works well. They add a noise to the weights of fully-connected layers of the network and adjust the parameters of this noise during training using backpropagation. Of course, this method shouldn't be confused with 'the network decides where to explore more,' which is a much more complex approach that also has widespread support (for example, see articles about intrinsic motivation and count-based exploration methods [5] or [6]).

The authors propose two ways of adding the noise, both of which work according to their experiments, but have different computational overheads:

1. **Independent Gaussian noise**: For every weight in a fully-connected layer, we have a random value that we draw from the normal distribution. Parameters of the noise μ and σ are stored inside the layer and get trained using backpropagation, the same way that we train weights of the standard linear layer. The output of such a 'noisy layer' is calculated in the same way as in a linear layer.

2. **Factorized Gaussian noise**: To minimize the amount of random values to be sampled, the authors proposed keeping only two random vectors, one with the size of input and another with the size of the output of the layer. Then, a random matrix for the layer is created by calculating the outer product of the vectors.

Implementation

In PyTorch, both methods could be easily implemented in a very straightforward way. What we need to do is to create our own nn.Linear layer equivalent with additional random values sampled every time forward() gets called. I've implemented both noisy layers and their implementations are in Chapter07/lib/dqn_model.py, in classes NoisyLinear (for independent Gaussian noise) and NoisyFactorizedLinear (for factorized noise variant).

```
class NoisyLinear(nn.Linear):
    def __init__(self, in_features, out_features, sigma_init=0.017,
bias=True):
        super(NoisyLinear, self).__init__(in_features, out_features,
bias=bias)
        self.sigma_weight = nn.Parameter(torch.full((out_features,
in_features), sigma_init))
        self.register_buffer("epsilon_weight", torch.zeros(out_
features, in_features))
        if bias:
            self.sigma_bias = nn.Parameter(torch.full((out_features,),
sigma_init))
            self.register_buffer("epsilon_bias", torch.zeros(out_
features))
        self.reset_parameters()
```

In the constructor, we create a matrix for σ (values of μ will be stored in a matrix inherited from nn.Linear). To make sigmas trainable, we need to wrap the tensor in a nn.Parameter. The register_buffer method creates a tensor in the network which won't be updated during backpropagation, but will be handled by the nn.Module machinery (for example, it will be copied to GPU with the cuda() call). An extra parameter and buffer is created for the bias of the layer. The initial value for sigmas (0.017) was taken from the Noisy Networks article cited in the beginning of this section. At the end, we will call the reset_parameters() method, which was overridden from nn.Linear and is supposed to perform the initialization of the layer.

```
    def reset_parameters(self):
        std = math.sqrt(3 / self.in_features)
        self.weight.data.uniform_(-std, std)
        self.bias.data.uniform_(-std, std)
```

In the `reset_parameters` method, we perform initialization of the `nn.Linear` weight and bias according to the recommendations in the article.

```
def forward(self, input):
    self.epsilon_weight.normal_()
    bias = self.bias
    if bias is not None:
        self.epsilon_bias.normal_()
        bias = bias + self.sigma_bias * self.epsilon_bias
    return F.linear(input, self.weight + self.sigma_weight *
self.epsilon_weight, bias)
```

In the forward method, we sample random noise in both weight and bias buffers, and perform linear transformation of the input data in the same way that `nn.Linear` does. The factorized Gaussian noise works in a similar way and I haven't found much difference in the results. So, I'll just put its code below for completeness. If you're curious, you can find the details and equations in the article [4].

```
class NoisyFactorizedLinear(nn.Linear):
    def __init__(self, in_features, out_features, sigma_zero=0.4,
bias=True):
        super(NoisyFactorizedLinear, self).__init__(in_features,
out_features, bias=bias)
        sigma_init = sigma_zero / math.sqrt(in_features)
        self.sigma_weight = nn.Parameter(torch.full((out_features,
in_features), sigma_init))
        self.register_buffer("epsilon_input", torch.zeros
(1, in_features))
        self.register_buffer("epsilon_output", torch.zeros
(out_features, 1))
        if bias:
            self.sigma_bias = nn.Parameter(torch.full((out_features,),
sigma_init))

    def forward(self, input):
        self.epsison_input.normal_()
        self.epsilon_output.normal_()

        func = lambda x: torch.sign(x) * torch.sqrt(torch.abs(x))
        eps_in = func(self.epsilon_input)
        eps_out = func(self.epsilon_output)

        bias = self.bias
        if bias is not None:
            bias = bias + self.sigma_bias * eps_out.t()
```

```
            noise_v = torch.mul(eps_in, eps_out)
            return F.linear(input, self.weight + self.sigma_weight *
    noise_v, bias)
```

From the implementation point of view, that's it. What we now need to do, to turn classic DQN into a NoisyNet variant, is just replace nn.Linear (which are the two last layers in our DQN network) with the NoisyLinear layer (or `NoisyFactorizedLinear` if you wish). Of course, you have to remove all the code related to the epsilon-greedy strategy. To check the internal noise level during training, we can monitor the signal-to-noise ratio (SNR) of our noisy layers, which is a ratio of RMS(μ) / RMS(σ), where RMS is the root mean square of the corresponding weights. In our case, SNR shows how many times the stationary component of the noisy layer is larger than the injected noise.

Our training code for the NoisyNet sample is in `Chapter07/04_dqn_noisy_net.py`. Let's look at the part of the code which differs from the basic DQN version:

```
class NoisyDQN(nn.Module):
    def __init__(self, input_shape, n_actions):
        super(NoisyDQN, self).__init__()

        self.conv = nn.Sequential(
            nn.Conv2d(input_shape[0], 32, kernel_size=8, stride=4),
            nn.ReLU(),
            nn.Conv2d(32, 64, kernel_size=4, stride=2),
            nn.ReLU(),
            nn.Conv2d(64, 64, kernel_size=3, stride=1),
            nn.ReLU()
        )
```

The beginning of the noisy version of the DQN is the same as before. The difference is in the rest of the network.

```
        conv_out_size = self._get_conv_out(input_shape)
        self.noisy_layers = [
            model.NoisyLinear(conv_out_size, 512),
            model.NoisyLinear(512, n_actions)
        ]
        self.fc = nn.Sequential(
            self.noisy_layers[0],
            nn.ReLU(),
            self.noisy_layers[1]
        )
```

Noisy layers are created with the same shape as their linear counterparts. We put them into the list to be able to access them later.

```
def _get_conv_out(self, shape):
    o = self.conv(torch.zeros(1, *shape))
    return int(np.prod(o.size()))

def forward(self, x):
    fx = x.float() / 256
    conv_out = self.conv(fx).view(fx.size()[0], -1)
    return self.fc(conv_out)
```

Functions to get the shape of the convolution part and `forward()` are the same as before. One extra function we have in the class is the calculation of the SNR for noisy layers.

```
def noisy_layers_sigma_snr(self):
    return [
        ((layer.weight ** 2).mean().sqrt() / (layer.sigma_weight
 ** 2).mean().sqrt()).data.cpu().numpy()[0]
        for layer in self.noisy_layers
    ]
```

The training loop is also exactly the same as before, except for one extra piece: every 500 frames we query SNR values for noisy layers from the network and write them in TensorBoard.

```
if frame_idx % 500 == 0:
    snr_vals = net.noisy_layers_sigma_snr()
    for layer_idx, sigma_l2 in enumerate(snr_vals):
        writer.add_scalar("sigma_snr_layer_%d" %
        (layer_idx+1),
                            sigma_l2, frame_idx)
```

Results

After the training, TensorBoard charts show much better training dynamics. The model was able to reach the mean score of 18 in less than 600k frames seen.

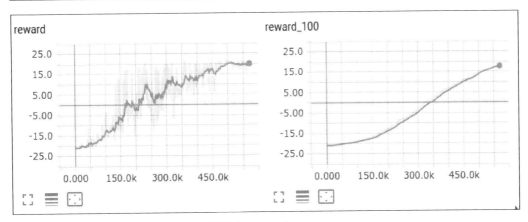

Figure 7: Noisy networks convergence

In comparison to the basic DQN, this is a major improvement (the dark line is a noisy DQN and light is a basic DQN). In the chart below, the first 1M frames are shown.

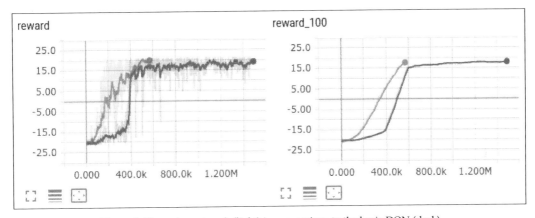

Figure 8: The noisy network (light) in comparison to the basic DQN (dark)

After checking the SNR chart, you may notice that both layers have decreased the noise level very quickly. The first layer went from 1 to almost 1/2.5 ratio of noise. The second layer is even more interesting, as its noise level decreased from 1/3 in the beginning to 1/16, but after 250k frames, which is roughly the same time as when raw rewards climbed close to the 20 score, the level of the noise in the last layer started to increase back, pushing the agent to explore the environment more. This makes a lot of sense, as after reaching high score levels, the agent basically knows how to play at a good level, but still needs to 'polish' its actions to improve the results even more.

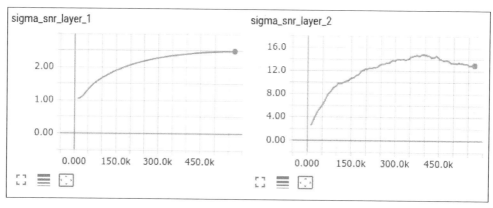

Figure 9: Noise-level changes during the training

Prioritized replay buffer

The next very useful idea on how to improve DQN training was proposed in 2015 in the paper, *Prioritized Experience Replay ([7] Schaul and others, 2015)*. This method tries to improve the efficiency of samples in the replay buffer by prioritizing those samples according to the training loss.

The basic DQN used the replay buffer to break the correlation between immediate transitions in our episodes. As we discussed in *Chapter 6, Deep Q-Networks*, the examples we experience during the episode will be highly correlated, as most of the time the environment is "smooth" and doesn't change much according to our actions. However, the SGD method assumes that the data we use for training has a i.i.d. property. To solve this problem, the classic DQN method used a large buffer of transitions, randomly sampled to get the next training batch.

The authors of the paper questioned this uniform random sample policy and proved that by assigning priorities to buffer samples, according to training loss and sampling the buffer proportional to those priorities, we can significantly improve convergence and the policy quality of the DQN. This method can be seen as "train more on data that surprises you". The tricky point here is to keep the balance of training on an 'unusual' sample and training on the rest of the buffer. If we focus only on a small subset of the buffer, we can lose our i.i.d. property and simply overfit on this subset.

From the mathematical point of view, the priority of every sample in the buffer is calculated as $P(i) = \frac{p_i^\alpha}{\sum_k p_k^\alpha}$, where p_i is the priority of the i-th sample in the buffer and α is the number that shows how much emphasis we give to the priority. If $\alpha = 0$, our sampling will become uniform as in the classic DQN method. Larger values for α put more stress on samples with higher priority. So, it's another hyperparameter to tune and the starting value of α proposed by the paper is 0.6.

There are several options proposed in the paper for how to define the priority and the most popular is to make it proportional to the loss for this particular example in the Bellman update. New samples added to the buffer need to be assigned a maximum value of priority, to be sure that they'll be sampled soon.

By adjusting the priorities for the samples, we're introducing the bias in our data distribution (we sample some transitions much more frequently than others), which needs to be compensated for in order for SGD to work. To get this result, the authors of the study used sample weights, which needed to be multiplied to the individual sample loss. The value of weight for each sample is defined as $w_i = (N \cdot P(i))^{-\beta}$, where β is another hyperparameter, which should be between 0 and 1. With $\beta = 1$, the bias introduced by the sampling is fully compensated, but the authors have shown that it's good for convergence to start with some β between 0 and 1 and slowly increase it to 1 during the training.

Implementation

To implement this method, we have to introduce several changes in our code. First of all, we need a new replay buffer that will track priorities, sample a batch according to them, calculate weights and let us update priorities after the loss has become known. The second change will be the loss function itself. Now we not only need to incorporate weights for every sample, but we need to pass loss values back to the replay buffer to adjust the priorities of sampled transitions.

In the example file `Chapter07/05_dqn_prio_replay.py`, we have all those changes implemented. For the sake of simplicity, the new priority replay buffer class uses a very similar storage scheme as our previous replay buffer. Unfortunately, new requirements for prioritization makes it impossible to implement sampling in O(1) time to buffer size. If we're using simple lists, every time that we sample a new batch we need to process all the priorities, which makes our sampling O(N) to the buffer size. It's not a big deal if our buffer is small, such as 100k samples, but may become an issue for real-life large buffers of millions of transitions. There are other storage schemes that support efficient sampling in O(log N) time, for example, using the segment tree data structure. You can find such implementation in the OpenAI Baselines project, `https://github.com/openai/baselines`.

Let's look at our example of the priority replay buffer.

```
PRIO_REPLAY_ALPHA = 0.6
BETA_START = 0.4
BETA_FRAMES = 100000
```

In the beginning, we're defining the value for α for samples' prioritization and parameters for β change the schedule. Our beta will be changed from 0.4 to 1.0 during first 100k frames.

```
class PrioReplayBuffer:
    def __init__(self, exp_source, buf_size, prob_alpha=0.6):
        self.exp_source_iter = iter(exp_source)
        self.prob_alpha = prob_alpha
        self.capacity = buf_size
        self.pos = 0
        self.buffer = []
        self.priorities = np.zeros((buf_size, ), dtype=np.float32)
```

The class for the priority replay buffer stores samples in a circular buffer (it allows us to keep a fixed amount of entries without reallocating the list) and NumPy array to keep priorities. We also store the iterator to the experience source object, to pull the samples from the environment.

```
    def __len__(self):
        return len(self.buffer)

    def populate(self, count):
        max_prio = self.priorities.max() if self.buffer else 1.0
        for _ in range(count):
            sample = next(self.exp_source_iter)
            if len(self.buffer) < self.capacity:
```

```
        self.buffer.append(sample)
    else:
        self.buffer[self.pos] = sample
    self.priorities[self.pos] = max_prio
    self.pos = (self.pos + 1) % self.capacity
```

The `populate()` method needs to pull the given amount of transitions from the `ExperienceSource` object and store them in the buffer. As our storage for the transitions is implemented as a circular buffer, we have two different situations with this buffer:

1. When our buffer hasn't reached the maximum capacity, we just need to append a new transition to the buffer.

2. If the buffer is already full, we need to overwrite the oldest transition, which is tracked by the pos class field, and adjust this position module's buffer size.

```
def sample(self, batch_size, beta=0.4):
    if len(self.buffer) == self.capacity:
        prios = self.priorities
    else:
        prios = self.priorities[:self.pos]
    probs = prios ** self.prob_alpha
    probs /= probs.sum()
```

In the sample method, we need to convert priorities to probabilities using our α hyperparameter.

```
    indices = np.random.choice(len(self.buffer), batch_size,
p=probs)
    samples = [self.buffer[idx] for idx in indices]
```

Then, using those probabilities, we sample our buffer to obtain a batch of samples.

```
    total = len(self.buffer)
    weights = (total * probs[indices]) ** (-beta)
    weights /= weights.max()
    return samples, indices, weights
```

As a last step, we calculate weights for samples in the batch and return three objects: batch, indices and weights. Indices for batch samples are required to update priorities for sampled items.

```
def update_priorities(self, batch_indices, batch_priorities):
    for idx, prio in zip(batch_indices, batch_priorities):
        self.priorities[idx] = prio
```

The last function of the priority replay buffer allows us to update new priorities for the processed batch. It's the responsibility of the caller to use this function with the calculated losses for the batch.

The next custom function we have in our example is the loss calculation. As the MSELoss class in PyTorch doesn't support weights (which is understandable, as MSE is loss used in regression problems, but weighting of the samples is commonly utilized in classification losses), we need to calculate the MSE and explicitly multiply the result on weight.

```
def calc_loss(batch, batch_weights, net, tgt_net, gamma,
device="cpu"):
    states, actions, rewards, dones, next_states = common.unpack_
batch(batch)

    states_v = torch.tensor(states).to(device)
    next_states_v = torch.tensor(next_states).to(device)
    actions_v = torch.tensor(actions).to(device)
    rewards_v = torch.tensor(rewards).to(device)
    done_mask = torch.ByteTensor(dones).to(device)
    batch_weights_v = torch.tensor(batch_weights).to(device)

    state_action_values = net(states_v).gather(1, actions_v.
unsqueeze(-1)).squeeze(-1)
    next_state_values = tgt_net(next_states_v).max(1)[0]
    next_state_values[done_mask] = 0.0
```

The beginning of the function is exactly the same as before, except for the extra argument for samples' weights array, which need to be converted to a tensor and placed on the GPU.

```
    expected_state_action_values = next_state_values.detach() *
gamma + rewards_v
    losses_v = batch_weights_v * (state_action_values - expected_
state_action_values) ** 2
    return losses_v.mean(), losses_v + 1e-5
```

In the last part of the loss calculation, we implement the same MSE loss but write our expression explicitly, rather than using the library. This allows us to take into account weights of samples and keep individual loss values for every sample. Those values will be passed to the priority replay buffer to update priorities. Small values are added to every loss to handle the situation of zero loss value, which will lead to zero priority of entry.

Now, it's time for our training loop.

```
if __name__ == "__main__":
    params = common.HYPERPARAMS['pong']
    parser = argparse.ArgumentParser()
    parser.add_argument("--cuda", default=False, action="store_true",
help="Enable cuda")
    args = parser.parse_args()
    device = torch.device("cuda" if args.cuda else "cpu")

    env = gym.make(params['env_name'])
    env = ptan.common.wrappers.wrap_dqn(env)

    writer = SummaryWriter(comment="-" + params['run_name'] + "-prio-
replay")
    net = dqn_model.DQN(env.observation_space.shape, env.action_
space.n).to(device)
    tgt_net = ptan.agent.TargetNet(net)
    selector = ptan.actions.EpsilonGreedyActionSelector(epsilon=params
['epsilon_start'])
    epsilon_tracker = common.EpsilonTracker(selector, params)
    agent = ptan.agent.DQNAgent(net, selector, device=device)

    exp_source = ptan.experience.ExperienceSourceFirstLast(env, agent,
gamma=params['gamma'], steps_count=1)
    buffer = PrioReplayBuffer(exp_source, params['replay_size'], PRIO_
REPLAY_ALPHA)
    optimizer = optim.Adam(net.parameters(), lr=params['learning_
rate'])
```

The initialization section should be very familiar, as we've created everything we need, and the only difference is the usage of `PrioReplayBuffer` instead of a simple replay buffer.

```
    frame_idx = 0
    beta = BETA_START

    with common.RewardTracker(writer, params['stop_reward']) as
reward_tracker:
        while True:
            frame_idx += 1
            buffer.populate(1)
            epsilon_tracker.frame(frame_idx)
            beta = min(1.0, BETA_START + frame_idx * (1.0 - BETA_
START) / BETA_FRAMES)
```

In the training loop, as before, we pull one transition from the experience source and update the epsilon according to the schedule. We use the similar schedule to linearly increase the beta hyperparameter for priority replay buffer weights' adjustment.

```
new_rewards = exp_source.pop_total_rewards()
if new_rewards:
    writer.add_scalar("beta", beta, frame_idx)
    if reward_tracker.reward(new_rewards[0], frame_idx,
selector.epsilon):
        break

if len(buffer) < params['replay_initial']:
    continue
```

As before, we track the total reward for the completed episodes, now showing beta change over the time of training.

```
optimizer.zero_grad()
batch, batch_indices, batch_weights = buffer.
sample(params['batch_size'], beta)
loss_v, sample_prios_v = calc_loss(batch, batch_weights,
net, tgt_net.target_model, params['gamma'], device=device)
loss_v.backward()
optimizer.step()
buffer.update_priorities(batch_indices, sample_prios_v.
data.cpu().numpy())
```

The call of the optimizer is different from the basic DQN version. First of all, our sample from the buffer now returns not a single batch, but three values: batch, indices of samples and their weights. We pass both batch and weights to the loss function, the result of which is two things: the first is the accumulated loss value that we need to backpropagate, and the second is a tensor with individual loss values for every sample in the batch. We backpropagate the accumulated loss and ask our priority replay buffer to update the samples' priorities.

Results

This example can be trained as usual. The following are the reward dynamics in comparison to the basic DQN.

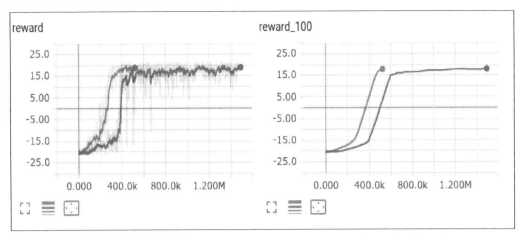

Figure 10: Prioritized replay buffer (upper) in comparison to basic DQN (lower)

As expected, prioritization in the replay buffer's samples shows better convergence dynamics.

Dueling DQN

This improvement to DQN was proposed in 2015, in the paper called *Dueling Network Architectures for Deep Reinforcement Learning ([8] Wang et al., 2015)*. The core observation of this paper lies in the fact that the Q-values $Q(s, a)$ our network is trying to approximate can be divided into quantities: the value of the state $V(s)$ and the advantage of actions in this state $A(s, a)$. We've seen quantity $V(s)$ before, as it was the core of the value iteration method from *Chapter 5, Tabular Learning and the Bellman Equation*. It just equals to the discounted expected reward achievable from this state. The advantage $A(s, a)$ is supposed to bridge the gap from $A(s)$ to $Q(s, a)$, as, by definition: $Q(s, a) = V(s) + A(s, a)$. In other words, the advantage $A(s, a)$ is just the delta, saying how much extra reward some particular action from the state brings us. Advantage could be positive or negative and, in general, can have any magnitude. For example, at some *tipping point*, the choice of one action over another can cost us lots of the total reward.

The above paper's contribution was an explicit separation of the value and the advantage in the network's architecture, which brought better training stability, faster convergence and better results on the Atari benchmark. The architecture difference from the classic DQN network is shown on the picture below. The classic DQN network (top) takes features from the convolution layer and, using fully-connected layers, transforms them into a vector of Q-values, one for each action. On the other hand, dueling DQN (bottom) takes convolution features and processes them using two independent paths: one path is responsible for $V(s)$ prediction, which is just a single number, and another path predicts individual advantage values, having the same dimension as Q-values in the classic case. After that, we add $V(s)$ to every value of $A(s, a)$ to obtain the $Q(s, a)$, which is used and trained as normal.

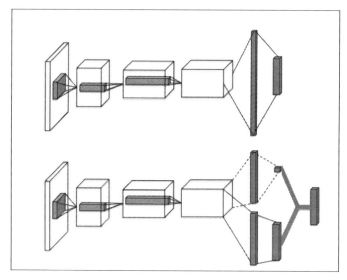

Figure 11: A basic DQN (top) and dueling architecture (bottom)

The above changes in the architecture are not enough to make sure that the network will learn $V(s)$ and $A(s, a)$ as we want it to. Nothing prevents the network, for example, from predicting some state $V(s) = 0$, and $A(s) = [1, 2, 3, 4]$, which is completely wrong, as the predicted $V(s)$ is not the expected value of the state. We have yet another constraint to be set: we want the mean value of the advantage of any state to be zero. In that case, the correct prediction for the above example will be $V(s) = 2.5$ and $A(s) = [-1.5, -0.5, 0.5, 1.5]$.

This constraint could be enforced in various ways, for example, via the loss function, but in the Dueling paper, the authors proposed a very elegant solution by subtracting from the Q expression in the network the mean value of the advantage, which effectively pulls the mean for advantage to zero: $Q(s,a) = V(s) + A(s,a) - \frac{1}{N}\sum_k A(s,k)$. This keeps the changes needed to be made in the classic DQN very simple: to convert it to the double DQN you need to change only the network architecture, without affecting other pieces of the implementation.

Implementation

A complete example is available in Chapter07/06_dqn_dueling.py, so here I'll show only the network class.

```
class DuelingDQN(nn.Module):
    def __init__(self, input_shape, n_actions):
        super(DuelingDQN, self).__init__()

        self.conv = nn.Sequential(
            nn.Conv2d(input_shape[0], 32, kernel_size=8, stride=4),
            nn.ReLU(),
            nn.Conv2d(32, 64, kernel_size=4, stride=2),
            nn.ReLU(),
            nn.Conv2d(64, 64, kernel_size=3, stride=1),
            nn.ReLU()
        )
```

The convolution layers are completely the same as before.

```
        conv_out_size = self._get_conv_out(input_shape)
        self.fc_adv = nn.Sequential(
            nn.Linear(conv_out_size, 512),
            nn.ReLU(),
            nn.Linear(512, n_actions)
        )
        self.fc_val = nn.Sequential(
            nn.Linear(conv_out_size, 512),
            nn.ReLU(),
            nn.Linear(512, 1)
        )
```

Instead of defining a single path of fully connected layers, we create two different transformations: one for advantages and one for value prediction.

```
def _get_conv_out(self, shape):
    o = self.conv(torch.zeros(1, *shape))
    return int(np.prod(o.size()))

def forward(self, x):
    fx = x.float() / 256
    conv_out = self.conv(fx).view(fx.size()[0], -1)
    val = self.fc_val(conv_out)
    adv = self.fc_adv(conv_out)
    return val + adv - adv.mean()
```

The changes in the `forward()` function are also very simple, thanks to PyTorch's expressiveness: we calculate value and advantage for our batch of samples and add them together, subtracting the mean of advantage to obtain the final Q-values.

Results

After training a dueling DQN, we can compare it to the classic DQN convergence on our Pong benchmark, as shown here.

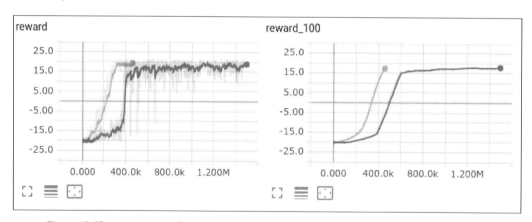

Figure 12: The convergence of a dueling architecture (light) in comparison to a basic DQN (dark)

Categorical DQN

The last and the most complicated method in our *DQN improvements toolbox* is from the very recent paper published by DeepMind in June 2017 called *A Distributional Perspective on Reinforcement Learning* (*[9] Bellemare, Dabney and Munos 2017*).

In the paper, the authors questioned the fundamental piece of Q-learning: Q-values and tried to replace them with more generic Q-value probability distribution. Let's try to understand the idea. Both the Q-learning and value iteration methods are working with the values of actions or states represented as simple numbers and showing how much total reward we can achieve from state or action. However, is it practical to squeeze all future possible reward into one number? In complicated environments, the future could be stochastic, giving us different values with different probabilities. For example, imagine the commuter scenario when you regularly drive from home to work. Most of the time, the traffic isn't that heavy and it takes you around 30 minutes to reach your destination. It's not exactly 30 minutes, but on average it's 30. From time to time, something happens, like road repairs or an accident, and due to traffic jams it takes you three-times longer to get to work. The probability of your commute time can be represented as a distribution of the 'commute time' random variable and is shown in the following chart.

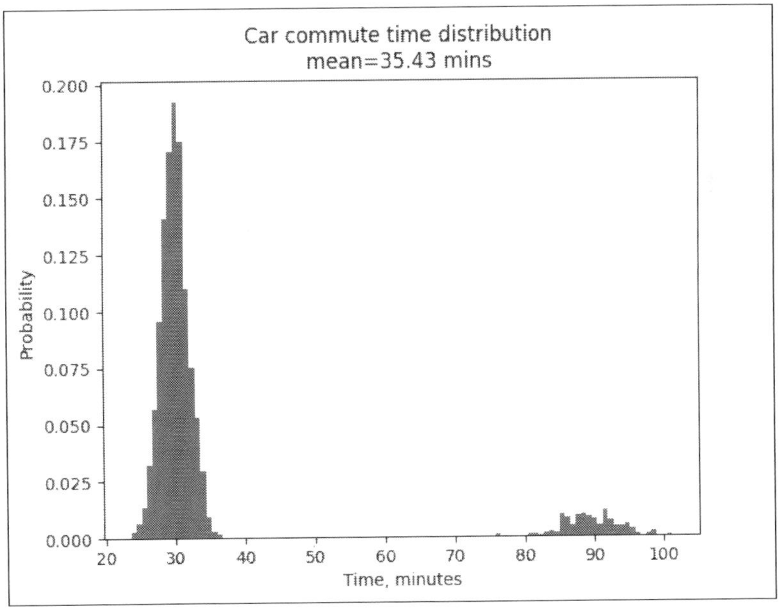

Figure 13: The probability distribution of commute time

Now imagine that you have an alternative way to get to work: train. It takes a bit longer, as you need to get from home to the train station and from the station to the office, but they're much more reliable. Say, for example, that the train commute time is 40 minutes on average with a small chance of train disruption, which adds 20 minutes of extra time to the journey. The distribution of the train commute is shown in the following graph.

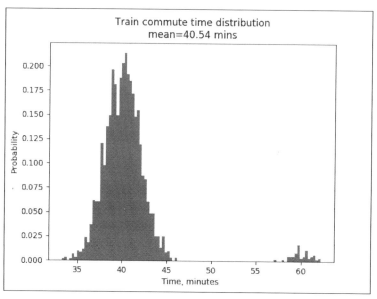

Figure 14: The probability distribution of train commute time

Imagine that now we want to make the decision on how to commute. If we know only the mean time for both car and train, a car looks more attractive, as on average it takes 35.43 minutes to travel, which is better than 40.54 minutes for the train. However, if we look at full distributions, we may decide to go by train, as even in the worst-case scenario it will be one hour of commuting versus one hour and 30 minutes. Switching to statistical language, car distribution has much higher **variance**, so, in situations when you really have to be at the office in 60 minutes max, the train is better.

Exactly the same idea was proposed by the authors of the paper, *Distributional Perspective On Reinforcement Learning* [9]. Why do we limit ourselves trying to predict an average value for an action, when the underlying value may have a complicated underlying distribution? Maybe it will help us to work with distributions directly.

The results presented in the paper show that, in fact, this idea could be helpful, but at the cost of introducing a more complicated method. I'm not going to put a strict mathematical definition here, but the overall idea is to predict the distribution of value for every action, similar to the distributions for our car/train example above. As a next step, the authors have shown that the Bellman equation can be generalized for a distribution case and it will have a form $Z(x, a) \overset{D}{=} R(x, a) + \gamma Z(x', a')$, which is very similar to the familiar Bellman equation, but now $Z(x, a)$, $R(x, a)$ are the probability distributions and not numbers.

The resulting distribution can be used to train our network to give better predictions of value distribution for every action of the given state, exactly the same way as with Q-learning. The only difference will be in the loss function, which now has to be replaced to something suitable for distributions' comparison. There are several alternatives available, for example Kullback-Leibler (KL)-divergence (or cross-entropy loss) used in classification problems or the Wasserstein metric. In the paper, the authors gave theoretical justification for the Wasserstein metric, but when they tried to apply it in practice, they faced limitations, so, in the end, the paper used KL-divergence. The paper is very recent, so it's quite probable that improvements to the methods will follow.

Implementation

As mentioned, the method is quite complex, so it took me a while to implement it and make sure it was working. The complete code is in `Chapter07/07_dqn_distrib.py`, which uses a function in `lib/common.py` that we haven't discussed before to perform distributions' projection. Before we start it, we need to say several words about the implementation logic.

The central part of the method is probability distribution, which we're approximating. There are lots of ways to represent the distribution, but the authors of the paper chose quite a generic *parametric distribution* that is basically a fixed amount of values placed regularly on a values range. The range of values should cover the range of possible accumulated discounted reward. In the paper, the authors did experiments with various amounts of atoms, but the best results were obtained with the range being split on `N_ATOMS=51` intervals in the range of values from `Vmin=-10` to `Vmax=10`.

For every atom (we have 51 of them), our network predicts the probability that future discounted value will fall into this atom's range. The central part of the method is the code, which performs the contraction of distribution of the next state's best action using gamma, adds local reward to the distribution and projects the results back into our original atoms. The following is the function that does exactly this:

```
def distr_projection(next_distr, rewards, dones, Vmin, Vmax,
n_atoms, gamma):
    batch_size = len(rewards)
    proj_distr = np.zeros((batch_size, n_atoms), dtype=np.float32)
    delta_z = (Vmax - Vmin) / (n_atoms - 1)
```

In the beginning, we allocate the array that will keep the result of the projection. This function expects the batch of distributions with a shape (batch_size, n_atoms), array of rewards, flags for completed episodes and our hyperparameters: Vmin, Vmax, n_atoms, and gamma. The delta_z variable is the width of every atom in our value range.

```
for atom in range(n_atoms):
        tz_j = np.minimum(Vmax, np.maximum(Vmin, rewards +
    (Vmin + atom * delta_z) * gamma))
```

In the preceding code, we iterate over every atom in the original distribution that we have and calculate the place that this atom will be projected by the Bellman operator, taking into account our value bounds. For example, the very first atom, with index 0, corresponds with value Vmin=-10, but for the sample with reward +1 will be projected into value -10 * 0.99 + 1 = -8.9. In other words, it will be shifted to the right (assume our gamma=0.99). If the value falls beyond our value range given by Vmin and Vmax, we clip it to the bounds.

```
b_j = (tz_j - Vmin) / delta_z
```

In the next line, we calculate the atom numbers that our samples have projected. Of course, samples can be projected between the atoms. In such situations, we'll spread value in the original distribution at the source atom, between the two atoms that it falls between. This spreading should be carefully handled, as our target atom can land exactly at some atom's position. In that case, we just need to add the source distribution value to the target atom.

```
l = np.floor(b_j).astype(np.int64)
u = np.ceil(b_j).astype(np.int64)
eq_mask = u == l
proj_distr[eq_mask, l[eq_mask]] += next_distr[eq_mask, atom]
```

The above code handles the situation when the projected atom lands exactly on the target atom. Otherwise, b_j won't be the integer value and variables l and u (which correspond to the indices of atoms below and above the projected point).

```
        ne_mask = u != l
        proj_distr[ne_mask, l[ne_mask]] += next_distr[ne_mask, atom] *
(u - b_j)[ne_mask]
        proj_distr[ne_mask, u[ne_mask]] += next_distr[ne_mask, atom] *
(b_j - l)[ne_mask]
```

When the projected point lands between atoms, we need to spread the probability of the source atom between atoms below and above. This is carried out by two lines in the above code and, of course, we need to properly handle the final transitions of episodes. In that case, our projection shouldn't take into account the next distribution and will just have a 1 probability corresponding to the reward obtained. However, we need, again, to take into account our atoms and properly distribute this probability if the reward value falls between the atoms. This case is handled by the code branch below, which zeroes resulting distribution for samples with the done flag set and then calculates the resulting projection.

```
    if dones.any():
        proj_distr[dones] = 0.0
        tz_j = np.minimum(Vmax, np.maximum(Vmin, rewards[dones]))
        b_j = (tz_j - Vmin) / delta_z
        l = np.floor(b_j).astype(np.int64)
        u = np.ceil(b_j).astype(np.int64)
        eq_mask = u == l
        eq_dones = dones.copy()
        eq_dones[dones] = eq_mask
        if eq_dones.any():
            proj_distr[eq_dones, l] = 1.0
        ne_mask = u != l
        ne_dones = dones.copy()
        ne_dones[dones] = ne_mask
        if ne_dones.any():
            proj_distr[ne_dones, l] = (u - b_j)[ne_mask]
            proj_distr[ne_dones, u] = (b_j - l)[ne_mask]
    return proj_distr
```

To give you an illustration of what this function does, let's look at artificially-made distributions processed by this function. I've used them to debug the function and make sure that it works as intended. The code for these checks is in `Chapter07/adhoc/distr_test.py`.

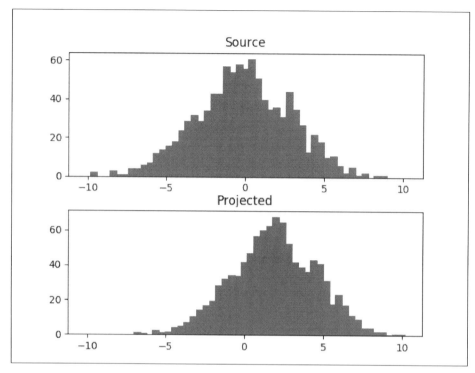

Figure 15: The sample of probability distribution transformation applied to normal distribution

The first illustration below corresponds to the normal distribution projected with *gamma=0.9* and shifted to the right with *reward=2*. In the situation when we pass done=True with the same data, the result will be different. In such cases, source distribution will be ignored completely and the result will have only reward projected.

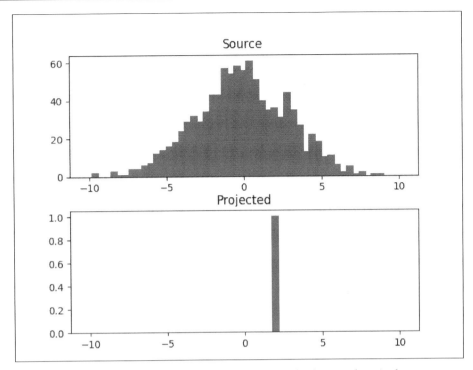

Figure 16: The projection of distribution for the final step in the episode

Now let's look at the main source of the method in Chapter07/07_dqn_distrib.py.

```
SAVE_STATES_IMG = False
SAVE_TRANSITIONS_IMG = False

if SAVE_STATES_IMG or SAVE_TRANSITIONS_IMG:
    import matplotlib as mpl
    mpl.use("Agg")
    import matplotlib.pylab as plt
```

In the beginning, we switch matplotlib into "headless" mode, which is when it doesn't require display for plotting. The code has special debug mode flags, which enable the saving of probability distributions to simplify debugging and the visualization of the training process (they are disabled by default).

```
Vmax = 10
Vmin = -10
N_ATOMS = 51
DELTA_Z = (Vmax - Vmin) / (N_ATOMS - 1)
```

Then we define our constants, which includes the range of value distribution Vmax, Vmin, number of atoms, and width of every atom.

```
STATES_TO_EVALUATE = 1000
EVAL_EVERY_FRAME = 100
```

The next two constants define how many states we keep in our held-out buffer to perform mean value calculation and how frequently this mean value will be updated. This is useful for evaluating the training progress because as our agent becomes better and better at the game, its Q-values grow.

```
SAVE_STATES_IMG = False
SAVE_TRANSITIONS_IMG = False
```

Those two flags enable the saving of distribution images, which is useful for debugging, but significantly slows down the training process. If the first flag is enabled every 10k frames, we save the predicted distributions for all actions for the first 200 states in our held-out buffer. Resulting images show how distributions of those states converge from uniform distribution in the beginning to something more realistic and Gaussian-like. The second flag enables the saving of projection distributions for batches with non-zero rewards or terminal episodes, which is really helpful for spotting bugs in distribution projection code and useful for visualizing the internals of the method.

```
class DistributionalDQN(nn.Module):
    def __init__(self, input_shape, n_actions):
        super(DistributionalDQN, self).__init__()

        self.conv = nn.Sequential(
            nn.Conv2d(input_shape[0], 32, kernel_size=8, stride=4),
            nn.ReLU(),
            nn.Conv2d(32, 64, kernel_size=4, stride=2),
            nn.ReLU(),
            nn.Conv2d(64, 64, kernel_size=3, stride=1),
            nn.ReLU()
        )

        conv_out_size = self._get_conv_out(input_shape)
        self.fc = nn.Sequential(
            nn.Linear(conv_out_size, 512),
            nn.ReLU(),
            nn.Linear(512, n_actions * N_ATOMS)
        )
```

```
            self.register_buffer("supports", torch.arange
   (Vmin, Vmax+DELTA_Z, DELTA_Z))
            self.softmax = nn.Softmax(dim=1)
```

The major difference in the NN constructor is the output of the net. Now, it's not the tensor of size `n_actions`; it's a matrix of `n_actions * n_atoms` elements, containing probability distributions for every action. With batch dimension, the resulting output has three dimensions. We also register the torch tensor with our atom's values to be able to use it later.

```
def _get_conv_out(self, shape):
    o = self.conv(torch.zeros(1, *shape))
    return int(np.prod(o.size()))

def forward(self, x):
    batch_size = x.size()[0]
    fx = x.float() / 256
    conv_out = self.conv(fx).view(batch_size, -1)
    fc_out = self.fc(conv_out)
    return fc_out.view(batch_size, -1, N_ATOMS)
```

The `forward()` function is mostly the same when compared to baseline DQN, except the final shape, which needs to be adjusted. However, `forward()` is not enough for our purposes. Besides raw distribution, we'll need both distributions and Q-values from the batch of states. To avoid multiple NN transformation, we'll define the function `both()`, which returns both raw distribution and Q-values. Q-values will be used to make decisions on actions. Of course, using distributions means that we can have different strategies for action selections, but greedy policy in regards to Q-values makes the method comparable to the standard DQN version.

```
def both(self, x):
    cat_out = self(x)
    probs = self.apply_softmax(cat_out)
    weights = probs * self.supports
    res = weights.sum(dim=2)
    return cat_out, res
```

To obtain Q-values from the distribution, we just need to calculate the weighted sum of the normalized distribution and atom's values. The result will be the expected value from the distribution.

```
def qvals(self, x):
    return self.both(x)[1]

def apply_softmax(self, t):
    return self.softmax(t.view(-1, N_ATOMS)).view(t.size())
```

The remaining two functions are simple utility functions. The first calculates only Q-values, while the second applies `softmax` to the output tensor, keeping the proper shape of the tensor.

```
def calc_loss(batch, net, tgt_net, gamma, device="cpu", save_
prefix=None):
    states, actions, rewards, dones, next_states = common.unpack_
batch(batch)
    batch_size = len(batch)

    states_v = torch.tensor(states).to(device)
    actions_v = torch.tensor(actions).to(device)
    next_states_v = torch.tensor(next_states).to(device)
```

The loss function for the categorical DQN (the authors also call it C51, by the number of atoms used) starts the same way as before: we unpack the batch and convert arrays to tensors.

```
    # next state distribution
    next_distr_v, next_qvals_v = tgt_net.both(next_states_v)
    next_actions = next_qvals_v.max(1)[1].data.cpu().numpy()
    next_distr = tgt_net.apply_softmax(next_distr_v).data.cpu().
numpy()
```

Later, we'll need both probability distributions and Q-values for the next states, so we use the `both()` call to the network, obtain the best actions to take in the next state, apply `softmax` to the distribution, and convert it to the array.

```
    next_best_distr = next_distr[range(batch_size), next_actions]
    dones = dones.astype(np.bool)
    proj_distr = common.distr_projection(next_best_distr, rewards,
dones, Vmin, Vmax, N_ATOMS, gamma)
```

Then, we extract distributions of the best actions and perform their projection using the Bellman operator. The result of the projection will be target distribution about what we want our network output to look like.

```
    distr_v = net(states_v)
    state_action_values = distr_v[range(batch_size), actions_v.data]
    state_log_sm_v = F.log_softmax(state_action_values, dim=1)
    proj_distr_v = torch.tensor(proj_distr).to(device)
    loss_v = -state_log_sm_v * proj_distr_v
    return loss_v.sum(dim=1).mean()
```

At the end of the function, we need to compute the output of the network and calculate KL-divergence between projected distribution and the network's output for the taken actions. KL-divergence shows how much two distributions differ and is defined $D_{KL}(P\|Q) = -\sum_i p_i \log q_i$.

To calculate the logarithm of probability, we use the PyTorch function `log_softmax`, which performs both `log` and `softmax` in a numerical and stable way. The training loop is the same as before, with one exception in `ptan.DQNAgent` creation, which needs to use function `qvals()`, instead of the model itself.

```
agent = ptan.agent.DQNAgent(lambda x: net.qvals(x), selector,
device=device)
```

Results

The plot with the results are as follows, with the upper line corresponding to the basic DQN and lower line being from the C51 training.

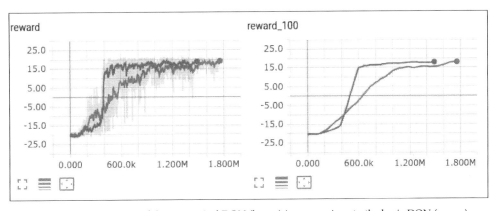

Figure 17: Convergence of the categorical DQN (lower) in comparison to the basic DQN (upper)

As you can see, categorical DQN is the only method of convergence dynamic, which, in the beginning is *worse* than the classic DQN. However, there is one factor that protects this new method: Pong is too simple a game to draw conclusions. In the Categorical DQN paper, the authors reported state-of-the-art scores for more than half of the games from the Atari benchmark (Pong is not among them).

It might be interesting to look into the dynamics of the probability distribution during the training. The code has two flags, SAVE_STATES_IMG and SAVE_TRANSITIONS_IMG (disabled by default), which enable the saving of probability distribution images during training. For example, on the image below is shown probability distribution for all six actions for one state at the beginning of training (after 30k frames).

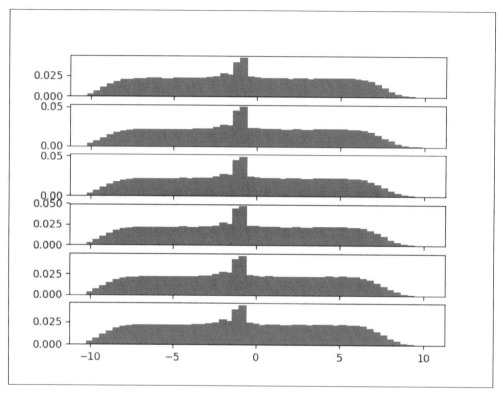

Figure 18: Probability distribution at the beginning of training

All the distributions are very wide (as the network hasn't converged yet) and the peak in the middle corresponds to the negative reward that the network expects to get from its actions. The same state after 500k frames of training is shown in the following figure:

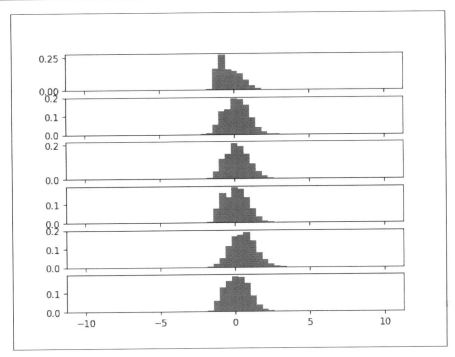

Figure 19: Probability distribution produced by the trained network

Now we can see that different actions have different distributions. The first action (which corresponds to the NOOP, that is *do nothing* action) has distribution shifted to the left, so doing nothing in this state usually leads to losing. The fifth action, which is RIGHTFIRE, has the mean value shifted to the right, so this action leads to a better score.

Combining everything

We've now seen all DQN improvements mentioned in the paper *[1] Rainbow: Combining Improvements in Deep Reinforcement Learning*. Let's combine all of them into one hybrid method. First of all, we need to define our network architecture and the three methods that have contributed to it:

- **Categorical DQN**: Our network will predict the value probability distribution of actions.
- **Dueling DQN**: Our network will have two separate paths for value of state distribution and advantage distribution. On the output, both paths will be summed together, providing the final value probability distributions for actions. To force advantage distribution to have a zero mean, we'll subtract distribution with mean advantage in every atom.

- **NoisyNet**: Our linear layers in the value and advantage paths will be noisy variants of `nn.Linear`.

In addition to network architecture changes, we'll use prioritized replay buffer to keep environment transitions and sample them proportionally to KL-divergence. Finally, we'll unroll the Bellman equation to **n-steps** and use the **double DQN** action selection process to prevent the overestimation of values of states.

Implementation

The preceding list of modifications may look complicated, but, in fact, all of the methods fit with each other quite nicely. The complete example is in the `Chapter07/08_dqn_rainbow.py file`:

```
# n-step
REWARD_STEPS = 2

# priority replay
PRIO_REPLAY_ALPHA = 0.6
BETA_START = 0.4
BETA_FRAMES = 100000

# C51
Vmax = 10
Vmin = -10
N_ATOMS = 51
DELTA_Z = (Vmax - Vmin) / (N_ATOMS - 1)
```

As usual, we define hyperparameters for all methods that we'll use (imports are omitted to save space).

```
class RainbowDQN(nn.Module):
    def __init__(self, input_shape, n_actions):
        super(RainbowDQN, self).__init__()

        self.conv = nn.Sequential(
            nn.Conv2d(input_shape[0], 32, kernel_size=8, stride=4),
            nn.ReLU(),
            nn.Conv2d(32, 64, kernel_size=4, stride=2),
            nn.ReLU(),
            nn.Conv2d(64, 64, kernel_size=3, stride=1),
            nn.ReLU()
        )
```

```
        conv_out_size = self._get_conv_out(input_shape)
        self.fc_val = nn.Sequential(
            dqn_model.NoisyLinear(conv_out_size, 512),
            nn.ReLU(),
            dqn_model.NoisyLinear(512, N_ATOMS)
        )

        self.fc_adv = nn.Sequential(
            dqn_model.NoisyLinear(conv_out_size, 512),
            nn.ReLU(),
            dqn_model.NoisyLinear(512, n_actions * N_ATOMS)
        )

        self.register_buffer("supports", torch.arange(Vmin,
    Vmax+DELTA_Z, DELTA_Z))
        self.softmax = nn.Softmax(dim=1)
```

The constructor of our network shouldn't surprise you much, as we've seen it before. It combines dueling DQN, NoisyNet, and the categorical DQN into one architecture. A value network path predicts the distribution of values for the input state, thus giving us a single vector of N_ATOMS for every batch sample. The advantage path produces the distribution for every action that we have in the game.

```
    def _get_conv_out(self, shape):
        o = self.conv(torch.zeros(1, *shape))
        return int(np.prod(o.size()))

    def forward(self, x):
        batch_size = x.size()[0]
        fx = x.float() / 256
        conv_out = self.conv(fx).view(batch_size, -1)
        val_out = self.fc_val(conv_out).view(batch_size, 1, N_ATOMS)
        adv_out = self.fc_adv(conv_out).view(batch_size, -1, N_ATOMS)
        adv_mean = adv_out.mean(dim=1, keepdim=True)
        return val_out + adv_out - adv_mean
```

The forward pass produces value distribution for actions, which are similar to Q-values in categorical DQN. By accurately reshaping the output from both the value and advantage paths, our return expression becomes very simple, thanks to PyTorch's broadcasting of tensors.

The idea is to make all values that we want to add have the same count of dimensions. For example, the value path will be reshaped into (batch_size, 1, N_ATOMS), so the second dimension will be broadcasted to all actions in the advantage path. The baseline advantage that we need to subtract is obtained by calculating the mean advantage for every atom over all actions. The keepdim=True argument asks the mean() call to keep the second dimension, which produces the tensor of (batch_size, 1, N_ATOMS). So, baseline advantage will be broadcasted too.

```
def both(self, x):
    cat_out = self(x)
    probs = self.apply_softmax(cat_out)
    weights = probs * self.supports
    res = weights.sum(dim=2)
    return cat_out, res

def qvals(self, x):
    return self.both(x)[1]
```

The preceding functions are used to be able to combine probability distributions into Q-values, without calling the network several times.

```
def apply_softmax(self, t):
    return self.softmax(t.view(-1, N_ATOMS)).view(t.size())
```

The final function applies softmax to the output probability distribution.

```
def calc_loss(batch, batch_weights, net, tgt_net, gamma,
device="cpu"):
    states, actions, rewards, dones, next_states = common.unpack_
batch(batch)
    batch_size = len(batch)

    states_v = torch.tensor(states).to(device)
    actions_v = torch.tensor(actions).to(device)
    next_states_v = torch.tensor(next_states).to(device)
    batch_weights_v = torch.tensor(batch_weights).to(device)
```

Our loss function accepts the same set of arguments as we've seen in prioritized replay buffer. In addition to batch array with training data, we pass weights for every sample.

```
    distr_v, qvals_v = net.both(torch.cat((states_v, next_states_v)))
    next_qvals_v = qvals_v[batch_size:]
    distr_v = distr_v[:batch_size]
```

Here we use a small trick to speed up our calculations a bit. As the double DQN method requires us to use our main network to select actions but use the target network to obtain values (in our case, value distributions) for those actions, we need to pass to our main network both the current states and the next states. Earlier, we calculated the network output in two calls, which is not very efficient on GPU. Now, we concatenate both current states and next states into one tensor and obtain the result in one network pass, splitting the result later. We need to calculate both Q-values and raw values' distributions, as our action selection policy is still greedy: we choose the action with the largest Q-value.

```
next_actions_v = next_qvals_v.max(1)[1]
next_distr_v = tgt_net(next_states_v)
next_best_distr_v = next_distr_v[range(batch_size), next_
actions_v.data]
next_best_distr_v = tgt_net.apply_softmax(next_best_distr_v)
next_best_distr = next_best_distr_v.data.cpu().numpy()
```

In the preceding lines, we decide on actions to take in the next state and obtain the distribution of those actions using our target network. So, the above net/ tgt_net shuffling implements the double DQN method. Then we apply softmax to distribution for those best actions and copy the data into CPU to perform the Bellman projection.

```
dones = dones.astype(np.bool)
proj_distr = common.distr_projection(next_best_distr, rewards,
dones, Vmin, Vmax, N_ATOMS, gamma)
```

In the preceding code, we calculate the projected distribution using the Bellman equation. This result will be used as a target in our KL-divergence.

```
state_action_values = distr_v[range(batch_size), actions_v.data]
state_log_sm_v = F.log_softmax(state_action_values, dim=1)
```

Here we obtain the distributions for taken actions and apply log_softmax to calculate the loss.

```
proj_distr_v = torch.tensor(proj_distr)
loss_v = -state_log_sm_v * proj_distr_v
loss_v = batch_weights_v * loss_v.sum(dim=1)
return loss_v.mean(), loss_v + 1e-5
```

In the last lines of the function, we calculate the KL-divergence loss, multiply it by weights and return two quantities: combined loss to be used in the optimizer step and individual loss values for batch, which will be used as priorities in the replay buffer. The rest of the module contains initialization and the training loop and should be familiar to you.

```
if __name__ == "__main__":
    params = common.HYPERPARAMS['pong']
    parser = argparse.ArgumentParser()
    parser.add_argument("--cuda", default=False, action="store_true",
help="Enable cuda")
    args = parser.parse_args()
    device = torch.device("cuda" if args.cuda else "cpu")

    env = gym.make(params['env_name'])
    env = ptan.common.wrappers.wrap_dqn(env)

    writer = SummaryWriter(comment="-" + params['run_name'] +
"-rainbow")
    net = RainbowDQN(env.observation_space.shape, env.action_space.n).
to(device)
    tgt_net = ptan.agent.TargetNet(net)
    agent = ptan.agent.DQNAgent(lambda x: net.qvals(x), ptan.actions.
ArgmaxActionSelector(), device=device)

    exp_source = ptan.experience.ExperienceSourceFirstLast(env, agent,
gamma=params['gamma'], steps_count=REWARD_STEPS)
    buffer = ptan.experience.PrioritizedReplayBuffer(exp_source,
params['replay_size'], PRIO_REPLAY_ALPHA)
    optimizer = optim.Adam(net.parameters(), lr=params['learning_
rate'])
```

In the preceding code we create everything we need, including our custom network, experience source, prioritized replay buffer and optimizer.

```
    frame_idx = 0
    beta = BETA_START

    with common.RewardTracker(writer, params['stop_reward']) as
reward_tracker:
        while True:
            frame_idx += 1
            buffer.populate(1)
            beta = min(1.0, BETA_START + frame_idx * (1.0 - BETA_
START) / BETA_FRAMES)
```

```
        new_rewards = exp_source.pop_total_rewards()
        if new_rewards:
            if reward_tracker.reward(new_rewards[0], frame_idx):
                break

        if len(buffer) < params['replay_initial']:
            continue

        optimizer.zero_grad()
        batch, batch_indices, batch_weights = buffer.
sample(params['batch_size'], beta)
        loss_v, sample_prios_v = calc_loss(batch, batch_
weights, net, tgt_net.target_model, params['gamma'] ** REWARD_STEPS,
device=device)
        loss_v.backward()
        optimizer.step()
        buffer.update_priorities(batch_indices, sample_prios_v.
data.cpu().numpy())

        if frame_idx % params['target_net_sync'] == 0:
            tgt_net.sync()
```

Results

Training dynamics for the aggregated agent are shown here.

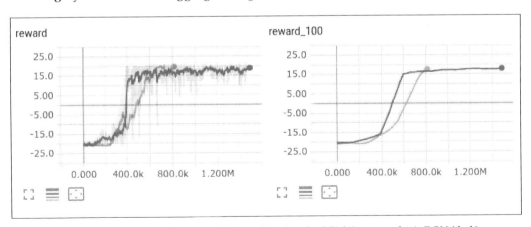

Figure 20: Convergence dynamics of the combined method (light) versus a basic DQN (dark)

If you put all of our methods into perspective, on the Pong game the aggregated agent doesn't have the best training dynamics, for example dueling DQN or NoisyNets alone converge a bit faster. However, Pong is not very complicated and was chosen as a benchmark for this chapter due to its simplicity and fast convergence. As an extra exercise, you can check those methods on different games from the Atari suite.

In the `lib/common.py` module, you can find hyperparameters closer to the settings used by the researchers in their benchmarks, but keep in mind that reaching state-of-the-art results on a complex game can take 50-100M frames, which can be a week of training.

Summary

In this chapter, we walked through and implemented lots of DQN improvements discovered by researchers since the first DQN paper was published in 2015. This list is far from complete. First of all, for the list of methods, I've used the paper, *[1] Rainbow: Combining Improvements in Deep Reinforcement Learning*, which was published by DeepMind, so the list of methods is definitely biased to DeepMind papers. Secondly, RL is so active nowadays that new papers come out almost every day, which makes it very hard to keep up with, even if we limit ourselves to one kind of RL model such as a DQN. The goal of this chapter was to give you a practical view of different ideas that the field has developed.

In the next chapter, we will apply our DQN knowledge to a real-life scenario of stocks trading.

References

1. *Matteo Hessel, Joseph Modayil, Hado van Hasselt, Tom Schaul, Georg Ostrovski, Will Dabney, Dan Horgan, Bilal Piot, Mohammad Azar, David Silver, 2017, Rainbow: Combining Improvements in Deep Reinforcement Learning. arXiv:1710.02298*

2. *Sutton, R.S. 1988, Learning to Predict by the Methods of Temporal Differences, Machine Learning 3(1):9-44*

3. *Hado Van Hasselt, Arthur Guez, David Silver, 2015, Deep Reinforcement Learning with Double Q-Learning. arXiv:1509.06461v3*

4. *Meire Fortunato, Mohammad Gheshlaghi Azar, Bilal Pilot, Jacob Menick, Ian Osband, Alex Graves, Vlad Mnih, Remi Munos, Demis Hassabis, Olivier Pietquin, Charles Blundell, Shane Legg, 2017, Noisy Networks for Exploration arXiv:1706.10295v1*

5. *Marc Bellemare, Sriram Srinivasan, Georg Ostrovski, Tom Schaus, David Saxton, Remi Munos 2016, Unifying Count-Based Exploration and Intrinsic Motivation arXiv:1606.01868v2*

6. *Jarryd Martin, Suraj Narayanan Sasikumar, Tom Everitt, Marcus Hutter, 2017, Count-Based Exploration in Feature Space for Reinforcement Learning arXiv:1706.08090*

7. *Tom Schaul, John Quan, Ioannis Antonoglou, David Silver, 2015, Prioritized Experience Replay arXiv:1511.05952*

8. *Ziyu Wang, Tom Schaul, Matteo Hessel, Hado van Hasselt, Marc Lanctot, Nando de Freitas, 2015, Dueling Network Architectures for Deep Reinforcement Learning arXiv:1511.06581*

9. *Marc G. Bellemare, Will Dabney, Rémi Munos, 2017, A Distributional Perspective on Reinforcement Learning arXiv:1707.06887*

8
Stocks Trading Using RL

Rather than learning new methods to solve toy **reinforcement learning (RL)** problems in this chapter, we'll try to utilize our **deep Q-network (DQN)** knowledge to deal with the much more practical problem of financial trading. I can't promise that the code will make you super rich on the stock market or Forex, because the goal is much less ambitious: to demonstrate how to go beyond the Atari games and apply RL to a different practical domain.

In this chapter, we'll implement our own OpenAI Gym environment, which simulates the stock market, and apply the DQN method that we've just learned in *Chapters 6, Deep Q-Networks,* and *Chapter 7, DQN Extensions,* to train the agent that will trade stocks to maximize the profit.

Trading

There are lots of financial instruments traded on markets every day: goods, stocks, and currencies. Even weather forecasts can be bought or sold using so-called "weather derivatives," which is just a consequence of the complexity of the modern world and financial markets. If your income depends on future weather conditions, like a business growing crops, then you might want to hedge the risks by buying weather derivatives. All these different items have a price which is changed over time. Trading is an activity of buying and selling financial instruments with different goals, like making profit (investment), gaining protection from future price movement (hedging) or just getting what you need (like buying steel for your manufacture or exchanging USD to JPY to pay a contract).

Since the first financial market was established, people have been trying to predict future price movements, as this promises lots of benefits, like "profit from nowhere" or protecting capital from sudden market movements. This problem is known to be complex and there are lots of financial consultants, investment funds, banks, and individual traders who are trying to predict the market and find the best moments to buy and sell to maximize profit.

The question is: can we look at the problem from the RL angle? We have some observation of the market and we want to make a decision: buy, sell, or wait. If we buy before the price goes up, our profit will be positive, otherwise, we'll get a negative reward. What we're trying to do is to get as much profit as possible. The connections between market trading and RL are quite obvious.

Data

In our example, we'll use the Russian stock market prices for the period of 2015-2016, which is placed in `Chapter08/data/ch08-small-quotes.tgz` and has to be unpacked before model training.

Inside the archive, we have CSV files with M1 bars, which means that every row in the CSV corresponds to a single minute in time and price movement during this minute is captured with four prices: open, high, low, and close. Here, an open price is the price at the beginning of the minute, high is the maximum price during the interval, low is the minimum price, and the close price is the last price of the minute time interval. Every minute interval is called **bar** and allows us to have an idea of price movement within the interval. For example, in the `YNDX_160101_161231.csv` file (which is Yandex company stocks for 2016), we have 130k lines of this form:

```
<DATE>,<TIME>,<OPEN>,<HIGH>,<LOW>,<CLOSE>,<VOL>
20160104,100100,1148.9000000,1148.9000000,1148.9000000,1148.9000000,0
20160104,100200,1148.9000000,1148.9000000,1148.9000000,1148.9000000,50
20160104,100300,1149.0000000,1149.0000000,1149.0000000,1149.0000000,33
20160104,100400,1149.0000000,1149.0000000,1149.0000000,1149.0000000,4
20160104,100500,1153.0000000,1153.0000000,1153.0000000,1153.0000000,0
20160104,100600,1156.9000000,1157.9000000,1153.0000000,1153.0000000,43
20160104,100700,1150.6000000,1150.6000000,1150.4000000,1150.4000000,5
20160104,100800,1150.2000000,1150.2000000,1150.2000000,1150.2000000,4
. . .
```

The first two columns are the date and time for the minute, the next four columns are open, high, low, and close prices and the last value represents the amount of buy and sell orders performed during the bar. The exact interpretation of this number is stock and market-dependent, but usually, volumes give you an idea about how active the market was.

The typical way to represent those prices is called a **candlestick chart**, where every bar is shown as a candle. Part of Yandex's quotes for one day in February 2016 is shown in the following chart. Every file in the archive contains the M1 data for one year and it will be used in this chapter's example:

Figure 1: Price data for Yandex in February 2016

Problem statements and key decisions

The finance domain is large and complex, so you can easily spend several years learning something new every day. In our example, we'll just scratch the surface a bit with our RL tools and our problem will be formulated as simply as possible, using price as an observation. We will investigate whether it will be possible for our agent to learn when the best time is to buy one single share and then close the position to maximize the profit. The purpose of this example is to show how flexible the RL model can be and what the first steps are that you usually need to take to apply RL to a real-life use case.

As you already know, to formulate RL problems three things are needed: **observation** of the environment, possible **actions,** and a **reward** system. In previous chapters, all three were already given to us and the internal machinery of the environment was hidden. Now we're in a different situation, so we need to decide ourselves what our agent will see and what set of actions it can take. The reward system is also not given as a strict set of rules, rather it is guided by our feelings and knowledge of the domain, but we still have lots of flexibility here.

Flexibility, in this case, is good and bad at the same time. It's good that we have the freedom to pass some information to the agent that we feel will be important to learn efficiently. For example, you can pass to the trading agent not only prices but also the information about news or important statistics to be published (which is known to influence financial markets a lot). The bad part is that this flexibility usually means that to find a good agent, you need to try lots of variants of data representation and it's not always obvious which will work better. In our case, we'll implement the basic trading agent in its simplest form. The observation will include the following information:

- N past bars, where each have open, high, low, and close prices
- An indication that the share was bought some time ago (it will be possible to have only one share at a time)
- Profit or loss we currently have from our current position (the share bought)

At every step, which will be after every minute's bar, the agent can take one of the following actions:

- **Do nothing**: Skip the bar without taking actions
- **Buy a share**: If the agent has already got the share, nothing will be bought, otherwise we'll pay the commission, which is usually some small percentage of the current price
- **Close the position**: If we've got no share previously bought, nothing will happen, otherwise we'll pay the commission for the trade

The reward that the agent receives could be expressed in various ways. On the one hand, we can split the reward into multiple steps during our ownership of the share. In that case, the reward on every step will be equal to the last bar's movement. On the other hand, the agent can receive reward only after the **close** action and receive full reward at once. At the first sight, both variants should have the same final result, but maybe with different convergence speed. However, in practice, the difference could be dramatic. We'll implement both variants to have a chance to compare them.

One last decision to make is how to represent the prices in our environment observation. Ideally, we would like our agent to be independent on actual price values and take into account relative movement, such as "stock has grown 1% during the last bar" or "stock has lost 5%." This makes sense, as different stocks' prices can vary, but they can have similar movement patterns. In finance, there exists a branch of analytics called "technical analysis," which studies such patterns to help to make predictions from them. We would like our system to be able to discover them (if they exist). To achieve this, we'll convert every bar "open, high, low, and close" prices to three numbers showing high, low, and close prices represented as a percentage to the open price.

This representation has its own drawbacks, as we're potentially losing the information about key price levels. For example, it's known that markets have a tendency to bounce from round price numbers (like $8000 per bitcoin) and levels which were turning points in the past. However, as already stated, we're not implementing "Wall Street Killer" here, but playing with the data and checking the concept. The representation in the form of relative price movement will help the system to find repeating patterns in the price level (if they exist, of course), regardless of the absolute price position. Potentially, the **neural network** (**NN**) could learn this on its own (it's just the mean price which needs to be subtracted from the absolute price values), but relative representation simplifies the NN's task.

The trading environment

As we have lots of code that is supposed to work with OpenAI Gym, we'll implement the trading functionality following Gym's `Env` class API, which should be familiar to you. Our environment is implemented in the `StocksEnv` class in the `Chapter08/lib/environ.py` module. It uses several internal classes to keep its state and encode observations. Let's first look at the public API class.

```
class Actions(enum.Enum):
    Skip = 0
    Buy = 1
    Close = 2
```

We encode all available actions as an enumerator's fields. We support a very simple set of actions with only three options: do nothing, buy a single share, and close the existing position.

```
class StocksEnv(gym.Env):
    metadata = {'render.modes': ['human']}
```

This metadata field is required the for `gym.Env` compatibility. We don't provide render functionality, so you can ignore this.

```
    @classmethod
    def from_dir(cls, data_dir, **kwargs):
        prices = {file: data.load_relative(file) for file in
data.price_files(data_dir)}
        return StocksEnv(prices, **kwargs)
```

Our environment class provides two ways to create its instance. The first way is to call the class method `from_dir` with data directory as the argument. In that case, it will load all quotes from CSV files in the directory and construct the environment. To deal with price data in our form, we have several helper functions in `Chapter08/lib/data.py`. Another way is to construct the class instance directly. In that case, you should pass the `prices` dictionary which has to map the quote tag to the `data.Prices` tuple. This object has five fields containing open, high, low, close, and volume time series in the NumPy array format. You can construct such objects using `data.py` library functions, like `data.load_relative`.

```
def __init__(self, prices, bars_count=DEFAULT_BARS_COUNT,
             commission=DEFAULT_COMMISSION_PERC,
  reset_on_close=True, state_1d=False,
             random_ofs_on_reset=True, reward_on_close=False,
  volumes=False):
```

The constructor of the environment accepts lots of arguments to tweak the environment's behavior and observation representation:

- `prices`: Contains one or more stock prices for one or more instruments as a `dict`, where keys are the instrument's name and value is a container object `data.Prices` which holds price data arrays.

- `bars_count`: The count of bars that we pass in observation. By default, this is 10 bars.

- `commission`: The percentage of the stock price we have to pay to the broker on buying and selling the stock. By default, it's 0.1%.

- `reset_on_close`: If this parameter is set to `True`, which it is by default, every time the agent asks us to close the existing position (in other words, sell a share), we stop the episode. Otherwise, the episode will continue until the end of our time series, which is one year of data.

- `conv_1d`: This boolean argument, switches between different representations of price data in the observation passed to the agent. If it is set to `True`, observations have a 2D shape, with different price components for subsequent bars organized in rows. For example, high prices (max price for the bar) are placed on the first row, low prices on the second and close prices on the third. This representation is suitable for doing 1D convolution on time series, where every row in the data has the same meaning as different color planes (red, green, or blue) in Atari 2D images. If we set this option to `False`, we have one single array of data with every bar's components placed together. This organization is convenient for fully-connected network architecture. Both representations are illustrated in Figure 2.

- `random_ofs_on_reset`: If the parameter is `True` (by default), on every reset of the environment, the random offset in time series will be chosen. Otherwise, we'll start from the beginning of the data.

- `reward_on_close`: This Boolean parameter switches between two reward schemes discussed above. If it is set to `True`, the agent will receive reward only on the "close" action issue. Otherwise, we'll give a small reward every bar, corresponding to price movement during that bar.

- `volumes`: This argument switches on volumes in observations and is disabled by default.

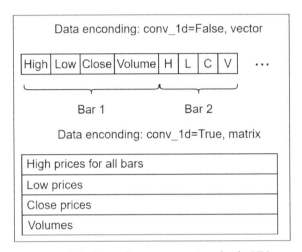

Figure 2: Different data representations for the NN

Now will continue looking on environment constructor:

```
assert isinstance(prices, dict)
self._prices = prices
if state_1d:
    self._state = State1D(bars_count, commission,
reset_on_close, reward_on_close=reward_on_close,
                              volumes=volumes)
    else:
        self._state = State(bars_count, commission, reset_on_
close, reward_on_close=reward_on_close,
volumes=volumes)
    self.action_space = gym.spaces.Discrete(n=len(Actions))
    self.observation_space = gym.spaces.Box(low=-np.inf,
high=np.inf, shape=self._state.shape, dtype=np.float32)
    self.random_ofs_on_reset = random_ofs_on_reset
    self._seed()
```

Most of the functionality of the StocksEnv class is implemented in two internal classes: State and State1D. They are responsible for observation preparation and our bought share state and reward. They are implementing a different representation of our data in the observations and we'll take a look at their code later. In the constructor, we create the state object, action space, and observation space fields that are required by Gym.

```
def reset(self):
    # make selection of the instrument and it's offset. Then
reset the state
    self._instrument =
self.np_random.choice(list(self._prices.keys()))
    prices = self._prices[self._instrument]
    bars = self._state.bars_count
    if self.random_ofs_on_reset:
        offset = self.np_random.choice(prices.high.shape[0]-
bars*10) + bars
    else:
        offset = bars
    self._state.reset(prices, offset)
    return self._state.encode()
```

This method defines the reset() functionality for our environment. According to the gym.Env semantics, we randomly switch the time series that we'll work on and select the starting offset in this time series. The selected price and offset are passed to our internal state instance, which then asks for an initial observation, using its encode() function.

```
def step(self, action_idx):
    action = Actions(action_idx)
    reward, done = self._state.step(action)
    obs = self._state.encode()
    info = {"instrument": self._instrument, "offset":
self._state._offset}
    return obs, reward, done, info
```

This method has to handle the action chosen by the agent and return the next observation, reward, and done flag. All real functionality is implemented in our state classes, so this method is a very simple wrapper around the call to state methods.

```
def render(self, mode='human', close=False):
    pass

def close(self):
    pass
```

The API for `gym.Env` allows you to define the `render()` method handler, which is supposed to render the current state in human or machine-readable format. Generally, this method is supposed to be used to peek inside the environment state and is useful for debugging or tracing the agent's behavior. For example, the market environment could render current prices as a chart to visualize what the agent sees at that moment. Our environment doesn't support rendering, so this method does nothing. Another method is `close()`, which gets called on the environment's destruction to free the allocated resources.

```
def seed(self, seed=None):
    self.np_random, seed1 = seeding.np_random(seed)
    seed2 = seeding.hash_seed(seed1 + 1) % 2 ** 31
    return [seed1, seed2]
```

This method is part of Gym's magic related to Python random number generator problems. For example, when you create several environments at the same time, their random number generators could be initialized with the same seed (which is the current timestamp, by default). It's not very relevant for our code (as we're using only one environment instance for DQN), but will become useful in the next part of the book when we go to the **Asynchronous Advantage Actor-Critic (A3C)** method, which is supposed to use several environments concurrently.

Let's now look at the internal `environ.State` class, which implements most of the environment's functionality.

```
class State:
    def __init__(self, bars_count, commission_perc,
reset_on_close, reward_on_close=True, volumes=True):
        assert isinstance(bars_count, int)
        assert bars_count > 0
        assert isinstance(commission_perc, float)
        assert commission_perc >= 0.0
        assert isinstance(reset_on_close, bool)
        assert isinstance(reward_on_close, bool)
        self.bars_count = bars_count
        self.commission_perc = commission_perc
        self.reset_on_close = reset_on_close
        self.reward_on_close = reward_on_close
        self.volumes = volumes
```

The constructor does nothing more than just checking and remembering the arguments in the object's fields:

```
def reset(self, prices, offset):
    assert isinstance(prices, data.Prices)
    assert offset >= self.bars_count-1
```

```
            self.have_position = False
            self.open_price = 0.0
            self._prices = prices
            self._offset = offset
```

The `reset()` method is called every time that the environment is being asked to reset and has to save the passed prices data and starting offset. In the beginning, we don't have any shares bought, so our state has `have_position=False` and `open_price=0.0`.

```
        @property
        def shape(self):
            # [h, l, c] * bars + position_flag + rel_profit (since
    open)
            if self.volumes:
                return (4 * self.bars_count + 1 + 1, )
            else:
                return (3 * self.bars_count + 1 + 1, )
```

This property returns the shape of the state representation in a NumPy array. The `State` class is encoded into a single vector, which includes prices with optional volumes and two numbers indicating the presence of a bought share and position profit.

```
        def encode(self):
            """
            Convert current state into numpy array.
            """
            res = np.ndarray(shape=self.shape, dtype=np.float32)
            shift = 0
            for bar_idx in range(-self.bars_count+1, 1):
                res[shift] = self._prices.high[self._offset + bar_idx]
                shift += 1
                res[shift] = self._prices.low[self._offset + bar_idx]
                shift += 1
                res[shift] = self._prices.close[self._offset +
    bar_idx]
                shift += 1
                if self.volumes:
                    res[shift] = self._prices.volume[self._offset +
    bar_idx]
                    shift += 1
            res[shift] = float(self.have_position)
            shift += 1
            if not self.have_position:
                res[shift] = 0.0
```

```
        else:
            res[shift] = (self._cur_close() - self.open_price) /
self.open_price
        return res
```

The above method encodes prices at the current offset into a NumPy array, which will be the observation of the agent.

```
    def _cur_close(self):
        open = self._prices.open[self._offset]
        rel_close = self._prices.close[self._offset]
        return open * (1.0 + rel_close)
```

This helper method calculates the current bar's close price. Prices passed to the `State` class have the relative form in respect to open price: the high, low, and close components are relative ratios to the open price. This representation was already discussed when we talked about the training data and it will (probably) help our agent to learn price patterns that are independent of actual price value.

```
    def step(self, action):
        assert isinstance(action, Actions)
        reward = 0.0
        done = False
        close = self._cur_close()
```

This method is the most complicated piece of code in the `State` class, which is responsible for performing one step in our environment. On exit, it has to return the reward in a percentage and indication of the episode ending.

```
        if action == Actions.Buy and not self.have_position:
            self.have_position = True
            self.open_price = close
            reward -= self.commission_perc
```

If the agent has decided to buy a share, we change our state and pay the commission. In our state, we assume the instant order execution at the current bar's close price, which is a simplification on our side, as, normally, order could be executed on a different price, which is called "price slippage".

```
        elif action == Actions.Close and self.have_position:
            reward -= self.commission_perc
            done |= self.reset_on_close
            if self.reward_on_close:
                reward += 100.0 * (close - self.open_price) /
self.open_price
            self.have_position = False
            self.open_price = 0.0
```

If we have a position and the agent asks us to close it, we pay commission again, change the `done` flag if we're in `reset_on_close` mode, give a final reward for the whole position, and change our state.

```
self._offset += 1
prev_close = close
close = self._cur_close()
done |= self._offset >= self._prices.close.shape[0]-1

if self.have_position and not self.reward_on_close:
    reward += 100.0 * (close - prev_close) / prev_close

return reward, done
```

In the rest of the function, we modify the current offset and give the reward for the last bar movement. That's it for the `State` class, so let's look at `State1D`, which has the same behavior and just overrides the representation of the state passed to the agent.

```
class State1D(State):
    @property
    def shape(self):
        if self.volumes:
            return (6, self.bars_count)
        else:
            return (5, self.bars_count)
```

The shape of this representation is different, as our prices are encoded as a 2D matrix suitable for a 1D convolution operator.

```
def encode(self):
    res = np.zeros(shape=self.shape, dtype=np.float32)
    ofs = self.bars_count-1
    res[0] = self._prices.high[self._offset-
ofs:self._offset+1]
    res[1] = self._prices.low[self._offset-ofs:self._offset+1]
    res[2] = self._prices.close[self._offset-
ofs:self._offset+1]
    if self.volumes:
        res[3] = self._prices.volume[self._offset-
ofs:self._offset+1]
        dst = 4
    else:
        dst = 3
    if self.have_position:
        res[dst] = 1.0
```

```
        res[dst+1] = (self._cur_close() - self.open_price) /
self.open_price
        return res
```

The above method encodes the prices in our matrix, depending on the current offset, whether we need volumes or not and whether we have stock. That's it for our trading environment. Compatibility with the Gym API allows us to plug it into familiar classes that we used to handle the Atari games. Let's do that now.

Models

In this example, two architectures of DQN are used: a simple feed-forward network with three layers and a network with 1D convolution and a feature extractor, followed by two fully connected layers to output Q values. Both of them use the dueling architecture described in the previous chapter. Double DQN and two-step Bellman unrolling have also been used. The rest of the process is the same as in the classical DQN (from *Chapter 6, Deep Q-Networks*).

Both models are in `Chapter08/lib/models.py` and are very simple.

```
class SimpleFFDQN(nn.Module):
    def __init__(self, obs_len, actions_n):
        super(SimpleFFDQN, self).__init__()

        self.fc_val = nn.Sequential(
            nn.Linear(obs_len, 512),
            nn.ReLU(),
            nn.Linear(512, 512),
            nn.ReLU(),
            nn.Linear(512, 1)
        )

        self.fc_adv = nn.Sequential(
            nn.Linear(obs_len, 512),
            nn.ReLU(),
            nn.Linear(512, 512),
            nn.ReLU(),
            nn.Linear(512, actions_n)
        )

    def forward(self, x):
        val = self.fc_val(x)
        adv = self.fc_adv(x)
        return val + adv - adv.mean()
```

The convolutional model has a common feature extraction layer with the 1D convolution operations and two fully connected heads to output the value of the state and advantages for actions.

```python
class DQNConv1D(nn.Module):
    def __init__(self, shape, actions_n):
        super(DQNConv1D, self).__init__()

        self.conv = nn.Sequential(
            nn.Conv1d(shape[0], 128, 5),
            nn.ReLU(),
            nn.Conv1d(128, 128, 5),
            nn.ReLU(),
        )

        out_size = self._get_conv_out(shape)

        self.fc_val = nn.Sequential(
            nn.Linear(out_size, 512),
            nn.ReLU(),
            nn.Linear(512, 1)
        )

        self.fc_adv = nn.Sequential(
            nn.Linear(out_size, 512),
            nn.ReLU(),
            nn.Linear(512, actions_n)
        )

    def _get_conv_out(self, shape):
        o = self.conv( torch.zeros(1, *shape))
        return int(np.prod(o.size()))

    def forward(self, x):
        conv_out = self.conv(x).view(x.size()[0], -1)
        val = self.fc_val(conv_out)
        adv = self.fc_adv(conv_out)
        return val + adv - adv.mean()
```

Training code

We have two very similar training modules in this example: one for the feed-forward model and one for 1D convolutions. For both of them, there is nothing new added to our examples from *Chapter 7, DQN Extensions*:

- They're using epsilon-greedy action selection to perform exploration. The epsilon linearly decays over the first 1M steps from 1.0 to 0.1.

- A simple experience replay buffer of size 100k is being used, which is initially populated with 10k transitions.

- For every 1000 steps, we calculate the mean value for the fixed set of states to check the dynamics of the Q-values during the training.

- For every 100k steps, we perform validation: 100 episodes are played on the training data and on previously unseen quotes. Characteristics of orders are recorded in TensorBoard, such as the mean profit, the mean count of bars, and share held. This step allows us to check for overfitting conditions.

The training modules are in `Chapter08/train_model.py` (feed-forward model) and `Chapter08/train_model_conv.py` (with conv 1d features). Both versions accept the same command line options.

To start the training, you need to pass training data with the `--data` option, which could be an individual CSV file of the whole directory with files. By default, the training module uses Yandex quotes for 2016 (file `data/YNDX_160101_161231.csv`). For the validation data, there is an option `--valdata`, which takes Yandex 2015 quotes by default. Another required option will be `-r`, which is used to pass the name of the run. This name will be used in the TensorBoard run name and to create directories with saved models.

Results

Let's now take a look at the results.

The feed-forward model

The convergence on Yandex data for one year requires about 10M training steps, which can take a while (GTX 1080Ti trains at a speed of 230-250 steps per second). During training, we have several charts in TensorBoard showing us what's going on.

The following are two charts, **reward_100** and **steps_100**, with average reward (which is in percentages) and the average length of the episode for the last 100 episodes, respectively:

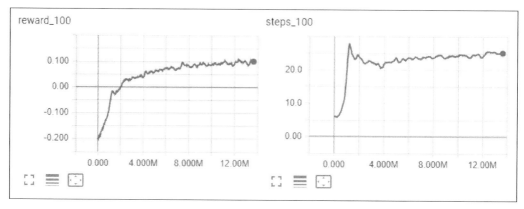

Figure 3: The reward plot for the feed-forward version

The charts show us two good things:

1. Our agent was able to figure out when to buy and sell the share to get positive reward (as we need to pay a commission of 0.1% on the open and close of the position, random actions will have -0.2% reward).

2. Over the training time, the length of the episode increased from seven bars to 25 and still continues to grow slowly, which means that the agent is holding the share longer and longer to increase the final profit.

Unfortunately, the preceding charts don't mean that the same agent will be profitable in the future, as there is no guarantee that the dynamics of quotes will be the same again. To check our strategy, we performed validation runs every 100k training steps. The validation was performed on two datasets: our training data and the previously unseen data from the same stock, but for a different time period. The results of the validation can be seen in the following figure:

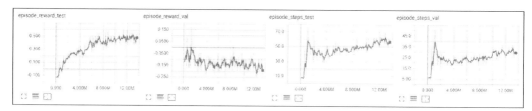

Figure 4: Test and validation dynamics during the training

On the test charts, (which are obtained from using the training data) we can see the same positive dynamics as in the **reward_100** and **steps_100** charts: the reward is positive and growing over time and the length of the episode is also growing. However, the validation reward chart, which is a result from the unseen data, shows the opposite dynamics: our reward is decreasing over time. This can be explained by the fact that the agent overfits to the training data and starts to behave worse on the unseen quotes. There are some spikes above the zero reward, but most of the time, our agent is losing money on the validation dataset. As mentioned before, we're not going to get this right overnight and the fact that the `episode_reward_val` line most of the time is above -0.2% (which is a broker commission in our environment), says that our agent is better than a random "buying and selling monkey".

During the training, our code saves models for later experiments. It does this every time the mean Q-values on our held-out states set updates the maximum. There is a tool which loads the model, trades on prices you've provided to it with the command-line option and draws the plots with the profit change over time. The tool is called `Chapter08/run_model.py` and can be used as shown below:

```
$ ./run_model.py -d data/YNDX_160101_161231.csv -m saves/ff-
YNDX16/mean_val-0.332.data -b 10 -n test
```

The options that the tool accepts are as follows:

- `-d`: This is the path to the quotes to use. On the preceding example, we apply the model to the data that it was trained on.
- `-m`: This is the path to the model file. By default, the training code saves it in `saves` dir.
- `-b`: This shows how many bars to pass to the model in the context. It has to match the count of bars used on training, which is 10 by default and can be changed in the training code.
- `-n`: This is the suffix to be prepended to the images produced.
- `--commission`: This allows you to redefine the broker's commission, which has a default of 0.1%.

At the end, the tool creates a chart of the total profit dynamics (in percentages). The following is the reward chart on Yandex 2016 quotes (used for training).

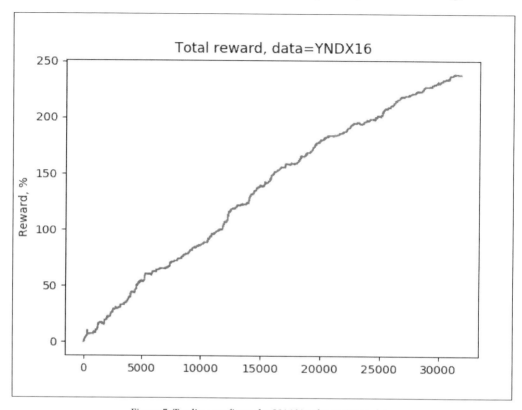

Figure 5: Trading profit on the 2016 Yandex training data

The result looks amazing: more than 200% profit in a year. However, let's look at what will happen with the 2015 data:

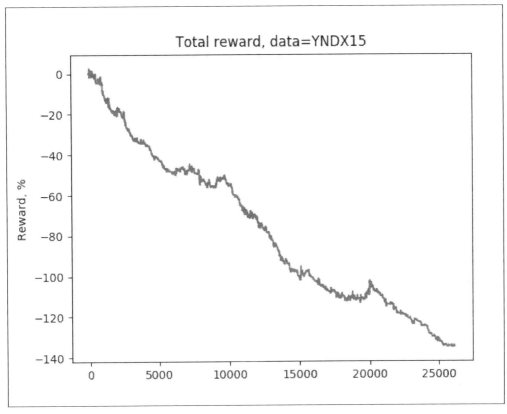

Figure 6: Trading profit on the 2015 Yandex validation data.

This result is much worse, as we've seen from the validation plots in TensorBoard. To check that our system is profitable with zero commission, we must rerun on the same data with the `--commission 0.0` option.

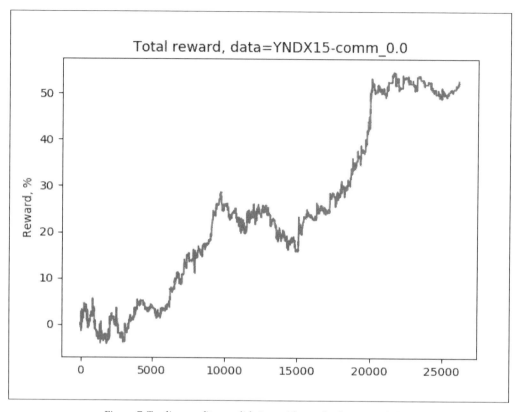

Figure 7: Trading profit on validation with zero broker commission

We have some bad days with drawdown, but the overall results are good: without commission our agent can be profitable. Of course, the commission is not the only issue. Our order simulation is very primitive and doesn't take into account real-life situations such as price spread and a slip in order execution.

The convolution model

The second model implemented in this example uses 1D convolution filters to extract features from the price data. This allows us to increase the number of bars in the context window that our agent sees on every step, without a significant increase in the network size. By default, the convolution model example uses 50 bars of context. The training code is in `Chapter08/train_model_conv.py`, and it accepts the same set of command-line parameters as the feed-forward version. On the following chart, there is a reward and count of steps for both the convolution (blue line) and feed-forward (brown line) models:

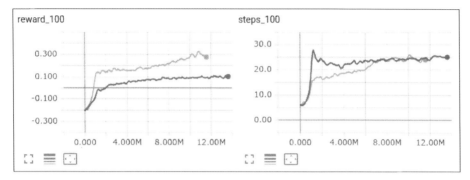

Figure 8: A comparison of reward dynamics between the convolution and feed-forward versions

As you can see, the convolution version trains much faster and has achieved better rewards using the same amount of episode steps. However, from the validation plots we can see the same situation as before: the agent is able to earn money on the training data, but it is much less profitable on the validation dataset:

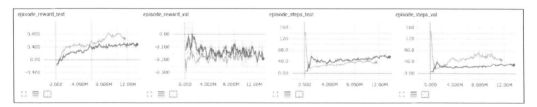

Figure 9: Validation data for both versions

Due to better fitting to the training data, the convolution agent behaves worse on the validation than the feed-forward agent. The reward charts created by `run_model.py` confirm that.

Below is the total reward on the training data. We can see that we have more profit than that in the feed-forward version (300% versus 250%).

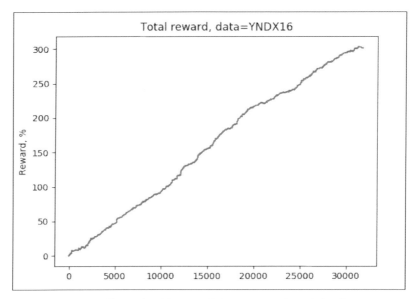

Figure 10: The profit of the convolution agent on the training data

However, the validation dataset, with commission 0.1%, shows consistent losses:

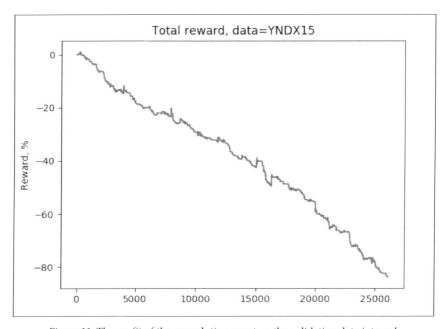

Figure 11: The profit of the convolution agent on the validation data interval

By disabling commission (as seen on the chart below) our convolution agent can earn some money, but less than that in the feed-forward version.

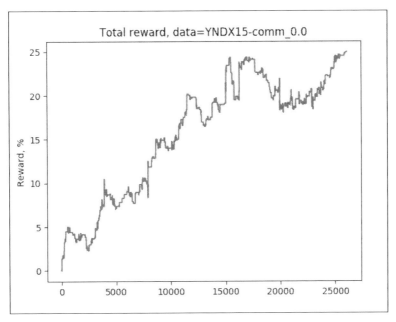

Figure 12: Profit on the validation data without broker commission

Things to try

As already mentioned, financial markets are large and complicated. The methods that we've tried are just the very beginning. Using RL to create a complete and profitable trading strategy is a large project, which can take several months of dedicated labor. However, there are things that we can try:

1. Our data representation is definitely not perfect. We don't take into account significant price levels (support and resistance), round price values, and others. Incorporating them into the observation could be a challenging problem.

2. Market prices are usually analyzed at different timeframes. Low-level data like one-minute bars are noisy (as they include lots of small price movements caused by individual trades), and it is like looking at the market using a microscope. At larger scales, such as one-hour or one-day bars, you can see large, long trends in data movement, which could be extremely important for price prediction.

3.   More training data is needed. One year of data for one stock is just 130k bars, which is almost nothing to capture all market situations. Ideally, a real-life agent should be trained on a much larger dataset, such as the prices for hundreds of stocks for the past 10 years?

4.   Experimenting with the network architecture. The convolution model has shown much faster convergence than the feed-forward model, but there are lots of things to optimize: the count of layers, kernel size, residual architecture, attention mechanism, and so on.

Summary

In this chapter, we saw a practical example of RL and implemented the trading agent and custom Gym environment. We tried two different architectures: a feed-forward network with price history on input and a 1D convolution network. Both architectures used the DQN method, with some extensions described in *Chapter 7, DQN Extensions*.

This is the last chapter in part two of the book. In part three, we'll talk about a different family of RL methods: policy gradients.

9
Policy Gradients – An Alternative

In this first chapter of part three of the book, we'll consider an alternative way to handle **Markov Decision Process (MDP)** problems, which forms a full family of methods called **Policy Gradients (PG)**. The chapter will present an overview of the methods, their motivation, and their strengths and weaknesses in comparison to the already familiar Q-learning. We will start with a simple PG method called REINFORCE and will try to apply it to our CartPole environment, comparing this with the **Deep Q-Networks (DQN)** approach.

Values and policy

Before we start talking about (PG), let's refresh our minds with the common characteristics of the methods covered in part two of this book. The central topic in Q-learning is the **value** of the state or action + state pair. Value is defined as the discounted total reward that we can gather from this state or by issuing this particular action from the state. If we know the value, our decision on every step becomes simple and obvious: we just act greedily in terms of value, and that guarantees us good total reward at the end of the episode. So, the values of states (in the case of the Value Iteration method) or state + action (in the case of Q-learning) stand between us and the best reward. To obtain these values, we've used the Bellman equation, which expresses the value on the current step via the values on the next step.

In *Chapter 1, What is Reinforcement Learning?*, we defined the entity that tells us what to do in every state as **policy**. As in Q-learning methods, when **values** are dictating to us how to behave, they are actually defining our policy. Formally, this could be written as $\pi(s) = \arg\max_a Q(s, a)$, which means that the result of our policy π at every state s is the action with the largest Q.

This policy-values connection was obvious, so we haven't put emphasis on the policy as a separate entity and have spent most of our time talking about values and the way to approximate them correctly. Now it's time to focus on this connection, as in part three of the book, we'll forget about values and turn our attention to the policy.

Why policy?

There are several reasons why policy might be an interesting topic to explore. First of all, **policy** is what we're looking for when we're solving a Reinforcement Learning (RL) problem. When the agent obtains the observation and needs to make a decision about what to do next, we need policy, not the value of the state or particular action. We do care about the total reward, but at every state, we may have little interest in the exact value of the state.

Imagine this situation: you're walking in the jungle and suddenly realize that there is a hungry tiger hiding in the bushes. You have several alternatives, such as run or hide or try to throw your backpack at him, but asking, "What's the exact value of the run action and is it larger than the value of the do nothing action?" is a bit silly. You don't care much about the value, because you need to make the decision on what to do fast and that's it. Our Q-learning approach tried to answer the policy question indirectly via approximating the values of the states and trying to choose the best alternative, but if we're not interested in values, why do extra work?

Another reason why policies may be more attractive than values is due to the environments with lots of actions or, in the extreme, with a **continuous** action space. To be able to decide on the best action to take having $Q(s, a)$, we need to solve a small optimization problem finding a, which maximizes $Q(s, a)$. In the case of an Atari game with several discrete actions, this wasn't a problem: we just approximated values of all actions and took the action with the largest Q. If our action is not a small discrete set, but has a scalar value attached to it, such as the steering wheel angle or the speed we want to run from the tiger, this optimization problem becomes hard, as Q is usually represented by a highly nonlinear neural network (NN), so finding the argument which maximizes the function's values can be tricky. In such cases, it's much more feasible to avoid values and work with the policy directly.

An extra vote in favor of policy learning is an environment with **stochasticity**. As we have seen in *Chapter 7, DQN Extensions*, in categorical DQN, our agent can benefit a lot from working with the distribution of Q-values, instead of expected mean values, as our network can more precisely capture underlying probability distribution. As we'll see in the next section, policy is naturally represented as the probability of actions, which is a step in the same direction as the categorical DQN method.

Policy representation

Now that we know the benefits of policy, we're ready to give it a try. So how do we represent the policy? In the case of Q-values, they were parametrized by the NN that returns values of actions as scalars. If we want our network to parametrize the actions, we have several options. The first and the simplest way could be just returning the identifier of the action (in the case of a discrete set of actions). However, this is not the best way to deal with a discrete set. A much more common solution, which is heavily used in classification tasks, is to return the probability distribution of our actions. In other words, for N mutually exclusive actions, we return N numbers representing the probability to take each action in the given state (which we pass as an input to the network). This representation is shown in the diagram below.

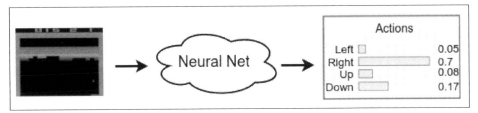

Figure 1: Policy approximation with an NN for a discrete set of actions

Such representation of actions as probability has the additional advantage of **smooth representation**: if we change our network weights a bit, the output of the network will also change. In the case of discrete numbers output, even a small adjustment of the weights can lead to a jump to the different action. However, if our output is probability distribution, a small change of weights will usually lead to a small change in output distribution, such as slightly increasing the probability of one action versus the others. This is a very nice property to have, as gradient optimization methods are all about tweaking the parameters of a model a bit to improve the results. In math notation, policy is usually represented as $\pi(s)$, so we'll use this notation as well.

Policy gradients

We defined our policy representation, but what we haven't seen so far is how we're going to change our network's parameters to improve the policy. If you remember from *Chapter 4, The Cross-Entropy Method*, in the cross-entropy method, we solved a very similar problem: our network took observations as inputs and returned the probability distribution of the actions. In fact, cross-entropy is a younger brother of the methods we'll discuss in this part of the book. To begin, we'll get acquainted with the method called REINFORCE, which has only minor differences from cross-entropy, but first we need to look at some mathematical notation that we'll use in this and the following chapters.

We define PG as $\mathcal{L} = -Q(s,a)\log \pi(a|s)$. Of course, there is a strong proof of this, but it's not that important. What interests us much more is the semantic of this expression.

PG defines the direction in which we need to change our network's parameters to improve the policy in terms of the accumulated total reward. The scale of the gradient is proportional to the value of the action taken, which is *Q(s, a)* in the formula above and the gradient itself is equal to the gradient of log-probability of the action taken. Intuitively, this means that we're trying to increase the probability of actions that have given us good total reward and decrease the probability of actions with bad final outcomes. Expectation E in the formula just means that we take several steps that we've made in the environment and average the gradient.

From a practical point of view, PG methods could be implemented as performing optimization of this loss function: $\mathcal{L} = -Q(s,a)\log \pi(a|s)$. The minus sign is important, as loss function is **minimized** during the **Stochastic Gradient Descent (SGD)**, but we want to **maximize** our policy gradient. You'll see code examples of PG methods later in this and the following chapters.

The REINFORCE method

The formula of PG that we've just seen is used by most of the policy-based methods, but the details can vary. One very important point is how exactly gradient scales *Q(s, a)* are calculated. In the cross-entropy method from *Chapter 4, The Cross-Entropy Method*, we played several episodes, calculated the total reward for each of them, and trained on transitions from episodes with a better-than-average reward. This training procedure is the PG method with *Q(s, a) = 1* for actions from *good* episodes (with large total reward) and *Q(s, a) = 0* for actions from worse episodes.

The cross-entropy method worked even with those simple assumptions, but the obvious improvement will be to use $Q(s, a)$ for training instead of just 0 and 1. So why should it help? The answer is a more fine-grained separation of episodes. For example, transitions of the episode with the total reward = 10 should contribute to the gradient more than transitions from the episode with the reward = 1. The second reason to use $Q(s, a)$ instead of just 0 or 1 constants is to increase probabilities of good actions in the beginning of the episode and decrease the actions closer to the end of episode. That's exactly the idea of the method called REINFORCE. Its steps are as follows:

1. Initialize the network with random weights

2. Play N full episodes, saving their (s, a, r, s') transitions

3. For every step t of every episode k, calculate the discounted total reward for subsequent steps $Q_{k,t} = \sum_{i=0} \gamma^i r_i$

4. Calculate the loss function for all transitions $\mathcal{L} = -\sum_{k,t} Q_{k,t} \log(\pi(s_{k,t}, a_{k,t}))$

5. Perform SGD update of weights minimizing the loss

6. Repeat from step 2 until converged

The algorithm above is different from Q-learning in several important aspects:

- No explicit exploration is needed. In Q-learning, we used an epsilon-greedy strategy to explore the environment and prevent our agent from getting stuck with non-optimal policy. Now, with probabilities returned by the network, the exploration is performed automatically. In the beginning, the network is initialized with random weights and the network returns uniform probability distribution. This distribution corresponds to random agent behavior.

- No replay buffer is used. PG methods belong to the on-policy methods class, which means that we can't train on data obtained from the old policy. This is both good and bad. The good part is that such methods usually converge faster. The bad side is they usually require much more interaction with the environment than off-policy methods such as DQN.

- No target network is needed. Here we use Q-values, but they're obtained from our experience in the environment. In DQN, we used the target network to break the correlation in Q-values approximation, but we're not approximating it anymore. Later, we'll see that the target network trick still can be useful in PG methods.

The CartPole example

To see the method in action, let's check the implementation of the REINFORCE method on the familiar CartPole environment. The full code of the example is in Chapter09/02_cartpole_reinforce.py.

```
GAMMA = 0.99
LEARNING_RATE = 0.01
EPISODES_TO_TRAIN = 4
```

In the beginning, we define hyperparameters (imports are omitted). The EPISODES_TO_TRAIN value specifies how many complete episodes we'll use for training.

```
class PGN(nn.Module):
    def __init__(self, input_size, n_actions):
        super(PGN, self).__init__()

        self.net = nn.Sequential(
            nn.Linear(input_size, 128),
            nn.ReLU(),
            nn.Linear(128, n_actions)
        )

    def forward(self, x):
        return self.net(x)
```

The network should also be familiar to you. Note that despite the fact our network returns probabilities, we're not applying softmax nonlinearity to the output. The reason behind this is that we'll use the PyTorch log_softmax function to calculate the logarithm of the softmax output at once. This way of calculation is much more numerically stable, but we need to remember that output from the network is not probability, but raw scores (usually called logits).

```
def calc_qvals(rewards):
    res = []
    sum_r = 0.0
    for r in reversed(rewards):
        sum_r *= GAMMA
        sum_r += r
        res.append(sum_r)
    return list(reversed(res))
```

This function is a bit tricky. It accepts a list of rewards for the whole episode and needs to calculate the discounted total reward for every step. To do this efficiently, we calculate the reward from the end of the local reward list. Indeed, the last step of the episode will have the total reward equal to its local reward. The step before the last will have the total reward of $r_{t-1} + \gamma r_t$ (if t is an index of the last step). Our `sum_r` variable contains the total reward for the previous steps, so to get the total reward for the previous step, we need to multiply `sum_r` by gamma and sum the local reward.

```
if __name__ == "__main__":
    env = gym.make("CartPole-v0")
    writer = SummaryWriter(comment="-cartpole-reinforce")

    net = PGN(env.observation_space.shape[0], env.action_space.n)
    print(net)

    agent = ptan.agent.PolicyAgent(net, preprocessor=ptan.agent.
float32_preprocessor,
                                   apply_softmax=True)
    exp_source = ptan.experience.ExperienceSourceFirstLast
(env, agent, gamma=GAMMA)

    optimizer = optim.Adam(net.parameters(), lr=LEARNING_RATE)
```

The preparation steps before the training loop also should be familiar to you. The only new element is the agent class from the `ptan` library. Here we are using `ptan.agent.PolicyAgent`, which needs to make a decision about actions for every observation. As our network now returns policy in the form of probabilities of the actions? to select the action to take, we need to obtain the probabilities from the network and then perform random sampling from this probability distribution.

When we worked with DQN, the output of the network was Q-values, so if some action had the value of 0.4 and another action 0.5, the second action was preferred 100% of the time. In the case of probability distribution, if the first action has a probability of 0.4 and the second 0.5, our agent should take the first action with 40% chance and the second with 50% chance. Of course, our network can decide to take the second action 100% of the time and in this case, it returns probability 0 for the first action and probability 1 for the second action.

This difference is important to understand, but the change in the implementation is not large. Our `PolicyAgent` internally calls the NumPy `random.choice` function with probabilities from the network. The argument `apply_softmax` argument instructs it to convert the network output to probabilities by calling softmax first. The third argument preprocessor is a way to get around the fact that the CartPole environment in Gym returns observation as `float64` instead of `float32` required by PyTorch.

```
total_rewards = []
done_episodes = 0

batch_episodes = 0
cur_rewards = []
batch_states, batch_actions, batch_qvals = [], [], []
```

Before we can start the training loop, we need several variables. The first group of these is used for reporting and contains the total rewards for the episodes and the count of completed episodes. The second group is used to gather the training data. The `cur_rewards list` contains local rewards for the currently-played episode. As this episode reaches the end, we calculate the discounted total rewards from local rewards using the `calc_qvals` function and append them to the `batch_qvals` list. The `batch_states` and `batch_actions lists` contain states and actions that we've seen from the last training.

```
for step_idx, exp in enumerate(exp_source):
    batch_states.append(exp.state)
    batch_actions.append(int(exp.action))
    cur_rewards.append(exp.reward)

    if exp.last_state is None:
        batch_qvals.extend(calc_qvals(cur_rewards))
        cur_rewards.clear()
        batch_episodes += 1
```

Above is the beginning of the training loop. Every experience that we get from the experience source contains state, action, local reward, and the next state. If the end of the episode has been reached, the next state will be `None`. For non-terminal experience entries, we just save state, action, and local reward in our lists. At the end of the episode, we convert the local rewards into Q-values and increment the episodes counter.

```
new_rewards = exp_source.pop_total_rewards()
if new_rewards:
    done_episodes += 1
    reward = new_rewards[0]
    total_rewards.append(reward)
```

```
        mean_rewards = float(np.mean(total_rewards[-100:]))
        print("%d: reward: %6.2f, mean_100: %6.2f, episodes: %d" % (
            step_idx, reward, mean_rewards, done_episodes))
        writer.add_scalar("reward", reward, step_idx)
        writer.add_scalar("reward_100", mean_rewards,
step_idx)
        writer.add_scalar("episodes", done_episodes, step_idx)
        if mean_rewards > 195:
            print("Solved in %d steps and %d episodes!" %
(step_idx, done_episodes))
            break
```

This part of the training loop is performed at the end of the episode and is responsible for the reporting of current progress and writing metrics to the TensorBoard.

```
    if batch_episodes < EPISODES_TO_TRAIN:
        continue

    optimizer.zero_grad()
    states_v = torch.FloatTensor(batch_states)
    batch_actions_t = torch.LongTensor(batch_actions)
    batch_qvals_v = torch.FloatTensor(batch_qvals)
```

When enough episodes have passed since the last training step, we perform optimization on the gathered examples. As a first step, we need to convert states, actions, and Q-values into appropriate PyTorch form.

```
    logits_v = net(states_v)
    log_prob_v = F.log_softmax(logits_v, dim=1)
    log_prob_actions_v = batch_qvals_v *
  log_prob_v[range(len(batch_states)), batch_actions_t]
    loss_v = -log_prob_actions_v.mean()
```

Then we calculate the loss from the steps. To do this, we ask our network to calculate states into logits and calculate logarithm + softmax of them. On the third line, we select log probabilities from the actions taken and scale them with Q-values. On the last line, we average those scaled values and do negation to obtain the loss to minimize. Once again, this minus sign is very important, as our PG needs to be maximized to improve the policy. As the optimizer in PyTorch does minimization in respect to the loss function, we need to negate the PG.

```
    loss_v.backward()
    optimizer.step()
```

```
        batch_episodes = 0
        batch_states.clear()
        batch_actions.clear()
        batch_qvals.clear()

   writer.close()
```

The rest of the code is clear: we perform backpropagation to gather gradients in our variables and ask the optimizer to perform a SGD update. At the end of the training loop, we reset the episodes counter and clear our lists for fresh data to gather.

Results

For reference, I've implemented DQN on the CartPole environment with almost the same hyperparameters as our REINFORCE example above. It's in Chapter09/01_cartpole_dqn.py. Both examples don't require any command-line arguments and should converge in less than a minute.

```
rl_book_samples/chapter09$ ./02_cartpole_reinforce.py
PGN (
   (net): Sequential (
      (0): Linear (4 -> 128)
      (1): ReLU ()
      (2): Linear (128 -> 2)
   )
)
63: reward:  62.00, mean_100:  62.00, episodes: 1
83: reward:  19.00, mean_100:  40.50, episodes: 2
99: reward:  15.00, mean_100:  32.00, episodes: 3
125: reward:   25.00, mean_100:  30.25, episodes: 4
154: reward:   28.00, mean_100:  29.80, episodes: 5
...
27676: reward: 200.00, mean_100: 193.58, episodes: 224
27877: reward: 200.00, mean_100: 194.07, episodes: 225
28078: reward: 200.00, mean_100: 194.07, episodes: 226
28279: reward: 200.00, mean_100: 194.53, episodes: 227
28480: reward: 200.00, mean_100: 195.09, episodes: 228
Solved in 28480 steps and 228 episodes!
```

The convergence dynamics for both DQN and REINFORCE are shown below.

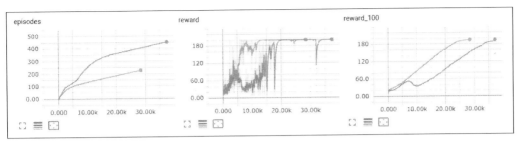

Figure 2: Convergence of DQN (orange) and REINFORCE (blue line)

As you can see, REINFORCE converges faster and requires less training steps and episodes to solve the CartPole environment. If you remember from *Chapter 4, The Cross-Entropy Method*, the cross-entropy method required about 40 batches of 16 episodes each to solve the CartPole environment, which is 640 episodes in total. The REINFORCE method is able to do the same in less than 300 episodes, which is a nice improvement.

Policy-based versus value-based methods

Let's now step back from the code we've just seen and talk about the differences that both the families of methods have:

- Policy methods are directly optimizing what we care about: our behavior. The value methods such as DQN are doing the same indirectly, learning the value first and providing to us policy based on this value.

- Policy methods are on-policy and require fresh samples from the environment. The value methods can benefit from old data, obtained from the old policy, human demonstration, and other sources.

- Policy methods are usually less sample-efficient, which means they require more interaction with the environment. The value methods can benefit from the large replay buffers. However, sample efficiency doesn't mean that value methods are more computationally efficient and very often it's the opposite. In the above example, during the training, we need to access our NN only once, to get the probabilities of actions. In DQN, we need to process two batch of states: one for the current state and another for the next state in the Bellman update.

As you can see, there is no strong preference of one family versus another. In some situations, policy methods will be the more natural choice, like in continuous control problems or cases when access to the environment is cheap and fast. However, there are lots of situations when value methods will shine, for example, the recent state-of-the-art results on Atari games achieved by DQN variants. Ideally, you should be familiar with both families equally and understand the strong and weak sides of both camps. In the next section, we'll talk about, REINFORCE method's limitations, ways to improve it, and how to apply the PG method to our favorite Pong game.

REINFORCE issues

In the previous section, we discussed the REINFORCE method, which is a natural extension of cross-entropy from *Chapter 4, The Cross-Entropy Method*. Unfortunately, both REINFORCE and cross-entropy still suffer from several problems, which make both of them limited to simple environments.

Full episodes are required

First of all, we still need to wait for the full episode to complete before we can start training. Even worse, both REINFORCE and cross-entropy behave better with more episodes used for training (just from the fact that more episodes mean more training data, which means more accurate PG). This situation is fine for short episodes in the CartPole, when in the beginning, we can barely handle the bar for more than 10 steps, but in Pong, it is completely different: every episode can lasts hundreds or even thousands of frames. It's equally bad from the training perspective, as our training batch becomes very large and from sample efficiency, when we need to communicate with the environment a lot just to perform a single training step.

The origin of the complete episodes requirement is to get as accurate a Q estimation as possible. When we talked about DQN, we saw that in practice, it's fine to replace the exact value for a discounted reward with our estimation using the one-step Bellman equation $Q(s, a) = r_a + \gamma V(s')$. To estimate $V(s)$, we've used our own Q-estimation, but in the case of PG, we don't have $V(s)$ or $Q(s, a)$ anymore.
$Q(s, a) = r_a + \gamma V(s')$

To overcome this, two approaches exist. On the one hand, we can ask our network to estimate $V(s)$ and use this estimation to obtain Q. This approach will be discussed in the next chapter and is called *Actor-Critic method*, which is the most popular method from the PG family.

On the other hand, we can do the Bellman equation unrolling N steps ahead, which will effectively exploit the fact that value contribution is decreasing when gamma is less than 1. Indeed, with gamma=0.9, value coefficient at the tenth step will be 0.9^{10}=0.35. At step 50, this coefficient becomes 0.9^{50}=0.00515, which is a really small contribution to the total reward. In the case of gamma=0.99, the required count of steps becomes larger, but we still can do this.

High gradients variance

In the PG formula $\nabla J \approx \mathbb{E}[Q(s,a)\nabla \log \pi(a|s)]$, we have a gradient proportional to the discounted reward from the given state. However, the range of this reward is heavily environment-dependent. For example, in the CartPole environment we're getting the reward of 1 for every timestamp we're holding the pole vertically. If we can do this for five steps, we'll get total (undiscounted) reward of 5. If our agent is smart and can hold the pole for, say, 100 steps, the total reward will be 100. The difference in value between those two scenarios is 20 times, which means that the scale between gradients of unsuccessful samples will be 20 times lower than that for more successful ones. Such a large difference can seriously affect our training dynamics, as one lucky episode will dominate in the final gradient.

In mathematical terms, our PGs have high variance and we need to do something about this in complex environments, otherwise, the training process can become unstable. The usual approach to handle this is subtracting a value called baseline from the Q. The possible choices of the baseline are as follows:

1. Some constant value, which normally is the mean of the discounted rewards
2. The moving average of the discounted rewards
3. Value of the state *V(s)*

Exploration

Even with the policy represented as probability distribution, there is a high chance that the agent will converge to some locally-optimal policy and stop exploring the environment. In DQN, we solved this using epsilon-greedy action selection: with probability epsilon, the agent took some random action instead of the action dictated by the current policy. We can use the same approach, of course, but PG allows us to follow a better path, called the entropy bonus.

In the information theory, the entropy is a measure of uncertainty in some system. Being applied to agent policy, entropy shows how much the agent is uncertain about which action to take. In math notation, entropy of the policy is defined as: $H(\pi) = -\sum \pi(a|s) \log \pi(a|s)$. The value of entropy is always greater than zero and has a single maximum when the policy is uniform. In other words, all actions have the same probability. Entropy becomes minimal when our policy has 1 for some action and 0 for all others, which means that the agent is absolutely sure what to do. To prevent our agent from being stuck in the local minimum, we are subtracting the entropy from the loss function, punishing the agent for being too certain about the action to take.

Correlation between samples

As we discussed in *Chapter 6, Deep Q-Networks*, training samples in one single episode are usually heavily correlated, which is bad for SGD training. In the case of DQN, we solved this issue by having a large replay buffer with 100k-1M observations that we sampled our training batch from. This solution is not applicable to the PG family anymore, due to the fact that those methods belong to the on-policy class. The implication is simple: using old samples generated by the old policy, we'll get PG for that old policy, not for our current one.

The obvious, but, unfortunately wrong solution would be to reduce the replay buffer size. It might work in some simple cases, but in general, we need fresh training data generated by our current policy. To solve this, parallel environments are normally used. The idea is simple: instead of communicating with one environment, we use several and use their transitions as training data.

PG on CartPole

Nowadays, almost nobody uses the vanilla PG method, as the much more stable Actor-Critic method exists, which will be the topic of the two following chapters. However, I still want to show the PG implementation, as it establishes very important concepts and metrics to check for the PG method's performance. So, we will start with a much simpler environment of CartPole, and in the next section, will check its performance on our favorite Pong environment. The complete code for the following example is available in Chapter09/04_cartpole_pg.py.

```
GAMMA = 0.99
LEARNING_RATE = 0.001
ENTROPY_BETA = 0.01
BATCH_SIZE = 8
REWARD_STEPS = 10
```

Besides already familiar hyperparameters, we have two new ones. Entropy beta value is the scale of the entropy bonus. The REWARD_STEPS value specifies how many steps ahead the Bellman equation is unrolled to estimate the discounted total reward of every transition.

```
class PGN(nn.Module):
    def __init__(self, input_size, n_actions):
        super(PGN, self).__init__()

        self.net = nn.Sequential(
            nn.Linear(input_size, 128),
            nn.ReLU(),
            nn.Linear(128, n_actions)
        )

    def forward(self, x):
        return self.net(x)
```

The network architecture is exactly the same as in the previous examples for CartPole: a two-layer network with 128 neurons in the hidden layer. The preparation code is also the same as before, except the experience source is asked to unroll the Bellman equation for 10 steps:

```
    exp_source = ptan.experience.ExperienceSourceFirstLast(env, agent,
gamma=GAMMA, steps_count=REWARD_STEPS)
```

In the training loop, we maintain the sum of the discounted reward for every transition and use it to calculate the baseline for policy scale.

```
    for step_idx, exp in enumerate(exp_source):
        reward_sum += exp.reward
        baseline = reward_sum / (step_idx + 1)
        writer.add_scalar("baseline", baseline, step_idx)
        batch_states.append(exp.state)
        batch_actions.append(int(exp.action))
        batch_scales.append(exp.reward - baseline)
```

In the loss calculation, we use the same code as before to calculate the policy loss (which is the negated PG).

```
        optimizer.zero_grad()
        logits_v = net(states_v)
        log_prob_v = F.log_softmax(logits_v, dim=1)
        log_prob_actions_v = batch_scale_v *
    log_prob_v[range(BATCH_SIZE), batch_actions_t]
        loss_policy_v = -log_prob_actions_v.mean()
```

Then we add the entropy bonus to the loss by calculating the entropy of the batch and subtracting it from the loss. As entropy has a maximum for uniform probability distribution and we want to push the training towards this maximum, we need to subtract from the loss.

```
prob_v = F.softmax(logits_v, dim=1)
entropy_v = -(prob_v * log_prob_v).sum(dim=1).mean()
entropy_loss_v = -ENTROPY_BETA * entropy_v
loss_v = loss_policy_v + entropy_loss_v

loss_v.backward()
optimizer.step()
```

Then, we calculate the Kullback-Leibler (KL)-divergence between the new and the old policy. KL-divergence is an information theory measurement of how one probability distribution diverges from another expected probability distribution. In our example, it is being used to compare the policy returned by the model before and after the optimization step. High spikes in KL are usually a bad sign, showing that our policy was pushed too far from the previous policy, which is a bad idea most of the time (as our NN is a very nonlinear function in a high-dimension space, so large changes in the model weight could have a very strong influence on policy).

```
new_logits_v = net(states_v)
new_prob_v = F.softmax(new_logits_v, dim=1)
kl_div_v = -((new_prob_v / prob_v).log() *
    prob_v).sum(dim=1).mean()
writer.add_scalar("kl", kl_div_v.item(), step_idx)
```

Finally, we calculate the statistics about the gradients on this training step. It's usually good practice to show the graph of maximum and L2-norm of gradients to get an idea about the training dynamics.

```
grad_max = 0.0
grad_means = 0.0
grad_count = 0
for p in net.parameters():
    grad_max = max(grad_max, p.grad.abs().max().item())
    grad_means += (p.grad ** 2).mean().sqrt().item()
    grad_count += 1
```

At the end of the training loop, we dump all values we'd like to monitor, to the TensorBoard.

```
        writer.add_scalar("baseline", baseline, step_idx)
        writer.add_scalar("entropy", entropy_v.item(), step_idx)
        writer.add_scalar("batch_scales", np.mean(batch_scales),
step_idx)
        writer.add_scalar("loss_entropy", entropy_loss_v.item(),
step_idx)
        writer.add_scalar("loss_policy", loss_policy_v.item(),
step_idx)
        writer.add_scalar("loss_total", loss_v.item(), step_idx)
        writer.add_scalar("grad_l2", grad_means / grad_count,
step_idx)
        writer.add_scalar("grad_max", grad_max, step_idx)

        batch_states.clear()
        batch_actions.clear()
        batch_scales.clear()
```

Results

In this example, we plot lots of charts in TensorBoard. Let's start with the familiar one: reward. As you can see below, the dynamics and performance are not very different from the REINFORCE method.

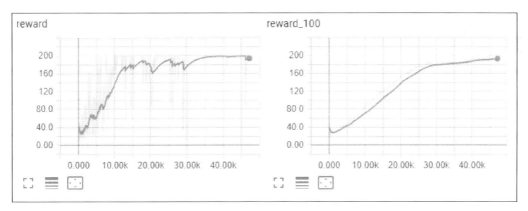

Figure 3: Reward dynamics for the PG method

The next two charts are related to our baseline and scales of PG. We expect the baseline to converge to $1 + 0.99 + 0.99^2 + \ldots + 0.99^9$, which is approximately 9.56. Scales of PG should oscillate around zero. That's exactly what we see in the following graph.

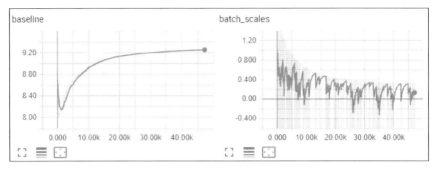

Figure 4: Baselines dynamics

The entropy is decreasing over time from 0.69 to 0.52. The starting value corresponds to the maximum entropy with two actions (which is, $-2 \cdot \frac{1}{2}\log\left(\frac{1}{2}\right) \approx 0.69$). The fact that the entropy is decreasing during the training shows that our policy is moving from the uniform distribution to more deterministic actions.

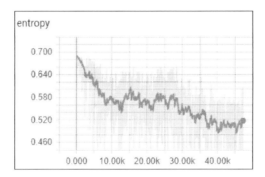

Figure 5: Entropy dynamics during the training

The next group of plots is related to loss, which includes policy loss, entropy loss, and their sum. The entropy loss is scaled and a mirrored version of the entropy chart above. The policy loss shows the mean scale and direction of the PG computed on batch. Here we should check the relative size of both, to prevent entropy loss dominating too much.

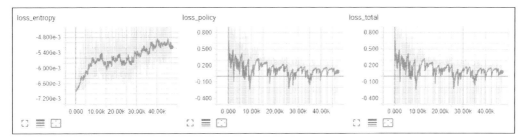

Figure 6: Loss dynamics

The final set of charts is the gradient's max, L2 values, and KL. Our gradients look healthy during the whole training: they are not too large and not too small, without huge spikes. The KL charts also look normal, as there are some spikes, but they don't exceed 1e-3.

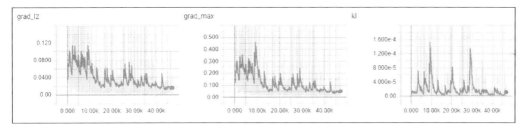

Figure 7: Gradients and KL divergence

PG on Pong

As covered in the previous section, the vanilla PG method works well on a simple CartPole environment, but surprisingly badly on more complicated environments. Even in the relatively simple Atari game Pong, our DQN was able to completely solve it in 1M frames and showed positive reward dynamics in just 100k frames, whereas PG failed to converge. Due to the instability of PG training, it became very hard to find good hyperparameters, which is still very sensitive to initialization.

This doesn't mean that the PGs are bad, because, as we'll see in the next chapter, just one tweak of the network architecture to get the better baseline in the gradients will turn PG into one of the best methods (Asynchronous Advantage Actor-Critic (A3C) method). Of course, there is a good chance that my hyperparameters are completely wrong or the code has some hidden bugs or whatever. Regardless, unsuccessful results still have value, at least as a demonstration of bad convergence dynamics. The complete code of the example is in Chapter09/05_pong_pg.py.

The three main differences from the previous example's code are as follows:

- The baseline is estimated with a moving average for 1M past transitions, instead of all examples
- Several concurrent environments are used
- Gradients are clipped to improve training stability

To make moving average calculations faster, a deque-backed buffer was created.

```
class MeanBuffer:
    def __init__(self, capacity):
        self.capacity = capacity
        self.deque = collections.deque(maxlen=capacity)
        self.sum = 0.0

    def add(self, val):
        if len(self.deque) == self.capacity:
            self.sum -= self.deque[0]
        self.deque.append(val)
        self.sum += val

    def mean(self):
        if not self.deque:
            return 0.0
        return self.sum / len(self.deque)
```

The second difference in this example is working with multiple environments and this functionality is supported by the ptan library. The only action we have to take is to pass the array of Env objects to the ExperienceSource class. All the rest is done automatically. In the case of several environments, the experience source asks them for transitions in round-robin, providing us with less-correlated training samples. The last difference from the CartPole example is gradient clipping, which is performed using the PyTorch clip_grad_norm function from the torch.nn.utils package.

The hyperparameters for the best variant are the following:

```
GAMMA = 0.99
LEARNING_RATE = 0.0001
ENTROPY_BETA = 0.01
BATCH_SIZE = 128

REWARD_STEPS = 10
BASELINE_STEPS = 1000000
```

```
GRAD_L2_CLIP = 0.1

ENV_COUNT = 32
```

Results

Okay, let's look at one of the best runs of the example. The following are the reward charts and you can see that during the training, rewards were almost constant for a while, then some growth started, which was interrupted by flat regions of minimal reward -21.

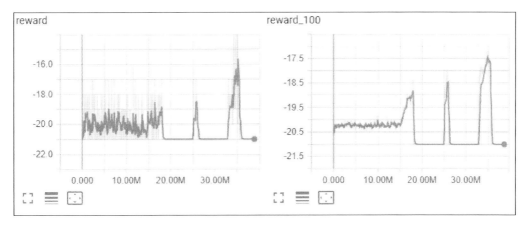

Figure 8: Reward plots for Pong

On the entropy plot, we can see that those flat regions correspond to periods when entropy was zero, which means that our agent had 100% certainty in its actions. During this time interval, gradients were zero too, so it's quite surprising that our training process was able to recover from those flat regions.

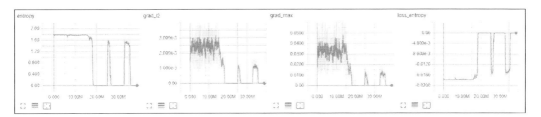

Figure 9: Another set of plots for Pong, using the PG method

The chart with baseline mostly follows the reward and has the same patterns.

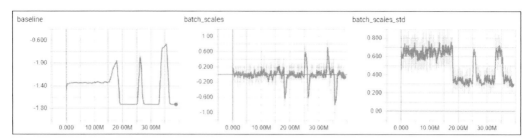

Figure 10: Baseline, scales, and standard deviation of scales

The KL plot has large spikes roughly at the moments to and from zero-entropy transitions, which shows that the policy suffered from heavy jumps in returning distributions.

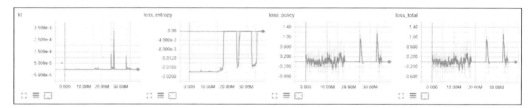

Figure 11: KL divergence and losses during training

Summary

In this chapter, we saw an alternative way of solving RL problems: PG, which is different in many ways from the familiar DQN method. We explored the basic method called REINFORCE, which is a generalization of our first method in RL-domain cross entropy. This method is simple, but, being applied to the Pong environment, didn't show good results.

In the next chapter, we'll consider ways to improve the stability of PG by combining both families of value-based and policy-based methods.

10

The Actor-Critic Method

In *Chapter 9, Policy Gradients – An Alternative*, we started to investigate an alternative to the familiar value-based methods family, called policy-based. In particular, we focused on the method called REINFORCE and its modification that uses a discounted reward to obtain the gradient of the policy (which gives us the direction to improve the policy). Both methods worked well for a small CartPole problem, but for a more complicated Pong environment, the convergence dynamic was painfully slow.

In this chapter, we'll discuss one more extension to the vanilla **Policy Gradient (PG)** method, which magically improves the stability and convergence speed of the new method. Despite the modification being only minor, the new method has its own name, **Actor-Critic**, and it's one of the most powerful methods in deep **Reinforcement Learning (RL)**.

Variance reduction

In the previous chapter, we briefly mentioned that one of the ways to improve the stability of PG methods is to reduce the variance of the gradient. Now let's try to understand why this is important and what it means to reduce the variance. In statistics, variance is the expected square deviation of a random variable from the expected value of this variable.

$$\mathrm{Var}[x] = \mathbb{E}[(x - \mathbb{E}[x])^2]$$

Variance shows us how far values are dispersed from the mean. When variance is high, the random variable can take values deviated widely from the mean. On the following plot, there is a normal (Gaussian) distribution with the same value of mean $\mu = 10$, but with different values for the variance.

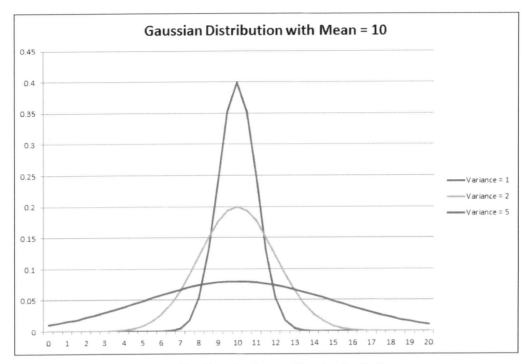

Figure 1: The effect of variance on Gaussian distribution

Now let's return to PG. It has already been stated in the previous chapter, that the method's idea is to increase the probability of good actions and decrease the chance of bad ones. In math notation, our PG was written as $\nabla J \approx \mathbb{E}[Q(s, a) \nabla \log \pi(a|s)]$. The scaling factor $Q(s, a)$ specifies how much we want to increase or decrease the probability of the action taken in the particular state. In the REINFORCE method, we used the discounted total reward as the scaling of the gradient. As an attempt to increase REINFORCE stability, we subtracted the mean reward from the gradient scale.

To understand why this helped, let's consider the very simple scenario of an optimization step on which we have three actions with different total discounted rewards: Q_1, Q_2, and Q_3. Now let's consider the policy gradient with regard to the relative values of those Qs.

As the first example, let both Q_1 and Q_2 be equal to some small positive number and Q_3 be a large negative number. So, actions at the first and second steps led to some small reward, but the third step was not very successful. The resulted **combined** gradient for all three steps will try to push our policy far from the action at step three and slightly toward the actions taken at step one and two, which is a totally reasonable thing to do.

Now let's imagine that our reward is always positive, only the value is different. This corresponds to adding some constant to all Q_1, Q_2, and Q_3. In this case, Q_1 and Q_2 become large positive numbers and Q_3 will have a small positive value. However, our policy update will become different! Next, we'll try hard to push our policy toward actions at the first and second step, and slightly push it towards an action at step three. So, strictly speaking, we're no longer trying to avoid the action taken for step three, despite the fact that the relative rewards are the same.

This dependency of our policy update on the constant added to the reward can slow down our training significantly, as we may require many more samples to *average out* the effect of such a shift in the PG. Even worse, as our total discounted reward changes over time, with the agent learning how to act better and better, our PG variance could also change. For example, in the Atari Pong environment, the average reward in the beginning is -21...-20, so all the actions look almost equally bad.

To overcome this, in the previous chapter, we subtracted the mean total reward from the Q-value and called this mean **baseline**. This trick normalized our PGs, as in the case of the average reward being -21, getting a reward of -20 looks like a win to the agent and it pushes its policy towards the taken actions.

CartPole variance

To check this theoretical conclusion in practice, let's plot the variance of the PG during the training for both the baseline version and the version without the baseline. The complete example is in `Chapter10/01_cartpole_pg.py` and most of the code is the same as in *Chapter 9, Policy Gradients – An Alternative*. Differences in this version are the following:

- It now accepts the command-line option `--baseline`, which enables the mean subtraction from the reward. By default, no baseline is used.

- On every training loop, we gather the gradients from the policy loss and use this data to calculate the variance.

To gather only the gradients from the policy loss and exclude the gradients from the entropy bonus added for exploration, we need to calculate the gradients in two stages. Luckily, PyTorch allows this to be done easily. Below, only the relevant part of the training loop is included to illustrate the idea.

```
optimizer.zero_grad()
logits_v = net(states_v)
log_prob_v = F.log_softmax(logits_v, dim=1)
log_prob_actions_v = batch_scale_v *
    log_prob_v[range(BATCH_SIZE), batch_actions_t]
loss_policy_v = -log_prob_actions_v.mean()
```

We calculate the policy loss as before, by calculating the log from the probabilities of taken actions and multiply it by policy scales (which are the total discounted reward, if we're not using the baseline or the total reward minus the baseline).

```
loss_policy_v.backward(retain_graph=True)
```

On the next step, we ask PyTorch to backpropagate the policy loss, calculating the gradients and keeping them in our model's buffers. As we've previously performed `optimizer.zero_grad()`, those buffers will contain only the gradients from the policy loss. One tricky thing here is the `retain_graph=True` option when we called `backward()`. It instructs PyTorch to keep the graph structure of the variables. Normally, this is destroyed by the `backward()` call, but in our case, this is not what we want. In general, retaining the graph could be useful when we need to backpropagate loss multiple times before the call to the optimizer. It's not a very common situation, but sometimes becomes handy.

```
grads = np.concatenate([p.grad.data.numpy().flatten()
                        for p in net.parameters()
                        if p.grad is not None])
```

Then, we iterate all parameters from our model (every parameter of our model is a tensor with gradients) and extract their grad field in a flattened NumPy array. This gives us one long array with all gradients from our model's variables. However, our parameter update should take into account not only policy gradient but also the gradient provided by our entropy bonus. To achieve this, we calculate the entropy loss and call `backward()` again. To be able to do this the second time, we need to pass `retain_graph=True`.

On the second `backward()` call, PyTorch will backpropagate our entropy loss and add the gradients to the internal gradients' buffers. So, what we now need to do is just ask our optimizer to perform the optimization step using those combined gradients.

```
prob_v = F.softmax(logits_v, dim=1)
entropy_v = -(prob_v * log_prob_v).sum(dim=1).mean()
```

```
entropy_loss_v = -ENTROPY_BETA * entropy_v
entropy_loss_v.backward()
optimizer.step()
```

Later, the only thing we need to do is to write statistics that we're interested in, into TensorBoard.

```
writer.add_scalar("grad_l2",
np.sqrt(np.mean(np.square(grads))), step_idx)
        writer.add_scalar("grad_max", np.max(np.abs(grads)),
step_idx)
        writer.add_scalar("grad_var", np.var(grads), step_idx)
```

By running this example twice, once with the `--baseline` command - line option and once without it, we get a plot of variance of our PG. The following are the charts for the reward dynamics:

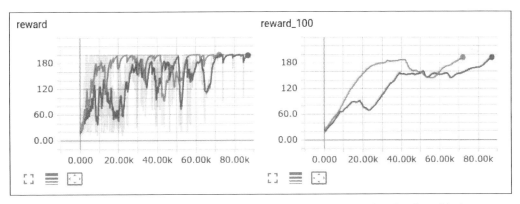

Figure 2: Convergence dynamics of the version with baseline (orange) and without (blue)

The following three charts show gradients' magnitude, maximum value, and variance:

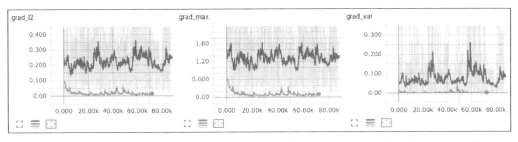

Figure 3: Gradient l2, max, and variance for the baseline subtracted (orange) and the basic version (blue)

As you can see, variance for the version with the baseline is two-to-three orders of magnitude lower than the version without one, which helps the system to converge faster.

Actor-critic

The next step in reducing the variance is making our baseline state-dependent (which, intuitively, is a good idea, as different states could have very different baselines). Indeed, to decide about the suitability of a particular action in some state, we're using the discounted total reward of the action. However, the total reward itself could be represented as a *value* of the state plus *advantage* of the action: $Q(s, a) = V(s) + A(s, a)$. We've seen this in *Chapter 7, DQN Extensions*, when we discussed DQN modifications, particularly dueling DQN.

So, why can't we use $V(s)$ as a baseline? In that case, the scale of our gradient will be just advantage $A(s, a)$, showing how this taken action is better in respect to the average state's value. In fact, we can do this, and it is a very good idea for improving the PG method. The only problem here is: we don't know the value of the $V(s)$ state to subtract it from the discounted total reward $Q(s, a)$. To solve this, let's use *another neural network*, which will approximate $V(s)$ for every observation. To train it, we can exploit the same training procedure we used in DQN methods: we'll carry out the Bellman step and then minimize the mean square error to improve $V(s)$ approximation.

When we know the value for any state (or, at least, have some approximation of it), we can use it to calculate the PG and update our policy network to increase probabilities for actions with good advantage values and decrease the chance of actions with bad advantage. The policy network (which returns probability distribution of actions) is called the *actor*, as it tells us what to do. Another network is called *critic*, as it allows us to understand how good our actions were. Below is an illustration of the architecture.

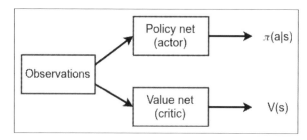

Figure 4: The A2C architecture

In practice, policy and value networks partially overlap, mostly due to the efficiency and convergence considerations. In this case, policy and value are implemented as different heads of the network, taking the output from the common body and transforming it into the probability distribution and a single number representing the value of the state. This helps both networks to share low-level features (such as convolution filters in the Atari agent), but combine them in a different way. This architecture is shown below.

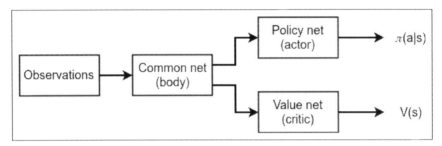

Figure 5: A2C architecture with a shared network body

From a training point of view, we complete these steps:

1. Initialize network parameters θ with random values

2. Play N steps in the environment using the current policy π_θ, saving state st, action at, reward rt

3. R = 0 if the end of the episode is reached or $V_\theta(s_t)$

4. For $i = t - 1 \ldots t_{start}$ (note that steps are processed backwards):
   - $R \leftarrow r_i + \gamma R$
   - Accumulate the PG $\partial\theta_\pi \leftarrow \partial\theta_\pi + \nabla_\theta \log \pi_\theta(a_i|s_i)(R - V_\theta(s_i))$
   - Accumulate the value gradients $\partial\theta_v \leftarrow \partial\theta_v + \frac{\partial(R - V_\theta(s_i))^2}{\partial\theta_v}$

5. Update network parameters using the accumulated gradients, moving in the direction of PG $\partial\theta_\pi$ and in the opposite direction of the value gradients $\partial\theta_v$

6. Repeat from step 2 until convergence is reached

The preceding algorithm is an outline, similar to those which are usually printed in research papers. In practice, some considerations need to be taken:

- Entropy bonus is usually added to improve exploration. It's typically written as an entropy value added to the loss function: $\mathcal{L}_H = \beta \sum_i \pi_\theta(s_i) \log \pi_\theta(s_i)$. This function has a minimum when probability distribution is uniform, so by adding it to the loss function, we're pushing our agent away from being too certain about its actions.

- Gradients accumulation is usually implemented as a loss function combining all three components: policy loss, value loss, and entropy loss. You should be careful with signs of these losses, as PGs? are showing you the direction of policy improvement, but both value and entropy losses should be minimized.

- To improve stability, it's worth using several environments, providing you with observations concurrently (when we have multiple environments and our training batch will be created from their observations). We'll look at several ways of doing this in the next chapter.

The preceding method is called Actor-Critic, or sometimes Advantage Actor-Critic, which is abbreviated as A2C for short. The version with several environments running in parallel is called Advantage Asynchronous Actor-Critic, which is also known as A3C. The A3C method will be the subject of the next chapter, but for now let's implement A2C.

A2C on Pong

In the previous chapter, we saw a (not very successful) attempt to solve our favorite Pong environment with PG. Let's try it again with the actor-critic method at hand.

```
GAMMA = 0.99
LEARNING_RATE = 0.001
ENTROPY_BETA = 0.01
BATCH_SIZE = 128
NUM_ENVS = 50

REWARD_STEPS = 4
CLIP_GRAD = 0.1
```

We're starting, as usual, by defining hyperparameters (imports are omitted). These values are not tuned, as we'll do this in the next section of this chapter. We have one new value here: CLIP_GRAD. This hyperparameter is specifying the threshold for gradient clipping, which, basically, prevents our gradients at optimization stage from becoming too large and pushing our policy too far. Clipping is implemented using the PyTorch functionality, but the idea is very simple: if the L2 norm of the gradient is larger than this hyperparameter, then the gradient vector is clipped to this value.

The REWARD_STEPS hyperparameter determines how many steps ahead we'll take to approximate the total discounted reward for every action. In PG, we used around 10 steps, but in A2C, we'll use our value approximation to get a state value for further steps, so it will be fine to decrease the number of steps.

```
class AtariA2C(nn.Module):
    def __init__(self, input_shape, n_actions):
        super(AtariA2C, self).__init__()

        self.conv = nn.Sequential(
            nn.Conv2d(input_shape[0], 32, kernel_size=8,
stride=4),
            nn.ReLU(),
            nn.Conv2d(32, 64, kernel_size=4, stride=2),
            nn.ReLU(),
            nn.Conv2d(64, 64, kernel_size=3, stride=1),
            nn.ReLU()
        )

        conv_out_size = self._get_conv_out(input_shape)
        self.policy = nn.Sequential(
            nn.Linear(conv_out_size, 512),
            nn.ReLU(),
            nn.Linear(512, n_actions)
        )

        self.value = nn.Sequential(
            nn.Linear(conv_out_size, 512),
            nn.ReLU(),
            nn.Linear(512, 1)
        )
```

Our network architecture has a shared convolution body and two heads: the first is returning the policy with probability distribution over our actions and the second head returns one single number, which will approximate the state's value. It might look similar to our dueling DQN architecture from *Chapter 7, DQN Extensions*, but our training procedure is different.

```
    def _get_conv_out(self, shape):
        o = self.conv(torch.zeros(1, *shape))
        return int(np.prod(o.size()))

    def forward(self, x):
        fx = x.float() / 256
        conv_out = self.conv(fx).view(fx.size()[0], -1)
        return self.policy(conv_out), self.value(conv_out)
```

The forward pass through the network returns a tuple of two tensors: policy and value. Now we have a large and important function, which takes the batch of environment transitions and returns three tensors: batch of states, batch of actions taken, and batch of Q-values calculated using the formula $Q(s,a) = \sum_{i=0}^{N-1} \gamma^i r_i + \gamma^N V(s_N)$. This Q-value will be used in two places: to calculate mean squared error (MSE) loss to improve the value approximation, in the same way as DQN, and to calculate the advantage of the action.

```
def unpack_batch(batch, net, device='cpu'):
    states = []
    actions = []
    rewards = []
    not_done_idx = []
    last_states = []
    for idx, exp in enumerate(batch):
        states.append(np.array(exp.state, copy=False))
        actions.append(int(exp.action))
        rewards.append(exp.reward)
        if exp.last_state is not None:
            not_done_idx.append(idx)
            last_states.append(np.array(exp.last_state,
copy=False))
```

In the first loop, we just walk through our batch of transitions and copy their fields into the lists. Note that the reward value already contains the discounted reward for `REWARD_STEPS` ahead, as we use the `ptan.ExperienceSourceFirstLast` class. We also need to handle situations of episode ending and remember indices of batch entries for the non-terminal episodes.

```
states_v = torch.FloatTensor(states).to(device)
actions_t = torch.LongTensor(actions).to(device)
```

In the preceding code, we convert the gathered state and actions into a PyTorch tensor and copy them into GPU if needed. The rest of the function calculates Q-values, taking into account the terminal episodes.

```
rewards_np = np.array(rewards, dtype=np.float32)
if not_done_idx:
    last_states_v = torch.FloatTensor(last_states).to(device)
    last_vals_v = net(last_states_v)[1]
    last_vals_np = last_vals_v.data.cpu().numpy()[:, 0]
    rewards_np[not_done_idx] += GAMMA ** REWARD_STEPS *
last_vals_np
```

The preceding code prepares the variable with the last state in our transition chain and queries our network for *V(s)* approximation. Then, this approximation is added to the discounted reward, multiplied by gamma exponentiated in a number of steps.

```
ref_vals_v = torch.FloatTensor(rewards_np).to(device)
return states_v, actions_t, ref_vals_v
```

In the beginning of the function, we pack our Q-values into the appropriate form and return.

```
if __name__ == "__main__":
    parser = argparse.ArgumentParser()
    parser.add_argument("--cuda", default=False,
action="store_true", help="Enable cuda")
    parser.add_argument("-n", "--name", required=True,
help="Name of the run")
    args = parser.parse_args()
    device = torch.device("cuda" if args.cuda else "cpu")

    make_env = lambda: ptan.common.wrappers.wrap_dqn(gym.make
("PongNoFrameskip-v4"))
    envs = [make_env() for _ in range(NUM_ENVS)]
    writer = SummaryWriter(comment="-pong-a2c_" + args.name)
```

The preparation code for the training loop is the same as usual, except that we're now using the array of environments to gather experience, instead of one environment.

```
    net = AtariA2C(envs[0].observation_space.shape,
envs[0].action_space.n).to(device)
    print(net)

    agent = ptan.agent.PolicyAgent(lambda x: net(x)[0],
apply_softmax=True, device=device)
    exp_source = ptan.experience.ExperienceSourceFirstLast(envs,
agent, gamma=GAMMA, steps_count=REWARD_STEPS)

    optimizer = optim.Adam(net.parameters(), lr=LEARNING_RATE,
eps=1e-3)
```

One very important detail here is passing the `eps` parameter to the optimizer. If you're familiar with the **Adam** algorithm, you may know that epsilon is a small number added to the denominator to prevent zero division situations. Normally, this value is set to some small number such as 1e-8 or 1e-10, but, in our case, these values turned out to be too small. I have no mathematically strict explanation for this, but with a default value of epsilon, the method does not converge at all. Very likely, the division to a small value of 1e-8 makes the gradients too large, which turns out to be fatal for training stability.

```
batch = []

with common.RewardTracker(writer, stop_reward=18) as tracker:
    with ptan.common.utils.TBMeanTracker(writer,
batch_size=10) as tb_tracker:
        for step_idx, exp in enumerate(exp_source):
            batch.append(exp)

            # handle new rewards
            new_rewards = exp_source.pop_total_rewards()
            if new_rewards:
                if tracker.reward(new_rewards[0], step_idx):
                    break

            if len(batch) < BATCH_SIZE:
                continue
```

In the training loop, we're using two wrappers. The first is already familiar to you: `common.RewardTracker`, which computes the mean reward for the last 100 episodes and tells us when this mean reward exceeds the desired threshold. Another wrapper, `TBMeanTracker`, is from the ptan library and is responsible for writing into TensorBoard the mean of the measured parameters for the last 10 steps. This is helpful when training can take millions of steps, so we don't want to write millions of points into TensorBoard, but rather write smoothed values every 10 steps. The next code chunk is responsible for our losses calculation, which is a core of the A2C method.

```
            states_v, actions_t, vals_ref_v = \
unpack_batch(batch, net, device=device)
            batch.clear()

            optimizer.zero_grad()
            logits_v, value_v = net(states_v)
```

In the beginning, we unpack our batch using the function we described earlier and ask our network to return policy and values for this batch. Policy is returned in unnormalized form, so to convert it into probability distribution, we need to apply softmax to it. We postpone this step to use `log_softmax`, as it is more numerically stable.

```
loss_value_v = F.mse_loss(value_v.squeeze(-1),
vals_ref_v)
```

The value loss part is almost trivial: we just calculate the MSE between the value returned by our network and the approximation we performed using the Bellman equation unrolled four steps forward.

```
log_prob_v = F.log_softmax(logits_v, dim=1)
adv_v = vals_ref_v - value_v.detach()
log_prob_actions_v = adv_v *
log_prob_v[range(BATCH_SIZE), actions_t]
loss_policy_v = -log_prob_actions_v.mean()
```

Here, we calculate the policy loss to obtain the PG. The first two steps are to obtain a log of our policy and calculate the advantage of actions, which is $A(s, a) = Q(s, a) - V(s)$. The call to `value_v.detach()` is important, as we don't want to propagate the PG into our value approximation head. Then we take the log of probability for the actions taken and scale them with advantage. Our PG loss value will be equal to the negated mean of this scaled log of policy, as PG directs us toward policy improvement, but loss value is supposed to be minimized.

```
prob_v = F.softmax(logits_v, dim=1)
entropy_loss_v = ENTROPY_BETA * (prob_v *
log_prob_v).sum(dim=1).mean()
```

The last piece of our loss function is entropy loss, which equals to the scaled entropy of our policy, taken with the opposite sign (entropy is calculated as $H(\pi) = -\sum \pi \log \pi$.

```
loss_policy_v.backward(retain_graph=True)
grads = np.concatenate([p.grad.data.cpu().numpy().
flatten()
                                    for p in net.parameters()
                                    if p.grad is not None])
```

In the preceding code, we calculate and extract gradients of our policy, which will be used to track the maximum gradient, its variance and L2 norm.

```
                    loss_v = entropy_loss_v + loss_value_v
                    loss_v.backward()
                    nn_utils.clip_grad_norm_(net.parameters(),
CLIP_GRAD)
                    optimizer.step()
                    loss_v += loss_policy_v
```

As a final step of our training, we backpropagate the entropy loss an, the value loss, and clip gradients and ask our optimizer to update the network.

```
                    tb_tracker.track("advantage", adv_v, step_idx)
                    tb_tracker.track("values", value_v, step_idx)
                    tb_tracker.track("batch_rewards", vals_ref_v,
step_idx)
                    tb_tracker.track("loss_entropy", entropy_loss_v,
step_idx)
                    tb_tracker.track("loss_policy", loss_policy_v,
step_idx)
                    tb_tracker.track("loss_value", loss_value_v, step_idx)
                    tb_tracker.track("loss_total", loss_v, step_idx)
                    tb_tracker.track("grad_l2", np.sqrt(np.mean
(np.square(grads))), step_idx)
                    tb_tracker.track("grad_max", np.max(np.abs(grads)),
 step_idx)
                    tb_tracker.track("grad_var", np.var(grads),
step_idx)
```

At the end of the training loop, we track all values that we're going to monitor in the TensorBoard. There are plenty of them and we'll discuss them in the next section.

A2C on Pong results

To start the training, run `02_pong_a2c.py` with the `--cuda` and `-n` options (which provides a name of the run for TensorBoard):

```
rl_book_samples/Chapter10$ ./02_pong_a2c.py --cuda -n t2
AtariA2C (
  (conv): Sequential (
    (0): Conv2d(4, 32, kernel_size=(8, 8), stride=(4, 4))
    (1): ReLU ()
```

```
    (2): Conv2d(32, 64, kernel_size=(4, 4), stride=(2, 2))
    (3): ReLU ()
    (4): Conv2d(64, 64, kernel_size=(3, 3), stride=(1, 1))
    (5): ReLU ()
  )
  (policy): Sequential (
    (0): Linear (3136 -> 512)
    (1): ReLU ()
    (2): Linear (512 -> 6)
  )
  (value): Sequential (
    (0): Linear (3136 -> 512)
    (1): ReLU ()
    (2): Linear (512 -> 1)
  )
)
37799: done 1 games, mean reward -21.000, speed 722.89 f/s
39065: done 2 games, mean reward -21.000, speed 749.92 f/s
39076: done 3 games, mean reward -21.000, speed 755.26 f/s
...
```

As a word of warning: the training process is lengthy. With the original hyperparameters, it requires more than 8M frames to solve, which is approximately three hours on GPU. In the next section of the chapter, we'll tweak the parameters to improve the convergence speed, but, for now, it's three hours. To improve the situation even more, in the next chapter, we'll look at the distributed version, which performs the environment in a separate process, but first let's focus on our plots in TensorBoard.

First of all, the reward dynamics look much better than in the example from the previous chapter:

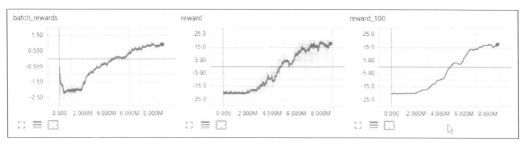

Figure 6: Convergence dynamics of the A2C method

The first plot, batch_rewards, shows Q-values approximated using the Bellman equation and an overall positive dynamic in Q approximation. The next two plots are the total undiscounted reward and the same reward, but averaged for the last 100 episodes. This shows that our training process is improving more-or-less consistently over time.

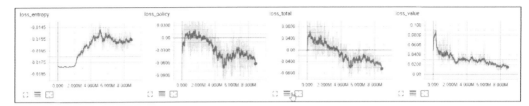

Figure 7: Loss components during the training

The next four charts are related to our loss and include individual loss components and the total loss. Here we can see various things. First of all, our value loss is decreasing consistently, which shows that our $V(s)$ approximation is improving during the training. The second observation we can share is that our entropy loss is growing, but it doesn't dominate in the total loss. This basically means that our agent becomes more confident in its actions, as policy becomes less uniform. The last thing to note here is that policy loss is decreasing most of the time and policy loss is correlated to the total loss, which is good, as we're interested in the PG first of all.

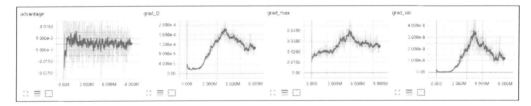

Figure 8: Advantage and gradients' metrics during the training

The last bunch of plots displays the advantage value and PG metrics. The advantage is a scale of our PGs and it equals to $Q(s, a) - V(s)$. We expect it to oscillate around zero and the chart meets our expectations. The gradient charts demonstrate that our gradients are not too small and not too large. Variance is very small in the beginning of the training (for 1.5M of frames), but starts to grow later, which means that our policy is changing.

Tuning hyperparameters

In the previous section, we had Pong solved in three hours of optimization and 9M frames. Now it's a good time to tweak our hyperparameters to speed up convergence. The golden rule here is to tweak one option at a time and make conclusions carefully, as the whole process is stochastic.

In this section, we'll start with the original hyperparameters and perform the following experiments:

- Increasing the learning rate
- Increasing the entropy beta
- Changing the count of environments that we're using to gather experience
- Tweaking the size of the batch

Strictly speaking, the experiments below weren't proper hyperparameter tuning, just an attempt to get a better understanding of how A2C convergence dynamics depend on the parameters. To find the best set of parameters, the full grid search or random sampling of values could give much better results, but will require much more time and resources to conduct.

Learning rate

Our starting **learning rate (LR)** is 0.001 and we can expect that a larger learning rate will lead to faster convergence. This turned out to be true in my tests, but only to a certain extent: convergence speed increased up to 0.003, but for larger values, the system didn't converge at all.

The performance results are as follows:

- LR=0.002: 4.8M frames, 1.5 hours
- LR=0.003: 3.6M frames, 1 hour
- LR=0.004: hasn't converged
- LR=0.005: hasn't converged

The reward dynamics and the value loss are shown on the following charts. Larger values of LR led to lower value loss, which suggests that using two optimizers for policy and value heads (with different learning rates) might lead to more stable learning.

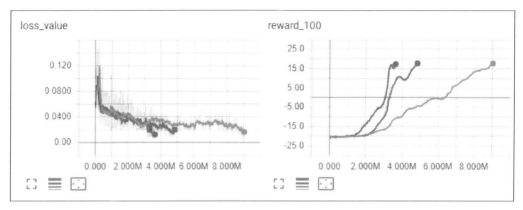

Figure 9: Experiments with different learning rates (faster convergence corresponds to large learning rates)

Entropy beta

I've tried two values for entropy loss scale: 0.02 and 0.03. The first value improved the speed, but the second made it worse again, so the optimal lies somewhere between them. The results were as follows:

- beta=0.02: 6.8M frames, 2 hours
- beta=0.03: 12M frames, 4 hours

Count of environments

It's not obvious what count of environments will work best, so I've tried several counts both lesser and greater than our initial value of 50. The results are contradictory, but it appears that with more environments, we get faster convergence:

- Envs=40: 8.6M frames, 3 hours
- Envs=30: 6.2M frames, 2 hours (looks like a lucky seed)
- Envs=20: 9.5M frames, 3 hours
- Envs=10: hasn't converged
- Envs=60: 11.6M frames, 4 hours (looks like an unlucky seed)
- Envs=70: 7.7M frames, 2.5 hours

Batch size

The experiments with batch size produced an unexpected result: smaller batch size leads to faster convergence, but with a very small batch, the reward doesn't grow. This is logical from an RL point of view, as with smaller batches, we perform more frequent updates of the network and we require less observations, but this is counter-intuitive for deep learning, as a larger batch normally brings more i.i.d training data:

- Batch=64: 4.9M frames, 1.7 hours
- Batch=32: 3.8M frames, 1.5 hours
- Batch=16, doesn't converge

Summary

In this chapter, we saw one of the most widely used methods in deep RL: A2C, which wisely combines the PG update with value of the state approximation. We introduced the idea behind A2C by analyzing the effect of the baseline on the statistics and convergence of gradients. Then we checked the extension of the baseline idea: A2C, where a separate network head provides us with the baseline for the current state.

In the next chapter, we will look at ways to perform the same algorithm in a distributed way.

11

Asynchronous Advantage Actor-Critic

This chapter is dedicated to the extension of the **Actor-Critic (A2C)** method that we discussed in detail in the previous chapter. The extension adds true asynchronous environment interaction. The full name is **Asynchronous Advantage Actor-Critic**, which is normally abbreviated to A3C. This method is one of the most widely used by RL practitioners. We will take a look at two approaches for adding asynchronous behavior to the basic A2C method.

Correlation and sample efficiency

One of the approaches to improving the stability of the **Policy Gradient (PG)** family of methods is to use multiple environments in parallel. The reason behind this is the fundamental problem we discussed in *Chapter 6*, *Deep Q-Networks*, when we talked about the correlation between samples, which breaks the **independent and identically distributed (i.i.d)** assumption, which is critical for **Stochastic Gradient Descent (SGD)** optimization. The negative consequence of such correlation is very high variance in gradients, which means that our training batch contains very similar examples, all of them pushing our network in the same direction. However, this may be totally the wrong direction in the global sense, as all those examples could be from one single lucky or unlucky episode.

With our **Deep Q-Network (DQN)**, we solved the issue by storing a large amount of previous states in the replay buffer and sampling our training batch from this buffer. If the buffer is large enough, the random sample from it is a much better representation of the states' distribution at large. Unfortunately, this solution won't work for PG methods, as most of them are on-policy, which means that we have to train on samples generated by our current policy, so, *remembering old transitions* is not possible anymore. You can try to do this, but the resulting PG will be for that old policy used to generate the samples, not for your current policy that you want to update.

For several years, this issue was in the focus of researchers and several ways to address it were proposed, but the problem is still far from being solved. The most commonly used solution is gathering transitions using several parallel environments, all of them exploiting the current policy. This breaks the correlation within one single episode, as we now train on several episodes obtained from different environments. At the same time, we are still using our current policy. The one very large disadvantage of this is **sample inefficiency**, as we basically throw away all experience that we've just got after one single training. It's very simple to compare DQN with PG approaches. For example, if, for DQN, we've used 1M samples of replay buffer and a training batch size of 32 samples for every new frame, every single transition will approximately be used 32 times before it is pushed from the experience replay. For the priority replay buffer, discussed in *Chapter 7, DQN Extensions*, this number could be much higher, as the sample probability is not uniform. In the case of PG, every single experience obtained from the environment could be used only once, as our method requires fresh data, so data efficiency of PG methods could be an order of magnitude lower than the value-based off-policy methods.

On the other hand, our A2C agent converged on **Pong** in 8M frames, which is just eight times more than 1M frames for basic DQN in *Chapter 6, Deep Q-Networks*, and *Chapter 7, DQN Extensions*. So, this shows us that PG methods are not completely useless; they're just different and have their own specificities that you need to take into account on method selection. If your environment is cheap in terms of the agent interaction (the environment is fast, has a low memory footprint, allows parallelization, and so on), PG methods could be a better choice. On the other hand, if the environment is expensive and obtaining a large amount of experience could slow down the training process, the value-based methods could be a smarter way to go.

Adding an extra A to A2C

From the practical point of view, communicating with several parallel environments is simple and we've already done this in the previous chapter, but haven't stated it explicitly. In the A2C agent, we passed an array of Gym environments into the `ExperienceSource` class, which switched it into the round-robin data gathering mode: every time we asked for a transition from the experience source, the class uses the next environment from our array (of course, keeping the state for every environment). This simple approach is equivalent to parallel communication with environments, but with one single difference: communication is not parallel in the strict sense, but performed in a serial way. However, samples from our experience source are shuffled. This idea is shown in the following diagram:

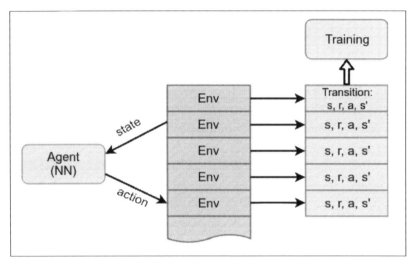

Figure 1: Agent training from multiple environments in parallel

This method worked fine and helped us to get convergence in the A2C method, but it is still not perfect in terms of computing resource utilization. Even the modest workstation nowadays has several CPU cores, which could be used for computation, such as training and environment interaction. On the other hand, parallel programming is harder than the traditional paradigm, when you have a clear stream of execution. Luckily, Python is a very expressive and flexible language with lots of third-party libraries, which allows you to do parallel programming without much trouble. Another piece of good news is that PyTorch natively supports parallel programming in its `torch.multiprocessing` module. Parallel and distributed programming is a very wide topic, which is far beyond the scope of this book. Here we'll just scratch the surface of the large domain of parallelization, but there is much more to learn.

With regard to actor-critic parallelization, two approaches exist:

1. **Data parallelism**: We can have several processes, each of them communicating with one or more environments and providing us with transitions (s, r, a, s'). All those samples are gathered together in one single training process, which calculates losses and performs an SGD update. Then, the updated neural network parameters need to be broadcasted to all other processes to use in future environment communications.

2. **Gradients parallelism**: As the goal of the training process is the calculation of gradients to update our network, we can have several processes calculating gradients on their own training samples. Then, these gradients can be summed together to perform the SGD update in one process. Of course, updated network weights also need to be propagated to all workers to keep data on-policy.

Both approaches are illustrated in diagrams below.

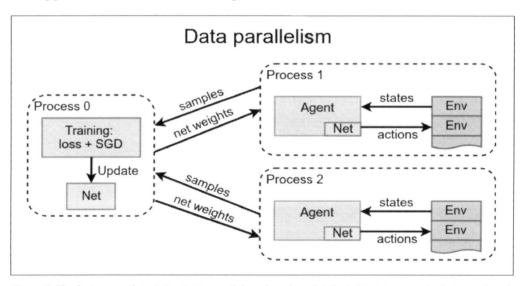

Figure 2: The first approach to Actor-Critic parallelism, based on distributed training samples being gathered

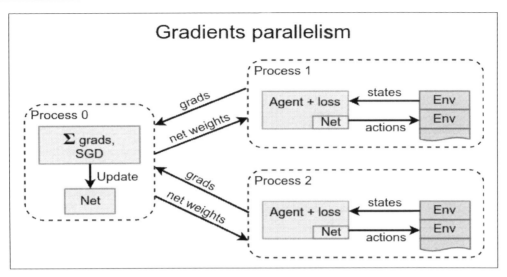

Figure 3: The second approach to parallelism, gathering gradients for the model

The difference between the two methods might not look very significant from the diagrams, but you need to be aware of the computation cost. The heaviest operation in A3C optimization is the training process, which consists of loss calculation from data samples (forward pass) and calculation of gradients with respect to this loss. The SGD optimization step is quite lightweight, basically just adding the scaled gradients to the network's weights. By moving the computation of loss and gradients in the second approach from the central process, we eliminated the major potential bottleneck and made the whole process significantly more scalable.

In practice, the choice of the method mainly depends on your resources and your goals. If you have one single optimization problem and lots of distributed computation resources, such as a couple of dozen GPUs spread over several machines in the networks, then gradients parallelism is the best approach to speed up your training. However, in the case of one single GPU, both methods will show you similar performance, and the first approach is generally simpler to implement, as you don't need to mess with low-level gradient values. In this chapter, we'll implement both methods on our favorite Pong game to see the difference between the approaches and look at PyTorch multiprocessing capabilities.

Multiprocessing in Python

Python includes the `multiprocessing` (most of the time abbreviated to just `mp`) module to support process-level parallelism and the required communication primitives. In our example, we'll use the two main classes from this module:

- `mp.Queue`: Concurrent multi-producer, multi-consumer FIFO queue with transparent serialization and deserialization of objects placed in the queue

- `mp.Process`: A piece of code that is run in the child process and methods to control it from the parent's process

PyTorch provides its own thin wrapper around the `multiprocessing` module, which adds the proper handling of tensors and variables on CUDA devices and shared memory. It provides exactly the same functionality as the `multiprocessing` module from the standard library, so all you need to do is to use `import torch.multiprocessing` instead of `import multiprocessing`.

A3C – data parallelism

The first version of A3C parallelization that we'll check (which was outlined on Figure 2) has both one main process which carries out training and several children processes communicating with environments and gathering experience to train on. For simplicity and efficiency, the **neural network** (**NN**) weights broadcasting from the trainer process is not implemented. Instead of explicitly gathering and sending weights to children, the network is shared between all processes using PyTorch built-in capabilities, allowing us to use the same `nn.Module` instance with all its weights in different processes by calling the `share_memory()` method on NN creation. Under the hood, this method has zero overhead for CUDA (as GPU memory is shared among all host's processes) or shared memory IPC in the case of CPU computation. In both cases, the method improves performance, but limits our example for one single machine using one single GPU card for training and data gathering. It's not very limiting for our Pong example, but if you need larger scalability, the example should be extended with explicit sharing of network weights.

The complete code is in the `Chapter11/01_a3c_data.py` file and it uses the `Chapter11/lib/common.py` module with the following functionality pieces:

- `class AtariA2C(nn.Module)`: This implements the Actor-Critic NN module

- `class RewardTracker`: This handles full episode undiscounted reward, writes it into TensorBoard, and checks for the *game solved* condition

- `unpack_batch(batch, net, last_val_gamma)`: This function converts a batch of transitions (state, reward, action, and last_state) for *n* episode steps into data suitable for training

We have already seen the code of those classes and functions in the previous chapters, so we won't repeat them here. Now let's check the code of the main modules, which includes the function for children subprocesses and the main training loop.

```
#!/usr/bin/env python3
import gym
import ptan
import numpy as np
import argparse
import collections
from tensorboardX import SummaryWriter

import torch.nn.utils as nn_utils
import torch.nn.functional as F
import torch.optim as optim
import torch.multiprocessing as mp

from lib import common
```

In the beginning, we're importing the required modules. There is nothing new here except that we are importing the `torch.multiprocessing` library.

```
GAMMA = 0.99
LEARNING_RATE = 0.001
ENTROPY_BETA = 0.01
BATCH_SIZE = 128

REWARD_STEPS = 4
CLIP_GRAD = 0.1

PROCESSES_COUNT = 4
NUM_ENVS = 15

ENV_NAME = "PongNoFrameskip-v4"
NAME = 'pong'
REWARD_BOUND = 18
```

In hyperparameters, we have two new values:

- `PROCESSES_COUNT` specifies the number of children processes that will gather training data for us. This activity is mostly CPU-bound, as the heaviest operation here is Atari frames preprocessing, so this value is set equal to the amount of CPU cores on my machine.

- `NUM_ENVS` is the number of environments every child process will use to gather data. This number multiplied by the number of processes is the total amount of parallel environments that we'll get our training data from.

```
def make_env():
    return ptan.common.wrappers.wrap_dqn(gym.make(ENV_NAME))


TotalReward = collections.namedtuple('TotalReward', field_
names='reward')
```

Before we get to the child process function, we need the environment construction function and a tiny wrapper that we'll use to send the total episode reward into the main training process.

```
def data_func(net, device, train_queue):
    envs = [make_env() for _ in range(NUM_ENVS)]
    agent = ptan.agent.PolicyAgent(lambda x: net(x)[0],
      device=device, apply_softmax=True)
    exp_source = ptan.experience.ExperienceSourceFirstLast(envs,
      agent, gamma=GAMMA, steps_count=REWARD_STEPS)

    for exp in exp_source:
        new_rewards = exp_source.pop_total_rewards()
        if new_rewards:
          train_queue.put(TotalReward
            (reward=np.mean(new_rewards)))
        train_queue.put(exp)
```

The preceding function is very simple but it is special, as it will be executed in the children process (we'll use the `mp.Process` class to launch those processes in the main code block). We pass it three arguments: our NN, the device to be used to perform computation (`cpu` or `cuda` string), and the queue we'll use to send data from the child process to our master process, which will perform training. The queue is used in the many-producers and one-consumer mode and can contain two different types of objects:

- `TotalReward`: This is a preceding object that we've defined, which has only one field reward, which is a float value of the total undiscounted reward for the completed episode.
- `ptan.experience.ExperienceFirstLast`: This is an object that wraps the first state in subsequence of `REWARD_STEPS`, action taken, the discounted reward for this subsequence, and the last state. This is our experience that we'll use for training.

That's it about the children processes, so now let's check the starting code for the main process and the training loop.

```
if __name__ == "__main__":
    mp.set_start_method('spawn')
    parser = argparse.ArgumentParser()
    parser.add_argument("--cuda", default=False,
        action="store_true", help="Enable cuda")
    parser.add_argument("-n", "--name", required=True,
        help="Name of the run")
    args = parser.parse_args()
    device = "cuda" if args.cuda else "cpu"
    writer = SummaryWriter(comment="-a3c-data_" + NAME + "_" +
args.name)
```

In the beginning, we take familiar steps, except for one single call to `mp.set_start_method`, which instructs the `multiprocessing` module about the kind of parallelism we want to use. The native multiprocessing library in Python supports several ways to start subprocesses, but due to PyTorch multiprocessing limitations, spawn is the best option.

```
env = make_env()
net = common.AtariA2C(env.observation_space.shape,
    env.action_space.n).to(device)
net.share_memory()
optimizer = optim.Adam(net.parameters(),

    lr=LEARNING_RATE, eps=1e-3)
```

After that, we create our NN, move it to the CUDA device and ask it to share its weights. CUDA tensors are shared by default, but for CPU mode, a call to `share_memory` is required.

```
train_queue = mp.Queue(maxsize=PROCESSES_COUNT)
data_proc_list = []
for _ in range(PROCESSES_COUNT):
    data_proc = mp.Process(target=data_func,
        args=(net, device, train_queue))
    data_proc.start()
    data_proc_list.append(data_proc)
```

Then we have to start our children processes, but before that, we create the queue that will be used by them to deliver to us data. The argument to the queue constructor specifies the maximum queue capacity. All attempts to push a new item to the full queue will be blocked, which is very convenient for us to keep our data samples on-policy. After the queue creation, we start the required amount of processes using the `mp.Process` class and keep them for correct shutdown in a list. Right after the `mp.Process.start()` call, our `data_func` function will be executed by the child process.

```
        batch = []
        step_idx = 0

        try:
            with common.RewardTracker(writer,
    stop_reward=REWARD_BOUND) as tracker:
                with ptan.common.utils.TBMeanTracker(writer,
    batch_size=100) as tb_tracker:
                    while True:
                        train_entry = train_queue.get()
                        if isinstance(train_entry, TotalReward):
                            if tracker.reward(train_entry.reward,
    step_idx):
                                break
                            continue
```

In the beginning of the training loop, we get the next entry from the queue and handle possible `TotalReward` objects, which we pass to the reward tracker.

```
                        step_idx += 1
                        batch.append(train_entry)
                        if len(batch) < BATCH_SIZE:
                            continue
```

As we can have only two types of objects in the queue (`TotalReward` and experience transitions), we need to check entry obtained from the queue only once. After the `TotalReward` entries are handled, we put experience objects into the batch accumulated until the required batch size.

```
                        states_v, actions_t, vals_ref_v = \
                            common.unpack_batch(batch, net,
    last_val_gamma=GAMMA**REWARD_STEPS, device=device)
                        batch.clear()
```

As we get the required amount of experience samples, we convert them into training data using the `unpack_bach` function and clear the batch. One thing to note: as our experience samples represent four steps subsequences (as REWARD_STEPS is 4), we need to use a proper discount factor of γ^4 for the last $V(s)$ reward term. The rest of the training loop is standard actor-critic loss calculation, which is performed in exactly the same way as in the previous chapter: we calculate the logits of the policy and value estimation using our current network and calculate policy, value, and entropy losses.

```
optimizer.zero_grad()
logits_v, value_v = net(states_v)

loss_value_v = F.mse_loss(value_v.squeeze(-1),
    vals_ref_v)

log_prob_v = F.log_softmax(logits_v, dim=1)
adv_v = vals_ref_v - value_v.detach()
log_prob_actions_v = adv_v *
    log_prob_v[range(BATCH_SIZE), actions_t]
loss_policy_v = -log_prob_actions_v.mean()

prob_v = F.softmax(logits_v, dim=1)
entropy_loss_v = ENTROPY_BETA * (prob_v *
    log_prob_v).sum(dim=1).mean()

loss_v = entropy_loss_v + loss_value_v +
    loss_policy_v
loss_v.backward()
nn_utils.clip_grad_norm_(net.parameters(),
    CLIP_GRAD)
optimizer.step()
```

As the last step, we pass the calculated tensors to the TensorBoard `tracker` class, which will perform the averaging and storing of the data that we want to monitor.

```
tb_tracker.track("advantage", adv_v, step_idx)
tb_tracker.track("values", value_v, step_idx)
tb_tracker.track("batch_rewards", vals_ref_v,
    step_idx)
tb_tracker.track("loss_entropy",
    entropy_loss_v, step_idx)
tb_tracker.track("loss_policy", loss_policy_v,
    step_idx)
tb_tracker.track("loss_value", loss_value_v,
    step_idx)
```

```
                    tb_tracker.track("loss_total", loss_v,
                        step_idx)
        finally:
            for p in data_proc_list:
                p.terminate()
                p.join()
```

In the last `finally` block, which can be executed due to an exception (*Ctrl + C,* for example) or *game solved* condition, we terminate the child processes and wait for them. This is required to make sure that there are no leftover processes.

Results

Start the example as usual, and after some delay, it should begin writing performance and the mean reward data. On GTX 1080Ti and 4-core machine, it shows the speed of about 1800 frames per second, which is a nice improvement on the 600 f/s we got in the previous chapter.

```
rl_book_samples/Chapter11$ ./01_a3c_data.py --cuda -n final
44830: done 1 games, mean reward -21.000, speed 1618.10 f/s
44856: done 2 games, mean reward -21.000, speed 2053.09 f/s
45037: done 3 games, mean reward -21.000, speed 2036.78 f/s
45351: done 4 games, mean reward -21.000, speed 1894.14 f/s
45562: done 5 games, mean reward -21.000, speed 2204.78 f/s
45573: done 6 games, mean reward -21.000, speed 629.41 f/s
...
```

In terms of convergence dynamics, the new version is similar to A2C with parallel environments and solves Pong in 7M-8M observations from the environment. However, those 8M frames are processed in slightly more than one hour, instead of waiting for three hours.

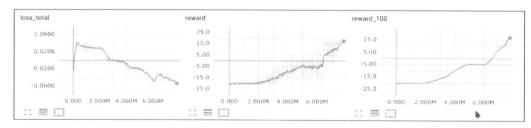

Figure 4: Convergence dynamics of the data parallel version of A3C on Pong

A3C – gradients parallelism

The next approach that we will consider to parallelize A2C implementation will have several child processes, but instead of feeding training data to the central training loop, they will calculate the gradients using their local training data and send those gradients to the central master process. This process is responsible for combining those gradients together (which is basically just summing them) and performing an SGD update on the shared network.

The difference might look minor, but this approach is much more scalable, especially if you have several powerful nodes with multiple GPUs connected with the network. In this case, the central process in the data-parallel model quickly becomes a bottleneck, as the loss calculation and backpropagation are computationally demanding. Gradient parallelization allows for the spreading of the load on several GPUs, performing only a relatively simple operation of gradient combination in the central place.

The complete example is in the `Chapter11/02_a3c_grad.py` file and it uses the same `Chapter11/lib/common.py` file as in our previous example.

```
GAMMA = 0.99
LEARNING_RATE = 0.001
ENTROPY_BETA = 0.01

REWARD_STEPS = 4
CLIP_GRAD = 0.1

PROCESSES_COUNT = 4
NUM_ENVS = 15

GRAD_BATCH = 64
TRAIN_BATCH = 2
ENV_NAME = "PongNoFrameskip-v4"
NAME = 'pong'
REWARD_BOUND = 18
```

As usual, we are defining the hyperparameters, which are mostly the same as in the previous example, except BATCH_SIZE is replaced by two parameters: GRAD_BATCH and TRAIN_BATCH. The value of GRAD_BATCH defines the size of the batch used by every child process to compute the loss and get the value of gradients. The second parameter, TRAIN_BATCH, specifies how many gradient batches from the child processes will be combined on every SGD iteration. Every entry produced by the child process has the same shape as our network parameters and we sum up TRAIN_BATCH values of them together. So, for every optimization step, we use the TRAIN_BATCH * GRAD_BATCH training samples. As the loss calculation and backpropagation are quite heavy operations, we use large GRAD_BATCH to make them more efficient. Due to this large batch, we should keep TRAIN_BATCH relatively low to keep our network update on-policy.

```
def make_env():
    return ptan.common.wrappers.wrap_dqn(gym.make(ENV_NAME))


def grads_func(proc_name, net, device, train_queue):
    envs = [make_env() for _ in range(NUM_ENVS)]

    agent = ptan.agent.PolicyAgent(lambda x: net(x)[0],
      device=device, apply_softmax=True)
    exp_source = ptan.experience.ExperienceSourceFirstLast(envs,
      agent, gamma=GAMMA, steps_count=REWARD_STEPS)

    batch = []
    frame_idx = 0
    writer = SummaryWriter(comment=proc_name)
```

The preceding is the function executed by the child process, which is much more complicated than in our data-parallel example. As a compensation, the training loop in the main process becomes almost trivial. On creation of the child process, we pass several arguments to the function:

- The name of the process, which is used to create the TensorBoard writer. In this example, every child process writes its own TensorBoard data set.

- The shared neural network.

- A device to perform computations (cpu or cuda string).

- The queue used to deliver the calculated gradients to the central process.

Our child process function looks very similar to the main training loop in the data-parallel version, which is not surprising, as the responsibilities of our child process increased. However, instead of asking the optimizer to update the network, we gather gradients and send them into the queue. The rest of the code is almost the same.

```
    with common.RewardTracker(writer, stop_reward=REWARD_BOUND) as
tracker:
        with ptan.common.utils.TBMeanTracker(writer,
batch_size=100) as tb_tracker:
            for exp in exp_source:
                frame_idx += 1
                new_rewards = exp_source.pop_total_rewards()
                if new_rewards and tracker.reward(new_rewards[0],
frame_idx):
                    break

                batch.append(exp)
                if len(batch) < GRAD_BATCH:
                    continue
```

Up to this point, we've gathered the batch with transitions and handled the end of episode rewards.

```
                states_v, actions_t, vals_ref_v = \
                    common.unpack_batch(batch, net,
last_val_gamma=GAMMA**REWARD_STEPS, device=device)
                batch.clear()

                net.zero_grad()
                logits_v, value_v = net(states_v)
                loss_value_v = F.mse_loss(value_v.squeeze(-1),
vals_ref_v)

                log_prob_v = F.log_softmax(logits_v, dim=1)
                adv_v = vals_ref_v - value_v.detach()
                log_prob_actions_v = adv_v *
log_prob_v[range(GRAD_BATCH), actions_t]
                loss_policy_v = -log_prob_actions_v.mean()

                prob_v = F.softmax(logits_v, dim=1)
                entropy_loss_v = ENTROPY_BETA * (prob_v *
```

```
log_prob_v).sum(dim=1).mean()

                    loss_v = entropy_loss_v + loss_value_v +
loss_policy_v
                    loss_v.backward()
```

In the preceding section, we calculate the combined loss from the training data and perform backpropagation of the loss, which effectively stores gradients in the `Tensor.grad` field for every network parameter. This could be done without bothering with synchronization with other workers, as our network's parameters are shared, but the gradients are locally allocated by every process.

```
            tb_tracker.track("advantage", adv_v, frame_idx)
            tb_tracker.track("values", value_v, frame_idx)
            tb_tracker.track("batch_rewards", vals_ref_v,
              frame_idx)
            tb_tracker.track("loss_entropy", entropy_loss_v,
              frame_idx)
            tb_tracker.track("loss_policy", loss_policy_v,
              frame_idx)
            tb_tracker.track("loss_value", loss_value_v,
              frame_idx)
            tb_tracker.track("loss_total", loss_v, frame_idx)
```

In the preceding code, we're sending our intermediate values, that we're going to monitor during the training, to TensorBoard.

```
            nn_utils.clip_grad_norm(net.parameters(),
              CLIP_GRAD)
            grads = [param.grad.data.cpu().numpy() if
              param.grad is not None else None
                    for param in net.parameters()]
            train_queue.put(grads)
```

At the end of the loop, we need to clip the gradients and extract them from the network's parameters into a separate buffer (to prevent them from being corrupted by the next iteration of the loop).

```
        train_queue.put(None)
```

The last line in `grads_func` puts `None` into the queue, signaling that this child process has reached the *game solved* state and training should be stopped.

```
if __name__ == "__main__":
    mp.set_start_method('spawn')
    parser = argparse.ArgumentParser()
```

```
parser.add_argument("--cuda", default=False,
    action="store_true", help="Enable cuda")
parser.add_argument("-n", "--name", required=True,
    help="Name of the run")
args = parser.parse_args()
device = "cuda" if args.cuda else "cpu"

env = make_env()
net = common.AtariA2C(env.observation_space.shape,
    env.action_space.n).to(device)
net.share_memory()
```

The main process starts with the creation of the network and sharing of its weights.

```
optimizer = optim.Adam(net.parameters(), lr=LEARNING_RATE,
    eps=1e-3)

train_queue = mp.Queue(maxsize=PROCESSES_COUNT)
data_proc_list = []
for proc_idx in range(PROCESSES_COUNT):
    proc_name = "-a3c-grad_" + NAME + "_" + args.name + "#%d"
        % proc_idx
    data_proc = mp.Process(target=grads_func, args=(proc_name,
        net, device, train_queue))
    data_proc.start()
    data_proc_list.append(data_proc)
```

Then, as before, we create the communication queue and spawn the required count of child processes.

```
batch = []
step_idx = 0
grad_buffer = None

try:
    while True:
        train_entry = train_queue.get()
        if train_entry is None:
            break
```

The major difference between the data-parallel version of A3C lies in the training loop, which is much simpler here, as children processes have done all heavy calculations for us. In the beginning of the loop, we handle the situation when one of the processes has reached the required mean reward to stop the training. In this case, we just exit the loop.

```
step_idx += 1

if grad_buffer is None:
    grad_buffer = train_entry
else:
    for tgt_grad, grad in zip(grad_buffer,train_entry):
        tgt_grad += grad
```

To average the gradients from different children, we call the optimizer's step() function for every TRAIN_BATCH gradient obtained. For intermediate steps, we just sum up the corresponding gradients together.

```
if step_idx % TRAIN_BATCH == 0:
    for param, grad in zip(net.parameters(),grad_buffer):
        grad_v = torch.FloatTensor(grad).to(device)
        param.grad = grad_v

    nn_utils.clip_grad_norm_(net.parameters(),CLIP_GRAD)
    optimizer.step()
    grad_buffer = None
```

When we have accumulated enough gradient pieces, we convert the sum of the gradients into the PyTorch FloatTensor and assign them to the grad field of the network parameters. After that, all we need to do is to call the optimizer's step() method to update the network parameters, using the accumulated gradients.

```
finally:
    for p in data_proc_list:
        p.terminate()
        p.join()
```

On the exit from the training loop, we stop all children processes to make sure that we terminated them, even if *Ctrl + C* was pressed to stop the optimization. This is needed to prevent zombie processes from occupying GPU resources.

Results

This example can be started the same way as before, and after a while, it should start displaying speed and mean reward; however, you need to be aware that displayed information is local for every child process, which means that speed, the count of games completed, and number of frames need to be multiplied by the amount of processes. My benchmarks have shown speed to be around 550-600 frames per second for every child, which gives 2200-2400 f/s in total.

```
rl_book_samples/Chapter11$ ./02_a3c_grad.py --cuda -n final
11278: done 1 games, mean reward -21.000, speed 520.23 f/s
11640: done 2 games, mean reward -21.000, speed 610.54 f/s
11773: done 3 games, mean reward -21.000, speed 485.09 f/s
11803: done 4 games, mean reward -21.000, speed 359.42 f/s
11765: done 1 games, mean reward -21.000, speed 519.08 f/s
11771: done 2 games, mean reward -21.000, speed 531.22 f/s
...
```

Convergence dynamics are also very similar to the previous version. The total number of observations is about 8M-10M, which requires one and a half hours to complete.

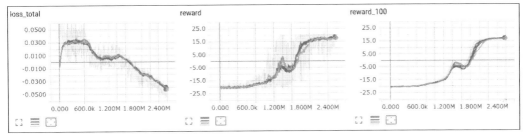

Figure 5: Convergence of gradient-based parallelization of A3C on Pong

Summary

In this chapter, we discussed why it is important for PG methods to gather training data from multiple environments, due to their on-policy nature. We also implemented two different approaches to A3C, in order to parallelize and stabilize the training process. Parallelization will rise once again in this book, when we discuss black-box methods (*Chapter 16, Black-Box Optimization in RL*). In the upcoming chapters, we'll take a look at practical problems that could be solved using PG methods, which will wrap up the PG part of the book.

12
Chatbots Training with RL

In this chapter, we'll take a look at another practical application of **Deep Reinforcement Learning** (**Deep RL**), which has become popular over the Past two years: the training of natural language models with RL methods. It started with a paper called *Recurrent Models of Visual Attention*, published in 2014, and has been successfully applied to a wide variety of problems from the **Natural Language Processing** (**NLP**) domain.

To understand the method, we will begin with a brief introduction to the NLP basics, including **Recurrent Neural Networks** (**RNNs**), **word embeddings,** and the **seq2seq** model. Then we'll discuss similarities between the NLP and RL problems and take a look at original ideas on how to improve NLP seq2seq training using RL methods. The core of the chapter is a dialogue system trained on the movie dialogues dataset.

Chatbots overview

One of the many trending topics of 2017 was AI-driven chatbots. There are various opinions on the subject, ranging from *completely useless stuff*, to *an absolutely brilliant idea*, but one thing is hard to question: chatbots open up new ways for people to communicate with computers which are much more human-like and natural than the old-style interfaces that we are all used to.

At its core, a chatbot is a computer program that uses natural language to communicate with other parties (humans or other computer programs) in a form of *dialogue*. There could be lots of different forms of such a scenario, namely one chatbot talking to a user, or many bots talking to each other, and so on. For example, there might be a technical support bot that can answer free-text questions from users. However, usually chatbots share common properties of a dialogue interaction (the user asks a question, but the chatbot can ask clarifying questions to get the missing information) and a free form of **natural language** (which makes it different from phone menus, for example, when you have a fixed *Press N to get to X category*, or *Enter your bank account number to check the balance* option given to the user).

Natural language understanding was a long-term science fiction concept. In films, you can just chat with your starship's computer to get useful and relevant information about the recent alien invasion, without pressing any button. This scenario was exploited by authors for decades, but in real life, such interactions with computers started to become a reality only recently. You still cannot talk to your starship, but you can at least switch on and off your toaster without pushing buttons, which is undoubtedly a major step forward!

The reason why it took computers so long to understand language is simply due to the complexity of language itself. Even in trivial scenarios, like saying, *Toaster, switch on!* you can imagine several ways to formulate your order and it's usually very hard to capture all those ways and corner cases in advance using normal computer-programming techniques. Unfortunately, traditional computer programming requires you to give computers exact, explicit instructions and one single corner case, or fuzziness in the input, could make your super-sophisticated code fail.

The recent advances in **Machine Learning** (**ML**) and **Deep Learning** (**DL**), with all its applications, is the first real step in the direction of breaking this strictness in computer programming by replacing it with a different idea: letting computers find patterns in data by themselves. This approach turned out to be quite successful in some domains and now everybody is very excited about the new methods and their potential applications. DL resurrection started in computer vision, then continued in the NLP domain and you definitely can expect more and more new, successful, and useful applications in the future.

So, returning to our chatbots, natural language complexity was the major blocker in practical applications. For a long time chatbots were mostly toy examples created by bored engineers for their entertainment. One of the oldest, and definitely the most popular example of such a system, is ELIZA, created in the 1960s (`https://en.wikipedia.org/wiki/ELIZA`). Despite the fact that ELIZA was quite successful at mimicking a psychotherapist, it had zero understanding of the user's phrases and just included a small set of manually created patterns and typical replies given to the user's input. This approach was a major way forward in implementing such systems in a pre-DL era, when it was a common belief that we just needed to add more patterns capturing the real language corner cases and after some time, computers would be able to understand the human language. Unfortunately, this idea turned out to be impractical, as the number of rules and contradicting examples that humans need to handle is too large and complex to be created manually.

The ML approach allows you to attack the complexity of the problem from a different direction. Instead of manually creating lots of rules to handle the user's input, you gather lots of training data and allow the ML algorithm to find the best way to solve the problem. This approach has its own specific details related to the NLP domain and we'll take a brief overview of them in the next section of the chapter. For now, what is much more important is that software developers discovered the ability to work with natural language in the same way that they work with other, much more computer-friendly formal things, such as document formats, network protocols or computer language grammars. This is still not trivial, requiring lots of work and sometimes you step into uncharted territory, but at least this approach works sometimes and doesn't require you to lock hundreds of linguists in one room for a decade to gather NLP rules!

From a chatbots perspective, they are still very new and experimental, but the overall idea is to allow computers to communicate with the user in the form of free-text dialogue instead of more formal ways. For example, let's take internet shopping as a case study. When you want to buy something, you go to the internet store, such as Amazon or eBay, and look through categories or use the website search to find the product that you want. However, this scenario has several problems. First of all, large web stores could have millions of items falling into thousands of categories in a very nondeterministic way. A simple child's toy can belong to several categories, like *puzzles, educational games,* and *5-10 years old* at the same time. On the other hand, if you don't know exactly what you want, or at least to which category it belongs to, you can easily spend hours browsing endless lists of similar items hoping that you'll find something that you're looking for. Search engines of websites solve this issue only partially, as you can get a meaningful amount of results only if you know some unique combination of words or the right brand name to search.

A different view on the problem would be a chatbot that can ask the user questions about his or her intentions, price range, and purpose to limit the search. Of course, this approach is not universal and shouldn't be seen as a 100% replacement for modern websites with search, catalogs, and other UI solutions developed over time, but it can provide a nice alternative in some use cases and serve some percentage of users better than old-style interaction methods.

Deep NLP basics

Hopefully, you're excited about chatbots and their potential applications, so let's now get to the boring details of NLP building blocks and standard approaches. As with almost everything in ML, deep NLP is experiencing hype and is evolving at a fast pace, so this section just scratches the surface and covers the most common and standard building blocks. For a more detailed description, Richard Socher's online course *CS224d* (`http://cs224d.stanford.edu`) is a really good starting point.

Recurrent Neural Networks

NLP has its own specificities that make it different from computer vision or other domains. One such feature is the processing of variable-length objects. At various levels, NLP is dealing with objects that could have different lengths, for example, a word in a language could contain several characters. Sentences are formed from variable-length word sequences. Paragraphs or documents consist of varying amounts of sentences. Such variability is not NLP-specific and can arise in different domains, like in signal processing or video processing. Even standard computer vision problems could be seen as a sequence of some objects, like an image captioning problem when a **Neural Network (NN)** can focus on various amounts of regions of the same image to better describe the image.

One of the standard building blocks are RNNs. The idea of an RNN is a network with fixed input and output, which is being applied to the sequence of objects and can pass information along this sequence. This information is called **hidden state** and is normally just a vector of numbers of some size.

On the following diagram, we have an RNN with one input which is a vector of numbers, the output of which is another vector. What makes it different from a standard feed-forward or convolution network is two extra gates: one input and one output. Extra input feeds the hidden state from the previous item into the RNN unit and the extra output provides a transformed hidden state to the next sequence.

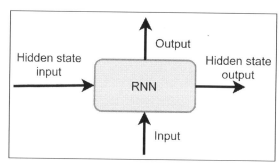

Figure 1: The structure of an RNN building block

This is supposed to solve our variable-length issue and, in fact, it does. As an RNN has two inputs, it could be applied to input sequences of any length, just by passing the hidden state produced by the previous entry to the next one. In Figure 2, an RNN is applied to the sentence *this is a cat*, producing the output for every word in the sequence. During the application, we have the same RNN applied to every input item, but by having the hidden state, it can now pass information along the sequence. This is similar to the convolution neural networks, when we have the same set of filters applied to various locations of the image, but the difference is that the convolution network cannot pass the hidden state.

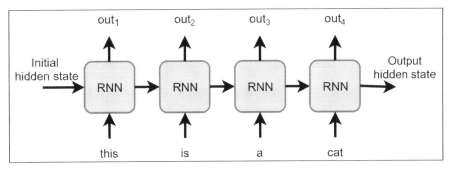

Figure 2: How an RNN is applied to a sentence

Despite the simplicity of this model, it adds an extra degree of freedom to the standard feed-forward NN model. The feed-forward networks are determined by their input and always produce the same output for some fixed input (in testing mode, of course, not during the training). An RNN's output depends not only on the input but on the hidden state, which could be changed by the network itself. So, the network could pass some information from the beginning of the sequence to the end and produce different output for the same input in different contexts. This context-dependency is very important in NLP, as in natural language, one single word could have a completely different meaning in different contexts and the meaning of a whole sentence could be changed by one single word.

Of course, such flexibility comes with its own cost. RNNs usually require more time to train and can produce some weird behavior, like loss oscillations or sudden amnesia during the training. However, the research community has already done a lot of work and is still working hard to make RNNs more practical and stable, so RNNs can be seen as a standard building block of the systems that need to process variable-length input.

Embeddings

Another standard building block of modern DL-driven NLP is **word embeddings**, which is also called word2vec. The idea comes from the problem of representing our language sequences in NNs. Normally, NNs work with fixed-sized vectors of numbers, but in NLP we normally have words or characters as input to the model.

One of the solutions would be one-hot encoding of our dictionary, when every word has its own position in the input vector and we set this number to 1 when we encounter this word in the input sequence. This is a standard approach in NNs when you have to deal with some not-very-large discrete set of items and want to represent them in a NN-friendly way. Unfortunately, one-hot encoding is not working very well for several reasons.

First of all, our input set is usually not small. If we want to encode only the most commonly used English dictionary, it will contain at least several thousand words. The Oxford English dictionary has 170,000 commonly-used words and 50,000 obsolete and rare words. This is only established vocabulary, not counting slang, new words, scientific terms, abbreviations, mistypes, jokes, Twitter memes, and so on. And this is only for the English language!

The second problem related to one-hot representation of words is the uneven frequency of vocabulary. There are relatively small sets of very frequent words, like *a*, *cat*, and so on, but a very large set of much more rarely-used words, like *covfefe* or *bibliopole*, and those rare words can occur only once or twice in a very large text corpus. So, our one-hot representation is very inefficient in terms of space.

Another issue with simple one-hot representation is not capturing a word's relations. For example, some words are synonyms and have the same meaning, but they will be represented by different vectors. Some words are used very frequently together, like *united nations* or *fair trade,* and this fact is also not captured in one-hot representation.

To overcome all this, we can use word embeddings, which map every word in some vocabulary into a dense, fixed-length vector of numbers. These numbers are not random but trained on a large corpus of text to capture the context of words. A detailed description of word embeddings is beyond the scope of this book, but this is a really powerful and widely-used NLP technique to represent words, characters and other objects in some sequence. For now, you can think about them as just mapping from words into number vectors and this mapping is convenient for the network to distinguish words from each other.

To obtain this mapping, two methods exist. First of all, you can download pre-trained vectors for the language that you need. There are several sources of embeddings available, just search on Google *glove pretrained vectors* or *word2vec pretrained* (GloVE and word2vec are different methods used to train such vectors, which produce similar results).

Another way to obtain embeddings is to train them on your own dataset. To do this, you can either use special tools, such as `fasttext`, which is open-sourced by Facebook, or just initialize embeddings randomly and allow your model to adjust them during normal training.

Encoder-Decoder

Another model widely used in NLP is called **Encoder-Decoder** and also **seq2seq**. It originally comes from machine translation, when your system needs to accept a sequence of words on the source language and produce another sequence on the target language. The idea behind seq2seq is to use an RNN to process an input sequence and *encode* this sequence into some fixed-length representation. This RNN is called an **encoder**. Then you feed the encoded vector into another RNN, called a **decoder**, which has to produce the resulting sequence in the target language. An example of this idea is shown as follows, where we are translating an English sentence into Russian:

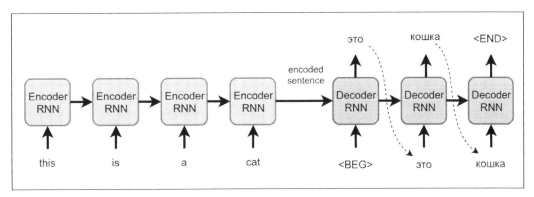

Figure 3: Encoder-Decoder architecture in machine translation

This model (with lots of modern tweaks and extensions) is still a major workhorse of machine translation but is general enough to be applicable to a much wider set of domains, for example, audio processing, image annotation, video captioning and others. In our chatbot example, we'll use it to generate reply phrases when given the input sequence of words.

Training of seq2seq

That's all very interesting, but how is it related to RL? The connection lies in the training process of the seq2seq model, but before we come to the modern RL approaches to the problem, we need to say a couple of words about the standard way of carrying out the training.

Log-likelihood training

Imagine that we need to create a machine translation system from one language (say, French) into another language (English) using the seq2seq model. Let's assume that we have a good, large dataset of sample translations with French-English sentences that we're going to train our model on. How do we do this?

The encoding part is obvious: we just apply our encoder RNN to the first sentence in the training pair, which produces an encoded representation of the sentence. The obvious candidate for this representation will be the hidden state returned from the last RNN application. At encoding stage, we ignore the RNN's outputs, taking into account only the hidden state from the last RNN application. We also extend our sentence with the special token <END>, which signals to the encoder the end of the sentence. This process is shown in the following diagram:

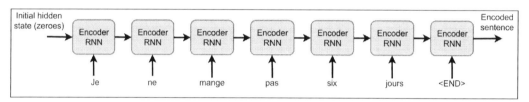

Figure 4: The encoding step

To start decoding, we pass the encoded representation to the decoder's input hidden state and pass the token <BEG> as a signal to begin decoding. In this step, the decoder RNN has to return to us the first token of the translated sentence. However, in the beginning of training, when both the encoder and decoder RNNs are initialized with random weights, the decoder's output will be random and our goal will be to push it toward the correct translation using **Stochastic Gradient Descent (SGD)**.

The traditional approach is to treat this problem as classification, when our decoder needs to return probability distribution over the tokens in the current position of the decoded sentence. Normally, this is done by transforming the decoder's output using the shallow feed-forward network and producing a vector, whose length is the size of our dictionary. Then we take this probability distribution and standard loss for classification problems: cross-entropy (also known as log-likelihood loss).

That's clear with the first token in the decoded sequence, which should be produced by the <BEG> token given on the input, but what about the rest of the sequence? There are two options here. The first alternative is to feed tokens from the reference sentence. For example, if we have training pair *Je ne mange pas six jours -> I haven't eaten for six days*, we feed tokens (I, haven't, eaten...) to the decoder and then use cross-entropy loss between the RNN's output and the next token in the sentence. This training mode is called **teacher forcing,** and at every step we feed a token from the correct translation, asking the RNN to produce the correct next token. This process is shown in the following diagram:

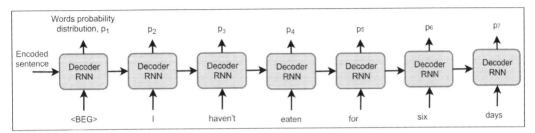

Figure 5: How the encoded vector is decoded in the teacher-forcing mode

The loss expression for the preceding example will be calculated as follows:

```
L = xentropy(p1,"I") + xentropy(p2,"haven't") + xentropy(p3,"eaten")
+ xentropy(p4,"for") + xentropy(p5,"six") + xentropy(p6,"days") +
xentropy(p7,"<END>")
```

As both the decoder and encoder are differentiable NNs, we can just backpropagate the loss to push both of them towards the better classification of this example in the future, the same way that we train the image classifier, for example.

Unfortunately, the preceding procedure doesn't solve the seq2seq training problem completely and the issue is related to the way the model was used. During the training, we know both input and the desired output sequences, so we can feed the valid output sequence to the decoder, which is being asked only to produce the next token of the sequence.

After the model has been trained, we won't have a target sequence (as this sequence is supposed to be produced by the model). So, the simplest way to use the model will be to encode the input sequence using the encoder and then ask the decoder to generate one item of the output at a time, feeding the produced token into the input of the decoder.

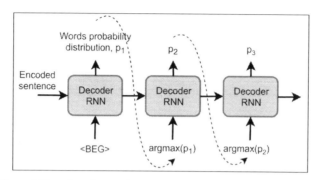

Figure 6: How decoding in the curriculum learning mode is performed

This passing of the previous result into the input might look natural, but there is a danger here. During the training, we haven't asked our decoder RNN to use its own output as input, so one single mistake during the generation may confuse the decoder and lead to the garbage output.

To overcome this, a second approach to seq2seq training exists, called **curriculum learning**. This method uses the same cross-entropy loss, but instead of passing the full target sequence as the decoder's input, we just ask the decoder to decode the sequence in the same way as we're going to use it after training. This process is illustrated on the preceding diagram. This adds robustness to the decoder, which gives a better result on the practical application of the model. As a downside, this mode may lead to very long training, as our decoder learns how to produce the desired output token-by-token. To compensate for this, in practice we usually train a model using both teacher and curriculum learning, just randomly choosing between those two for every batch.

Bilingual evaluation understudy (BLEU) score

Before we get into the main topic of this chapter (RL for seq2seq), we need to introduce the metric used to compare the quality of machine translation output commonly used in NLP problems. The metric, called **BLEU**, is one of the standard ways to compare the output sequence produced by the machine with some set of reference outputs. It allows multiple reference outputs to be used (one sentence could be translated in various ways) and at its core it calculates the ratio of unigrams, bigrams, and so on, shared between produced output and reference sentences.

Other alternatives exist, such as CIDEr and ROGUE. In this example, we will use BLEU implemented in the `nltk` Python library (the `nltk.translate.bleu_score package`).

RL in seq2seq

RL and text generation might look very different, but there are connections which could be used to improve the quality of the trained seq2seq models. The first thing to note is that our decoder outputs the probability distribution at every step, which is very similar to **Policy Gradient (PG)** models. From this perspective, our decoder could be seen as an agent trying to decide which token to produce at every step. There are several advantages of such interpretation of the decoding process.

First of all, by treating our decoding process as stochastic, we can automatically take into account multiple target sequences. For example, there are many possible replies to the *hello! How are you?* phrase, and all of them are correct. By optimizing the log-likelihood objective, our model will try to learn some average of all those replies, but the average of the phrases *I'm fine, thanks!* and *not very good* will not necessarily be a meaningful phrase. By returning the probability distribution and sampling the next token from it, our agent potentially could learn how to produce all possible variants, instead of learning some averaged answer.

The second benefit is optimizing the objective that we care about. In log-likelihood training, we're minimizing the cross-entropy between the produced tokens and tokens from the reference, but in machine translation, and many other NLP problems, we don't really care about log-likelihood: we want to maximize the BLEU score of the produced sequence. Unfortunately, the BLEU score is not differentiable, so we can't backpropagate on it. However, PG methods such as REINFORCE (from *Chapter 9, Policy Gradients – An Alternative*) work even when the reward is not differentiable: we just push up the probabilities of successful episodes and decrease for worse ones.

The third advantage we can exploit is in the fact that our sequence generation process is defined by us and we know its internals. By introducing stochasticity into the process of decoding, we can repeat the decoding process several times, gathering different decoding scenarios from the single training sample. This can be beneficial when our training dataset is limited, which is almost always the case, unless you're a Google or Facebook employee.

To understand how to switch our training from log-likelihood objective to an RL scenario, let's look at both from the mathematical point of view. Log-likelihood estimation means maximizing the sum $\sum_{i=1}^{N} \log p_{model}(y_i|x_i)$ by tweaking the model's parameter, which is exactly the same as minimization of **Kullback–Leibler (KL)**-divergence between the data probability distribution and probability distribution parameterized by the model, which could be written as a maximization of $\mathbb{E}_{x \sim p_{data}} \log p_{model}(x)$.

On the other hand, the REINFORCE method has the objective to maximize $\mathbb{E}_{s \sim data, a \sim \pi(a|s)} Q(s, a) \log \pi(a|s)$. The connection is obvious and the difference between the two is just the scale before the logarithm and the way we're selecting actions (which are tokens in our dictionary).

In practice, REINFORCE for seq2seq training could be written as the following algorithm:

1. For every sample in the dataset, obtain the encoded representation E, using the encoder RNN

2. Initialize the current token with the special `begin` token: `T = '<BEG>'`

3. Initialize the output sequence with the empty sequence: `Out = []`

4. While `T != '<END>'`

    ◦ Get the probability distribution of the tokens and the new hidden state, passing the current token and the hidden state: p, H = Decoder(T, E)

    ◦ Sample output token T_{out} from the probability distribution

    ◦ Remember the probability distribution p

    ◦ Append T_{out} to the output sequence Out += T_{out}

    ◦ Set the current token T ←T_{out}, E ← H

5. Calculate BLEU or another metric between Out and the reference sequences: Q = BLEU(Out, Out$_{ref}$))

6. Estimate the gradients $\nabla J = \sum_T Q \nabla \log p(T)$

7. Update the model using SGD

8. Repeat until converged

Self-critical sequence training

The described approach, despite its positive sides, has also several complications. First of all, it's almost useless to train from scratch. Even for simple dialogs, the output sequence usually has at least five or more words, each taken from the dictionary of several thousand words. The number of different phrases of size five, with a dictionary of 1000 words equals 5^{1000}, which is slightly less than 10^{700}. So, the probability of obtaining the correct reply in the beginning of the training (when our weights for both encoder and decoder are random) is negligibly small. To overcome this, we can combine both log-likelihood and RL approaches and pretrain our model with the log-likelihood objective first (switching between teacher forcing and curriculum learning) and after the model gets to some level of quality, switch to the REINFORCE method to fine-tune the model. In general, this could be seen as a uniform approach to complex RL problems, when a large action space makes it infeasible to start with a randomly-behaving agent, as the chance of such an agent randomly reaching the goal is negligible. There are lots of research happening around the incorporation of externally generated samples into the RL training process and using log-likelihood pretraining on correct actions is one of the approaches.

Another issue with the vanilla REINFORCE method is the high variance of the gradients that we've discussed in the *Chapter 10, The Actor-Critic Method*. As you might remember, to solve the issue we used the **Actor-Critic (A2C)** method, which used the dedicated estimation of the state's value as a variance. We can apply the A2C method that way, of course, by extending our decoder with another head and returning BLEU score estimation given the decoded sequence, but there is a better approach. In the paper a *Self-Critical Sequence Training for Image Captionings* [1], published by S. Rennie and E. Marcherett and others in 2016, a better baseline was proposed.

To obtain the baseline, the authors of the paper used the decoder in argmax mode to generate a sequence, which then was used to calculate the similarity metric like BLEU or similar. Switching to argmax mode makes the decoder process fully deterministic and provides the baseline for the REINFORCE policy gradient in the formula:

$$\nabla J = \mathbb{E}[(Q(s) - b(s))\nabla \log p(a|s)]$$

In the following section, we'll implement and train a simple chatbot from the movies dataset.

The chatbot example

In the beginning of this chapter, we talked a bit about chatbots and NLP, so let's try to implement something simple using seq2seq and RL training. In total, there are two large groups of chatbots distinguished: **entertainment human-mimicking** and **goal-oriented** chatbots. The first group is supposed to entertain a user giving human-like replies to a user's phrases, without fully understanding them. The latter category is much harder to implement and is supposed to solve a user's problem: provide information, change reservations or switch on and off your home toaster. Most of the latest efforts in the industry are focused on the goal-oriented group, but the problem is far from being fully solved yet. As this chapter is supposed to give a short example of the methods described, we'll focus on training an entertainment bot using an online dataset with phrases extracted from movies.

Despite the simplicity of this problem, this example is large in terms of code and the new concepts that we have, so whole code of the example is not included in the book. We'll focus only on the central modules responsible for model training and usage, but lots of functions will be covered as an overview.

The example structure

The complete example is in the rl_book_samples/Chapter12 folder and contains the following parts:

- data: A directory with the get_data.sh script to download and unpack the dataset that we'll use in the example. The dataset archive is 10 MB, contains structured dialogs extracted from various sources, and is known as the **Cornell Movie-Dialogs Corpus**, which is available here: https://www.cs.cornell.edu/~cristian/Cornell_Movie-Dialogs_Corpus.html.

- libbots: A directory with Python modules shared between various example's components. Those modules are described in the next chapter.

- tests: A directory with unit tests for library modules.

- The root folder contains two programs to train the model: train_crossent.py, which is used to train the model in the beginning and train_scst.py, which is used to fine-tune the pretrained model using the REINFORCE algorithm.

- A script to display various statistics and data from the dataset: cor_reader.py.

- A script to apply the trained model to the dataset, displaying quality metrics: data_test.py.

- A script to use the model against a user-provided phrase: `use_model.py`.

- A bot for Telegram messenger, which uses the pretrained model: `telegram_bot.py`.

We will start with the data-related parts of the example, then look at both training scripts, before finishing by covering the model usage.

Modules: cornell.py and data.py

Two library modules working with the dataset used to train the model are `cornell.py` and `data.py`. Both are related to data processing and are used to transform the dataset into a form suitable for training but working on different layers.

The `cornell.py` file includes low-level functions to parse data in the Cornell Movie-Dialogs Corpus format and represents it in a form suitable for later processing. The main goal of the module is to load a list of dialogs from movies. As the dataset contains metadata about the movies, we can filter dialogs to be loaded by various criteria, but only a genre filter is implemented. In the list of dialogs returned, every dialog is represented as a list of phrases and every phrase is a list of lowercase words (which are called **tokens**). For example, a phrase could be `["hi", "!", "how", "are", "you", "?"]`.

The conversion of sentences to the list of tokens is called tokenization in NLP and even this step by itself can be a tricky process, as you need to handle punctuation, abbreviations, quotes, apostrophes, and other natural language specifics. Luckily, the `nltk` library includes several tokenizers, so going from a sentence to a list of tokens is just a matter of calling the appropriate function, which significantly simplifies our task. The main function in `cornell.py` used outside of it is the function `load_dialogues()`, which is supposed to load dialogue data with an optional genre filter.

The `data.py` module works on a higher level and doesn't include any dataset-specific knowledge. It provides the following functionality, which is used almost everywhere in the example:

- Working with mappings from tokens in their integer IDs: saving and loading from the file (`save_emb_dict()` and `load_emb_dict()` functions), encoding the list of tokens into a list of IDs (`encode_words()`), decoding the list of integer IDs into tokens (`decode_words()`) and generating the dictionary mapping from the training data (`phrase_pairs_dict()`)

- Working with the training data: iterating batches of given size (`iterate_batches()`) and splitting data into training/testing parts (`split_train_test()`)

- Loading dialogs data and converting it into phrase-reply pairs suitable for training: `load_data()` function

On data loading and dictionary creation, we also add special tokens with the pre-defined IDs:

- A token for unknown words `#UNK`, used for all out-of-dictionary tokens
- A token for the beginning of the sequence `#BEG`, prepended to all sequences
- A token for the end of the sequence `#END`

Besides the optional genre filter, which could be used to limit data size during experiments, several other filters are applied to the loaded data. The first filter limits the maximum number of tokens in training pairs. RNN training can be expensive in terms of the number of operations and memory usage, so I left only the training pairs with 20 tokens for the first and the second training entry. This also helps for convergence speed, as the variability of dialogs with short sentences is much less, so it's easier for our RNN to train on this data. This also has a downside of our model producing only short replies.

The second filter applied to the data is related to the dictionary. The amount of words in the dictionary has significant influence on the performance and GPU memory needed, as both our embedding matrix (keeping embeddings vectors for every dict token) and decoder output projection matrix (which converts the decoder RNN's output into the probability distribution) have dictionary size as one of the dimensions. So, by reducing the amount of words in our dictionary, we can reduce memory and improve the training speed. To get this during the data loading, we calculate the count of occurrences for every word in the dictionary and map all words which have met less than 10 times to an unknown token. Later, all the training pairs with an unknown token are removed from the training set.

BLEU score and utils.py

To calculate the BLEU score, the `nltk` library is used, but to make the BLEU calculation a bit more convenient, two wrapper functions are implemented: `calc_bleu(candidate_seq, reference_seq)`, which calculates the score when we have one candidate and one reference sequence and `calc_bleu_many(candidate_seq, reference_sequences)`, which is used to get the score when we have several reference sequences to compare against our candidate. In the case of several candidates, the best BLEU score is calculated and returned.

Also, to reflect the short phrases in our dataset, BLEU is calculated for unigrams and bigrams only. The following is the code of the `utils.py` module, which is responsible for BLEU calculations and an extra two functions used to tokenize the sentences and convert the list of tokens back into a string.

```
import string
from nltk.translate import bleu_score
from nltk.tokenize import TweetTokenizer


def calc_bleu_many(cand_seq, ref_sequences):
    sf = bleu_score.SmoothingFunction()
    return bleu_score.sentence_bleu(ref_sequences, cand_seq,
                                    smoothing_function=sf.method1,
                                    weights=(0.5, 0.5))


def calc_bleu(cand_seq, ref_seq):
    return calc_bleu_many(cand_seq, [ref_seq])


def tokenize(s):
    return TweetTokenizer(preserve_case=False).tokenize(s)


def untokenize(words):
    return "".join([" " + i if not i.startswith("'") and i not in
string.punctuation else i for i in words]).strip()
```

Model

The functions related to the training process and the model itself are defined in the `libbots/model.py` file. It is important for understanding the training process, so the code with comments is shown as follows.

```
HIDDEN_STATE_SIZE = 512
EMBEDDING_DIM = 50
```

Two hyperparameters are defining the size of the hidden state used by both the encoder and decoder RNNs. In the PyTorch implementation of RNNs, this value defines three parameters at once:

- Dimension of the hidden state expected on the input and returned as the output of the RNN unit

- Dimension of the output returned from the RNN. Despite being the same dimension, the output of the RNN is different from the hidden state

- Internal count of neurons used for RNN transformation

The second hyperparameter, EMBEDDING_DIM, defines the dimensionality of our embeddings, which is a set of vectors used to represent every token in our dictionary. For this example, we are not using the pre-trained embeddings like GLoVe or word2vec but will train them alongside the model. As our encoder and decoder are both accept tokens on the input, this dimensionality of embeddings also defines the size of the RNN's input.

```
class PhraseModel(nn.Module):
    def __init__(self, emb_size, dict_size, hid_size):
        super(PhraseModel, self).__init__()

        self.emb = nn.Embedding(num_embeddings=dict_size,
embedding_dim=emb_size)
        self.encoder = nn.LSTM(input_size=emb_size,
hidden_size=hid_size,
                               num_layers=1, batch_first=True)
        self.decoder = nn.LSTM(input_size=emb_size,
hidden_size=hid_size,
                               num_layers=1, batch_first=True)
        self.output = nn.Sequential(
            nn.Linear(hid_size, dict_size)
        )
```

In the model's constructor, we create embedding, encoder, decoder and output projection components. As RNN implementation, LSTM is used. The batch_first argument specifies that the batch will be provided as the first dimension of the input tensor to the RNN. The projection layer is a linear transformation, which converts the output from the decoder into dictionary probability distribution.

The rest of the model is methods that are used to perform different transformations of the data using our seq2seq model. Strictly speaking, this class breaks PyTorch convention to override the forward method to apply the network to the data. This is intentional, to emphasize the fact that the seq2seq model is not possible to interpret as a single transformation of input data to output. In our example, we'll use the model in different ways, for example, processing the target sequence in teacher-forcing mode or decoding the sequence one-by-one using argmax or performing one single decoding step. As base class nn.Module.forward method is just responsible for calling hooks (which we're not using in our example), it's fine to avoid forward method redefinition.

```
def encode(self, x):
    _, hid = self.encoder(x)
    return hid
```

The preceding method performs the simplest operation in our model: it encodes the input sequence and returns the hidden state from the last step of the encoder RNN. In PyTorch, all RNN classes return the tuple of two objects as a result. The first component of the tuple is output of the RNN for every application of the RNN and the second is the hidden state from the last item in the input sequence. We're not interested in the encoder's output, so we just return the hidden state.

```
def get_encoded_item(self, encoded, index):
    # For RNN
    # return encoded[:, index:index+1]
    # For LSTM
    return encoded[0][:, index:index+1].contiguous(), \
           encoded[1][:, index:index+1].contiguous()
```

The preceding function is a utility method used to get access to the hidden state of the individual component of the input batch. It is required, because we're encoding the whole batch of sequences in one call (using the `encode()` method), but decoding is performed for every batch sequence individually. This method is used to extract the hidden state of index'th element of the batch. The details of this extraction are RNN-implementation dependent. LSTM, for example, has hidden state represented as a tuple of two tensors: the cell state and the hidden state. However, simple RNN implementation, like vanilla `torch.nn.RNN` class or the more complicated `torch.nn.GRU`, both have hidden state as a single tensor. So, this knowledge is encapsulated in this method, which should be adjusted if you switch encoder and decoder underlying RNN type.

The rest of the methods are solely related to the decoding process in its different forms.

```
def decode_teacher(self, hid, input_seq):
    # Method assumes batch of size=1
    out, _ = self.decoder(input_seq, hid)
    out = self.output(out.data)
    return out
```

The simplest and the most efficient way to perform decoding is teacher-forcing mode. In this mode, we simply apply the decoder RNN to the reference sequence (reply phrase of the training sample). In teacher-forcing mode, the input for every step is known in advance and the only dependency that the RNN has between steps is its hidden state, which allows us to perform RNN transformation very efficiently, without transferring data from and to the GPU and implemented in the underlying CuDNN library.

This is not the case for other decoding methods, when the output of every decoder step defines the input for the next step. This connection between output and input is done in Python code, so decoding is performed step-by step, not necessarily transferring the data (as all our tensors are already in GPU memory), but the control is defined by Python code and not by the highly-optimized CuDNN library.

```
def decode_one(self, hid, input_x):
    out, new_hid = self.decoder(input_x.unsqueeze(0), hid)
    out = self.output(out)
    return out.squeeze(dim=0), new_hid
```

The preceding method performs one single decoding step for one example. We pass the hidden state for the decoder (which is set to the encoded sequence at the first step) and input the tensor with the embeddings vector for the input token. Then, the result from the decoder is passed through the output projection to obtain the raw scores for every token in the dictionary. It's not a probability distribution, as we do not pass the output through the softmax function, just the raw scores (also called logits). The result of the function is those logits and the new hidden state returned by the decoder.

```
    def decode_chain_argmax(self, hid, begin_emb, seq_len, stop_at_
token=None):
        res_logits = []
        res_tokens = []
        cur_emb = begin_emb
```

The `decode_chain_argmax()` method performs decoding of an encoded sequence, using `argmax` as a transition from probability distribution to a token index produced. The function arguments are as follows:

- `hid`: The hidden state returned by the encoder for the input sequence.

- `begin_emb`: The embedding vector for the #BEG token used to start decoding.

- `seq_len`: The maximum length of the decoded sequence. The resulting sequence could be shorter if the decoder returns #END token, but never could be longer. It helps to stop decoding when the decoder starts to repeat itself infinitely, which might happen at the beginning of training.

- `stop_at_token`: Optional token ID (normally #END token) that stops the decoding process.

This function is supposed to return two values: a tensor with resulting logits returned by the decoder on every step and the list of token IDs produced. The first value is used for training, as we need the output tensors to calculate the loss, while the second value is passed to the quality metric function, which is the BLEU score in this case.

```
for _ in range(seq_len):
    out_logits, hid = self.decode_one(hid, cur_emb)
    out_token_v = torch.max(out_logits, dim=1)[1]
    out_token = out_token_v.data.cpu().numpy()[0]

    cur_emb = net.emb(out_token_v)

    res_logits.append(out_logits)
    res_tokens.append(out_token)
    if stop_at_token is not None and out_token ==
stop_at_token:
        break
return torch.cat(res_logits), res_tokens
```

At every decoding loop iteration, we apply the decoder RNN to one single token, passing the current hidden state for the decoder (in the beginning it equals to the encoded vector) and embedding vector for the current token. The output from the decoder RNN is a tuple with logits (unnormalized probabilities for every word in the dictionary) and the new hidden state. To go from logits to the decoded token ID, we use the argmax function as the name of the method. Then we obtain embeddings for the decoded token, save logits and token ID in the resulting lists and check for stop conditions.

```
def decode_chain_sampling(self, hid, begin_emb, seq_len,
stop_at_token=None):
    res_logits = []
    res_actions = []
    cur_emb = begin_emb

    for _ in range(seq_len):
        out_logits, hid = self.decode_one(hid, cur_emb)
        out_probs_v = F.softmax(out_logits, dim=1)
        out_probs = out_probs_v.data.cpu().numpy()[0]
        action = int(np.random.choice(out_probs.shape[0],
p=out_probs))
```

```
        action_v = torch.LongTensor([action]).to(action_v.device)
        cur_emb = net.emb(action_v)

        res_logits.append(out_logits)
        res_actions.append(action)
        if stop_at_token is not None and action == stop_at_token:
            break
    return torch.cat(res_logits), res_actions
```

The next and the last function to perform decoding of the sequence does almost the same as `decode_chain_argmax()`, but, instead of argmax, it performs the random sampling from the returned probability distribution. The rest of the logic is the same.

Besides the `PhraseModel` class, the `model.py` file contains several functions used to prepare the input to the model, which has to be in a tensor form for PyTorch RNN machinery to work properly.

```
def pack_batch_no_out(batch, embeddings, device="cpu"):
    assert isinstance(batch, list)
    # Sort descending (CuDNN requirements)
    batch.sort(key=lambda s: len(s[0]), reverse=True)
    input_idx, output_idx = zip(*batch)
```

This function packs the input batch (which is a list of (`phrase`, `replay`) tuples) into the form suitable for encoding and `decode_chain_*` functions. As the first step, we sort the batch by the first phrase's length in decreasing order. This is a requirement of the CuDNN library used by PyTorch as a CUDA backend.

```
    # create padded matrix of inputs
    lens = list(map(len, input_idx))
    input_mat = np.zeros((len(batch), lens[0]), dtype=np.int64)
    for idx, x in enumerate(input_idx):
        input_mat[idx, :len(x)] = x
```

Then we create a matrix with [batch, max_input_phrase] dimensions and copy our input phrases there. This form is called **padded sequence**, because our sequences of variable length are padded with zeros to the longest sequence.

```
    input_v = torch.tensor(input_mat).to(device)
    input_seq = rnn_utils.pack_padded_sequence(input_v, lens,
batch_first=True)
```

As the next step, we wrap this matrix into a PyTorch tensor and use a special function from the PyTorch RNN module to convert this matrix from the padded form into the so-called **packed form**. In the packed form, our sequences are stored column-wise (that is, in a transposed form), keeping the length of every column. For example, in the first row we have all first tokens from all sequences. In the second row, we have tokens from the second position for sequences longer than 1, and so on. This representation allows CuDNN to perform RNN processing very efficiently, handling our batch of sequences at once.

```
# lookup embeddings
r = embeddings(input_seq.data)
emb_input_seq = rnn_utils.PackedSequence(r, input_seq.batch_sizes)
return emb_input_seq, input_idx, output_idx
```

At the end of the function, we convert our data from the integer token IDs into embeddings, which could be done in one step, as our token IDs have already been packed into the tensor. Then we return the result tuple with three items: the packed sequence to be passed to the encoder and two lists of lists with the integer token IDs for the input and output sequences.

```
def pack_input(input_data, embeddings, device="cpu"):
    input_v = torch.LongTensor([input_data]).to(device)
    r = embeddings(input_v)
    return rnn_utils.pack_padded_sequence(r, [len(input_data)],
batch_first=True)
```

The preceding function is used to convert the encoded phrase (as the list of token IDs) into the packed sequence suitable to pass to the RNN.

```
def pack_batch(batch, embeddings, device="cpu"):
    emb_input_seq, input_idx, output_idx = pack_batch_no_out
(batch, embeddings, device)
    output_seq_list = []
    for out in output_idx:
        output_seq_list.append(pack_input(out[:-1],
embeddings, device))
    return emb_input_seq, output_seq_list, input_idx, output_idx
```

The next function uses the `pack_batch_no_out()` method, but, in addition, converts the output indices into the list of packed sequences to be used in the teacher-forcing mode of training. Those sequences have the #END token stripped.

```
def seq_bleu(model_out, ref_seq):
    model_seq = torch.max(model_out.data, dim=1)[1]
    model_seq = model_seq.cpu().numpy()
    return utils.calc_bleu(model_seq, ref_seq)
```

Finally, the last function in `model.py`, which calculates the BLEU score from the tensor with logits, is produced by the decoder in teacher-forcing mode. Its logic is simple: it just calls argmax to obtain sequence indices and then uses the BLEU calculation function from the `utils.py` module.

Training: cross-entropy

To train the first approximation of the model, the cross-entropy method is used and implemented in `train_crossent.py`. During the training, we randomly switch between the teacher-forcing mode (when we give the target sequence on the decoder's input) and argmax chain decoding (when we decode the sequence one step at a time, choosing the token with the highest probability in the output distribution). The decision between those two training modes is taken randomly with the fixed probability of 50%. This allows for combining the characteristics of both methods: fast convergence from teacher forcing and stable decoding from curriculum learning.

```
SAVES_DIR = "saves"

BATCH_SIZE = 32
LEARNING_RATE = 1e-3
MAX_EPOCHES = 100

log = logging.getLogger("train")

TEACHER_PROB = 0.5
```

In the beginning, we define hyperparameters specific to the cross-entropy training step. The value of TEACHER_PROB defines the probability of teacher-forcing training being chosen randomly for every training sample.

```
def run_test(test_data, net, end_token, device="cpu"):
    bleu_sum = 0.0
    bleu_count = 0
    for p1, p2 in test_data:
        input_seq = model.pack_input(p1, net.emb, device)
        enc = net.encode(input_seq)
        _, tokens = net.decode_chain_argmax(enc, input_seq.data[0:1],
                                            seq_len=data.MAX_TOKENS,
                                            stop_at_token=end_token)
        bleu_sum += utils.calc_bleu(tokens, p2[1:])
        bleu_count += 1
    return bleu_sum / bleu_count
```

The `run_test` method is called every epoch to calculate the mean BLEU score for the held-out test dataset, which is 5% of loaded data by default.

```
if __name__ == "__main__":
    logging.basicConfig(format="%(asctime)-15s %(levelname)s
%(message)s", level=logging.INFO)
    parser = argparse.ArgumentParser()
    parser.add_argument("--data", required=True, help="Category to use
for training. "
                                                      "Empty string to
train on full dataset")
    parser.add_argument("--cuda", action='store_true', default=False,
                        help="Enable cuda")
    parser.add_argument("-n", "--name", required=True, help="Name of
the run")
    args = parser.parse_args()
    device = torch.device("cuda" if args.cuda else "cpu")

    saves_path = os.path.join(SAVES_DIR, args.name)
    os.makedirs(saves_path, exist_ok=True)
```

The program allows specifying the genre of films that we want to train on and the name of the current training, which is used in a TensorBoard comment and as a name of the directory for the periodical model checkpoints.

```
    phrase_pairs, emb_dict = data.load_data(genre_filter=args.data)
    log.info("Obtained %d phrase pairs with %d uniq words",
             len(phrase_pairs), len(emb_dict))
    data.save_emb_dict(saves_path, emb_dict)
    end_token = emb_dict[data.END_TOKEN]
    train_data = data.encode_phrase_pairs(phrase_pairs, emb_dict)
```

When the arguments have been parsed, we load the dataset for the provided genre, save the embeddings dictionary (which is a mapping from the token's string to the integer ID of the token) and encode the phrase pairs. At this point, our data is a list of tuples with two entries and every entry is a list of token integer IDs.

```
    rand = np.random.RandomState(data.SHUFFLE_SEED)
    rand.shuffle(train_data)
    log.info("Training data converted, got %d samples", len
(train_data))
    train_data, test_data = data.split_train_test(train_data)
    log.info("Train set has %d phrases, test %d", len(train_data),
len(test_data))
```

After the data has been loaded, we split it to train/test parts, then we shuffle the data using a fixed random seed (to be able to repeat the same shuffle at the RL training stage).

```
    net = model.PhraseModel(emb_size=model.EMBEDDING_DIM,
dict_size=len(emb_dict),
                            hid_size=model.HIDDEN_STATE_SIZE).
to(device)
    log.info("Model: %s", net)
    writer = SummaryWriter(comment="-" + args.name)
    optimiser = optim.Adam(net.parameters(), lr=LEARNING_RATE)
    best_bleu = None
```

Then we create the model, passing it the dimensionality of the embeddings, size of the dictionary and the hidden size of the encoder and decoder.

```
    for epoch in range(MAX_EPOCHES):
        losses = []
        bleu_sum = 0.0
        bleu_count = 0
        for batch in data.iterate_batches(train_data, BATCH_SIZE):
            optimiser.zero_grad()
            input_seq, out_seq_list, _, out_idx = model.pack_
batch(batch, net.emb, device)
            enc = net.encode(input_seq)
```

Our training loop performs the fixed number of epochs and each of them is an iteration over the batches of pairs of the encoded phrases. For the every batch, we pack it using `model.pack_batch()`, which returns the packed input sequence, packed output sequence and two lists of input and output token indices of the batch. To get the encoded representation for every input sequence in the batch, we call `net.encode()`, which just passes the input sequence through our encoder and returns the hidden state from the last RNN application. This hidden state has a shape of [batch_size, `model.HIDDEN_STATE_SIZE`], which is [16, 512] by default.

```
        net_results = []
        net_targets = []
        for idx, out_seq in enumerate(out_seq_list):
            ref_indices = out_idx[idx][1:]
            enc_item = net.get_encoded_item(enc, idx)
```

Then, we decode every sequence in our batch individually. Maybe it is possible to parallelize this loop somehow, but it will make the example less readable. For every sequence in the batch, we get a reference sequence of token IDs (without training the #BEG token) and the encoded representation of the input sequence created by the encoder.

```
            if random.random() < TEACHER_PROB:
                r = net.decode_teacher(enc_item, out_seq)
                bleu_sum += model.seq_bleu(r, ref_indices)
            else:
                r, seq = net.decode_chain_argmax(enc_item,
    out_seq.data[0:1],
                                                 len(ref_indices))
                bleu_sum += utils.calc_bleu(seq, ref_indices)
```

In the preceding code, we randomly decide which method of decoding to use:
teacher-forcing or curriculum learning. They differ only in the model's method called
and the way we compute the BLEU score. For the teacher-forcing mode, the `decode_
teacher()` method returns the tensor of logits of size [out_seq_len, dict_size], so,
to calculate the BLEU score, we need to use the function from the `model.py` module.
In the case of curriculum learning, implemented by the `decode_chain_argmax()`
method, it returns both a logits tensor and list of token IDs of the output sequence.
This allows us to calculate the BLEU score directly.

```
            net_results.append(r)
            net_targets.extend(ref_indices)
            bleu_count += 1
```

At the end of sequence processing, we append the resulting logits and reference
indices to be used later on in the loss calculation.

```
        results_v = torch.cat(net_results)
        targets_v = torch.LongTensor(net_targets).to(device)
        loss_v = F.cross_entropy(results_v, targets_v)
        loss_v.backward()
        optimiser.step()
        losses.append(loss_v.item())
```

To calculate the cross-entropy loss, we convert the list of logits tensors into one single
tensor and convert the list with reference token IDs into a PyTorch tensor, putting
it in GPU memory. Then what we need to do is just calculate the cross-entropy loss,
perform the backpropagation and ask the optimizer to adjust the model. This ends
the processing of one single batch.

```
        bleu = bleu_sum / bleu_count
        bleu_test = run_test(test_data, net, end_token, device)
        log.info("Epoch %d: mean loss %.3f, mean BLEU %.3f,
    test BLEU %.3f",
                 epoch, np.mean(losses), bleu, bleu_test)
        writer.add_scalar("loss", np.mean(losses), epoch)
        writer.add_scalar("bleu", bleu, epoch)
        writer.add_scalar("bleu_test", bleu_test, epoch)
```

When all the batches have been processed, we calculate the mean BLEU score from the training, run a test on the held-out dataset and report our metrics.

```
if best_bleu is None or best_bleu < bleu_test:
    if best_bleu is not None:
        out_name = os.path.join(saves_path, "pre_
bleu_%.3f_%02d.dat" %
                                (bleu_test, epoch))
        torch.save(net.state_dict(), out_name)
        log.info("Best BLEU updated %.3f", bleu_test)
    best_bleu = bleu_test

if epoch % 10 == 0:
    out_name = os.path.join(saves_path, "epoch_%03d_%.3f_%.3f.
dat" %
                            (epoch, bleu, bleu_test))
    torch.save(net.state_dict(), out_name)
```

To be able to fine-tune the model, we save the model's weights with the best test BLEU score seen so far. We also save the checkpoint file every 10 iterations.

Running the training

That's it for our training code. To start it you need to pass the name of the run in the command line and provide the genre filter. The complete dataset is quite large (617 movies in total) and may require lots of time to train, even on GPU. For example, on GTX 1080Ti every epoch takes about 16 minutes, which is 18 hours for 100 epoches.

By applying the genre filter, you can train on a subset of the movies, for example, the genre *comedy* includes 159 movies, bringing us 22k training phrase pairs, which is smaller than 150k phrase pairs from the complete dataset. The dictionary size with the *comedy* filter is also much smaller (4905 words versus 11131 words in the complete data). This decreases epoch time from 16 minutes to 3 minutes.

To make the training set even smaller, you can use the *family* genre, which has only 16 movies with 3000 phrase pairs and 772 words. In this case, 100 epoches takes only 30 minutes. For example, here's how to start training for the *comedy* genre. This process writes checkpoints into directory `saves/crossent-comedy`, while TensorBoard metrics are written in the runs directory.

```
rl_book_samples/Chapter12$ ./train_crossent.py --cuda --data comedy -n
crossent-comedy
2018-01-15 12:35:35,072 INFO Loaded 159 movies with genre comedy
2018-01-15 12:35:35,073 INFO Read and tokenise phrases...
2018-01-15 12:35:39,785 INFO Loaded 93039 phrases
2018-01-15 12:35:40,057 INFO Loaded 24716 dialogues with 93039
phrases, generating training pairs
2018-01-15 12:35:40,118 INFO Counting freq of words...
2018-01-15 12:35:40,469 INFO Data has 31774 uniq words, 4913 of them
occur more than 10
2018-01-15 12:35:40,660 INFO Obtained 47644 phrase pairs with 4905
uniq words
2018-01-15 12:35:40,992 INFO Training data converted, got 26491
samples
2018-01-15 12:35:40,992 INFO Train set has 25166 phrases, test 1325
2018-01-15 12:35:43,320 INFO Model: PhraseModel (
  (emb): Embedding(4905, 50)
  (encoder): LSTM(50, 512, batch_first=True)
  (decoder): LSTM(50, 512, batch_first=True)
  (output): Sequential (
    (0): Linear (512 -> 4905)
  )
)
2018-01-15 12:39:17,656 INFO Epoch 0: mean loss 5.000, mean BLEU
0.164, test BLEU 0.122
2018-01-15 12:42:49,997 INFO Epoch 1: mean loss 4.671, mean BLEU
0.178, test BLEU 0.078
2018-01-15 12:46:23,016 INFO Epoch 2: mean loss 4.537, mean BLEU
0.179, test BLEU 0.088
```

For the cross-entropy training, there are three metrics written into the TensorBoard: loss, train BLEU score and test BLEU score. Below are the plots for the *comedy* genre, which took six hours to train.

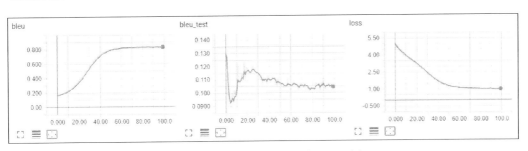

Figure 6: Cross-entropy training on the 'comedy' genre

As you can see, the BLEU score for the training data is consistently growing, saturating around 0.83, but the BLEU score for the testing dataset stopped improving after the 25th epoch and is much less impressive than training data BLEU score. There are two reasons for this. First of all, our dataset is not large and representative enough for our training process to generalize reply phrases to get a good score on the test dataset. In the *comedy* genre, we have 25,166 training pairs and 1325 testing pairs, so there is a high chance for testing pairs to contain phrases which are totally new and not related to the training pairs. This happens due to the high variability of the dialogs that we have and we'll take a look at our data in the next section.

The second possible reason for the low test BLEU could be the fact that cross-entropy training doesn't take into account phrases with several possible replies. As we'll see in the next section, our data contains phrases with several alternatives as a reply. Cross-entropy tries to find such model's weights, which will produce output sequences matching the desired output, but if your desired output is random, there is not much that the model can do about that.

Another reason for the low test score could be lack of proper regularization in the model, which should help to prevent overfitting. This is left as an exercise for you to check the effect.

Checking the data

It's always a good idea to look at your dataset from various angles, like counting statistics, plotting various characteristics of data or just eyeballing your data to get a better understanding of your problem and potential issues. The tool `cor_reader.py` supports the minimalistic functionality for data analysis. By running it with `--show-genres` option, you'll get all genres from the dataset with a number of movies in each, sorted by the count of movies in order of decreasing size. The top 10 of them are shown as follows:

```
rl_book_samples/Chapter12$ ./cor_reader.py --show-genres
Genres:
drama: 320
thriller: 269
action: 168
comedy: 162
crime: 147
romance: 132
sci-fi: 120
```

```
adventure: 116
mystery: 102
horror: 99
```

The `--show-dials` option displays dialogs from the movies without any preprocessing, in the order they appear in the database. The number of dialogs is large, so it's worth passing the `-g` option to filter by genre. For example, let's look at two dialogs from the comedy movies.

```
rl_book_samples/Chapter12$ ./cor_reader.py -g comedy --show-dials |
head -n 10
Dialog 0 with 4 phrases:
can we make this quick? roxanne korrine and andrew barrett are having
an incredibly horrendous public break - up on the quad . again .
well , i thought we'd start with pronunciation , if that's okay with
you .
not the hacking and gagging and spitting part . please .
okay ... then how ' bout we try out some french cuisine . saturday ?
night ?

Dialog 1 with two phrases:
you're asking me out . that's so cute . what's your name again ?
forget it .
```

By passing the `--show-train` option, you can check the training pairs, grouped by the first phrase and sorted in descending order by the count of replies. This data already has the frequency of words (at least 10 occurrences) and phrase length (at most 20 tokens) filter applied. The following is a part of the output for the family genre.

```
rl_book_samples/Chapter12$ ./cor_reader.py -g family --show-train |
head -n 20
Training pairs (558 total)
0: #BEG yes . #END
 : #BEG but you will not ... be safe ... #END
 : #BEG oh ... oh well then , one more won't matter . #END
 : #BEG vada you've gotta stop this , there's absolutely nothing wrong
with you ! #END
 : #BEG good . #END
 : #BEG he's getting big . vada , come here and sit down for a minute
. #END
 : #BEG who's that with your dad ? #END
```

```
    : #BEG for this . #END
    : #BEG didn't i tell you ? i'm always right , you know , my dear ...
aren't i ? #END
    : #BEG oh , i hope we got them in time . #END
    : #BEG oh - - now look at him ! this is terrible ! #END
1: #BEG no . #END
    : #BEG were they pretty ? #END
    : #BEG it's there . #END
    : #BEG why do you think she says that ? #END
    : #BEG come here , sit down . #END
    : #BEG what's wrong with your eyes ? #END
    : #BEG maybe we should , just to see what's the big deal . #END
    : #BEG why not ? #END
```

As you can see, even in a small subset of the data, there are phrases with multiple reply candidates. The last option, supported by cor_reader.py, is --show-dict-freq, which counts the frequency of words and shows them sorted by the count of occurrences.

```
rl_book_samples/Chapter12$ ./cor_reader.py -g family --show-dict-freq
| head -n 10
Frequency stats for 772 tokens in the dict
.: 1907
,: 1175
?: 1148
you: 840
!: 758
i: 653
-: 578
the: 506
a: 414
```

Testing the trained model

Okay, enough about the data, let's now play with our models. During the training, both training tools (train_crossent.py and train_scst.py) periodically save the model, which is done in two different situations: when the BLEU score on the test dataset updates the maximum and every 10 epoches. Both kinds of models have the same format (produced by the torch.save() method) and contain the model's weights. Except the weights, I save the token to integer ID mapping, which will be used by tools to preprocess the phrases.

To experiment with models, two utils exists. The first one is `data_test.py`, which loads the model and applies it to all phrases from the given genre and reports the average BLEU score. Before the testing, phrase pairs are grouped by the first phrase. For example, following is the result for two models, trained on the comedy genre. The first one was trained by the cross-entropy method and the second one was fine-tuned by RL methods.

```
rl_book_samples/Chapter12$ ./data_test.py --data comedy -m saves/
xe-comedy/epoch_030_0.567_0.114.dat
2018-01-15 15:25:43,097 INFO Loaded 159 movies with genre comedy
2018-01-15 15:25:43,097 INFO Read and tokenise phrases...
2018-01-15 15:25:47,814 INFO Loaded 93039 phrases
2018-01-15 15:25:48,084 INFO Loaded 24716 dialogues with 93039
phrases, generating training pairs
2018-01-15 15:25:48,144 INFO Counting freq of words...
2018-01-15 15:25:48,497 INFO Data has 31774 uniq words, 4913 of them
occur more than 10
2018-01-15 15:25:48,688 INFO Obtained 47644 phrase pairs with 4905
uniq words
2018-01-15 15:29:54,990 INFO Processed 22767 phrases, mean BLEU =
0.5283

rl_book_samples/Chapter12$ ./data_test.py --data comedy -m saves/
sc-comedy-e40-no-skip/epoch_080_0.841_0.124.dat
2018-01-15 15:31:47,931 INFO Loaded 159 movies with genre comedy
2018-01-15 15:31:47,931 INFO Read and tokenise phrases...
2018-01-15 15:31:52,617 INFO Loaded 93039 phrases
2018-01-15 15:31:52,887 INFO Loaded 24716 dialogues with 93039
phrases, generating training pairs
2018-01-15 15:31:52,947 INFO Counting freq of words...
2018-01-15 15:31:53,299 INFO Data has 31774 uniq words, 4913 of them
occur more than 10
2018-01-15 15:31:53,492 INFO Obtained 47644 phrase pairs with 4905
uniq words
2018-01-15 15:36:11,085 INFO Processed 22767 phrases, mean BLEU =
0.8066
```

The second way to experiment with a model is the script `use_model.py`, which allows you to pass any string to the model and ask it to generate the reply.

```
rl_book_samples/Chapter12$ ./use_model.py -m saves/sc-comedy-e40-
no-skip/epoch_080_0.841_0.124.dat -s 'how are you?'
very well. thank you.
```

By passing a number to the `--self` option, you can ask the model to process its own reply as input, in other words to generate the dialogue.

```
rl_book_samples/Chapter12$ ./use_model.py -m saves/sc-comedy-e40-no-
skip/epoch_080_0.841_0.124.dat -s 'how are you?' --self 10
very well. thank you.
okay ... it's fine.
hey ...
shut up.
fair enough.
so?
so, i saw my draw.
what are you talking about?
just one.
i have a car.
```

By default, the generation is performed using argmax, so the model's output is always defined by the input tokens. It's not always what we want, so we can add randomness to the output by passing the `--sample` option. In that case, on every decoder step the next token will be sampled from returned probability distribution.

```
rl_book_samples/Chapter12$ ./use_model.py -m saves/sc-comedy-e40-no-
skip/epoch_080_0.841_0.124.dat -s 'how are you?' --self 2 --sample
very well.
very well.
rl_book_samples/Chapter12$ ./use_model.py -m saves/sc-comedy-e40-no-
skip/epoch_080_0.841_0.124.dat -s 'how are you?' --self 2 --sample
very well. thank you.
ok.
```

Training: SCST

As we've already discussed, RL training methods applied to the seq2seq problem can potentially improve the final model. The main reasons are:

- Better handling of multiple target sequences. For example, *hi!* could be replied with *hi!, hello, not interested* or something else. The RL point of view is to treat our decoder as a process of selecting actions when every action is a token to be generated, which fits better to the problem.

- Optimizing the BLEU score directly instead of cross-entropy loss. Using the BLEU score for the generated sequence as a gradient scale, we can push our model towards the successful sequences and decrease the probability of unsuccessful ones.

- By repeating the decoding process, we can generate more episodes to train on, which will lead to better gradient estimation.

- Additionally, using the self-critical sequence training approach, we can get the baseline almost for free, without increasing the complexity of our model, which could improve the convergence even more

All this looks quite promising, so let's check it. RL training is implemented as a separate training step in the tool `train_scst.py`. It requires the model file saved by `train_crossentropy.py` to be passed in a command line.

```
SAVES_DIR = "saves"

BATCH_SIZE = 16
LEARNING_RATE = 1e-4
MAX_EPOCHES = 10000
```

As usual, we start with hyperparameters (imports were omitted). This training script has the same set of hyperparameters, the only difference is smaller batch size, as GPU memory requirements for SCST are higher and have a smaller learning rate.

```
log = logging.getLogger("train")


def run_test(test_data, net, end_token, device="cpu"):
    bleu_sum = 0.0
    bleu_count = 0
    for p1, p2 in test_data:
        input_seq = model.pack_input(p1, net.emb, device)
        enc = net.encode(input_seq)
        _, tokens = net.decode_chain_argmax(enc, input_seq.data[0:1],
seq_len=data.MAX_TOKENS,
                                            stop_at_token=end_token)
        ref_indices = [
            indices[1:]
            for indices in p2
        ]
        bleu_sum += utils.calc_bleu_many(tokens, ref_indices)
        bleu_count += 1
    return bleu_sum / bleu_count
```

Preceding is the function which is run every epoch to calculate the BLEU score on the test dataset. It is almost the same as in `train_crossent.py`, as the only difference is in test data, which is now grouped by the first phrase. So, the shape of the data is now [(first_phrase, [second_phrases])]. As before, we need to strip the #BEG token from every second phrase, but the BLEU score is now calculated by another function, which accepts several reference sequences and returns the best score from them.

```
if __name__ == "__main__":
    logging.basicConfig(format="%(asctime)-15s %(levelname)s
%(message)s", level=logging.INFO)
    parser = argparse.ArgumentParser()
    parser.add_argument("--data", required=True, help="Category to use
for training. Empty string to train on full dataset")
    parser.add_argument("--cuda", action='store_true', default=False,
help="Enable cuda")
    parser.add_argument("-n", "--name", required=True, help="Name of
the run")
    parser.add_argument("-l", "--load", required=True, help="Load
model and continue in RL mode")
    parser.add_argument("--samples", type=int, default=4, help="Count
of samples in prob mode")
    parser.add_argument("--disable-skip", default=False,
action='store_true', help="Disable skipping of samples with high
argmax BLEU")
    args = parser.parse_args()
    device = torch.device("cuda" if args.cuda else "cpu")
```

The tool now accepts three new command-line arguments: option `-l` is passed to provide the file name with the model to load, while option `--samples` is used to change the amount of decoding iterations performed for every train sample. Using more samples leads to more accurate PG estimation but increases GPU memory requirements. The last new option `--disable-skip` could be used to disable skipping of training samples with high BLEU score (by default the threshold is 0.99). This skipping functionality significantly increases the training speed, as we train only on training samples with bad sequences generated in argmax mode, but my experiments have shown that disabling this skipping leads to better model quality.

```
    saves_path = os.path.join(SAVES_DIR, args.name)
    os.makedirs(saves_path, exist_ok=True)

    phrase_pairs, emb_dict = data.load_data(genre_filter=args.data)
    log.info("Obtained %d phrase pairs with %d uniq words",
len(phrase_pairs), len(emb_dict))
    data.save_emb_dict(saves_path, emb_dict)
    end_token = emb_dict[data.END_TOKEN]
```

```
    train_data = data.encode_phrase_pairs(phrase_pairs, emb_dict)
    rand = np.random.RandomState(data.SHUFFLE_SEED)
    rand.shuffle(train_data)
    train_data, test_data = data.split_train_test(train_data)
    log.info("Training data converted, got %d samples", len
(train_data))
```

Then, we load the training data the same way we did in cross-entropy training. The extra code is in the two lines below, which are used to group the training data by the first phrase.

```
    train_data = data.group_train_data(train_data)
    test_data = data.group_train_data(test_data)
    log.info("Train set has %d phrases, test %d", len(train_data),
len(test_data))

    rev_emb_dict = {idx: word for word, idx in emb_dict.items()}

    net = model.PhraseModel(emb_size=model.EMBEDDING_DIM, dict_
size=len(emb_dict), hid_size=model.HIDDEN_STATE_SIZE).to(device)
    log.info("Model: %s", net)

    writer = SummaryWriter(comment="-" + args.name)
    net.load_state_dict(torch.load(args.load))
    log.info("Model loaded from %s, continue training in RL mode...",
args.load)
```

When the data is loaded, we create the model and load its weights from the given file.

```
    beg_token = torch.LongTensor([emb_dict[data.BEGIN_TOKEN]]).
to(device)
```

Before we start the training, we need a special tensor with ID of #BEG token. It will be used to look up the embeddings and pass the result to the decoder.

```
    with ptan.common.utils.TBMeanTracker(writer, batch_size=100)
as tb_tracker:
        optimiser = optim.Adam(net.parameters(), lr=LEARNING_RATE,
eps=1e-3)
        batch_idx = 0
        best_bleu = None
        for epoch in range(MAX_EPOCHES):
            random.shuffle(train_data)
            dial_shown = False
```

```
total_samples = 0
skipped_samples = 0
bleus_argmax = []
bleus_sample = []
```

For every epoch, we count the total amount of samples and count the skipped samples (due to the high BLEU score). To track the BLEU change during the training, we keep arrays with the BLEU score of argmax-generated sequences and sequences generated by doing sampling.

```
for batch in data.iterate_batches(train_data, BATCH_SIZE):
    batch_idx += 1
    optimiser.zero_grad()
    input_seq, input_batch, output_batch = model.pack_
batch_no_out(batch, net.emb, device)
    enc = net.encode(input_seq)

    net_policies = []
    net_actions = []
    net_advantages = []
    beg_embedding = net.emb(beg_token)
```

In the beginning of every batch, we pack the batch and encode all first sequences of the batch by calling net.encode(). Then we declare several lists, which will be populated during the individual decoding of batch entries.

```
for idx, inp_idx in enumerate(input_batch):
    total_samples += 1
    ref_indices = [
        indices[1:]
        for indices in output_batch[idx]
    ]
    item_enc = net.get_encoded_item(enc, idx)
```

In the preceding loop, we start processing individual entries in a batch: strip the #BEG token from reference sequences and obtain an individual entry of encoded batch.

```
        r_argmax, actions = net.decode_chain_argmax
(item_enc, beg_embedding, data.MAX_TOKENS, stop_at_token=end_token)
        argmax_bleu = utils.calc_bleu_many
(actions, ref_indices)
        bleus_argmax.append(argmax_bleu)
```

As a next step, we decode the batch entry in argmax mode and calculate its BLEU score. This score will be used as a baseline in the REINFORCE PG estimation later.

```
if not args.disable_skip and argmax_bleu > 0.99:
    skipped_samples += 1
    continue
```

In case we have sample skipping enabled, and argmax BLEU is higher than the threshold (threshold of 0.99 means near to perfect match of the sequences), we stop with this batch entry and go to the next.

```
if not dial_shown:
    log.info("Input: %s", utils.untokenize
(data.decode_words(inp_idx, rev_emb_dict)))
    ref_words = [utils.untokenize
(data.decode_words(ref, rev_emb_dict)) for ref in ref_indices]
    log.info("Refer: %s", " ~~|~~ ".join
(ref_words))
    log.info("Argmax: %s, bleu=%.4f",
utils.untokenize(data.decode_words(actions, rev_emb_dict)),
                argmax_bleu)
```

The preceding code piece is executed once every epoch and provides a random sample of input sequence, reference sequences and the result of the decoder (sequence and BLEU score). It's useless for the training process, but provides us with information during the training.

Then we need to perform several rounds of decoding of the batch entry using the random sampling. By default, the count of such rounds is 4, but this is tunable using the command-line option.

```
for _ in range(args.samples):
    r_sample, actions = net.decode_chain_
sampling(item_enc, beg_embedding,

data.MAX_TOKENS, stop_at_token=end_token)
    sample_bleu = utils.calc_bleu_many
(actions, ref_indices)
```

The sampling decoding call has the same set of arguments as for the argmax decoding, followed by the same call to the `calc_bleu_many()` function to obtain the BLEU score.

```
if not dial_shown:
    log.info("Sample: %s, bleu=%.4f",
utils.untokenize(data.decode_words(actions, rev_emb_dict)),
                sample_bleu)
```

```
                    net_policies.append(r_sample)
                    net_actions.extend(actions)
                    net_advantages.extend([sample_bleu - argmax_
bleu] * len(actions))

                    bleus_sample.append(sample_bleu)
```

At the rest of the decoding loop, we show the decoded sequence if we need to and populate our lists. To get the advantage of the decoding round, we subtract the BLEU score obtained by the argmax method from the result of the random sampling decoding.

```
                    dial_shown = True

            if not net_policies:
                continue
```

When we're done with a batch, we have several lists: the list with logits from every step of the decoder, the list of taken actions for those steps (which are, in fact, tokens chosen) and the list of advantages for every step.

```
            policies_v = torch.cat(net_policies)
            actions_t = torch.LongTensor(net_actions).to(device)
            adv_v = torch.FloatTensor(net_advantages).to(device)
```

The returned logits are already in GPU memory, so we can use the `torch.cat()` function to combine them into the single tensor. The other two lists need to be converted and copied on GPU.

```
            log_prob_v = F.log_softmax(policies_v, dim=1)
            log_prob_actions_v = adv_v * log_prob_v[range
    (len(net_actions)), actions_t]
            loss_policy_v = -log_prob_actions_v.mean()

            loss_v = loss_policy_v
            loss_v.backward()
            optimiser.step()
```

When everything is ready, we can calculate PG by applying `log(softmax())` and choose values from the chosen actions, scaled by their advantages. The negative mean of those scaled logarithms will be our loss that we ask the optimizer to minimize.

```
            tb_tracker.track("advantage", adv_v, batch_idx)
            tb_tracker.track("loss_policy", loss_policy_v,
    batch_idx)
```

As the last steps in the batch processing loop, we send the advantage and the loss value to TensorBoard.

```
bleu_test = run_test(test_data, net, end_token, device)
bleu = np.mean(bleus_argmax)
writer.add_scalar("bleu_test", bleu_test, batch_idx)
writer.add_scalar("bleu_argmax", bleu, batch_idx)
writer.add_scalar("bleu_sample", np.mean(bleus_sample),
batch_idx)
writer.add_scalar("skipped_samples", skipped_samples /
total_samples, batch_idx)
writer.add_scalar("epoch", batch_idx, epoch)
log.info("Epoch %d, test BLEU: %.3f", epoch, bleu_test)
```

The preceding code is executed at the end of every epoch and calculates the BLEU score for the test dataset and reports it, together with the BLEU scores obtained during the training, to TensorBoard.

```
if best_bleu is None or best_bleu < bleu_test:
    best_bleu = bleu_test
    log.info("Best bleu updated: %.4f", bleu_test)
    torch.save(net.state_dict(), os.path.join(saves_path,
"bleu_%.3f_%02d.dat" % (bleu_test, epoch)))
    if epoch % 10 == 0:
        torch.save(net.state_dict(), os.path.join(saves_path,
"epoch_%03d_%.3f_%.3f.dat" % (epoch, bleu, bleu_test)))
```

As before, we write a model checkpoint every time that the test BLEU score updates the maximum or every 10 epochs.

Running the SCST training

To run the training, you need the model saved by the cross-entropy training passed with the -l argument. The genre your model was trained on has to match the flag passed to SCST training.

```
rl_book_samples/Chapter12$ ./train_scst.py --cuda --data comedy -l
saves/xe-comedy/epoch_040_0.720_0.111.dat -n sc-comedy-test
2018-01-16 11:09:40,942 INFO Loaded 159 movies with genre comedy
2018-01-16 11:09:40,942 INFO Read and tokenise phrases...
2018-01-16 11:09:45,640 INFO Loaded 93039 phrases
2018-01-16 11:09:45,913 INFO Loaded 24716 dialogues with 93039
phrases, generating training pairs
2018-01-16 11:09:45,975 INFO Counting freq of words...
2018-01-16 11:09:46,327 INFO Data has 31774 uniq words, 4913 of them
occur more than 10
```

```
2018-01-16 11:09:46,519 INFO Obtained 47644 phrase pairs with 4905
uniq words
2018-01-16 11:09:46,855 INFO Training data converted, got 25166
samples
2018-01-16 11:09:46,957 INFO Train set has 21672 phrases, test 1253
2018-01-16 11:09:49,272 INFO Model: PhraseModel (
  (emb): Embedding(4905, 50)
  (encoder): LSTM(50, 512, batch_first=True)
  (decoder): LSTM(50, 512, batch_first=True)
  (output): Sequential (
    (0): Linear (512 -> 4905)
  )
)
2018-01-16 11:09:49,458 INFO Model loaded from saves/xe-comedy/
epoch_040_0.720_0.111.dat, continue training in RL mode...
2018-01-16 11:09:49,989 INFO Input: #BEG like i said, it's a business
deal ... #END
2018-01-16 11:09:49,989 INFO Refer: damn, you are the real thing ...
#END
2018-01-16 11:09:49,989 INFO Argmax: yeah ... #END, bleu=0.0781
2018-01-16 11:09:49,996 INFO Sample: yeah. #END, bleu=0.0175
2018-01-16 11:09:50,006 INFO Sample: yeah said ... #END, bleu=0.1170
2018-01-16 11:09:50,038 INFO Sample: yeah,! what about show show ...?
... where? #END, bleu=0.0439
2018-01-16 11:09:50,048 INFO Sample: yeah white ... #END, bleu=0.1170
```

Results

From my experiments, RL fine-tuning is able to improve both the test BLEU score and the train BLEU score. For example, the following is the cross-entropy training on the comedy genre.

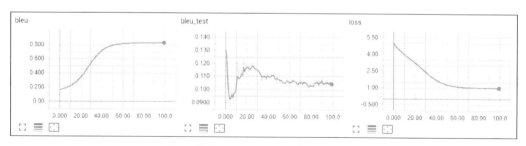

Figure 7: Cross-entropy training dynamics

From those charts, you can see that the best test BLEU score was 0.124 and training BLEU stopped improving at 0.83. By fine-tuning the model, saved at epoch 40 (with train BLEU 0.72 and test BLEU 0.111), it was able to reach train BLEU of 0.88. From the dynamics of the train BLEU, it looks like it can grow further, but just requires more time. I wasn't patient enough, as even reaching this point took 200 epoches, which is more than one day. The charts are as follows:

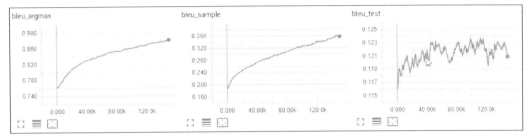

Figure 8: SCST training

Separating training from the same model, but without skipping training samples with a high BLEU score from argmax decoding (with option `--disable-skip`), I was able to reach 0.127 BLEU on the test set, which is not very impressive, but as already explained, it's hard to get good generalization on such few dialog samples.

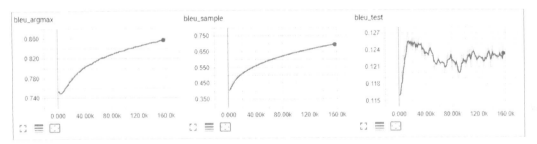

Figure 9: SCST without skipping samples

Telegram bot

As a final step, the Telegram chatbot using the trained model was implemented. To be able to run it you need to install the `python-telegram-bot` extra package into your virtual environment using `pip install`.

Another step you need to take to start the bot is to obtain the API token by registering the new bot. The complete process is described in the documentation `https://core.telegram.org/bots#6-botfather`. The resulting token is a string of the form `110201543:AAHdqTcvCH1vGWJxfSeofSAs0K5PALDsaw`. The bot requires this string to be placed in a configuration file in `~/.config/rl_Chapter12_bot.ini` and the structure of this file is shown in the telegram bot source code as follows.

The logic of the bot is not very different from the other two tools used to experiment with the model: it receives the phrase from the user and replies with the sequence generated by the decoder.

```python
#!/usr/bin/env python3
# This module requires python-telegram-bot
import os
import sys
import logging
import configparser
import argparse

try:
    import telegram.ext
except ImportError:
    print("You need python-telegram-bot package installed to start the
bot")
    sys.exit()

from libbots import data, model, utils

import torch

# Configuration file with the following contents
# [telegram]
# api=API_KEY
CONFIG_DEFAULT = "~/.config/rl_Chapter12_bot.ini"

log = logging.getLogger("telegram")


if __name__ == "__main__":
    logging.basicConfig(format="%(asctime)-15s %(levelname)
s %(message)s", level=logging.INFO)
    parser = argparse.ArgumentParser()
    parser.add_argument("--config", default=CONFIG_DEFAULT,
                        help="Configuration file for the bot,
default=" + CONFIG_DEFAULT)
    parser.add_argument("-m", "--model", required=True, help=
"Model to load")
    parser.add_argument("--sample", default=False, action='store_
true', help="Enable sampling mode")
    prog_args = parser.parse_args()
```

The bot supports two modes of operations: argmax decoding, which is used by default and sample mode. In argmax, the bot's replies on the same phrase are always the same. When the sampling is enabled, during decoding we sample from the returned probability distribution on every step, which increases the variability of the bot's replies.

```
conf = configparser.ConfigParser()
if not conf.read(os.path.expanduser(prog_args.config)):
    log.error("Configuration file %s not found", prog_args.config)
    sys.exit()

emb_dict = data.load_emb_dict(os.path.dirname(prog_args.model))
log.info("Loaded embedded dict with %d entries", len(emb_dict))
rev_emb_dict = {idx: word for word, idx in emb_dict.items()}
end_token = emb_dict[data.END_TOKEN]

net = model.PhraseModel(emb_size=model.EMBEDDING_DIM, dict_
size=len(emb_dict), hid_size=model.HIDDEN_STATE_SIZE)
net.load_state_dict(torch.load(prog_args.model))
```

In the preceding code, we parse the configuration file to get the Telegram API token, load embeddings and initialize the model with weights. We don't need to load the dataset, as no training is needed.

```
def bot_func(bot, update, args):
    text = " ".join(args)
    words = utils.tokenize(text)
    seq_1 = data.encode_words(words, emb_dict)
    input_seq = model.pack_input(seq_1, net.emb)
    enc = net.encode(input_seq)
```

This function is called by the `python-telegram-bot` library to notify it about the user sending a phrase to the bot. Here we obtain the phrase, tokenize it and convert to the form suitable for the model. Then, the encoder is used to obtain the initial hidden state for the decoder.

```
if prog_args.sample:
    _, tokens = net.decode_chain_sampling(enc, input_seq.
data[0:1], seq_len=data.MAX_TOKENS, stop_at_token=end_token)
else:
    _, tokens = net.decode_chain_argmax(enc, input_seq.
data[0:1], seq_len=data.MAX_TOKENS, stop_at_token=end_token)
```

Next, we call one of the decoding methods, depending on the program command line arguments. The result that we get in both cases is the sequence of integer token IDs of the decoded sequence.

```
if tokens[-1] == end_token:
    tokens = tokens[:-1]
reply = data.decode_words(tokens, rev_emb_dict)
if reply:
    reply_text = utils.untokenize(reply)
    bot.send_message(chat_id=update.message.chat_id,
text=reply_text)
```

When we've got the decoded sequence, the only thing we need to do is to decode it back in text form using our dictionary and send the reply to the user.

```
updater = telegram.ext.Updater(conf['telegram']['api'])
updater.dispatcher.add_handler(telegram.ext.CommandHandler
('bot', bot_func, pass_args=True))

log.info("Bot initialized, started serving")
updater.start_polling()
updater.idle()
```

The last piece of code is `python-telegram-bot` machinery to register our bot function. To trigger it, you need to use the command/bot phrase in the telegram chat. The following is an example of one conversation generated by the trained model.

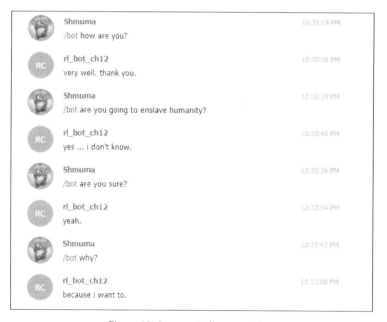

Figure 10: A generated conversation

Summary

Despite its simplicity, and the toy-like example in this chapter, seq2seq is a very widely used model in NLP and other domains, so the alternative RL approach could potentially be applicable to a wide range of problems. In this chapter, we've just scratched the surface of deep NLP models and ideas, which goes well beyond the scope of this book. We covered the basics of NLP models, such as RNN and the seq2seq model and different ways that it could be trained.

In the next chapter, we'll take a look at another example of the application of RL methods in another domain: automating web navigation tasks.

13
Web Navigation

This chapter takes a look at another practical application of **Reinforcement Learning (RL)**: web navigation and browser automation. We'll discuss why web navigation is important and how it can be solved with an RL approach. Next, we will take a deep look at one very interesting, but a commonly overlooked and a bit of abandoned RL benchmark, which was implemented by OpenAI and called **Mini World of Bits**.

Web navigation

When the web was invented, it started as several text-only web pages interconnected by hyperlinks. If you're curious, here is the first web page home: `http://info.cern.ch/`, with text and links. The only thing you can do is to read and click on links to go between pages. Several years later, in 1995, IETF published HTML 2.0 specification and it had lots of extensions to the original version invented by *Tim Berners-Lee*. Among these extensions it included forms and form elements that allowed web page authors to add activity to their websites. Users could enter and change text, toggle checkboxes, select drop-down lists, and push buttons. The set of controls was similar to the minimalistic set of GUI application's controls. There was one single difference: all this happened inside the browser's window and both the data and UI controls that users interacted with were defined by the server's page, but not by the local application installed.

Fast-forward 22 years and now we have JavaScript, HTML5 canvas, and office applications working inside our browser. The boundary between the desktop and the web is so thin and blurry that you may not even know whether the app you're using is a HTML page or a native app. However, it is still the browser which understands HTML and talks HTTP to the outside world.

At its core, **web navigation** is defined as a process of a user interacting with the website or websites. The user can click on links, type text, or do any other actions to reach some goal, such as sending an email, finding out the exact years of the French Revolution or checking recent Facebook notifications. All this will be done using web navigation, so there is a question: can our program learn how to do the same?

Browser automation and RL

From another angle, the problem of automating website interaction was attacked for a long time in an attempt to solve the very practical tasks of **website testing** and **web scraping**. Website testing is needed when you have some complicated website that you (or other people) have developed and you want to ensure that it does what it is supposed to do. For example, if you have a login page that was redesigned and is ready to be deployed on a live website, then you may want to be sure that this new design does sane things in case a wrong password entered, the user clicks on **I forgot my password** and so on. A complex website could potentially include hundreds or thousands of use cases that should be tested on every release, so all such functions should be automated.

Web scraping solves the problem of extracting some data from websites at scale. For example, if you want to build a system that aggregates all prices for all pizza places in your town, you will potentially need to deal with hundreds of different websites, which could be problematic to build and maintain. Web scraping tools are trying to solve the problem of interacting with websites. Their functionality can vary from simple HTTP requests and subsequent HTML parsing, to full emulation of the user moving the mouse, clicking buttons, thinking, and so on.

The standard approach to browser automation normally allows you to control the real browser, such as Chrome, or FireFox, with your program, which can observe the web page data, like DOM tree and an object's location on the screen and issue the actions, like moving the mouse, pressing some keys, pushing the "Back" button or just executing some JavaScript code. The connections to the RL problem setup is obvious: our agent interacts with the web page and browser by issuing actions and observing some state. The reward is not that clear and intuitively should be task-specific, like successfully filling some form or reaching the page with the desired information.

Practical applications of a system that could learn browser tasks are related to the above-mentioned use cases. For example, in web testing for very large websites, it's very tedious to define the testing process using low-level browser actions like "move the mouse five pixels to the left, then press the left button." What you want to do is to give the system some demonstrations and let it generalize and repeat the shown actions in all similar situations or at least make it robust enough for UI redesign, button text change, and so on. Additionally, there are lots of cases when you don't know the problem in advance, for example when you want the system to explore the weak points of the website, like security vulnerabilities. In that case, the RL agent could try lots of weird actions very quickly, much faster than humans could. Of course, the action space for security testing is enormous, so random clicking won't be very competitive with experienced human testers. In that case, the RL-based system could, potentially, combine the prior knowledge and experience of humans but still keep the ability to explore and learn from this exploration.

Another potential domain that could benefit from RL browser automation is scraping and web data extraction in general. For example, you might want to extract some data from hundreds of thousands of different websites, like hotel websites, car renting agents, or other businesses around the world. Very often, before you get to the desired data, a form with parameters needs to be filled, which becomes a very nontrivial task given the different websites' design, layout, and natural language flexibility. With such a task at hand, an RL agent can save tons of time and effort by extracting the data reliably and at scale.

Mini World of Bits benchmark

Potential practical applications of browser automation with RL are attractive, but have one very serious drawback: they're too large to be used for research and the comparison of methods. In fact, the implementation of a full-sized web scraping system could take months of effort by a team and most of the issues will not be directly related to RL, like data gathering, browser engine communication, input and output representation and tons of other questions that the real production system development consists of.

By solving all those issues, we can easily miss the forest by looking at the trees. That's why researchers love benchmark datasets, like MNIST, ImageNet, the Atari suite and lots of others. However, not every problem makes a good benchmark. On the one hand, it should be simple enough to allow quick experimentations and the comparison between methods. On the other hand, the benchmark has to be challenging and leave room for improvements. For example, Atari benchmarks consist of a wide variety of games, from very simple games, which could be solved in half an hour (like Pong) to quite complex games that haven't been properly solved yet (like Montezuma Revenge, which requires the complex planning of actions).

To the best of my knowledge, there is only one such a benchmark for the browser automation domain, which makes it even worse that this benchmark was undeservedly forgotten about by the RL community. As an attempt to fix this issue, we'll take a look at the benchmark in this chapter. Let's talk about its history first.

In December 2016, OpenAI published a dataset called **Mini World of Bits** (**MiniWoB**) that contains 80 browser-based tasks. These tasks are observed on a pixel level (strictly speaking, besides pixels, a text description of tasks is given to the agent) and are supposed to be communicated with the mouse and keyboard actions using the VNC (`https://en.wikipedia.org/wiki/Virtual_Network_Computin`) client. VNC is a standard remote-desktop protocol when the VNC server allows clients to connect and work with a server's GUI applications using the mouse and keyboard via the network. These 80 tasks vary a lot in terms of complexity and the actions required from the agent. Some tasks are very simple, even for RL, like "Click on the dialog's close button", or "Push the single button", but some require multiple steps, for example, "Open collapsed groups and click on the link with some text", or "Select a specific date using the date picker tool" (and this date is randomly generated every episode). Some of the tasks are simple for humans, but require character recognition, for example, "Mark checkboxes with this text" (and the text is generated randomly). Screenshots of some MiniWoB problems are shown in the following figure:

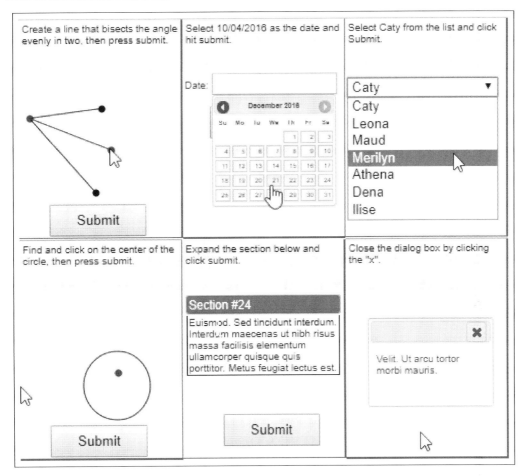

Figure 1: MiniWoB environments

Unfortunately, despite the brilliant idea and challenging nature of MiniWoB, it was almost abandoned by OpenAI right after the initial release. As an attempt to right a wrong, in this chapter we'll take a closer look at this benchmark and learn how to write an agent solving some of the tasks. We will also discuss how to extract, preprocess, and incorporate human demonstrations into the training process and check their effect on the final performance of the agents. Before jumping into the RL part of the agent, we need to understand how MiniWoB works. To do this, we need to take a closer look at OpenAI Gym's extension called OpenAI Universe.

OpenAI Universe

OpenAI Universe is available in OpenAI's GitHub repository `https://github.com/openai/universe` and its core idea is to wrap general GUI applications into an RL environment using the same core classes provided by Gym. To achieve this, it uses the VNC protocol to connect with the VNC server running inside the docker container, exposing the mouse and keyboard actions to the RL agent and providing the GUI application image as an observation. The reward is provided by an external small "rewarder" daemon running inside the same container and giving the agent scalar reward value based on this rewarder judgement. It is possible to launch several containers locally, or over the network, to gather episodes data in parallel, in the same way that we started several Atari emulators to increase the convergence of the **Actor-Critic (A2C)** method in *Chapter 11, Asynchronous Advantage Actor-Critic.* The architecture is illustrated in the following diagram:

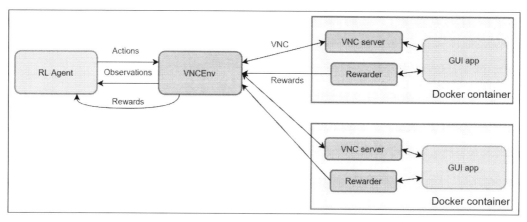

Figure 2: OpenAI Universe architecture

This architecture allows quick integration of third-party applications into the RL framework, as you don't need to make any changes in the app itself, only package it as a docker container and write a relatively-small rewarder daemon, which uses a simple text protocol to communicate. On the other side, this approach is much more resource demanding, in comparison with, for example, Atari games, when the emulator is relatively lightweight and works completely inside the RL agent's process. The VNC approach requires a VNC server to be started side-by-side with the application and the rate of RL agent communication with the application is defined by the VNC server speed and network throughput (in the case of remote docker containers).

Installation

To start using the OpenAI Universe, you need to install its Python package inside your environment. Please be careful with the version that you're installing. At the time of writing, the command `pip install universe` installs the old version 0.21.3, which requires the old Gym 0.7.2. To prevent a downgrade, you need to install the latest version 0.21.5 from GitHub using the command `pip install git+https://github.com/openai/universe`. For convenience, I provided the `environment.yml` environment definition file for Anaconda, so, to quickly create the environment `rl_book_ch13` with all requirements, just run the command `conda env create -f Chapter13/environment.yml`. After this command, you need to run the `pip install` command preceding to install OpenAI Universe from GitHub.

Another component, which is required by Universe, is Docker, which is a standard method running lightweight containers, available on most modern operating systems. To install it, refer to Docker's website `https://www.docker.com`. OpenAI Universe gives you the flexibility of where and how to start the containers, so your agent can connect to one or many remote machines with Docker installed. To check that docker is up and running, try command `docker ps`, which shows running containers.

Actions and observations

In contrast to Atari games, or other Gym environments that we've worked with so far, OpenAI Universe exposes a much more generic action space. Atari games used six-to-seven discrete actions, corresponding to the controller's buttons and joystick directions. CartPole's action space is even smaller, with just two actions available. VNC gives our agent much more flexibility in terms of what it can do. First of all, the full keyboard, with control keys and up/down state of every key is exposed. So, your agent can decide to press 10 buttons simultaneously and it will be totally fine from a VNC point of view. The second part of the action space is the mouse, when you can move the mouse to any coordinate and control the state of its buttons. This significantly increases the dimensionality of the action space that the agent needs to learn how to handle.

Besides the larger action space, the OpenAI Universe environment has slightly different environment semantics compared to the Gym environments. The difference is in two aspects. The first is the so-called **vectorized** representation of observations, actions, and reward. As you can see on *Figure 2*, one environment could be connected to several Docker containers running the same application and gathering parallel experience from them. Such parallel communication allows **Policy Gradient (PG)** methods to obtain more diverse training samples, but now we need to specify which exact application we need to send the action with the `env.step()` call. To solve this, OpenAI Universe environment's `step()` method requires not a single action, but a list of actions for every connected container. The return from this function is also vectorized and now consists of a tuple of lists: `(observations, rewards, done_flags, infos)`.

The second difference is dictated by the VNC protocol's asynchronous manner of observations and actions. In the Atari environment, every call to `step()` triggers the request to the emulator to move forward one clock tick (which is 1/25 of second), so our agent could block the emulator for a while and it would be completely transparent for the running game. With VNC, this is not the case. As the GUI application is running in parallel to our client, we cannot block it anymore. If our agent decides to think for a while, it can miss observations that happened during that time.

Another implication of this asynchronous nature of the observations is the situation when the container is not ready yet or in the middle of resetting. In that case, the specific observation can be `None` and those situations need to be handled by the agent.

Environment creation

To create the OpenAI Universe environment, you need, as before, to call `gym.make()` with the environment ID. For example, a very simple problem from the MiniWoB set is `wob.mini.ClickDialog-v0`, which requires you to close the dialog by clicking on the **X** button. However, before the environment can be used, you need to configure it: specifying where and how many Docker instances you want. There is a special method of the environment called `configure()`. This method needs to be called before any other methods of the environment and it accepts several arguments. The most important arguments are as follows:

- `remotes`: A parameter, which could be a number or a string. If it's specified as a number, it gives the amount of local containers needed to be started for the environment. As a string, this parameter can specify the URL of already-running containers that the environment needs to connect in the form of `vnc://host1:port1+port2,host2:port1+port2`. The first port is a VNC protocol port (`5900` by default). The second port is a port of the rewarder daemon, which is by default `15900`. Both ports could be redefined on the Docker container launch.

- `fps`: An argument giving the expected frames per second for the agent's observations.

- `vnc_kwargs`: An argument, which has to be a dict, with extra VNC protocol parameters, defining the compression level and the quality of the image to be transferred to the agent. Those parameters are very important for performance, especially for containers running in the cloud.

To illustrate this, let's consider a very simple program that starts one single container with the `ClickDialog` problem and obtains its first observation as an image. This example is available in `Chapter13/adhoc/wob_create.py`.

```
#!/usr/bin/env python3
import gym
import universe
import time

from PIL import Image
```

This example is very simple, so we need only a very small set of packages. The importing of the `universe` package is required despite it not being used, as with this import it registers its environments in Gym.

```
if __name__ == "__main__":
    env = gym.make("wob.mini.ClickDialog-v0")

    env.configure(remotes=1, fps=5, vnc_kwargs={
        'encoding': 'tight', 'compress_level': 0,
        'fine_quality_level': 100, 'subsample_level': 0
    })
    obs = env.reset()
```

We create our environment and ask it to configure itself. The passed arguments specify only one local container will be started, five frames per second, and the VNC connection without image compression. This will mean that a large amount of traffic is passed between the VNC server and VNC client, which prevents compression artefacts from appearing in the image. This could be required for MiniWoB problems showing text using a relatively small font size.

```
while obs[0] is None:
    a = env.action_space.sample()
    obs, reward, is_done, info = env.step([a])
    print("Env is still resetting...")
    time.sleep(1)
```

While our single observation is None (we expect only one observation in a returned list, as we've asked only for one remote container), we pass random actions to the environment, waiting for the image to appear:

```
print(obs[0].keys())
im = Image.fromarray(obs[0]['vision'])
im.save("image.png")
env.close()
```

When, finally, we have got the image from the server, we save it as a PNG file, as shown below. In MiniWoB problems, the image is not the only observation we get. In fact, observation from the environment is a dict with two entries: vision, containing a NumPy array with screen pixels and text, containing the text description of the problem. For some problems, only the image is required, but for some tasks from the MiniWoB suite, the text includes essential information for solving the problem, like which color area to click on or what dates need to be selected.

The following image was cropped, as the original resolution of the observation is 1024 x 768.

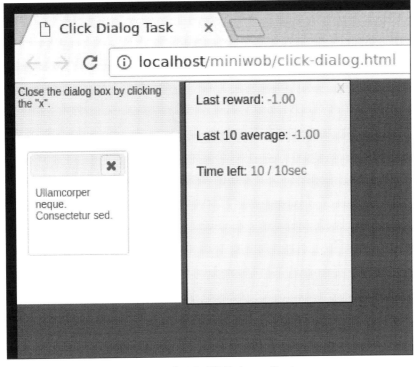

Figure 3: Part of a MiniWoB observation image

MiniWoB stability

My experiments with the original MiniWoB Docker image, published by OpenAI, have shown one serious issue: sometimes the server-side Python script, which controls the browser inside the container, crashes. This leads to training problems, as our environment loses connection to the container and the training stops. The solution for this issue is a one-line change, but it is complicated by the fact that OpenAI doesn't support MiniWoB and doesn't accept the fixes, so, to resolve the issue, I had to apply the patch inside the container. There is another small patch related to human demonstration, which fixes the issue with recording files being overwritten between episodes. The patched image with both fixes was pushed into my Docker Hub repository and is available as the `shmuma/miniwob:v2` label, so you can use it instead of the original `quay.io/openai/universe.world-of-bits:0.20.0` image. If you're curious, I've placed the patches and instructions on how to apply them in the code samples repository `Chapter13/wob_fixes`.

Simple clicking approach

As the first demo, let's implement a simple **Asynchronous Advantage Actor-Critic (A3C)** agent, which decides where it should click on given the image observation. This approach can solve only a small subset of the full MiniWoB suite and we'll discuss restrictions of this approach later. For now, it will allow us to get a better understanding of the problem.

As with the previous chapter, due to size of the code, I won't put a complete source code here. We'll focus on the most important functions and give the rest as an overview. The complete source code is available in the GitHub repository `https://github.com/PacktPublishing/Deep-Reinforcement-Learning-Hands-On`.

Grid actions

When we talked about OpenAI Universe's architecture and organization, it was mentioned that the richness and flexibility of the action space creates lots of challenges for the RL agent. MiniWoB's active area inside the browser is just 160x210 (exactly the same dimension that the Atari emulator has), but even with such a small area, our agent could be asked to move the mouse, perform clicks, drag objects, and so on. Just the mouse alone could be problematic to master, as, in the extreme case, there could be an almost infinite amount of different actions that the agent could perform, like pressing the mouse button at some point and dragging the mouse to a different location. In our example, we'll simplify our problem a lot by just considering clicks at some fixed grid points inside the active webpage area. The sketch of our action space is given as follows:

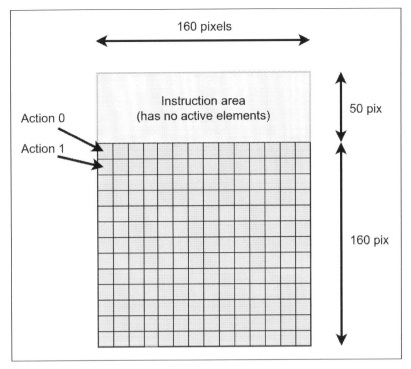

Figure 4: A grid action space

This approach is already implemented in the OpenAI Universe as an action wrapper `universe.wrappers.experimental.action_space.SoftmaxClickMouse`. It has all the defaults pre-set for MiniWoB environments, which is an 160x210 region shifted 10 pixels to the right and 75 pixels down (to get rid of the browser's frames). The grid of actions is 10x10, which gives 256 final actions to choose from.

Besides the action preprocessor, we definitely need an observation preprocessor, as the input image from VNC environment is a 1024x768x3 tensor, but the active area of MiniWoB is just 210x160. There is no suitable cropper defined, so I've implemented it myself as a class `lib.wob_vnc.MiniWoBCropper` that is in the `Chapter13/lib/wob_vnc.py` library module. Its code is very simple and is shown as follows:

```
WIDTH = 160
HEIGHT = 210
X_OFS = 10
Y_OFS = 75
```

```
class MiniWoBCropper(vectorized.ObservationWrapper):
    def __init__(self, env, keep_text=False):
        super(MiniWoBCropper, self).__init__(env)
        self.keep_text = keep_text


    def _observation(self, observation_n):
        res = []
        for obs in observation_n:
            if obs is None:
                res.append(obs)
                continue
            img = obs['vision'][Y_OFS:Y_OFS+HEIGHT, X_OFS:X_OFS+WIDTH, :]
            img = np.transpose(img, (2, 0, 1))
            if self.keep_text:
                text = " ".join(map(lambda d: d.get('instruction',
''), obs.get('text', [{}])))
                res.append((img, text))
            else:
                res.append(img)
        return res
```

The optional `keep_text` argument in the constructor enables the mode to preserve the text description of the problem. We don't need it at the moment and our first version of the agent will always keep it disabled. In this mode, `MiniWoBCropper` returns the NumPy array with shape (3, 210, 160).

Example overview

With decisions about actions and observations made, our next steps are straightforward. We'll use the A3C method to train the agent, which should decide from the 160 x 210 observation which grid cell to click. Besides the policy, which is a probability distribution over 256 grid cells, our agent estimates the value of the state, which will be used as a baseline in PG estimation.

There are several modules in this example:

- `Chapter13/lib/common.py`: Methods shared among examples in this chapters, including the already-familiar `RewardTracker` and `unpack_batch` function

- `Chapter13/lib/model_vnc.py`: Includes a definition of the model, which will be shown in the next section

- `Chapter13/lib/wob_vnc.py`: Includes MiniWoB-specific code, like the observation cropper, environment configuration method and other utility functions
- `Chapter13/wob_click_train.py`: The script used to train the model
- `Chapter13/wob_click_play.py`: The script loads the model weights and uses them against the single environment, recording observations and counting stats about the reward

Model

The model is very straightforward and uses the same patterns that we've seen in other A3C examples. I haven't spent much time optimizing and fine-tuning the architecture and hyperparameters, so it's likely that the final result could be improved significantly. Following is the model definition with two convolution layers, a single-layered policy and value heads.

```python
class Model(nn.Module):
    def __init__(self, input_shape, n_actions):
        super(Model, self).__init__()

        self.conv = nn.Sequential(
            nn.Conv2d(input_shape[0], 64, 5, stride=5),
            nn.ReLU(),
            nn.Conv2d(64, 64, 3, stride=2),
            nn.ReLU(),
        )

        conv_out_size = self._get_conv_out(input_shape)

        self.policy = nn.Sequential(
            nn.Linear(conv_out_size, n_actions),
        )

        self.value = nn.Sequential(
            nn.Linear(conv_out_size, 1),
        )

    def _get_conv_out(self, shape):
        o = self.conv(torch.zeros(1, *shape))
        return int(np.prod(o.size()))
```

```
    def forward(self, x):
        fx = x.float() / 256
        conv_out = self.conv(fx).view(fx.size()[0], -1)
        return self.policy(conv_out), self.value(conv_out)
```

Training code

The training script is in `Chapter13/wob_click_train.py` and also should be very
familiar but contains several OpenAI Universe and MiniWoB-specific pieces, so I put
it here. This script can work in two modes: with and without human demonstrations.
Currently we're considering only training from scratch, but some code is related to
demonstrations and should be ignored for now. We'll look at it in the appropriate
section later.

```
#!/usr/bin/env python3
import os
import gym
import random
import universe
import argparse
import numpy as np
from tensorboardX import SummaryWriter

from lib import wob_vnc, model_vnc, common, vnc_demo

import ptan

import torch
import torch.nn.utils as nn_utils
import torch.nn.functional as F
import torch.optim as optim
```

There is not much to say about the used modules, except the new `universe`. It
might look unused, but you still need to import it, as on import it registers new
environments in Gym's repository, so they become available on the `gym.make()` call.

```
REMOTES_COUNT = 8
ENV_NAME = "wob.mini.ClickDialog-v0"

GAMMA = 0.99
REWARD_STEPS = 2
BATCH_SIZE = 16
LEARNING_RATE = 0.0001
ENTROPY_BETA = 0.001
```

```
CLIP_GRAD = 0.05

DEMO_PROB = 0.5

SAVES_DIR = "saves"
```

The hyperparameters section is also mostly the same, except that a couple of hyperparameters are new. First of all, REMOTES_COUNT specifies the amount of Docker containers that we'll try to connect. By default, our training script assumes that those containers have already started on one single machine and we can connect to them on pre-defined ports (5900..5907 for VNC connection and 15900..15907 for the rewarder daemon). We'll look at the details of starting containers in the next section.

The parameter ENV_NAME specifies the problem that we'll try to attack and it could be redefined with the command line arguments. The problem ClickDialog is very simple and gives the reward to the agent for clicking on the dialog's close button.

```
if __name__ == "__main__":
    parser = argparse.ArgumentParser()
    parser.add_argument("-n", "--name", required=True, help="Name of
the run")
    parser.add_argument("--cuda", default=False, action='store_true',
help="CUDA mode")
    parser.add_argument("--port-ofs", type=int, default=0,
help="Offset for container's ports, default=0")
    parser.add_argument("--env", default=ENV_NAME, help="Environment
name to solve, default=" + ENV_NAME)
    parser.add_argument("--demo", help="Demo dir to load. Default=No
demo")
    parser.add_argument("--host", default='localhost', help="Host with
docker containers")
    args = parser.parse_args()
    device = torch.device("cuda" if args.cuda else "cpu")
```

We have quite a large amount of command-line options and using them you can tweak the training behavior. There is only one required option to pass the name of the run, which will be used for TensorBoard and directory to save the model's weights. The parameter --demo should be ignored for now, as it is related to human demonstrations.

```
    env_name = args.env
    if not env_name.startswith('wob.mini.'):
        env_name = "wob.mini." + env_name
```

```
name = env_name.split('.')[-1] + "_" + args.name
writer = SummaryWriter(comment="-wob_click_" + name)
saves_path = os.path.join(SAVES_DIR, name)
os.makedirs(saves_path, exist_ok=True)
```

After arguments are parsed, we normalize the environment name (all MiniWoB environments start with the `wob.mini.` prefix, so we don't require it to be specified in the command line), start the TensorBoard writer and create the directory for the models.

```
demo_samples = None
if args.demo:
    demo_samples = vnc_demo.load_demo(args.demo, env_name)
    if not demo_samples:
        demo_samples = None
    else:
        print("Loaded %d demo samples, will use them during
 training" % len(demo_samples))
```

The preceding piece of code is related to demonstrations and should be ignored for now.

```
env = gym.make(env_name)
env = universe.wrappers.experimental.SoftmaxClickMouse(env)
env = wob_vnc.MiniWoBCropper(env)
wob_vnc.configure(env, wob_vnc.remotes_url(port_ofs=args.port_ofs,
 hostname=args.host, count=REMOTES_COUNT))
```

To prepare the environment, we ask Gym to create it, wrap it into the `SoftmaxClickMouse` wrapper described before and then apply our cropper. However, this environment is not ready to be used yet. To complete the initialization, we need to configure it using utility functions in the `wob_vnc` module. Their goal is to call the `env.configure()` method with arguments specifying VNC connection parameters, like image quality and compression level and the addresses of Docker containers that we want to connect. Those connection endpoints are specified in a URL of special form, generated by the function `wob_vnc.remotes_url()`. This URL has the form of `vnc://host:port1+port2,host:port1+port2` and allows one single environment to communicate with any amount of Docker containers running on the multiple hosts.

```
net = model_vnc.Model(input_shape=wob_vnc.WOB_SHAPE,
 n_actions=env.action_space.n).to(device)
    print(net)
    optimizer = optim.Adam(net.parameters(), lr=LEARNING_RATE,
 eps=1e-3)
```

```
    agent = ptan.agent.PolicyAgent(lambda x: net(x)[0], device=device,
apply_softmax=True)
    exp_source = ptan.experience.ExperienceSourceFirstLast(
        [env], agent, gamma=GAMMA, steps_count=REWARD_STEPS,
vectorized=True)
```

Before the training can be started, we create the model, the agent and experience source from the PTAN library. The only new thing here is the argument `vectorized=True`, which tells the experience source that our environment is vectorized and returns multiple results in one call.

```
    best_reward = None
    with common.RewardTracker(writer) as tracker:
        with ptan.common.utils.TBMeanTracker(writer, batch_size=10)
as tb_tracker:
            batch = []
            for step_idx, exp in enumerate(exp_source):
                rewards_steps = exp_source.pop_rewards_steps()
                if rewards_steps:
                    rewards, steps = zip(*rewards_steps)
                    tb_tracker.track("episode_steps", np.mean(steps),
step_idx)

                    mean_reward = tracker.reward(np.mean(rewards),
step_idx)
                    if mean_reward is not None:
                        if best_reward is None or mean_reward > best_
reward:
                            if best_reward is not None:
                                name = "best_%.3f_%d.dat" % (mean_
reward, step_idx)
                                fname = os.path.join(saves_path, name)
                                torch.save(net.state_dict(), fname)
                                print("Best reward updated: %.3f ->
%.3f" % (best_reward, mean_reward))
                            best_reward = mean_reward
                batch.append(exp)
                if len(batch) < BATCH_SIZE:
                    continue
```

In the beginning of the training loop, we ask our experience source for new experience objects and pack them into the batch. In the meantime, we track the average undiscounted reward and, if it updates the maximum, we save the model's weight.

```
if demo_samples and random.random() < DEMO_PROB:
    random.shuffle(demo_samples)
    demo_batch = demo_samples[:BATCH_SIZE]
    model_vnc.train_demo(net, optimizer, demo_batch,
writer, step_idx,
                                        preprocessor=ptan.agent.
default_states_preprocessor,
                                        device=device)
```

The preceding piece of code is relevant to demonstrations and should be ignored for now.

```
states_v, actions_t, vals_ref_v = \
        common.unpack_batch(batch, net, last_val_
gamma=GAMMA ** REWARD_STEPS,
                                device=device)
    batch.clear()
```

When the batch is complete, we unpack it into individual tensors and perform the A2C training procedure: calculate value loss to improve the value head estimation and calculate the PG using value as a baseline for advantage.

```
optimizer.zero_grad()
logits_v, value_v = net(states_v)

loss_value_v = F.mse_loss(value_v, vals_ref_v)

log_prob_v = F.log_softmax(logits_v, dim=1)
adv_v = vals_ref_v - value_v.detach()
log_prob_actions_v = adv_v * log_prob_v[range
(BATCH_SIZE), actions_t]
loss_policy_v = -log_prob_actions_v.mean()

prob_v = F.softmax(logits_v, dim=1)
entropy_loss_v = ENTROPY_BETA * (prob_v * log_prob_v).
sum(dim=1).mean()
```

To improve exploration, we add the entropy loss calculated as a scaled negative entropy of the policy.

```
loss_v = loss_policy_v + entropy_loss_v + loss_value_v
loss_v.backward()
```

```
                  nn_utils.clip_grad_norm(net.parameters(), CLIP_GRAD)
                  optimizer.step()

                  tb_tracker.track("advantage", adv_v, step_idx)
                  tb_tracker.track("values", value_v, step_idx)
                  tb_tracker.track("batch_rewards", vals_ref_v, step_
idx)
                  tb_tracker.track("loss_entropy", entropy_loss_v, step_
idx)
                  tb_tracker.track("loss_policy", loss_policy_v, step_
idx)
                  tb_tracker.track("loss_value", loss_value_v, step_idx)
                  tb_tracker.track("loss_total", loss_v, step_idx)
```

Then we track the key quantities with TensorBoard to be able to monitor them during the training.

Starting containers

Before the training can be started, you need to have docker containers with MiniWoB started. OpenAI Universe provides an option to start them automatically and to do this you need to pass the integer value to `env.configure()` call, for example, `env.configure(remotes=4)` will start locally four Docker containers with MiniWoB.

Despite the simplicity of this start mode, it has several disadvantages:

- You have no control over the containers' location, so all containers will be started locally. This is not convenient when you want them to be started on a remote machine or multiple machines.

- By default, OpenAI Universe starts the container published in quay.io (at the time of writing, it's image `quay.io/openai/universe.world-of-bits` with version 0.20.0), which has a serious bug in the reward calculation. Due to this, your training process can crash from time to time, which is not good when training can take days. There is an option to `env.configure()`, called `docker_image`, which allows you to redefine the image used to start, but you need to hard-code the image into the code.

- The starting tuple of containers has an overhead, so your training has to wait before all the containers start.

As an alternative, I find it much more flexible to start Docker containers in advance. In that case, you need to pass to `env.configure()` a URL pointing the environment to the hosts and ports that it has to be connected with. To start the container, you need to run the command `docker run -d -p 5900:5900 -p 15900:15900 --privileged --ipc host --cap-add SYS_ADMIN <CONTAINER_ID> <ARGS>`. The meaning of the arguments are as follows:

1. `-d`: Starts the container in *detach* mode. To be able to see the container's logs, you can replace this option with `-t`. In that case, the container will be started interactively and could be stopped with *Ctrl + C*.

2. `-p SRC_PORT:TGT_PORT`: Forwards the src port from the container's host to the target port inside the container. This option allows you to start several MiniWoB containers on one machine. Every container starts the VNC server listening on port `5900` and rewarder daemon on port `15900`. Argument `-p 5900:5900` makes the VNC server available on port `5900` on the host machine (machine running the container). For the second container, you should pass `-p 5901:5900`, which makes it available on port `5901`, instead of the occupied `5900`. The same is true for rewarder: inside the container it listens on port `15900`. By providing the `-p` option, you can forward connections from your host machine to the container's port.

3. `--privileged`: This option allows the container to access the host's devices. As for why MiniWoB gets started with this option, maybe there are some VNC server requirements.

4. `--ipc host`: Enables containers to share the IPC (interprocess communications) namespace with the host.

5. `--cap-add SYS_ADMIN`: Extends the container's capabilities to perform extended configuration of the host's settings.

6. `<CONTAINER_ID>`: Identifier of the container. Should be `shmuma/miniwob:v2` which is a patched version of the original `quay.io/openai/universe.world-of-bits:0.20.0`. More details were given in the preceding section of *MiniWoB stability*.

7. `<ARGS>`: You can pass extra arguments to the container to change its mode of operation. We'll need them later, for recording human demonstrations. For now, it can be empty.

That's it! Our training script expects eight containers to be running, sitting on ports `5900-5907` and `15900-15907`. For example, to start them I use the following commands (also available as `Chapter13/adhoc/start_docker.sh`)

```
docker run -d -p 5900:5900 -p 15900:15900 --privileged --ipc host --cap-
add SYS_ADMIN shmuma/miniwob:v2

docker run -d -p 5901:5900 -p 15901:15900 --privileged --ipc host --cap-
add SYS_ADMIN shmuma/miniwob:v2

docker run -d -p 5902:5900 -p 15902:15900 --privileged --ipc host --cap-
add SYS_ADMIN shmuma/miniwob:v2

docker run -d -p 5903:5900 -p 15903:15900 --privileged --ipc host --cap-
add SYS_ADMIN shmuma/miniwob:v2

docker run -d -p 5904:5900 -p 15904:15900 --privileged --ipc host --cap-
add SYS_ADMIN shmuma/miniwob:v2

docker run -d -p 5905:5900 -p 15905:15900 --privileged --ipc host --cap-
add SYS_ADMIN shmuma/miniwob:v2

docker run -d -p 5906:5900 -p 15906:15900 --privileged --ipc host --cap-
add SYS_ADMIN shmuma/miniwob:v2

docker run -d -p 5907:5900 -p 15907:15900 --privileged --ipc host --cap-
add SYS_ADMIN shmuma/miniwob:v2
```

All of them will be started in the background and could be seen with the `docker ps` command:

```
CONTAINER ID        IMAGE               COMMAND
CREATED             STATUS              PORTS
NAMES
ecf5d17c5419        92756d1f08ac        "/app/universe-envs/w"    23 hours
ago        Up 23 hours        0.0.0.0:5907->5900/tcp, 0.0.0.0:15907-
>15900/tcp    elegant_bohr

8aaaeeb28e11        92756d1f08ac        "/app/universe-envs/w"    23 hours
ago        Up 23 hours        0.0.0.0:5906->5900/tcp, 0.0.0.0:15906-
>15900/tcp    tiny_shirley

e8028af83bb2        92756d1f08ac        "/app/universe-envs/w"    23 hours
ago        Up 23 hours        0.0.0.0:5905->5900/tcp, 0.0.0.0:15905-
>15900/tcp    gloomy_chandrasekhar

9164b9dd4449        92756d1f08ac        "/app/universe-envs/w"    23 hours
ago        Up 23 hours        0.0.0.0:5904->5900/tcp, 0.0.0.0:15904-
>15900/tcp    sad_minsky

bb6817065e82        92756d1f08ac        "/app/universe-envs/w"    23 hours
ago        Up 23 hours        0.0.0.0:5903->5900/tcp, 0.0.0.0:15903-
>15900/tcp    sleepy_pasteur

5dfb6a4e784c        92756d1f08ac        "/app/universe-envs/w"    23 hours
ago        Up 23 hours        0.0.0.0:5902->5900/tcp, 0.0.0.0:15902-
>15900/tcp    gloomy_thompson .
```

```
bacb19a24647        92756d1f08ac         "/app/universe-envs/w"   23 hours
ago       Up 23 hours        0.0.0.0:5901->5900/tcp, 0.0.0.0:15901-
>15900/tcp   goofy_dubinsky

34861292023d        92756d1f08ac         "/app/universe-envs/w"   23 hours
ago       Up 23 hours        0.0.0.0:5900->5900/tcp, 0.0.0.0:15900-
>15900/tcp   backstabbing_lamport
```

Training process

When containers have started and are ready to be used, you can start training.
In the beginning, it shows messages about connection status, but finally it should
start reporting about the episodes' statistics.

```
rl_book_samples/Chapter13$ ./wob_click_train.py -n t2 --cuda

[2018-01-29 14:27:48,545] Making new env: wob.mini.ClickDialog-v0

[2018-01-29 14:27:48,547] Using SoftmaxClickMouse with action_region=
(10, 125, 170, 285), noclick_regions=[]

[2018-01-29 14:27:48,547] SoftmaxClickMouse noclick regions removed
0 of 256 actions

[2018-01-29 14:27:48,548] Writing logs to file: /tmp/universe-9018.log

[2018-01-29 14:27:48,548] Using the golang VNC implementation

[2018-01-29 14:27:48,548] Using VNCSession arguments: {'compress_level':
0, 'subsample_level': 0, 'encoding': 'tight', 'start_timeout': 21,
'fine_quality_level': 100}. (Customize by running "env.configure
(vnc_kwargs={...})"

[2018-01-29 14:27:48,579] [0] Connecting to environment: vnc://
localhost:5900 password=openai.
```

If desired, you can manually connect to the container's VNC server, using a VNC
client, such as TurboVNC. Most environments provide a convenient in-browser
VNC client: `http://localhost:15900/viewer/?password=openai`

```
...

[2018-01-29 14:27:52,218] Throttle fell behind by 1.06s; lost 5.32 frames

[2018-01-29 14:27:52,955] [1:localhost:5901] Initial reset complete:
episode_id=17803

37: done 1 games, mean reward 0.686, speed 11.77 f/s

52: done 2 games, mean reward 0.447, speed 28.29 f/s

72: done 3 games, mean reward -0.035, speed 33.24 f/s

98: done 4 games, mean reward -0.130, speed 25.92 f/s

125: done 5 games, mean reward -0.015, speed 33.64 f/s

146: done 6 games, mean reward 0.137, speed 26.18 f/s
```

By default, the training process starts the `ClickDialog-v0` environment, which should take 100k-200k to reach the mean reward 0.8-0.99. The convergence dynamics are shown in the following graph:

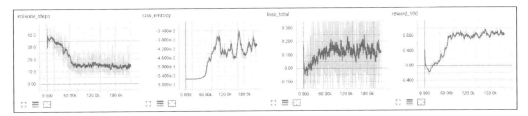

Figure 5: Convergence of the ClickDialog environment

The **episode_steps** chart shows the mean count of actions that the agent should carry out before the end of the episode. Ideally, for this problem, the count should be 1, as the only action that the agent needs to take is to click on dialog's close button. However, in fact, the agent sees seven-to-nine frames before the episode ends. This happens for two reasons: the cross on the dialog close button can appear with some delay and the browser inside the container adds a time gap before the agent clicks and the rewarder notices this. Anyway, in approximately 100k frames (which is about half an hour with eight containers), the training procedure converged to quite a good policy, which can close the dialog most of the time.

Checking the learned policy

To be able to peek inside the agent's activity, there is a tool which loads model weights from the file and runs several episodes, recording the screenshots with the agent's observations and actions selected. The tool is called `Chapter13/wob_click_play.py` and it connects to the first container (port `5900` and `15900`), running on the local machine and accepting the following arguments:

- `-m`: The filename with the model to be loaded.
- `--save <IMG_PREFIX>`: If specified it saves every observation in a separate file. The argument is the path prefix.
- `--count`: Sets the count of episodes to run.
- `--env`: Sets the environment name to be used, which by default is `ClickDialog-v0`.
- `--verbose`: Shows every step with reward, done and internal info.

This is useful for examining (or even debugging) the agent's behavior for different states during training. For example, checking the best model trained on `ClickDialog` shows us this:

```
rl_book_samples/Chapter13$ ./wob_click_play.py -m saves/ClickDialog-v0_
t1/best_1.047_209563.dat --count 5

[2018-01-29 15:43:57,188] [0:localhost:5900] Sending reset for env_
id=wob.mini.ClickDialog-v0 fps=60 episode_id=0

[2018-01-29 15:44:01,223] [0:localhost:5900] Initial reset complete:
episode_id=288

Round 0 done

Round 1 done

Round 2 done

Round 3 done

Round 4 done

Done 5 rounds, mean steps 6.40, mean reward 0.734
```

To check the agent's actions, you can pass `--save` option with the prefix of the images to be written. The actions that the agent performs are shown as a blue circle at the point of click on. The area on the right contains the technical information about the last reward and time left before timeout. For example, one of the saved images is shown as follows:

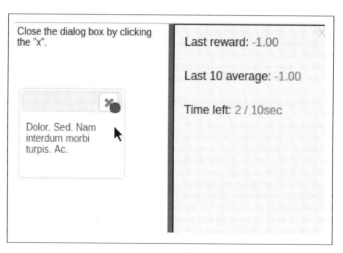

Figure 6: A screenshot of the agent in action

Issues with simple clicking

Unfortunately, the demonstrated approach can only be used to solve relatively simple problems, like `ClickDialog`. If you try to use it for more complicated tasks, the convergence is unlikely. There could be multiple reasons for this. First of all, our agent is stateless, which basically means that it makes the decision about the action only from the observation, without taking into account its previous actions. You may remember in *Chapter 1, What is Reinforcement Learning?* that we discussed the Markov property of the **Markov Decision Process (MDP)** and that this Markov property allowed us to discard all previous history, keeping only the current observation. Even in relatively simple problems from MiniWoB, this Markov property could be violated. For example, there is a problem called `ClickButtonSequence-v0` (the screenshot is shown as follows), which requires our agent to first click on button **ONE** and then on button **TWO**. Even if our agent is lucky enough to randomly click in the required order, it won't be able to distinguish from the single image that button needs to be clicked next.

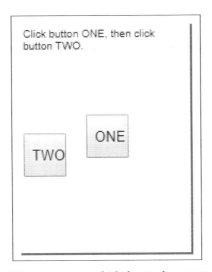

Figure 7: An example of the environment which the stateless agent could struggle to solve

Despite the simplicity of this problem, we cannot use our RL methods to solve it, because MDP formalism is not applicable anymore. Such problems are called Partially-Observable MDPs or POMDP and the usual approach for them is allowing the agent to keep some kind of state. The challenge here is to find the balance between keeping only minimal relevant information and overwhelming the agent with non-relevant information by adding everything into the observation.

Another issue that we can face with our example is that the data required to solve the problem might not be available in the image or could just be in an inconvenient form. For example, there are two problems: ClickTab and ClickCheckboxes. In the first one, you need to click on one of three tabs, but every time the tab that needs to be clicked is randomly chosen. Which tab needs to be clicked on is shown in a description (provided with an in-text field of observation and shown on the top of the environment's page), but our agent sees only pixels, which makes it complicated to connect the tiny number on the top with the outcome of the random click result. The situation is even worse with the ClickCheckboxes problem, when several checkboxes with randomly-generated text needs to be clicked. One of the possible options to prevent overfitting to the problem will be to use some kind of **OCR** (**optical character recognition**) net to convert the image in the observation into text form.

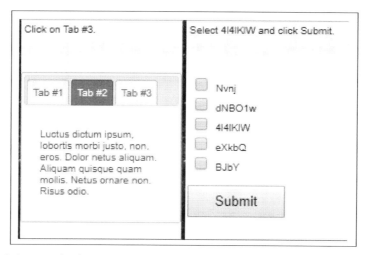

Figure 8: An example of environments where text description is important to action properly

Yet another issue could be related just to the dimensionality of the action space that the agent needs to explore. Even for single-click problems, the amount of actions could be very large, so it takes a long time for the agent to discover how to behave. One of the possible solutions here is incorporating demonstrations into the training. For example, on the following image there is a problem called CountSides-v0. The goal there is to click on the button that corresponds to the count of sides of the shape shown.

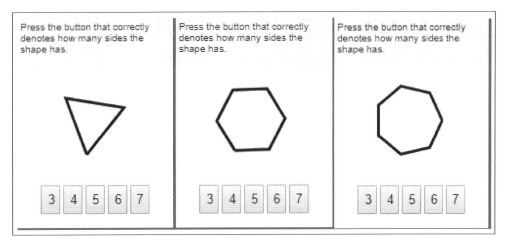

Figure 9: A screenshot of the CountSides environment

I've tried to train the agent from scratch and after a day of training, it has shown almost zero progress. However, after adding a couple of dozen examples of correct clicks, it successfully solved the problem in 15 minutes of training. Of course, maybe my hyperparameters were bad, but, still, the effect of the demonstrations is quite impressive. In the next example of this chapter, we'll take a look at how we can record and inject human demonstrations to improve the convergence.

Human demonstrations

The idea behind demonstrations is simple: to help our agent to discover the best way to solve the task, we show it some examples of actions that we think are required for the problem. Those examples could be not the best solution or 100% accurate, but they should be good enough to show the agent promising directions to explore.

In fact, this is a very natural thing to do and all human learning is based on some prior examples given by a teacher in class, your parents or other people. Those examples could be in a written form (recipe books) or given as demonstrations that you need to repeat several times to get it right (dance classes). Such forms of training are much more effective than random search. Just imagine how complicated and lengthy it would be to learn how to clean your teeth by trial-and-error alone. Of course, there is a danger from learning how to follow the demonstrations, which could be wrong or not the most efficient way to solve the problem, but overall, it's much more effective than random search.

All our previous examples used zero prior knowledge and started with random weights' initialization, which caused random actions to be performed at the beginning of the training. After some iterations, the agent discovered that some actions in some states give more promising results (via the Q-value or policy with higher advantage) and started to prefer those actions over the others. Finally, this process led to more or less optimal policy, which gave the agent high reward at the end. It worked well when our action space dimensionality was low and the environment's behavior wasn't very complex, but just doubling the actions' count caused at least twice the observations needed. In the case of our clicker agent, we have 256 different actions corresponding to 10x10 grids in the active area, which is 128 times more actions than we had in the CartPole environment. It is not surprising that the training process becomes lengthy and may fail to converge at all.

This issue of dimensionality could be addressed in various ways, like smarter exploration methods, training with better sampling efficiency (one-shot training), incorporating prior knowledge (transfer learning) and other means. There is lots of research activity focused on making RL better and faster and we can be sure that lots of breakthroughs are ahead. In this section, we'll try the more traditional approach of incorporating the demonstration recorded by humans into the training process.

You might remember our discussion about on-policy and off-policy methods (which were discussed in *Chapter 4, The Cross-Entropy Method* and *Chapter 7, DQN Extensions*). This is very relevant to our human demonstrations, because, strictly speaking, we cannot use off-policy data (human observation-actions pairs) with the on-policy method (A3C in our case). That happens due to the nature of on-policy methods: they estimate the PG using the samples gathered from the current policy. If we just push human-recorded samples into the training process, the estimated gradient will be relevant for human policy, but not our current policy given by the **Neural Network (NN)**. To solve this issue, we need to cheat a bit and look at our problem from the supervised learning angle. To be concrete, we'll use the log-likelihood objective to push our network towards taking actions from demonstrations.

Before we can go to the implementation details, we need to address a very important question: how do we obtain the demonstrations in the most convenient form?

Recording the demonstrations

There is no universal recipe for how to record the demonstration, as demonstration depends on the observation and action space details. However, from a higher perspective, we should save the information available for a human or another agent, whose actions we want to record, as well as actions taken by this agent. For example, if we want to obtain Atari game sessions played by somebody, we need to save the screen image, plus the button pressed on this screen.

In our case of the OpenAI Universe environment, there is an elegant solution, based on VNC protocol and used as a universal transport. To save the demonstrations, we need to capture the screen sent by the server to the VNC client, as well as mouse and keyboard actions sent by the client to the server. MiniWoB provides built-in functionality for this based on VNC protocol proxy, which is illustrated on the following scheme:

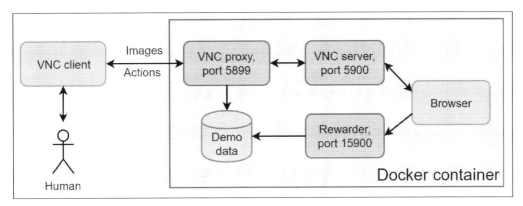

Figure 10: Demonstrating recording architecture

By default, VNC proxy is not started on the container's start, as there is a separate *demo mode*. To start the container with proxy enabled, you need to pass the arguments `demonstration -e ENV_NAME` to the container. You also will need to pass the port forwarding options to make port `5899` (that VNC proxy is listening to) available from outside. The whole command line used to start the container in recording mode for env `ClickTest2` is below (also available as `Chapter13/adhoc/start_docker_demo.sh`):

```
docker run -e TURK_DB='' -p 5899:5899 --privileged --ipc host --cap-add
SYS_ADMIN shmuma/miniwob:v2 demonstration -e wob.mini.ClickTest2-v0
```

The argument `TURK_DB` is required, which is probably related to **Mechanical Turk** used by OpenAI to gather human demonstrations for internal experiments. Unfortunately, OpenAI hasn't released those demonstrations, despite its promise to do so. So, the only way to get the demonstrations is to record them yourself.

Once the container is started, you can connect to it using any VNC client that you prefer. For all linux/windows/mac there are several alternatives available. You should connect to the host of your container, port `5899`. The connection password is **openai**. After connection, you should see the browser window with an environment that you've specified on the container start.

Now you can start solving the problem, but don't forget that all your actions will be recorded and will be used later during the training. So, your actions should be efficient and not include any non-relevant actions, like clicking at the wrong place, and so on. Of course, you can always do an experiment checking the robustness of the training to such noisy demonstrations. Time given for solving the problem is also limited, as for most of the environments it's 10 seconds. On expiration, the problem will start over and you will be given the reward of -1. If you don't see the mouse pointer, you should enable **Local mouse render** mode in your VNC client.

Once you've recorded some demonstrations, you can disconnect from the server and copy the recorded data. Remember that your recording will be preserved only while the container is alive. The recorded data is placed in /tmp/demo folder inside the container's filesystem, but you can see the files using docker exec command (following 80daf4b8f257 is an ID of a container started in demo mode):

```
$ docker exec -t 80daf4b8f257 ls -laR /tmp/demo
/tmp/demo:
total 20
drwxr-xr-x  3 root    root      4096 Jan 30 17:06 .
drwxrwxrwt 19 root    root      4096 Jan 30 17:07 ..
drwxr-xr-x  2 root    root      4096 Jan 30 17:07
1517332006-fprnte8qiy3af3-0
-rw-r--r--  1 nobody  nogroup     20 Jan 30 17:09 env_id.txt
-rw-r--r--  1 root    root       531 Jan 30 17:09 rewards.demo


/tmp/demo/1517332006-fprnte8qiy3af3-0:
total 35132
drwxr-xr-x 2 root root      4096 Jan 30 17:07 .
drwxr-xr-x 3 root root      4096 Jan 30 17:06 ..
-rw-r--r-- 1 root root     51187 Jan 30 17:07 client.fbs
-rw-r--r-- 1 root root        20 Jan 30 17:07 env_id.txt
-rw-r--r-- 1 root root      5888 Jan 30 17:07 rewards.demo
-rw-r--r-- 1 root root  35900918 Jan 30 17:07 server.fbs
```

One individual VNC session is saved inside the `/tmp/demo` folder in a separate subdir, so you can use the same container for several recording sessions. To copy the data, you can use the command `docker cp` command:

```
docker cp 80daf4b8f257:/tmp/demo .
```

Once you've got the raw data files, you can use them for training, but first let's talk about the data format.

Recording format

For every client connection, VNC proxy records four files:

* `env_id.txt`: A text file with the ID of the environment used to record the demonstration. This is very convenient for filtering when you have several demonstrations data directories.

* `rewards.demo`: A JSON file with events recorded by the rewarder daemon. This includes timestamped events from the environment, like text description change, reward obtained and others.

* `client.fbs`: A binary format with events sent by the client to the VNC server. Inside it contains timestamps of raw VNC protocol messages (called **Remote Framebuffer Protocol** or **RFP**).

* `server.fbs`: A binary format with data sent by the VNC server to the client. It has the same format as `client.fbs`, but the set of messages is different.

The trickiest files here are `client.fbs` and `server.fbs`, as they are binary and the format has no convenient reader (at least I'm not aware of such a library). The protocol of VNC is standardized in RFC6143 called The Remote Framebuffer Protocol which is available on the IETF website `https://tools.ietf.org/html/rfc6143`. This protocol defines the set of messages that the VNC client and server can exchange to provide a remote desktop to a user. The client can send the keyboard or mouse events and the server is responsible for sending the image of the desktop to allow the client to see an up-to-date view of the applications. To improve user experience over slow network links, the server optimizes the transfer by optionally compressing the image and sending only relevant (modified) parts of the GUI desktop.

To make demo recordings usable for RL agent training, we need to convert this VNC format into a set of images and user events issued at the time of the image. To achieve this, I've implemented a small VNC protocol parser using KaiTai binary parser language (project website `http://kaitai.io/`), which provides a convenient way to parse complex binary file formats using a declarative Yaml-formatted language. If you're curious, the source files for the client and server messages are in the `Chapter13/ksy` directory.

Python code, related to the demo format, is placed in module `Chapter13/lib/vnc_demo.py` which contains a high-level function loader for the demo directory and the set of lower-level methods used to interpret the internal binary format. The result returned by the loader function `vnc_demo.load_demo()` is the list of tuples. Every tuple contains a NumPy array with the observation used by the MiniWoB model and the index of the mouse action performed.

To check the demo data, there is a small utility `Chapter13/ahdoc/demo_dump.py`, which loads the demo directory with `client.fbs` and `server.fbs` and dumps demo samples as image files. The example of the command line used to convert the demonstrations that I've recorded into images is shown as follows:

```
rl_book_samples/Chapter13$ ./adhoc/demo_dump.py -d data/demo-CountSides/
-e wob.mini.CountSides-v0 -o count
[2018-01-30 12:44:11,794] Making new env: wob.mini.CountSides-v0
[2018-01-30 12:44:11,796] Using SoftmaxClickMouse with action_region=
(10, 125, 170, 285), noclick_regions=[]
[2018-01-30 12:44:11,797] SoftmaxClickMouse noclick regions removed
0 of 256 actions
Loaded 64 demo samples
[2018-01-30 12:44:12,191] Making new env: wob.mini.CountSides-v0
[2018-01-30 12:44:12,192] Using SoftmaxClickMouse with action_region=
(10, 125, 170, 285), noclick_regions=[]
[2018-01-30 12:44:12,192] SoftmaxClickMouse noclick regions removed
0 of 256 actions
```

This command produced 64 image files with the prefix `count`.

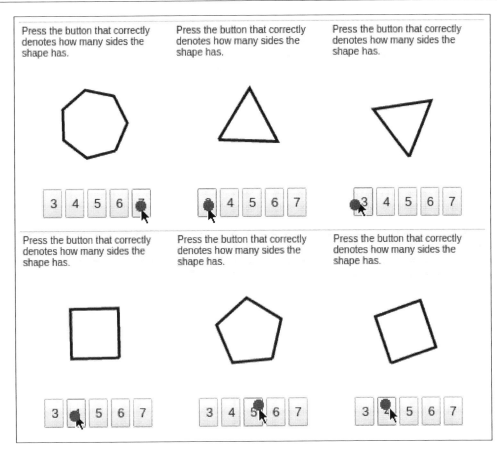

Figure 12: On every image the click point is shown as a blue circle

The binary data for this recording is available in Chapter13/demos/demo-CountSides.tar.gz and you need to unpack it before usage. It also needs to be said that my implementation of the VNC protocol reading is experimental, works only with files produced by VNC proxy used in the MiniWoB image 0.20.0 and is not pretending to fully comply with VNC protocol RFC. Furthermore, the reading process is hard-coded for our action space transformation and doesn't produce examples of mouse movements, keys pressed and other events. If you think it should be extended for a more generic case, you're always welcome to contribute.

Training using demonstrations

Now that we know how to record and load the demonstration data, we have only one question unanswered yet: how does our training process need to be modified to incorporate human demonstrations? The simplest solution, which nevertheless works surprisingly well, is to use the log-likelihood objective that we used in training our chatbot in *Chapter 12, Chatbots Training with RL*. To do so, we need to look at our A2C model as a classification problem producing the classification of input observation in its policy head. In its simplest form, the value head will be left untrained, but, in fact, it won't be hard to train it too: we know the rewards obtained during the demonstrations, so what is needed is calculating the discounted reward from every observation to the end of the episode.

To check how it was implemented, let's return to the code pieces we skipped during the description of `Chapter13/wob_click_train.py`. First of all, we can pass the directory with demonstration data by passing the `--demo <DIR>` option in the command line. This will enable the branch below, where we load the demonstration samples from the directory specified. Function `vnc_demo.load_demo()` is smart enough to automatically load demonstrations from any level of subdirectories, so you just need to pass the directory where your demonstrations are placed.

```
demo_samples = None
if args.demo:
    demo_samples = vnc_demo.load_demo(args.demo, env_name)
    if not demo_samples:
        demo_samples = None
    else:
        print("Loaded %d demo samples, will use them during
training" % len(demo_samples))
```

The second piece of code relevant to demonstration training is inside the training loop and is executed before any normal batch. The training from demonstrations is performed with some probability (by default it is 0.5) and is specified by the DEMO_ PROB hyperparameter.

```
if demo_samples and random.random() < DEMO_PROB:
    random.shuffle(demo_samples)
    demo_batch = demo_samples[:BATCH_SIZE]
    model_vnc.train_demo(net, optimizer, demo_batch,
writer, step_idx,
                                preprocessor=ptan.agent.
default_states_preprocessor, device=device)
```

The logic is simple: with DEMO_PROB chance we sample BATCH_SIZE samples from our demonstration data and perform the round of training of our network in the batch. The actual training is performed by the model_vnc.train_demo() function, which is shown as follows:

```
def train_demo(net, optimizer, batch, writer, step_idx, preprocessor,
device="cpu"):
    batch_obs, batch_act = zip(*batch)
    batch_v = preprocessor(batch_obs).to(device)
    optimizer.zero_grad()
    ref_actions_v = torch.LongTensor(batch_act).to(device)
    policy_v = net(batch_v)[0]
    loss_v = F.cross_entropy(policy_v, ref_actions_v)
    loss_v.backward()
    optimizer.step()
    writer.add_scalar("demo_loss", loss_v.data.cpu().numpy()[0],
step_idx)
```

The training code is also very simple and straightforward. We split our batch on observation and actions list, preprocess the observations to convert them into a PyTorch tensor and place them on GPU, then we ask our A2C network to return the policy and calculate the cross-entropy loss between the result and desired actions. From an optimization point of view, we're pushing our network towards the actions taken in the demonstrations.

Results

To check the effect of demonstrations, I've performed two sets of training on the CountSides problem with the same hyperparameters: one was done without demonstrations, another used 64 demonstration clicks. The difference was dramatic. Training performed *from scratch*, reached the best mean reward of -0.64 after 12 hours of training and the training dynamics didn't show any improvement. The training dynamics are shown as follows:

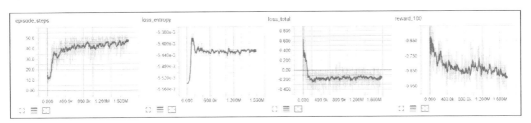

Figure 12: Training dynamics on the CountSides environment

With just 64 demonstration samples added, in just 45k frames the training was able to reach the mean reward of 1.75. High entropy loss shown as follows demonstrates that the agent became very sure about its actions.

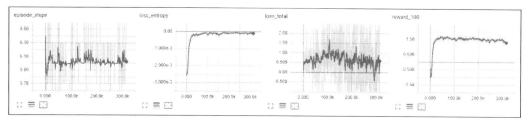

Figure 13: Training on the same environment with human demonstrations

To put things in perspective, below are the same charts combined.

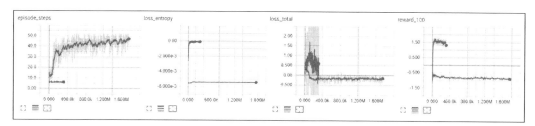

Figure 14: Comparison of training with (blue) and without (brown) demonstrations

TicTacToe problem

To check the effect of demonstrations on training, I've taken a more complex problem from MiniWoB, which is a TicTacToe game. I've recorded some demonstrations (available in `Chapter13/demos/demo-TicTacToe.tgz`), in total almost 200 actions, and some examples of them are as follows:

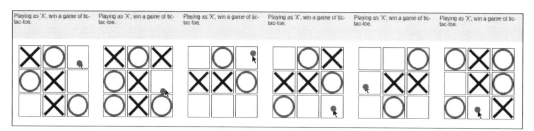

Figure 15: The TicTacToe environment with human actions

After one hour of training, the agent was able to reach the mean reward of -0.05, which means that it can win from time to time and for the rest of the games the agent can come to a draw. The training dynamics are shown below. To improve the exploration, demo training probability was decreased from 0.5 to 0.01 after 25k frames seen.

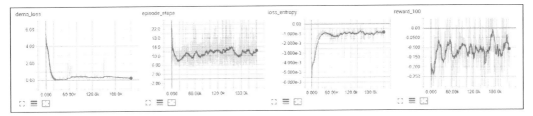

Figure 16: Training dynamics of the TicTacToe agent

Using `wob_click_play.py`, we can check the agent's actions step-by-step. For example, following are some games played by the best model with the mean reward of 0.187:

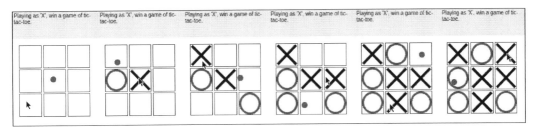

Figure 17: A game played by the agent

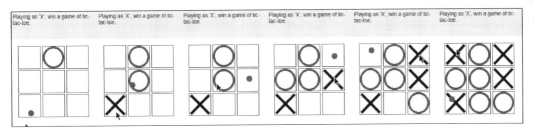

Figure 18: A second game played by the agent

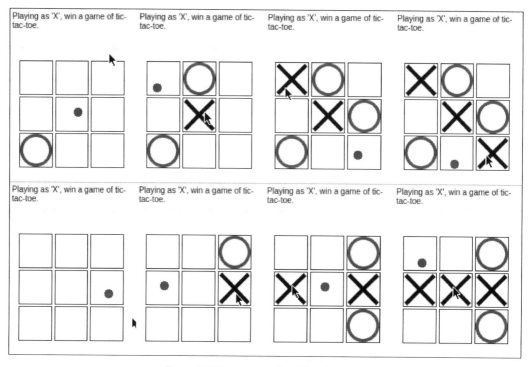

Figure 19: More games played by the agent

Adding text description

As the last example of this chapter, we'll add text description of the problem into observations of our model. We've already mentioned that some problems contain vital information given in a text description, like the index of tabs needed to be clicked or list of entries that the agent needs to check. The same information is shown on the top of the image observation, but pixels is not always the best representation of a simple text.

To take this text into account, we need to extend our model's input from an image only to an image and text data. We have worked with text in the previous chapter, so a **Recurrent Neural Network (RNN)** is quite an obvious choice (maybe not the best for such a toy problem but it is flexible and scalable). We are not going to cover this example in detail but will just focus on the most important points of the implementation (the whole code is in `Chapter13/wob_click_mm_train.py`). In comparison to our clicker model, text extension doesn't add too much.

First of all, we should ask the wrapper `MiniWoBCropper` to keep the text obtained from the observation. The complete source code of this class has already been shown earlier in this chapter. To keep the text, we should pass `keep_text=True` to the wrapper constructor, which makes this class return a tuple with a NumPy array and text string instead of just a NumPy array with the image.

Then, we need to prepare our model to be able to process such tuples, instead of a batch of NumPy arrays. This needs to be done in two places: in our agent (when we use the model to choose the action) and in the training code. To adapt the observation in a model-friendly way, we can use a special functionality of the PTAN library, called `preprocessor`. The core idea is very simple: `preprocessor` is a callable function which needs to convert the list of observations in a form that is ready to be passed to the model. By default, `preprocessor` converts the list of NumPy arrays into a PyTorch tensor and, optionally, copies it in GPU memory. However, sometimes more sophisticated transformations are required, like in our case, when we need to pack the images into the tensor, but text strings require special handling. In that case, you can redefine the default `preprocessor` and pass it into the `ptan.Agent` class. In theory, `preprocessor` functionality could be moved into the model itself, thanks to PyTorch flexibility, but default `preprocessor` simplifies our lives in cases when observations are just NumPy arrays. Following is the `preprocessor` class source code taken from the `Chapter13/lib/model_vnc.py` module.

```
class MultimodalPreprocessor:
    log = logging.getLogger("MulitmodalPreprocessor")

    def __init__(self, max_dict_size=MM_MAX_DICT_SIZE, device="cpu"):
        self.max_dict_size = max_dict_size
        self.token_to_id = {TOKEN_UNK: 0}
        self.next_id = 1
        self.tokenizer = TweetTokenizer(preserve_case=False)
        self.device = device
```

In the constructor, we create a mapping from token to identifier (which will be dynamically extended) and create the tokenizer from the `nltk` package.

```
    def __len__(self):
        return len(self.token_to_id)

    def __call__(self, batch):
        tokens_batch = []
        for img_obs, txt_obs in batch:
            tokens = self.tokenizer.tokenize(txt_obs)
            idx_obs = self.tokens_to_idx(tokens)
```

```
        tokens_batch.append((img_obs, idx_obs))
        # sort batch decreasing to seq len
        tokens_batch.sort(key=lambda p: len(p[1]), reverse=True)
        img_batch, seq_batch = zip(*tokens_batch)
        lens = list(map(len, seq_batch))
```

The goal of our preprocessor is to convert a batch of (image, text) tuples into two objects: the first has to be a tensor with image data of shape (batch_size, 3, 210, 160) and the second has to contain the batch of tokens from text descriptions in the form of a packed sequence. The packed sequence is a PyTorch data structure suitable for efficient processing with RNN and we've discussed it in *Chapter 12, Chatbots Training with RL*.

As the first step of our transformation, we tokenize text strings into tokens and convert every token into the list of integer IDs. Then we sort our batch on decrease of tokens' count, which is a requirement of underlying CuDNN library for efficient RNN processing.

```
        img_v = torch.FloatTensor(img_batch).to(self.device)
```

In the preceding line, we convert observation images into the single tensor.

```
        seq_arr = np.zeros(shape=(len(seq_batch),
    max(len(seq_batch[0]), 1)), dtype=np.int64)
        for idx, seq in enumerate(seq_batch):
            seq_arr[idx, :len(seq)] = seq
            # Map empty sequences into single #UNK token
            if len(seq) == 0:
                lens[idx] = 1
```

To create the packed sequence class, first we need to create a *padded sequence* tensor, which is a matrix of (batch_size, len_of_longest_seq). We copy IDs of our sequences into this matrix.

```
        seq_v = torch.LongTensor(seq_arr).to(self.device)
        seq_p = rnn_utils.pack_padded_sequence(seq_v, lens, batch_
    first=True)
        return img_v, seq_p
```

As a final step, we create the tensors from the NumPy matrix and convert them into *packed* form by using the PyTorch utility function. The result of the transformation is two objects: a tensor with images and a packed sequence with tokenized texts.

```
    def tokens_to_idx(self, tokens):
        res = []
        for token in tokens:
```

```
          idx = self.token_to_id.get(token)
          if idx is None:
              if self.next_id == self.max_dict_size:
                  self.log.warning("Maximum size of dict reached,
token '%s' converted to #UNK token", token)
                  idx = 0
              else:
                  idx = self.next_id
                  self.next_id += 1
                  self.token_to_id[token] = idx
          res.append(idx)
      return res
```

The preceding utility function has to convert the list of tokens into a list of IDs. The tricky thing is that we don't know in advance the size of dictionary from the text descriptions. One approach would be to work on character level and feed individual characters into the RNN, but it would cause too long sequences to be processed. The alternative solution is to hardcode some reasonable dictionary size, say 100 tokens, and dynamically assign token IDs to tokens that we've never seen before. In this implementation, the latter approach is used, but it could be not applicable to MiniWoB problems which contain randomly-generated strings in the text description.

```
    def save(self, file_name):
        with open(file_name, 'wb') as fd:
            pickle.dump(self.token_to_id, fd)
            pickle.dump(self.max_dict_size, fd)
            pickle.dump(self.next_id, fd)

    @classmethod
    def load(cls, file_name):
        with open(file_name, "rb") as fd:
            token_to_id = pickle.load(fd)
            max_dict_size = pickle.load(fd)
            next_id = pickle.load(fd)

            res = MultimodalPreprocessor(max_dict_size)
            res.token_to_id = token_to_id
            res.next_id = next_id
            return res
```

As our token-to-ID mapping is dynamically generated, our `preprocessor` has to provide a way to save and load this state in a file. The preceding two functions do that exactly. The next piece of the puzzle is the `model` class itself, which is an extension of our model used.

```python
class ModelMultimodal(nn.Module):
    def __init__(self, input_shape, n_actions, max_dict_size=MM_MAX_
DICT_SIZE):
        super(ModelMultimodal, self).__init__()

        self.conv = nn.Sequential(
            nn.Conv2d(input_shape[0], 64, 5, stride=5),
            nn.ReLU(),
            nn.Conv2d(64, 64, 3, stride=2),
            nn.ReLU(),
        )

        conv_out_size = self._get_conv_out(input_shape)

        self.emb = nn.Embedding(max_dict_size, MM_EMBEDDINGS_DIM)
        self.rnn = nn.LSTM(MM_EMBEDDINGS_DIM, MM_HIDDEN_SIZE, batch_
.first=True)

        self.policy = nn.Sequential(
            nn.Linear(conv_out_size + MM_HIDDEN_SIZE*2, n_actions),
        )

        self.value = nn.Sequential(
            nn.Linear(conv_out_size + MM_HIDDEN_SIZE*2, 1),
        )
```

The difference is in a new embedding layer, which converts integer token IDs into dense token vectors and LSTM RNN. The outputs from the convolution and RNN layers are concatenated and fed into the policy and value heads, so the dimensionality of their input is the image and text features combined.

```python
    def _get_conv_out(self, shape):
        o = self.conv(torch.zeros(1, *shape))
        return int(np.prod(o.size()))
```

```
    def _concat_features(self, img_out, rnn_hidden):
        batch_size = img_out.size()[0]
        if isinstance(rnn_hidden, tuple):
            flat_h = list(map(lambda t: t.view(batch_size, -1),
rnn_hidden))
            rnn_h = torch.cat(flat_h, dim=1)
        else:
            rnn_h = rnn_hidden.view(batch_size, -1)
        return torch.cat((img_out, rnn_h), dim=1)
```

The preceding function performs the concatenation of the image and RNN features into one single square tensor.

```
    def forward(self, x):
        x_img, x_text = x
        assert isinstance(x_text, rnn_utils.PackedSequence)

        # deal with text data
        emb_out = self.emb(x_text.data)
        emb_out_seq = rnn_utils.PackedSequence(emb_out, x_text.batch_
sizes)
        rnn_out, rnn_h = self.rnn(emb_out_seq)

        # extract image features
        fx = x_img.float() / 256
        conv_out = self.conv(fx).view(fx.size()[0], -1)

        feats = self._concat_features(conv_out, rnn_h)
        return self.policy(feats), self.value(feats)
```

In the forward function, we expect two objects prepared by the preprocessor: a tensor with input images and packed sequences of the batch. Images are processed with convolutions and text data is fed through the RNN, then both of the results are concatenated and policy and value results are calculated.

That's most of the new code. The training Python script wob_click_mm_train.py is mostly the copy of wob_click_train.py, with just a tiny difference of preprocessor created. keep_text=True was passed to the MiniWoBCropper() constructor and other small modifications.

Results

I ran several experiments on the environment `ClickButton-v0`, which has a goal to make a selection between several random buttons. Some of the recorded demonstrations are shown as follows:

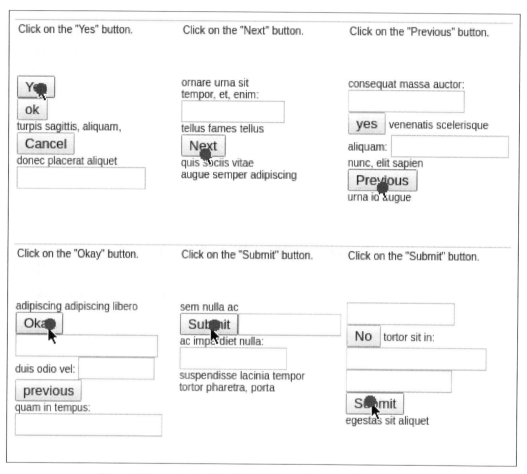

Figure 20: Screenshots of the ClickButton environment demonstrations

Even with demonstrations, a model without text description was able to reach the mean reward of 0.4, which is not much better than randomly clicking on any button in the dialog.

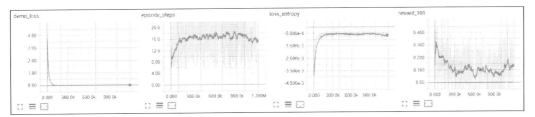

Figure 21: Convergence of the ClickButton agent without text description used during the training

However, the model enriched with features from the text description was able to perform much better and the best mean reward for 100 episodes was 0.7.

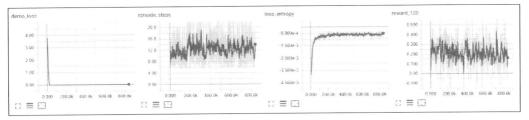

Figure 22: ClickButton environment training with text description

The reward dynamics of both models are quite noisy, which may signal that tuning hyperparameters and/or increasing the number of parallel environments could help.

Things to try

In this chapter, we've only just started playing with MiniWoB, by touching upon the six easiest environments from the full set of 80 problems, so there is plenty of uncharted territory ahead. If you want to practice, there are several items you can experiment with:

- Testing the robustness of demonstrations to noisy clicks.
- Implementing training of the value head of A2C based on demonstration data.
- Implementing more sophisticated mouse control, like *Move mouse N pixels left/right/top/bottom*.
- Using some pretrained OCR net (or train your own!) to extract text information from the observations.
- Taking other problems and trying to solve them. There are some quite tricky and fun problems, like *sort items using drag-n-drop*, or *repeat the pattern using checkboxes*.

Summary

In this chapter, we saw the practical application of RL methods for browser automation and used the MiniWoB benchmark from OpenAI. This chapter concludes part three of the book. The next part will be devoted to more complicated and recent methods related to continuous action spaces, non-gradient methods, and other more advanced methods of RL.

14

Continuous Action Space

This chapter kicks off the **advanced Reinforcement Learning (RL)** part of the book by taking a look at the problems that we've only briefly mentioned before: working with environments when our action space is not discrete. In this chapter, we'll become familiar with the challenges that arise in such cases and learn how to solve them.

Why a continuous space?

All the examples that we've seen so far in the book had a discrete action space, so you might have the wrong impression that discrete actions dominate the field. This is a very biased view, of course, and just reflects the selection of domains that we picked our test problems from. Besides Atari games and simple, classical RL problems, there are lots of tasks requiring more than just making a selection from a small and discrete set of things to do.

To give you an example, just imagine a simple robot with only one controllable joint, which can be rotated in some range of degrees. Usually, to control a physical joint, you have to specify either the desired position or the force applied. In both cases, you need to make a decision about a continuous value. This value is fundamentally different from a discrete action space, as the set of values that you can make a decision on is potentially infinite. For instance, you can ask the joint to move to a 13.5° angle or 13.512° angle and the results could be different. Of course, there are always some physical limitations of the system, and you cannot specify the action with infinite precision, but the size of potential values could be very large.

In fact, when you need to communicate with a physical world, a continuous action space is much more likely than having a discrete set of actions. For example, different kinds of robots control systems (such as a heating/cooling controller). The methods of RL could be applied to this domain, but there are some details that you need to take into consideration before using the **Asynchronous Advantage Actor-Critic** (**A3C**) or **Deep Q-Network** (**DQN**) methods.

In this chapter, we'll try to understand how to deal with this family of problems. This will act as a good starting point for you to begin learning about this very interesting and important domain of RL.

Action space

The fundamental and obvious difference with a continuous action space is its continuity. In contrast to a discrete action space, when the action is defined as a discrete mutually exclusive set of options to choose from, the continuous action has a value from some range. On every time step, the agent needs to select the concrete value for the action and pass it to the environment.

In Gym, a continuous action space is represented as the `gym.spaces.Box` class, which was described in *Chapter 2, OpenAI Gym*, when we talked about the observation space. You may remember that Box includes a set of values with a shape and bounds. For example, every observation from the Atari emulator was represented as `Box(low=0, high=255, shape=(210, 160, 3))`, which means 100,800 values organized as a 3D tensor, with values from the 0..255 range.

For the action space, it's unlikely that you'll work with such large numbers of actions. For example, the robot that we'll use as a testing environment has eight continuous actions, which correspond to eight motors, two in every robot's leg. For this environment, the action space will be defined as `Box(low=-1, high=1, shape= (8, ))`, which means eight values from the range -1..1 have to be selected at every timestamp to control the robot. In that case, the action passed to the `env.step()` at every step won't be an integer anymore: it will be a NumPy vector of some shape with individual action values. Of course, there could be more complicated cases when the action space is a combination of discrete and continuous actions, which may be represented with the `gym.spaces.Tuple` class.

Environments

Most of the environments that include continuous action spaces are related to the physical world, so physics simulations are normally used. There are lots of software packages that can simulate physical processes, from very simple, open-source tools to complex, commercial packages that can simulate multiphysics processes (such as fluid, burning, and strength simulations). In the case of robotics, one of the most popular packages is MuJoCo, which stands for **Multi-Joint Dynamics with Contact** (www.mujoco.org). This is a physics engine in which you can define the components of the system, their interaction and properties. Then the simulator is responsible for *solving the system* by taking into account your intervention and finding the parameters (usually the location, velocities, and accelerations) of the components. This makes it ideal as a playground for RL environments, as you can define fairly complicated systems (such as multipede robots or robotic arms or humanoids) and then feed the observation into the RL agent, getting actions back.

Unfortunately, MuJoCo isn't free and requires a license to be used. There is a trial one-month license available on websites, but after the trial, a license will be required. For students, MuJoCo developers provide a free license, but for post-university RL enthusiasts, buying a license could be overkill. Luckily, there is an open-source alternative, called PyBullet, which provides similar functionality (maybe at a cost of lower speed or accuracy) for free.

PyBullet is available at https://github.com/bulletphysics/bullet3 and can be installed by running pip install pybullet inside your virtual environment. The following code (which is available in Chapter14/01_check_env.py) allows you to check that PyBullet works and looks at the action space and renders an image of the environment that we'll use as a guinea pig in this chapter.

```
#!/usr/bin/env python3
import gym
import pybullet_envs

ENV_ID = "MinitaurBulletEnv-v0"
RENDER = True


if __name__ == "__main__":
    spec = gym.envs.registry.spec(ENV_ID)
    spec._kwargs['render'] = RENDER
    env = gym.make(ENV_ID)

    print(env.observation_space)
    print(env.action_space, env.action_space.sample())
```

```
print(env)
print(env.reset())
input("Press any key to exit\n")
env.close()
```

After starting the utility above, it should open the GUI window with our four-legged robot that we'll train how to move.

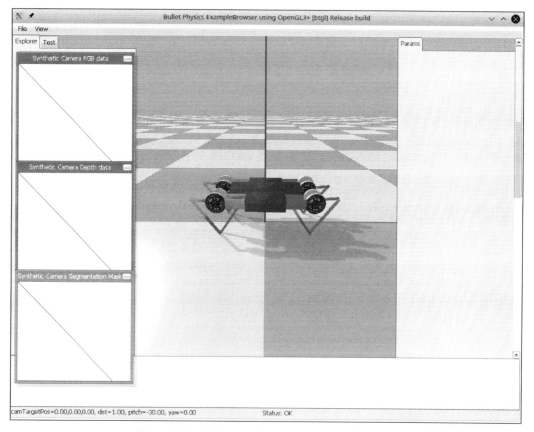

Figure 1: The Minitaur environment in the PyBullet GUI

This environment provides you with 28 numbers as observation. They correspond to different physical parameters of the robot: velocity, position, and acceleration (you can check the source code of `MinitaurBulletEnv-v0` for details). The action space is eight numbers, which define the parameters of the motors. There are two in every leg (one in every knee). The reward of this environment is the distance travelled by the robot minus the energy spent.

```
rl_book_samples/Chapter14$ ./01_check_env.py
[2018-02-05 15:02:14,305] Making new env: MinitaurBulletEnv-v0
pybullet build time: Feb 2 2018 08:30:15
...
Observation space: Box(28,)
Action space: Box(8,)
<TimeLimit<MinitaurBulletEnv<MinitaurBulletEnv-v0>>>
[ 1.47892781e+00 1.47092442e+00 1.47486159e+00 1.46795948e+00
  1.48735227e+00 1.49067837e+00 1.48767487e+00 1.48856073e+00
  1.22760518e+00 1.23364264e+00 1.23980635e+00 1.23808274e+00
  1.23863620e+00 1.20957165e+00 1.22914063e+00 1.21966631e+00
  5.27463590e-01 5.87924378e-01 5.56949063e-01 6.10125678e-01
  4.58817873e-01 4.37388898e-01 4.57652322e-01 4.52128593e-01
  -3.00935339e-03 1.04264007e-03 -2.26649036e-04 9.99994903e-01]
Press any key to exit
```

The Actor-Critic (A2C) method

The first method that we'll apply to our walking robot problem is A2C, which we experimented with in part three of the book. This choice of method is quite obvious, as A2C is very easy to adapt to the continuous action domain. As a quick refresher, A2C's idea is to estimate the gradient of our policy as

$\nabla J = \nabla_\theta \log \pi_\theta(a|s)(R - V_\theta(s))$. The π_θ policy is supposed to provide to us the probability distribution of actions given the observed state. The quantity $V_\theta(s)$ is called a critic, equals to the value of the state and is trained using the **Mean Square Error (MSE)** between the critic return and the value estimated by the Bellman equation. To improve exploration, the entropy bonus $L_H = \pi_\theta(s) \log \pi_\theta(s)$ is usually added to the loss.

Obviously, the value head of the actor-critic will be unchanged for continuous actions. The only thing that is affected is the representation of the policy. In the discrete cases that we've seen, we had only one action with several mutually exclusive discrete values. For such a case, the obvious representation of the policy was the probability distribution over all actions. In a continuous case, we usually have several actions, each of which can take a value from some range. With that in mind, the simplest policy representation will be just those values returned for every action. These values should not be confused with the value of the state $V(s)$, which means how many rewards we can get from the state. To illustrate the difference, let's imagine a simple car steering case, when we can only turn the wheel. The action at every moment will be the wheel angle (action value), but the value of every state will be the potential discounted reward from the state, which is a totally different thing.

Returning to our action representation options, if you remember from *Chapter 9, Policy Gradients – An Alternative*, the representation of an action as a concrete value has different disadvantages, mostly related to the exploration of the environment. A much better choice will be something stochastic. The simplest alternative will be the network returning parameters of the Gaussian distribution. For N actions, it will be two vectors of size N. The first is the mean values μ and the second vector will contain variances σ^2. In that case, our policy will be represented as a random N-dimensional vector of uncorrelated, normally distributed random variables and our network can make a selection about the mean and the variance of every variable.

By definition, the probability density function of the Gaussian distribution is $f(x|\mu,\sigma^2) = \frac{1}{\sqrt{2\pi\sigma^2}} e^{-\frac{(x-\mu)^2}{2\sigma^2}}$. We could directly use this formula to get the probabilities, but to improve numerical stability, it is worth doing some math and simplifying the expression for $\log \pi_\theta(a|s)$.

The final result will be this: $\log \pi_\theta(a|s) = -\frac{(x-\mu)^2}{2\sigma^2} - \log \sqrt{2\pi\sigma^2}$.

The entropy of the Gaussian distribution could be obtained using the differential entropy definition and will be $\ln \sqrt{2\pi e\sigma^2}$. Now we have everything we need to implement the A2C method. Let's do it.

Implementation

The complete source code is in Chapter14/02_train_a2c.py, Chapter14/lib/model.py and Chapter14/lib/common.py. Most of the code will already be familiar to you, so the following includes only the parts that differ. Let's start with the model class defined in Chapter14/lib/model.py.

```
HID_SIZE = 128

class ModelA2C(nn.Module):
    def __init__(self, obs_size, act_size):
        super(ModelA2C, self).__init__()

        self.base = nn.Sequential(
            nn.Linear(obs_size, HID_SIZE),
            nn.ReLU(),
        )
        self.mu = nn.Sequential(
            nn.Linear(HID_SIZE, act_size),
            nn.Tanh(),
        )
        self.var = nn.Sequential(
```

```
        nn.Linear(HID_SIZE, act_size),
        nn.Softplus(),
    )
    self.value = nn.Linear(HID_SIZE, 1)
```

As you can see, our network has three heads, instead of the normal two for a discrete variant of A2C. The first two heads return the mean value and the variance of the actions, while the last is the critic head returning the value of the state. The mean value returned has an activation function of a hyperbolic tangent, which is the squashed output to the range of -1..1. The variance is transformed with the softplus activation function, which is $log(1+e^x)$ and has the shape of a smoothed ReLU function. This activation helps to make our variance positive. The value head, as usual, has no activation function applied.

```
    def forward(self, x):
        base_out = self.base(x)
        return self.mu(base_out), self.var(base_out),
    self.value(base_out)
```

The transformation is obvious: we apply the common layer first, then we calculate individual heads.

```
    class AgentA2C(ptan.agent.BaseAgent):
        def __init__(self, net, device="cpu"):
            self.net = net
            self.device = device

        def __call__(self, states, agent_states):
            states_v = ptan.agent.float32_preprocessor(states).to(device)
            mu_v, var_v, _ = self.net(states_v)
            mu = mu_v.data.cpu().numpy()
            sigma = torch.sqrt(var_v).data.cpu().numpy()
            actions = np.random.normal(mu, sigma)
            actions = np.clip(actions, -1, 1)
            return actions, agent_states
```

The next step will be to implement the ptan agent class, which is used to convert the observation into actions. In the discrete case, we've used the ptan.agent.DQNAgent and ptan.agent.PolicyAgent classes, but for our problem, we need to write our own, which is not complicated: you just need to write a class, derived from ptan.agent.BaseAgent and override the __call__ method, which needs to convert observations into actions.

In the preceding class, we get the mean and the variance from the network and sample the normal distribution using NumPy functions. To prevent the actions from going outside of the environment's -1..1 bounds, we use `np.clip`, which replaces all values less than -1 with -1 and values more than 1 with 1. The `agent_states` argument is not used, but needs to be returned with the chosen actions, as our `BaseAgent` supports keeping the state of the agent (it will become handy in the next section, when we'll need to implement a random exploration using the **Ornstein-Uhlenbeck (OU)** process).

With the model and the agent at hand, we can now go to the training process, defined in `Chapter14/02_train_a2c.py`. It consists of the training loop and two functions. The first is used to perform periodical tests of our model on the separate testing environment. As during the testing, we don't need to do any exploration, we'll just use the mean value returned by the model directly, without any random sampling. The testing function is as follows:

```
def test_net(net, env, count=10, device="cpu"):
    rewards = 0.0
    steps = 0
    for _ in range(count):
        obs = env.reset()
        while True:
            obs_v = ptan.agent.float32_preprocessor([obs]).to(device)
            mu_v = net(obs_v)[0]
            action = mu_v.squeeze(dim=0).data.cpu().numpy()
            obs, reward, done, _ = env.step(action)
            rewards += reward
            steps += 1
            if done:
                break
    return rewards / count, steps / count
```

The second function defined in the training module implements the calculation of the logarithm of the taken actions given the policy. The formula for this was given above and the function is a straightforward implementation of it. The only tiny difference is in using the `torch.clamp()` function to prevent the division on zero when the returned variance is too small.

```
def calc_logprob(mu_v, var_v, actions_v):
    p1 = - ((mu_v - actions_v) ** 2) / (2*var_v.clamp(min=1e-3))
    p2 = - torch.log(torch.sqrt(2 * math.pi * var_v))
    return p1 + p2
```

The training loop, as usual, creates the network and the agent, then instantiates the two-step experience source and optimizer. The hyperparameters used are given as follows and weren't tweaked much, so there is plenty of room for optimization.

```
ENV_ID = "MinitaurBulletEnv-v0"
GAMMA = 0.99
REWARD_STEPS = 2
BATCH_SIZE = 32
LEARNING_RATE = 5e-5
ENTROPY_BETA = 1e-4


TEST_ITERS = 1000
```

The code used to perform the optimization step on the collected batch is very similar to the A2C training that we implemented in *Chapter 10, The Actor-Critic Method*, and *Chapter 11, Asynchronous Advantage Actor - Critic*. The difference is only in using our `calc_logprob` function and a different expression for the entropy bonus.

```
            states_v, actions_v, vals_ref_v = \
                common.unpack_batch_a2c(batch, net,
        last_val_gamma=GAMMA ** REWARD_STEPS, device=device)
            batch.clear()

            optimizer.zero_grad()
            mu_v, var_v, value_v = net(states_v)

            loss_value_v = F.mse_loss(value_v, vals_ref_v)

            adv_v = vals_ref_v.unsqueeze(dim=-1) -
        value_v.detach()
            log_prob_v = adv_v * calc_logprob(mu_v,
        var_v, actions_v)
            loss_policy_v = -log_prob_v.mean()
            entropy_loss_v = ENTROPY_BETA * (-(torch.log(2*math.
        pi*var_v) + 1)/2).mean()

            loss_v = loss_policy_v + entropy_loss_v + loss_value_v
            loss_v.backward()
            optimizer.step()
```

Every `TEST_ITERS` frames, testing of the model is performed and in the case of the best reward obtained, the model weights are saved.

Results

In comparison to other methods that we'll take a look at in this chapter, A2C shows the worst results, both in terms of the best reward and convergence speed. That's likely because of the single environment used to gather experience, which is a weak point of the PG methods. So, you may want to check the effect of several (eight or more) parallel environments on A2C.

To start the training, you need to pass the -n argument with the run name, which will be used in TensorBoard and a new directory to save the models. The --cuda option enables GPU usage, but due to the small dimensionality of the input and tiny network size, it gives only a marginal increase in speed. The sample output from the training is shown as follows:

```
Chapter14$ ./02_train_a2c.py -n test
pybullet build time: Feb 2 2018 08:26:19
ModelA2C (
   (base): Sequential (
      (0): Linear (28 -> 128)
      (1): ReLU ()
   )
   (mu): Sequential (
      (0): Linear (128 -> 8)
      (1): Tanh ()
   )
   (var): Sequential (
      (0): Linear (128 -> 8)
      (1): Softplus (beta=1, threshold=20)
   )
   (value): Linear (128 -> 1)
)
Test done is 20.32 sec, reward -0.786, steps 443
122: done 1 episodes, mean reward -0.473, speed 5.69 f/s
1123: done 2 episodes, mean reward -2.560, speed 27.54 f/s
1209: done 3 episodes, mean reward -1.838, speed 176.22 f/s
1388: done 4 episodes, mean reward -1.549, speed 137.63 f/s
```

After 13M of frames (almost two days), the training process has reached the best score of 1.188, which is not very impressive. Some of the tracked parameters are shown in the following diagram:

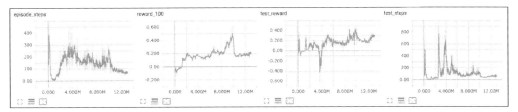

Figure 2: Training of the A2C agent on the Minitaur environment

The **episode_steps** chart shows the average count of steps performed in the episode before the end. The time limit of the environment is 1000 steps, so everything below that indicates that the episode was stopped due to environment checks (for most of the environments, these are checking for self-damage, which stops the simulation). The **test_reward** and **test_steps** charts show the mean reward and number of steps obtained during the testing.

Using models and recording videos

As we've seen before, the physical simulator can render the state of the environment, which makes it possible to see how our trained model behaves. To do that for our A2C models, there is a utility, Chapter14/03_play_a2c.py. Its logic is the same as in the test_net function, so its code is not shown here. To start it, you need to pass the -m option with the model file and -r with a directory name, which will be created to save the video. To render the image, PyBullet requires OpenGL, so to be able to record the video on a headless server, you need to use Xvfb: xvfb-run -s "-screen 0 640x480x24 +extension GLX" ./03_play_a2c.py -m model.dat -r dest-dir. There is a script that does this in Chapter14/adhoc/record_a2c.sh. For example, the best model that I got from A2C training produced this:

```
Chapter14$ ./adhoc/record_a2c.sh res/a2c-t1-long/a2c-t1/
best_+1.188_203000.dat a2c-res/
pybullet build time: Feb 2 2018 08:26:19
In 738 steps we got 1.261 reward
```

In the directory specified, there will be a recorded movie with the agent's activity.

Deterministic policy gradients

The next method that we'll take a look at is called deterministic policy gradients, which is a variation of the A2C method, but has a very nice property of being off-policy. The following is my very relaxed interpretation of the strict proofs. If you are interested in understanding the core of this method deeply, you may always refer to the article by David Silver and others called *Deterministic Policy Gradient Algorithms*, published in 2014 and the paper by Timothy P. Lillicrap and others called *Continuous Control with Deep Reinforcement Learning*, published in 2015.

The simplest way to illustrate the method is by comparison with the already familiar A2C. In this method, the actor estimates the stochastic policy, which returns the probability distribution over discrete actions or, as we've just seen in the previous section, the parameters of normal distribution. In both cases, our policy was *stochastic*, so, in other words, our action taken was sampled from this distribution. Deterministic policy gradients also belong to the A2C family, but the policy is *deterministic*, which means that it directly provides us with the action to take from the state. This makes it possible to apply the chain rule to the Q-value, and by maximizing the Q, the policy will be improved as well. To understand this, let's look at how the actor and critic are connected in a continuous action domain.

Let's start with an actor, as it is the simpler of the two. What we want from it is the action to take for every given state. In a continuous action domain, every action is a number, so the actor network will take the state as an input and return N values, one for every action. This mapping will be deterministic, as the same network always returns the same output if the input is the same (we're not going to use DropOut or something similar, just an ordinary feed-forward network).

Now let's look at the critic. The role of the critic is to estimate the Q-value, which is a discounted reward of the action taken in some state. However, our action is a vector of numbers, so our critic net now accepts two inputs: the state and the action. The output from the critic will be the single number, which corresponds to the Q-value. This architecture is different from the DQN, when our action space was discrete and, for efficiency, we returned values for all actions in one pass. This mapping is also deterministic.

So, what do we have? We have two functions, one is the actor, let's call it $\mu(s)$, which converts the state into the action and the other is the critic, by the state and the action giving us the Q-value: $Q(s, a)$. We can substitute the actor function into the critic and get the expression with only one input parameter of our state: $Q(s, \mu(s))$. In the end, **Neural Networks (NNs)** are just functions.

Now the output of the critic gives us the approximation of the entity we're interested in maximizing in the first place: the discounted total reward. This value depends not only on the input state, but also on parameters of the θ_μ actor and the θ_Q critic networks. At every step of our optimization, we want to change the actor's weights to improve the total reward that we want to get. In mathematical terms, we want the gradient of our policy.

In his deterministic policy gradient theorem, David Silver has proved that stochastic policy gradient is equivalent to the deterministic policy gradient. In other words, to improve the policy, we just need to calculate the gradient of the $Q(s, \mu(s))$ function. By applying the chain rule, we get the gradient: $\nabla_a Q(s, a) \nabla_{\theta_\mu} \mu(s)$.

Note that, despite both the A2C and **Deep Deterministic Policy Gradients (DDPG)** methods belonging to the A2C family, the way that critic is used is different. In A2C, we used the critic as a baseline for a reward from the experienced trajectories, so the critic is an optional piece (without it, we'll get the REINFORCE method) and is used to improve the stability. This happens as policy in A2C is **stochastic**, which builds a barrier in our backpropagation capabilities (we have no way to differentiate the random sampling step). In DDPG, the critic was used in a different way. As our policy is **deterministic**, we can now calculate the gradients from Q, obtained from the critic up to the actor's weights, so the whole system is differentiable and could be optimized end-to-end with **Stochastic Gradient Descent (SGD)**. To update the critic network, we can use the Bellman equation to find the approximation of $Q(s, a)$ and minimize the MSE objective.

All this may look a bit cryptic, but behind it stands quite a simple idea: the critic is updated as we did in A2C and the actor is updated in a way to maximize the critic's output. The beauty of this method is that it is off-policy, which means that we can now have a huge replay buffer and other tricks that we've used in DQN training. Nice, right?

Exploration

The price we have to pay for all this goodness is that our policy is now deterministic, so we have to explore the environment somehow. We can do this by adding noise to the actions returned by the actor before we pass them to the environment. There are several options here. The simplest method is just to add the random noise to the $\mu(s) + \epsilon \mathcal{N}$ actions. We'll use this way of exploration in the next method that we will consider in the chapter. A fancier approach to the exploration will be to use the above-mentioned stochastical model, which is very popular in the financial world and other domains dealing with stochastic processes: OU processes.

This process models the velocity of the massive Brownian particle under the influence of the friction and is defined by this stochastic differential equation: $\partial x_t = \theta(\mu - x_t)\partial t + \sigma \partial W$, where θ, μ, σ are parameters of the process and W_t is the Wiener process. In a discrete-time case, the OU process could be written as $x_{t+1} = x_t + \theta(\mu - x_t) + \sigma N$. This equation expresses the next value generated by the process via the previous value of the noise, adding normal noise N. In our exploration, we'll add the value of the OU process to the action returned by the actor.

Implementation

This example consists of three source files: Chapter14/lib/model.py contains the model and the ptan agent, while Chapter14/lib/common.py has a function used to unpack the batch, and Chapter14/04_train_ddpg.py has a start up code and the training loop. Here we'll show only the significant pieces of the code.

The model consists of two separate networks for the actor and critic and follows the architecture from the paper, *Continuous Control with Deep Reinforcement Learning*. The actor is extremely simple and is feed-forward with two hidden layers. The input is an observation vector, while the output is a vector with N values, one for each action. The output actions are transformed with hyperbolic tangent non-linearity to squeeze the values to the -1..1 range.

The critic is a bit unusual, as it includes two separate paths for observation and the actions, and those paths are concatenated together to be transformed into the critic output of one number. The following is a diagram with the structures of both networks:

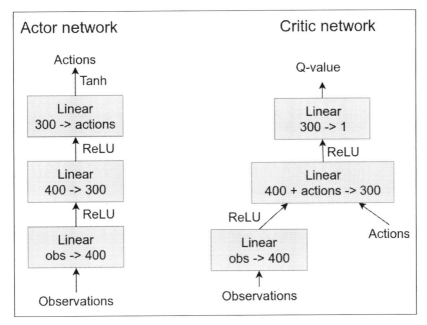

Figure 3: DDPG actor and critic networks

The code for both classes is simple and straightforward:

```
class DDPGActor(nn.Module):
    def __init__(self, obs_size, act_size):
        super(DDPGActor, self).__init__()

        self.net = nn.Sequential(
            nn.Linear(obs_size, 400), nn.ReLU(),
            nn.Linear(400, 300), nn.ReLU(),
            nn.Linear(300, act_size), nn.Tanh()
        )

    def forward(self, x):
        return self.net(x)


class DDPGCritic(nn.Module):
    def __init__(self, obs_size, act_size):
        super(DDPGCritic, self).__init__()
```

```
        self.obs_net = nn.Sequential(
            nn.Linear(obs_size, 400),
            nn.ReLU(),
        )

        self.out_net = nn.Sequential(
            nn.Linear(400 + act_size, 300), nn.ReLU(),
            nn.Linear(300, 1)
        )

    def forward(self, x, a):
        obs = self.obs_net(x)
        return self.out_net(torch.cat([obs, a], dim=1))
```

The `forward()` function of the critic first transforms the observations with its small network, then concatenates the output and given actions to transform them into one single value of Q. To use the actor network with the ptan experience source, we need to define the agent class that has to transform the observations into the actions. This class is the most convenient place to put our OU exploration process, but to do this properly, we should use the functionality of ptan agents that we haven't used so far: optional statefulness. The idea is simple: our agent transforms the observations into the actions, but what if it needs to remember something between the observations? All our examples have been stateless so far, but sometimes this is not enough. The issue with OU is that we have to track the OU values between the observations. Another very useful use case for stateful agents is **Partially-Observable Markov Decision Process (POMDP)**, which we briefly mentioned in *Chapter 13, Web Navigation*. The POMDP is an MDP when the state observed by the agent doesn't comply to the Markov property and doesn't include the full information to distinguish one state from the another. In that case, our agent needs to track the state along the trajectory to be able to take the action.

So, the code for the agent that implements the OU for exploration is as follows:

```
class AgentDDPG(ptan.agent.BaseAgent):
    def __init__(self, net, device="cpu", ou_enabled=True, ou_mu=0.0,
ou_teta=0.15, ou_sigma=0.2, ou_epsilon=1.0):
        self.net = net
        self.device = device
        self.ou_enabled = ou_enabled
        self.ou_mu = ou_mu
        self.ou_teta = ou_teta
        self.ou_sigma = ou_sigma
        self.ou_epsilon = ou_epsilon
```

The constructor accepts lots of parameters, most of which are the default values of OU taken from the paper of Timothy P. Lillycrap and others, 2015.

```
def initial_state(self):
    return None
```

This method is derived from the `BaseAgent` class and has to return the initial state of the agent when a new episode is started. As our initial state has to have the same dimension as actions (we want to have individual exploration trajectories for every action of the environment), we postpone the initialization of the state until the `__call__` method, as follows:

```
def __call__(self, states, agent_states):
    states_v = ptan.agent.float32_preprocessor(states).
to(self.device)
    mu_v = self.net(states_v)
    actions = mu_v.data.cpu().numpy()
```

This method is the core of the agent and the purpose of it is to convert the observed state and internal agent state into the action. As the first step, we convert the observations into the appropriate form and ask the actor network to convert them into deterministic actions. The rest of the method is for adding the exploration noise by applying the OU process.

```
if self.ou_enabled and self.ou_epsilon > 0:
    new_a_states = []
    for a_state, action in zip(agent_states, actions):
        if a_state is None:
            a_state = np.zeros(shape=action.shape,
dtype=np.float32)
        a_state += self.ou_teta * (self.ou_mu - a_state)
        a_state += self.ou_sigma *
np.random.normal(size=action.shape)
```

In this loop, we iterate over the batch of observations and the list of the agent states from the previous call and update the OU process value, which is a straightforward implementation of the preceding formula.

```
        action += self.ou_epsilon * a_state
        new_a_states.append(a_state)
```

To finalize the loop, we add the noise from the OU process to our actions and save the noise value for the next step.

```
    else:
        new_a_states = agent_states

    actions = np.clip(actions, -1, 1)
    return actions, new_a_states
```

Finally, we clip the actions to enforce them to fall into the -1..1 range, otherwise PyBullet will throw an exception. The final piece of the DDPG implementation is the training loop in the `Chapter14/04_train_ddpg.py` file. To improve the stability, we use the replay buffer with 100k transitions and target networks for both the actor and the critic. We discussed both in *Chapter 6, Deep Q-Networks*.

```
    act_net = model.DDPGActor(env.observation_space.shape[0],
env.action_space.shape[0]).to(device)
    crt_net = model.DDPGCritic(env.observation_space.shape[0],
env.action_space.shape[0]).to(device)
    tgt_act_net = ptan.agent.TargetNet(act_net)
    tgt_crt_net = ptan.agent.TargetNet(crt_net)
    agent = model.AgentDDPG(act_net, device=device)
    exp_source = ptan.experience.ExperienceSourceFirstLast
(env, agent, gamma=GAMMA, steps_count=1)
    buffer = ptan.experience.ExperienceReplayBuffer
(exp_source, buffer_size=REPLAY_SIZE)
    act_opt = optim.Adam(act_net.parameters(), lr=LEARNING_RATE)
    crt_opt = optim.Adam(crt_net.parameters(), lr=LEARNING_RATE)
```

We also use two different optimizers to simplify the way that we handle gradients for the actor and the critic training steps. The most interesting code is inside the training loop. On every iteration, we store the experience into the replay buffer and sample the training batch.

```
            batch = buffer.sample(BATCH_SIZE)
            states_v, actions_v, rewards_v, dones_mask,
last_states_v = \
                common.unpack_batch_ddpg(batch, device=device)
```

Then two separate training steps are performed. To train the critic, we need to calculate the target Q-value using the one-step Bellman equation, with the target critic network as the approximation of the next state.

```
            # train critic
            crt_opt.zero_grad()
            q_v = crt_net(states_v, actions_v)
            last_act_v = tgt_act_net.target_model(last_states_v)
            q_last_v = tgt_crt_net.target_model(last_states_v,
last_act_v)
            q_last_v[dones_mask] = 0.0
            q_ref_v = rewards_v.unsqueeze(dim=-1)
+ q_last_v * GAMMA
```

When we've got the reference, we can calculate the MSE loss and ask the critic's optimizer to tweak the critic weights. The whole process is similar to the training we've done for DQN, so nothing is really new here.

```
                critic_loss_v = F.mse_loss(q_v, q_ref_v.detach())
                critic_loss_v.backward()
```

```
                    crt_opt.step()
                    tb_tracker.track("loss_critic", critic_loss_v,
    frame_idx)
                    tb_tracker.track("critic_ref", q_ref_v.mean(),
    frame_idx)
```

On the actor training step, we need to update the actor's weights in a direction that will increase the critic's output. As both the actor and critic are represented as differentiable functions, what we need to do is just pass the actor's output to the critic and then minimize the negated value returned by the critic.

```
                    # train actor
                    act_opt.zero_grad()
                    cur_actions_v = act_net(states_v)
                    actor_loss_v = -crt_net(states_v, cur_actions_v)
                    actor_loss_v = actor_loss_v.mean()
```

This negated output of the critic could be used as a loss to backpropagate it to the critic network and, finally, the actor. We don't want to touch the critic's weights, so it's important to ask only the actor's optimizer to do the optimization step. The weights of the critic will still keep the gradients from this call, but they will be discarded on the next optimization step.

```
                    actor_loss_v.backward()
                    act_opt.step()
                    tb_tracker.track("loss_actor", actor_loss_v,
    frame_idx)
```

As the last step of the training loop, we perform the target nets update in an unusual way. Previously, we synced the weights from the optimized network into the target every n-steps. In continuous action problems, such syncing works worse than so-called *soft sync*. The soft sync is carried out on every step, but only a small ratio of the optimized network's weights are added to the target network. This makes a smooth and slow transition from old weight to the new ones.

```
                    tgt_act_net.alpha_sync(alpha=1 - 1e-3)
                    tgt_crt_net.alpha_sync(alpha=1 - 1e-3)
```

Results

The code could be started the same way as the A2C example: you need to pass the run name and optional --cuda flag. My experiments have shown ~30% speed increase from GPU, so, if you're in a hurry, using CUDA may be a good idea, but the increase is not that dramatic, as we've seen in case of Atari games.

After 5M observations, which took about a day, the DDPG algorithm was able to reach the mean reward of 3.943 on 10 test episodes, which is an improvement over the A2C result. The training dynamics are shown as follows.

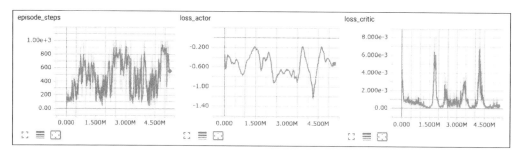

Figure 4: DDPG training dynamics

The `episode_steps` value shows the mean length of the episodes that we used for training. The critic loss is an MSE loss and it should be low, but the actor loss, as you will remember, is the negated critic's output, so the smaller it is, the better reward that the actor can (potentially) achieve. From the preceding charts, the training is not very stable and noisy.

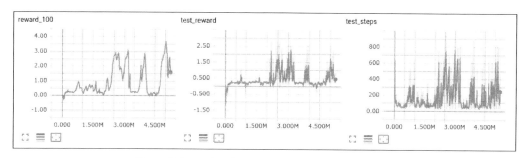

Figure 5: Reward and tests during the training of DDPG

The last three charts from the same run include the mean reward from the training episodes and the testing runs values. These charts are also quite noisy.

Recording videos

To check the trained agent in action, we can record video the same way as we recorded it for the A2C agent. For DDPG, there is a separate tool, Chapter14/05_play_ddpg.py, which is almost the same as for the A2C method, but just uses different classes for the actor. The result from my model is as follows:

```
rl_book_samples/Chapter14$ adhoc/record_ddpg.sh saves/ddpg-t5-simpler-
critic/best_+3.933_2484000.dat res/play-ddpg
pybullet build time: Feb 2 2018 08:26:19
In 1000 steps we got 5.346 reward
```

Distributional policy gradients

As the last method of this chapter, we'll take a look at the very recent paper by Gabriel Barth-Maron, Matthew W. Hoffman, and others, called *Distributional Policy Gradients*, published in 2018. At the time of writing, this paper hasn't been uploaded to ArXiV yet, as it was only submitted for a review for the conference ICLR 2018. It is available at `https://openreview.net/forum?id=SyZipzbCb`.

The full name of the method is Distributed Distributional Deep Deterministic Policy Gradients or D4PG for short. The authors proposed several improvements to the DDPG method we've just seen to improve stability, convergence, and sample efficiency.

First of all, they adapted the distributional representation of the Q-value proposed in the paper by Mark G.Bellemare, called *A Distributional Perspective on Reinforcement Learning*, published in 2017. We discussed this approach in *Chapter 7, DQN Extensions*, when we talked about DQN improvements, so refer to it or to the original paper for details. The core idea is to replace a single Q-value from the critic with a probability distribution. The Bellman equation is replaced with the Bellman operator, which transforms this distributional representation in a similar way.

The second improvement was the usage of the n-step Bellman equation, unrolling to speed up the convergence. We also discussed this in detail in *Chapter 7, DQN Extensions*. Another improvement versus the original DDPG method was the usage of the prioritized replay buffer instead of the uniformly-sampled buffer. So, strictly speaking, the authors took relevant improvements from the paper by Matteo Hassel and others, called *Rainbow: Combining Improvements in Deep Reinforcement Learning*, published in 2017, and adapted it to the DDPG method. The result was impressive: this combination showed the state-of-the-art results on the set of continuous control problems. Let's try to reimplement the method and check it ourselves.

Architecture

The most notable change is the critic's output. Instead of returning the single Q-value for the given state and the action, it now returns N_ATOMS values, corresponding to the probabilities of values from the pre-defined range. In my code, I've used N_ATOMS=51 and the distribution range of *Vmin=-10* and *Vmax=10*, so the critic returned 51 numbers, representing the probabilities of the discounted reward to fall into bins with bounds in [-10, -9.6, -9.2, …, 9.6, 10].

Another difference between D4PG and DDPG is the exploration. DDPG used the OU process for the exploration, but according to D4PG authors, they tried both OU and adding simple random noise to the actions, and the result was the same. So, they used a simpler approach for the exploration in the paper.

The last significant difference in the code will be related to the training, as D4PG uses cross-entropy loss to calculate the difference between two probability distributions: returned by the critic and obtained as a result of the Bellman operator. To make both distributions aligned to the same supporting atoms, distribution projection is used in the same way as in the original paper by Bellemare, and others, 2017.

Implementation

The complete source is in `Chapter14/06_train_d4pg.py`, `Chapter14/lib/model.py` and `Chapter14/lib/common.py`. As before, we start with the model class. The actor class has exactly the same architecture, so during the training class, DDPGActor was used. The critic has the same size and count of the hidden layers, but the output is not a single number, but N_ATOMS.

```python
class D4PGCritic(nn.Module):
    def __init__(self, obs_size, act_size, n_atoms, v_min, v_max):
        super(D4PGCritic, self).__init__()

        self.obs_net = nn.Sequential(
            nn.Linear(obs_size, 400),
            nn.ReLU(),
        )

        self.out_net = nn.Sequential(
            nn.Linear(400 + act_size, 300),
            nn.ReLU(),
            nn.Linear(300, n_atoms)
        )

        delta = (v_max - v_min) / (n_atoms - 1)
        self.register_buffer("supports", torch.arange
(v_min, v_max+delta, delta))
```

We also create a helper PyTorch buffer with reward supports, which will be used to get from the probability distribution to the single mean Q-value.

```python
    def forward(self, x, a):
        obs = self.obs_net(x)
        return self.out_net(torch.cat([obs, a], dim=1))

    def distr_to_q(self, distr):
        weights = F.softmax(distr, dim=1) * self.supports
        res = weights.sum(dim=1)
        return res.unsqueeze(dim=-1)
```

As you can see, softmax is not the part of the network, as we're going to use the more stable `log_softmax()` function during the training. Due to this, `softmax()` needs to be applied when we want to get actual probabilities. The agent class is much simpler for D4PG and has no state to track.

```
class AgentD4PG(ptan.agent.BaseAgent):
    def __init__(self, net, device="cpu", epsilon=0.3):
        self.net = net
        self.device = device
        self.epsilon = epsilon

    def __call__(self, states, agent_states):
        states_v = ptan.agent.float32_preprocessor(states).to(device)
        mu_v = self.net(states_v)
        actions = mu_v.data.cpu().numpy()
        actions += self.epsilon * np.random.normal(size=actions.shape)
        actions = np.clip(actions, -1, 1)
        return actions, agent_states
```

For every state to be converted to actions, the agent applies the actor network and adds the Gaussian noise to the actions, scaled by the epsilon value. In the training code, we have the hyperparameters shown as follows. I've used a smaller replay buffer of 100k and it worked fine (in the D4PG article the authors used 1M transitions in the buffer). The buffer was pre-populated with 10k samples from the environment, then the training started.

```
ENV_ID = "MinitaurBulletEnv-v0"
GAMMA = 0.99
BATCH_SIZE = 64
LEARNING_RATE = 1e-4
REPLAY_SIZE = 100000
REPLAY_INITIAL = 10000
REWARD_STEPS = 5

TEST_ITERS = 1000

Vmax = 10
Vmin = -10
N_ATOMS = 51
DELTA_Z = (Vmax - Vmin) / (N_ATOMS - 1)
```

For every training loop, we perform the same two steps as before: we train the critic and the actor. The difference is in the way that the loss for the critic is calculated.

```
                batch = buffer.sample(BATCH_SIZE)
                states_v, actions_v, rewards_v, dones_mask,
    last_states_v = \
                    common.unpack_batch_ddpg(batch, device=device)

                # train critic
                crt_opt.zero_grad()
                crt_distr_v = crt_net(states_v, actions_v)
                last_act_v = tgt_act_net.target_model(last_states_v)
                last_distr_v = F.softmax(tgt_crt_net.target_
    model(last_states_v, last_act_v), dim=1)
```

As the first step in the critic training, we ask it to return the probability distribution for states and actions taken. This probability distribution will be used as an input in the cross-entropy loss calculation. To get the target probability distribution, we need to calculate the distribution from the last states in the batch and then perform the Bellman projection of the distribution.

```
                proj_distr_v = distr_projection(last_distr_v,
    rewards_v, dones_mask, gamma=GAMMA**REWARD_STEPS, device=device)
```

This projection function is a bit complicated and will be explained after the training loop code. For now, it calculates the transformation of the last_states probability distribution, which is shifted according to the immediate reward and scaled to respect the discount factor. The result is the target probability distribution that we want our network to return. As there are no general cross-entropy loss functions in PyTorch, we calculate it manually, by multiplying the logarithm of input probability by the target probabilities.

```
                prob_dist_v = -F.log_softmax(crt_distr_v, dim=1) *
    proj_distr_v
                critic_loss_v = prob_dist_v.sum(dim=1).mean()
                critic_loss_v.backward()
                crt_opt.step()
```

The actor training is much simpler and the only difference from the DDPG method is the usage of the distr_to_q() function to convert from probability distribution to the single mean Q-value using support atoms.

```
                # train actor
                act_opt.zero_grad()
                cur_actions_v = act_net(states_v)
                crt_distr_v = crt_net(states_v, cur_actions_v)
                actor_loss_v = -crt_net.distr_to_q(crt_distr_v)
                actor_loss_v = actor_loss_v.mean()
```

```
            actor_loss_v.backward()
            act_opt.step()
            tb_tracker.track("loss_actor", actor_loss_v,
frame_idx)
```

Now comes the most complicated piece of code in D4PG implementation: the projection of the probability using the Bellman operator. It was already explained in *Chapter 7, DQN Extensions*, but the function is tricky, so let's do it again. The overall goal of the function is to calculate the result of the Bellman operator and project the resulting probability distribution to the same support atoms as the original distribution. The Bellman operator has a form of $Z(x,a) \overset{D}{=} R(x,a) + \gamma Z(x',a')$ and it is supposed to transform the probability distribution.

```
def distr_projection(next_distr_v, rewards_v, dones_mask_t,
gamma, device="cpu"):
    next_distr = next_distr_v.data.cpu().numpy()
    rewards = rewards_v.data.cpu().numpy()
    dones_mask = dones_mask_t.cpu().numpy().astype(np.bool)
    batch_size = len(rewards)
    proj_distr = np.zeros((batch_size, N_ATOMS), dtype=np.float32)
```

In the beginning, we convert the provided tensors to NumPy arrays and create an empty array for the resulting projected distribution.

```
    for atom in range(N_ATOMS):
        tz_j = np.minimum(Vmax, np.maximum(Vmin, rewards +
(Vmin + atom * DELTA_Z) * gamma))
```

In the loop, we iterate over our atoms and as the first step, calculate the place that this atom will be projected to by the Bellman operator, taking into account the value range $V_{min}...V_{max}$.

```
        b_j = (tz_j - Vmin) / DELTA_Z
```

The preceding line calculates the index of the atom that this projected value belongs to. Of course, the value may fall between the atoms, so in that case, we project the value proportionally to both atoms.

```
        l = np.floor(b_j).astype(np.int64)
        u = np.ceil(b_j).astype(np.int64)
        eq_mask = u == l
        proj_distr[eq_mask, l[eq_mask]] += next_distr[eq_mask, atom]
```

The preceding code handles the rare case when the project value lands exactly on the atom. In that case, we just add the value to the atom. Of course, we work with a batch, so some of the samples might comply to this case, but some might not. That's why we need to calculate the mask and filter with it.

```
        ne_mask = u != 1
        proj_distr[ne_mask, l[ne_mask]] += next_distr[ne_mask, atom] *
(u - b_j)[ne_mask]
        proj_distr[ne_mask, u[ne_mask]] += next_distr[ne_mask, atom] *
(b_j - l)[ne_mask]
```

As the final step of the loop, we need to process the case when the projected value is somewhere between two atoms. In that case, we calculate the proportion and distribute the projected value among two atoms.

```
if dones_mask.any():
    proj_distr[dones_mask] = 0.0
    tz_j = np.minimum(Vmax, np.maximum(Vmin, rewards[dones_mask]))
    b_j = (tz_j - Vmin) / DELTA_Z
```

In this branch, we handle the situation when the episode is over and our projected distribution will contain only one stripe corresponding to the atom of the reward that we've obtained. Here we do the same actions as before, but our source distribution is just reward.

```
    l = np.floor(b_j).astype(np.int64)
    u = np.ceil(b_j).astype(np.int64)
    eq_mask = u == l
    eq_dones = dones_mask.copy()
    eq_dones[dones_mask] = eq_mask
    if eq_dones.any():
        proj_distr[eq_dones, l] = 1.0
    ne_mask = u != l
    ne_dones = dones_mask.copy()
    ne_dones[dones_mask] = ne_mask
    if ne_dones.any():
        proj_distr[ne_dones, l] = (u - b_j)[ne_mask]
        proj_distr[ne_dones, u] = (b_j - l)[ne_mask]
```

At the end of the function, we pack the distribution into the PyTorch tensor and return it.

```
    return torch.FloatTensor(proj_distr).to(device)
```

Results

The method D4PG has shown the best result in both convergence speed and the reward obtained. In just five hours of training and less than 1M observations, it was able to reach the mean test reward of 12.799, which we can guess is close to the maximum in the environment. On the charts below are the dynamics for 2M observations.

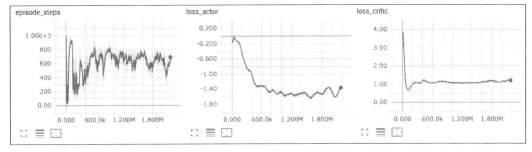

Figure 6: DDPG steps and losses during the training

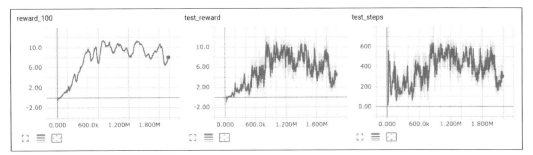

Figure 7: DDPG reward during the training and test

From the charts it can be seen that the agent found the best policy and stopped converging after 1M of frames. To record the video of the model activity, you can use the same `Chapter14/05_play_ddpg.py` utility, as the actor's architecture is exactly the same. The best video I've got from the trained model can be found here: `https://youtu.be/BMt40odLfyk`.

Things to try

Here is a list of things you can do to improve your understanding of the topic:

1. In the D4PG code, I used a simple replay buffer, which was enough to get good an improvement over DDPG. You can try to switch the example to the prioritized replay buffer in the same way as we did in *Chapter 7, DQN Extensions*, and check the effect.

2. There are lots of interesting and challenging environments around. For example, you can start with other PyBullet environments, but there is also **DeepMind Control Suite** (there was a paper about it published at the beginning of 2018, comparing the A3C, DDPG, and D4PG methods), MuJoCo-based environments in Gym and lots of others.

3. You can request the trial license of MuJoCo and compare its stability, performance and resulting policy with PyBullet.

4. Play with the very challenging *Learning how to run* competition from NIPS-2017, where you are given a simulator of the human body and your agent needs to figure out how to move it around.

Summary

In this chapter, we quickly skimmed through a very interesting domain of continuous control, using RL methods and checked three different algorithms on one problem of a four-legged robot. In our training, we used an emulator, but there are real models of this robot made by the Ghost Robotics company (you can check out the cool video on YouTube: `https://youtu.be/bnKOeMoibLg`).

We applied three training methods to this environment: A2C, DDPG, and D4PG (which has shown the best results). In the next chapter, we'll continue exploring the continuous action domain and will check a different set of improvements: trust region.

15
Trust Regions – TRPO, PPO, and ACKTR

In this chapter, we'll take a look at the approaches used to improve the stability of the stochastic policy gradient method. Some attempts have been made to make the policy improvement more stable and we'll focus on three methods: **Proximal Policy Optimization (PPO)**, **Trust Region Policy Optimization (TRPO)** and **Actor-Critic (A2C)** using **Kronecker-Factored Trust Region (ACKTR)**.

To compare them to the A2C baseline, we'll use several environments from the roboschool library created by OpenAI.

Introduction

The overall motivation of the methods that we'll take a look at is to improve the stability of the policy update during the training. Intuitively, there is a dilemma: on the one hand, we'd like to train as fast as we can, making large steps during the **Stochastic Gradient Descent (SGD)** update. On the other hand, a large update of the policy is usually a bad idea, as our policy is a very nonlinear thing, so a large update can ruin the policy we've just learned. Things can become even worse in the RL landscape, as making a bad update of the policy once won't be recovered by subsequent updates. Instead, the bad policy will bring us bad experience samples that we'll use on subsequent training steps, which could break our policy completely. Thus, we want to avoid making large updates by all means possible. One of the naive solutions would be to use a small learning rate to make baby steps during the SGD, but this would significantly slow down the convergence.

To break this vicious circle, several attempts have been made by researchers to estimate the effect that our policy update is going to have in terms of the future outcome. Of course, this is a very handwavy explanation, but it can help us to understand the idea, which could be helpful, as those methods are quite math-heavy (especially TRPO).

Roboschool

To experiment with the methods in this chapter, we'll use roboschool, which uses PyBullet as a physics engine and has 13 environments of various complexity. PyBullet has similar environments, but at the time of writing it wasn't possible to create several instances of the same environment due to internal OpenGL issue. In this chapter, we'll get in touch with two problems: RoboschoolHalfCheetah-v1, which models a two-legged creature and RoboschoolAnt-v1, which has four legs. The state and action spaces of them are very similar to the Minitaur environment that we saw in the previous chapter: the state includes characteristics from joints and actions are activations of those joints. The goal for both is to move as far as possible, minimizing the energy spent.

Figure 1: Screenshots of two roboschool environments: RoboschoolHalfCheetah and RoboschoolAnt

To install roboschool, you need to follow the instructions on `https://github.com/openai/roboschool`. This requires extra components to be installed in the system and a modified PyBullet to be built and used. After the installation of roboschool, you should be able to use `import roboschool` in your code to get access to the new environments.

Installation may not be very easy and smooth, and in my case exporting the `PKG_CONFIG_PATH` variable with the directory name `python-3.6.pc` was required. The full command was:

```
export PKG_CONFIG_PATH=/home/shmuma/anaconda3/envs/rl_book_samples-0.4.0/
lib/pkgconfig/
```

After this, the last step of roboschool installation went without issues.

A2C baseline

To establish the baseline results, we'll use the A2C method, in a very similar way to the code in the previous chapter. The complete source is in files `Chapter15/01_train_a2c.py` and `Chapter15/lib/model.py`. There are a few differences between this baseline and version we've used in the previous chapter. First of all, there are 16 parallel environments used to gather the experience during the training. The second difference is the model structure and the way that we perform exploration. To illustrate them, let's look at the model and the agent classes.

Both the actor and critic are placed in the separate networks without sharing weights. They follow the approach used in the previous chapter, when our critic estimates the mean and the variance for the actions, but now, variance is not a separate head of the base network, but just a single parameter of the model. This parameter will be adjusted during the training by SGD, but it doesn't depend on the observation.

```
HID_SIZE = 64


class ModelActor(nn.Module):
    def __init__(self, obs_size, act_size):
        super(ModelActor, self).__init__()

        self.mu = nn.Sequential(
            nn.Linear(obs_size, HID_SIZE),
            nn.Tanh(),
            nn.Linear(HID_SIZE, HID_SIZE),
            nn.Tanh(),
            nn.Linear(HID_SIZE, act_size),
            nn.Tanh(),
        )
        self.logstd = nn.Parameter(torch.zeros(act_size))

    def forward(self, x):
        return self.mu(x)
```

The actor network has two hidden layers of 64 neurons each with tanh nonlinearity. The variance is modeled as a separate network parameter and is interpreted as a logarithm of the standard deviation.

```python
class ModelCritic(nn.Module):
    def __init__(self, obs_size):
        super(ModelCritic, self).__init__()

        self.value = nn.Sequential(
            nn.Linear(obs_size, HID_SIZE),
            nn.ReLU(),
            nn.Linear(HID_SIZE, HID_SIZE),
            nn.ReLU(),
            nn.Linear(HID_SIZE, 1),
        )

    def forward(self, x):
        return self.value(x)
```

The critic network also has two hidden layers of the same size with one single output value, which is the estimation of *V(s)*, which is a discounted value of the state.

```python
class AgentA2C(ptan.agent.BaseAgent):
    def __init__(self, net, device="cpu"):
        self.net = net
        self.device = device

    def __call__(self, states, agent_states):
        states_v = ptan.agent.float32_preprocessor(states).to
(self.device)

        mu_v = self.net(states_v)
        mu = mu_v.data.cpu().numpy()
        logstd = self.net.logstd.data.cpu().numpy()
        actions = mu + np.exp(logstd) * np.random.normal
(size=logstd.shape)
        actions = np.clip(actions, -1, 1)
        return actions, agent_states
```

The agent which converts the state into the action also works by simply obtaining the predicted mean from the state and applying the noise with variance, dictated by the current value of the logstd parameter.

Results

By default, the RoboschoolHalfCheetah-v1 environment is used, but to change it you can pass the -e argument with the desired environment ID. Following is the chart with smoothed total reward obtained from the training environments (plot **reward_100**), averaged test score (from 10 tests) and episode length during the training on the HalfCheetah environment.

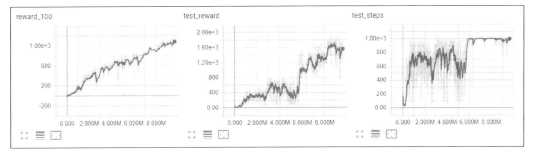

Figure 2: A2C convergence on HalfCheetah

This problem has a local minimum of policy, with ~700 score reward, when the model stands still, keeping the balance for 1000 steps. To obtain a larger reward, it needs to find out that running forward can give a larger reward, which took it almost 6M observations. The total training time is 15 hours.

RoboschoolAnt-v1 is slower, due to a longer simulation process, so it's likely that yet another day of training will be able to improve the policy. However, the charts are enough to get the idea of convergence stability and performance.

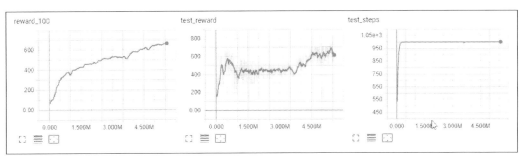

Figure 3: A2C convergence on Ant

Videos recording

As usual, there is a utility which can benchmark the trained model and record a video with the agent in action. It is in file `Chapter15/02_play.py` and can accept any model from the methods present in this chapter (as actor network is the same in all methods). You can also change the environment name using the `-e` command option.

Proximal Policy Optimization

Historically, this method came from the OpenAI team and was proposed long after TRPO (which is from 2015), but PPO is much simpler than TRPO, so we'll start from it. The paper in which it was proposed is by John Schulman et al and called *Proximal Policy Optimization Algorithms*, published in 2017 (arXiv:1707.06347).

The core improvement over the classical **Asynchronous Advantage Actor-Critic (A3C)** method is to change the expression used to estimate the PG. Instead of the gradient of logarithm probability of the action taken, the PPO method uses a different objective: the ratio between the new and the old policy scaled by the advantages.

In math form, the old A3C objective could be written as $J_\theta = \mathbb{E}_t[\nabla_\theta \log \pi_\theta(a_t|s_t) A_t]$. The new objective proposed by the PPO is $J_\theta = \mathbb{E}_t[\frac{\pi_\theta(a_t|s_t)}{\pi_{\theta_{old}}(a_t|s_t)} A_t]$. The reason behind changing the objective is the same as for the cross-entropy method from *Chapter 4, The Cross-Entropy Method*: importance sampling. However, if we just start to blindly maximize this value, it may lead to a very large update to the policy weights. To limit the update, the clipped objective is used. If we write the ratio between the new and the old policy as $r_t(\theta) = \frac{\pi_\theta(a_t|s_t)}{\pi_{\theta_{old}}(a_t|s_t)}$ the clipped objective could be written as $J_\theta^{clip} = \mathbb{E}_t[\min(r_t(\theta) A_t, clip(r_t(\theta), 1 - \epsilon, 1 + \epsilon) A_t)]$. This objective limits the ratio between the old and the new policy to be in the interval $[1 - \epsilon, 1 + \epsilon]$, so by varying ϵ we can limit the size of the update.

Another difference from the A3C method is the way that we estimate the advantage. In the A3C paper, the advantage obtained from the finite-horizon estimation of T steps is in the form: $A_t = -V(s_t) + r_t + \gamma r_{t+1} + \ldots + \gamma^{T-t+1} r_{T-1} + \gamma^{T-t} V(s_T)$. In the PPO paper, the authors used more general estimation in the form of, $A_t = \sigma_t + (\gamma\lambda)\sigma_{t+1} + (\gamma\lambda)^2 \sigma_{t+2} + \ldots + (\gamma\lambda)^{T-t+1} \sigma_{T-1}$ where $\sigma_t = r_t + \gamma V(s_{t+1}) - V(s_t)$. The original A3C estimation is a special case of the proposed method with $\lambda = 1$.

The PPO method also uses a slightly different training procedure, when a long sequence of samples is obtained from the environment and then advantage is estimated for the whole sequence, before several epochs of training are performed.

Implementation

The code of the sample is placed in two source code files: `Chapter15/04_train_ppo.py` and `Chapter15/lib/model.py`. The actor, the critic and the agent classes are exactly the same as we had in the A2C baseline. The differences are in the training procedure and the way that we calculate advantages, but let's start with hyperparameters.

```
ENV_ID = "RoboschoolHalfCheetah-v1"
GAMMA = 0.99
GAE_LAMBDA = 0.95
```

The value of `GAMMA` is already familiar, but `GAE_LAMBDA` is the new constant which specifies the lambda factor in the advantage estimator. The value of `0.95` was used in the PPO paper.

```
TRAJECTORY_SIZE = 2049
LEARNING_RATE_ACTOR = 1e-4
LEARNING_RATE_CRITIC = 1e-3
```

The method assumes that a large amount of transitions will be obtained from the environment for every subiteration (as mentioned in the previous section about PPO, during training it does several epochs over the sampled training batch). We also use two different optimizers for the actor and the critic (as they have no shared weights).

```
PPO_EPS = 0.2
PPO_EPOCHES = 10
PPO_BATCH_SIZE = 64
```

For every batch of `TRAJECTORY_SIZE` samples we perform `PPO_EPOCHES` iterations of PPO objective, with minibatches of 64 samples. The value `PPO_EPS` specifies the clipping value for the ratio of the new and the old policy.

```
TEST_ITERS = 1000
```

For every 1k observations obtained from the environment, we perform a test of 10 episodes to obtain the total reward and count of steps for the current policy. The function below takes the trajectory with steps and calculates advantages for the actor and reference values for the critic training. Our trajectory is not a single episode but can be several episodes concatenated together.

```
def calc_adv_ref(trajectory, net_crt, states_v, device="cpu"):
    values_v = net_crt(states_v)
    values = values_v.squeeze().data.cpu().numpy()
```

As the first step, we ask the critic to convert states into values.

```
last_gae = 0.0
result_adv = []
result_ref = []
for val, next_val, (exp,) in zip(reversed(values[:-1]),
    reversed(values[1:]), reversed(trajectory[:-1])):
```

This loop joins the values obtained and experience points. For every trajectory step, we need the current value (obtained from the current state) and the value for the next subsequent step (to perform the estimation using the Bellman equation). We also traverse the trajectory in the reverse order, to be able to calculate more recent values of the advantage in one step.

```
if exp.done:
    delta = exp.reward - val
    last_gae = delta
else:
    delta = exp.reward + GAMMA * next_val - val
    last_gae = delta + GAMMA * GAE_LAMBDA * last_gae
```

On every step, our action depends on the done flag for this step. If this is a terminal step of the episode, we have no prior reward to take into account (remember, we're processing trajectory in the reverse order). So, our value of delta on this step is just immediate reward minus the value predicted for the step. If the current step is not terminal, the delta will be equal to the immediate reward plus the discounted value from the subsequent step, minus the value for the current step. In the classic A3C method, this delta was used as an advantage estimation, but here, the smoothed version is used, so the advantage estimation (tracked in the `last_gae` variable) is calculated as the sum of deltas with discount factor $\gamma\lambda$.

```
result_adv.append(last_gae)
result_ref.append(last_gae + val)
```

The goal of the function is to calculate advantages and reference values for the critic, so we save them in lists.

```
adv_v = torch.FloatTensor(list(reversed(result_adv))).to(device)
ref_v = torch.FloatTensor(list(reversed(result_ref))).to(device)
return adv_v, ref_v
```

In the training loop, we gather the trajectory of the desired size using `ExperienceSource(steps_count=1)` class from the PTAN library. With such configuration, it provides us with individual steps from the environment in tuples `(state, action, reward, done)`.

```
trajectory.append(exp)
if len(trajectory) < TRAJECTORY_SIZE:
    continue

traj_states = [t[0].state for t in trajectory]
traj_actions = [t[0].action for t in trajectory]
traj_states_v = torch.FloatTensor(traj_states).to(device)
traj_actions_v = torch.FloatTensor(traj_actions).to(device)
traj_adv_v, traj_ref_v = calc_adv_ref(trajectory, net_crt, device=device)
```

When we've got trajectory large enough for training (which is given by the `TRAJECTORY_SIZE` hyperparameter above), we convert states and taken actions into tensors and use the already-described function to obtain advantages and reference values. Despite the fact that our trajectory is quite long, the observations of our test environments are quite short, so it's fine to process our batch in one step. In the case of Atari frames, such a batch could cause a GPU memory error.

In the next step, we calculate the logarithm of probability of the actions taken. This value will be used as $\pi_{\theta_{old}}$ in the objective of PPO. Additionally, we normalize the advantage's mean and variance to improve the training stability.

```
mu_v = net_act(traj_states_v)
old_logprob_v = calc_logprob(mu_v, net_act.logstd, traj_actions_v)
traj_adv_v = (traj_adv_v - torch.mean(traj_adv_v)) / torch.std(traj_adv_v)
```

Two subsequent lines drop the last entry from the trajectory, to reflect the fact that our advantages and reference values are one step shorter than the trajectory length (as we shifted values in the loop inside the `calc_adv_ref` function).

```
trajectory = trajectory[:-1]
old_logprob_v = old_logprob_v[:-1].detach()
```

When all the preparations have been done, we perform several epoches of training on our trajectory. For every batch, we extract the portions from the corresponding arrays and do the critic and the actor training separately.

```
for epoch in range(PPO_EPOCHES):
    for batch_ofs in range(0, len(trajectory), PPO_BATCH_
SIZE):
        states_v = traj_states_v[batch_ofs:batch_ofs +
PPO_BATCH_SIZE]
        actions_v = traj_actions_v[batch_ofs:batch_ofs +
PPO_BATCH_SIZE]
        batch_adv_v = traj_adv_v[batch_ofs:batch_ofs +
PPO_BATCH_SIZE].unsqueeze(-1)
        batch_ref_v = traj_ref_v[batch_ofs:batch_ofs +
PPO_BATCH_SIZE]
        batch_old_logprob_v = old_logprob_v[batch_
ofs:batch_ofs + PPO_BATCH_SIZE]
```

To train the critic, all we need to do is to calculate the **Mean Squared Error (MSE)** loss with the reference values calculated beforehand.

```
opt_crt.zero_grad()
value_v = net_crt(states_v)
loss_value_v = F.mse_loss(value_v.squeeze(-1),
batch_ref_v)

loss_value_v.backward()
opt_crt.step()
```

In the actor training, we minimize the negated clipped objective:

$\mathbb{E}_t[\min(r_t(\theta)A_t, clip(r_t(\theta), 1-\epsilon, 1+\epsilon)A_t)]$, where $r_t(\theta) = \frac{\pi_\theta(a_t|s_t)}{\pi_{\theta_{old}}(a_t|s_t)}$. The lines following is a straightforward implementation of this formula.

```
opt_act.zero_grad()
mu_v = net_act(states_v)
logprob_pi_v = calc_logprob(mu_v, net_act.logstd,
actions_v)
ratio_v = torch.exp(logprob_pi_v - batch_old_
logprob_v)
surr_obj_v = batch_adv_v * ratio_v
clipped_surr_v = batch_adv_v * torch.
clamp(ratio_v, 1.0 - PPO_EPS, 1.0 + PPO_EPS)
loss_policy_v = -torch.min(surr_obj_v, clipped_
surr_v).mean()

loss_policy_v.backward()
opt_act.step()
```

Results

Trained on both our test environments, the PPO method has shown a major improvement over the A2C method. The following charts shows the training progress on the RoboschoolHalfCheetah-v1 environment, when the methods were able to reach a 1k score after just two hours of training and 1.3M observations, which is much better than A2C with 10M observations and 15 hours to get the same result. The peak reward that the agent was able to obtain after 10 hours of training was more than 2600 and it looks like it can do better, as just some tweaks like **learning rate (LR)** decay are required.

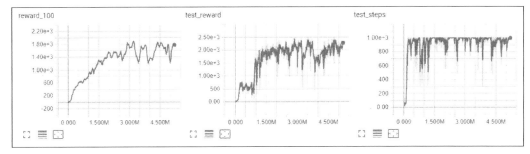

Figure 4: PPO convergence on HalfCheetah

On the RoboschoolAnt-v1, the reward increase was also almost linear and during the 20 hours the max test reward was 1848, which is also an improvement over the A2C method.

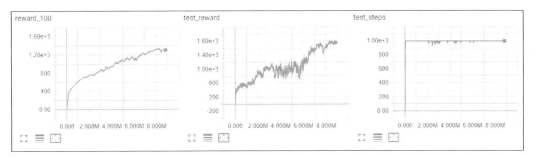

Figure 5: PPO on the Ant environment

Trust Region Policy Optimization

TRPO was proposed in 2015 by the Berkeley researchers in the paper by John Schulman et al called *Trust Region Policy Optimization* (arXiv:1502.05477). This paper was a step towards improving the stability and consistency of the stochastic policy gradient optimization and has shown good results on various control tasks.

Unfortunately, the paper and the method are quite math-heavy, so it can be hard to understand the details of the method. The same could be said about the implementation, which uses the conjugate gradients method to efficiently solve the constrained optimization problem.

As the first step, the TRPO method defines the discounted visitation frequencies of the state: $\rho_\pi(s) = P(s_0 = s) + \gamma P(s_1 = s) + \gamma^2 P(s_2 = s) + \dots$. In this equation, $P(s_i = s)$ equals to the sampled probability of state s to be met at position i of the sampled trajectories. Then, TRPO defines the optimization objective as $L_\pi(\tilde{\pi}) = \eta(\pi) + \sum_s \rho_\pi(s) \sum_a \tilde{\pi}(a|s) A_\pi(s, a)$ where $\eta(\pi) = \mathbb{E}[\sum_{t=0}^{\infty} \gamma^t r(s_t)]$ is the expected discount reward of the policy and $\tilde{\pi} = \arg\max_a A_\pi(s, a)$ defines the deterministic policy.

To address the issue with large policy updates, TRPO defines the additional constraint on the policy update, expressed as a maximum **Kullback-Leibler (KL)**-divergence between the old and the new policies, which could be written as $\bar{D}_{KL}^{\rho_{\theta_{old}}}(\theta_{old}, \theta) \leq \delta$.

Implementation

Most of the TRPO implementations available on GitHub, or other open-source repositories, are very similar to each other, probably because all of them grew from the original John Schulman TRPO implementation here `https://github.com/joschu/modular_rl`. My version of TRPO is also not very different and uses the core functions implementing the conjugate gradient method (used by TRPO to solve the constrained optimization problem) from this repository: `https://github.com/ikostrikov/pytorch-trpo`.

The complete example is in `Chapter15/03_train_trpo.py` and `Chapter15/lib/trpo.py` and the training loop is very similar to the PPO example: we sample the trajectory of transitions of the predefined length and calculate the advantage estimation using the smoothed formula given in the PPO section (historically, this estimator was proposed first in the TRPO paper). Next, we do one training step of the critic using MSE loss with the calculated reference value and one step of the TRPO update, which consists of finding the direction we should go by using the conjugate gradients method and doing a linear search along this direction to find a step which preserves the desired KL-divergence.

Following is the piece of the training loop which carries out both those steps:

```
# critic step
opt_crt.zero_grad()
value_v = net_crt(traj_states_v)
loss_value_v = F.mse_loss(value_v.squeeze(-1), traj_ref_v)
loss_value_v.backward()
opt_crt.step()
```

To perform the TRPO step, we need to provide two functions: the first will calculate the loss of the current actor policy, which uses the same ratio as in PPO of the new and the old policies multiplied by the advantage estimation. The second function has to calculate KL-divergence between the old and the current policy.

```
# actor step
def get_loss():
    mu_v = net_act(traj_states_v)
    logprob_v = calc_logprob(mu_v, net_act.logstd, traj_
actions_v)
    action_loss_v = -traj_adv_v.unsqueeze(dim=-1) * torch.
exp(logprob_v - old_logprob_v)
    return action_loss_v.mean()

def get_kl():
    mu_v = net_act(traj_states_v)
    logstd_v = net_act.logstd
    mu0_v = mu_v.detach()
    logstd0_v = logstd_v.detach()
    std_v = torch.exp(logstd_v)
    std0_v = std_v.detach()
    kl = logstd_v - logstd0_v + (std0_v ** 2 +
((mu0_v - mu_v) ** 2) / (2.0 * std_v ** 2)) - 0.5
    return kl.sum(1, keepdim=True)

trpo.trpo_step(net_act, get_loss, get_kl, TRPO_MAX_KL,
TRPO_DAMPING, device=device)
```

In other words, the PPO method is the TRPO which uses the simple clipping of the policy ratio to limit the policy update, instead of the complicated conjugate gradients and line search.

Results

From my experiments, TRPO has shown better results than the A2C baseline, but behaved worse than PPO. Very likely that is just due to untuned copy-pasted TRPO low-level machinery.

On the HalfCheetah test, TRPO was able to reach 1k reward after 5M observations and eight hours of training. In 13M observations it doubled the reward, which took it almost a day of working.

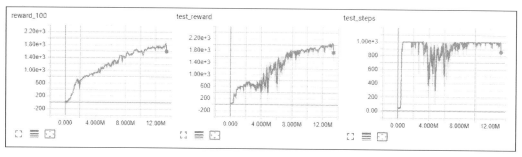

Figure 6: TRPO on the HalfCheetah environment

Training on the RoboschoolAnt-v1 was much less successful. After three hours and 1.5M steps, the agent got a reward of 700, but then the training process diverged.

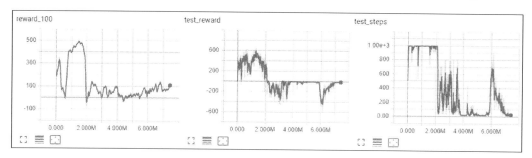

Figure 7: TRPO on the Ant environment

A2C using ACKTR

The third method that we'll compare uses a different approach to address SGD stability. In the paper by Yuhuai Wu and others called *Scalable Trust-Region Method for Deep Reinforcement Learning Using Kronecker-Factored Approximation* published in 2017 (arXiv:1708.05144), the authors combined the second-order optimization methods and trust region approach.

The idea of the second-order methods is to improve the traditional SGD by taking the second-order derivatives of the optimized function (in other words, its curvature) to improve the convergence of the optimization process. To make things more complicated, working with the second derivatives usually requires you to build and invert a Hessian matrix, which can be prohibitively large, so the practical methods typically approximate it in some way. This area is currently very active in research, as developing robust, scalable optimization methods is very important for the whole machine learning domain.

One of the second-order methods is called **Kronecker-factored** approximation (usually abbreviated as **KFAC**) which was proposed by James Martens and Roger Grosse in their paper *Optimizing Neural Networks with Kronecker-Factored Approximate Curvature*, published in 2015. However, a detailed description of this method is well beyond the scope of this book.

Implementation

As the KFAC method is quite recent, there is no optimizer for implementing this method included in PyTorch. The only available PyTorch prototype is from Ilya Kostrikov and available here: `https://github.com/ikostrikov/pytorch-a2c-ppo-acktr`. There is another version of KFAC for TensorFlow, which comes with OpenAI Baselines, but porting and testing it on PyTorch can be a hard thing to do.

For my experiments, I've taken the KFAC from the link above and adopted it to the existing code, which required replacing the optimizer and doing an extra `backward()` call to gather Fisher information. The critic was trained the same way as in A2C.

The complete example is in `Chapter15/05_train_acktr.py` and is not shown here, as it's basically the same as A2C. The only difference is that a different optimizer was used.

Results

On the RoboschoolAnt-v1 environment, the ACKTR method has shown better results than A2C, but worse than PPO. Of course, those results have to be taken with a grain of salt, as I haven't done much hyperparameters tuning here (which is left to the reader as an exercise) and the results can depend on the actual environment, so normally it's good practice to try different methods on your task at hand.

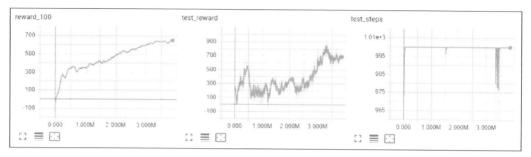

Figure 8: ACKTR on HalfCheetah

On the HalfCheetah environment, ACKTR behaved much less stably and was able to reach only a reward of 1k.

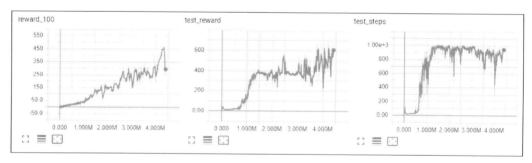

Figure 9: ACKTR on Ant

Summary

In this chapter, we've checked three different methods aiming to improve the stability of the stochastic policy gradient and compared them to A2C implementation on two continuous control problems. With methods from the previous chapter (DDPG and D4PG), they create basic tools to work with a continuous control domain.

In the next chapter, we'll switch to a different set of RL methods that have been becoming popular recently: black-box or gradient-free methods.

Black-Box Optimization in RL 16

In this chapter, we'll again change our perspective on Reinforcement Learning (RL) training and will switch to the so-called black-box optimizations, in particular the evolution strategies and genetic algorithms. These methods are at least a decade old, but recently several research studies were conducted, which showed the applicability of the methods to large-scale RL problems and their competitiveness with the value iteration and Policy Gradient (PG) methods.

Black-box methods

In the beginning, let's discuss the whole family of methods and how they differ from what we've seen so far. Black-box optimization methods are the general approach to the optimization problem, when you treat the objective that you're optimizing as a black box, without any assumption about the differentiability, value function, smoothness of the objective, and so on. The only requirement that those methods expose is the ability to calculate the **fitness function**, which should give us the measure of suitability of a particular instance of the optimized entity at hand.

One of the simplest examples of the method in this family is random search, which is when you randomly sample the thing you're looking for (in the case of RL it's the policy $\pi(a|s)$), then you check the fitness of this candidate, and if the result is good enough (according to some reward criteria), then you're done. Otherwise, you repeat the process again and again. Despite the simplicity and even naivety of this approach, especially in respect to the sophisticated methods that we've seen so far, this is a good example to illustrate the idea of the black-box methods. Furthermore, with some modifications, as we'll see shortly, this simple approach can be compared in terms of efficiency and the quality of the resulting policies to the Deep Q-Network (DQN) and PG methods.

Black-box methods have several very appealing properties:

1. They are at least two times faster than gradient-based methods, as we don't need to perform the backpropagation step to obtain the gradients.

2. There are very few assumptions about the optimized objective and the policy, which is treated as a black box. Traditional methods struggle with situations when your reward function is non-smooth or the policy contains steps with random choice. All of this is not an issue for black-box methods, as they don't expect much from the black-box internals.

3. The methods can generally be parallelized very well. For example, the above-mentioned random search can easily scale up to thousands of CPUs or GPUs working in parallel, without any dependency on each other. It's not the case for DQN or PG, when you need to accumulate gradients and propagate the current policy to all parallel workers, which decreases the parallelism.

The downside of the above is usually lower sample efficiency. In particular, the naive random search of the policy, parameterized with the Neural Network (NN) with half a million parameters, has very low probability to succeed. In this chapter, we'll discuss two approaches which were able to greatly improve the applicability of the black-box method in the domain of complex RL problems.

Evolution strategies

The subset of black-box optimization methods is called evolution strategies (ES) and has been inspired by the evolution process, where the most successful individuals have the highest influence on the overall direction of the search. There are many different methods that fall into this class and in this chapter, we'll consider the approach taken by OpenAI researchers Tim Salimans, Jonathan Ho, and others in their paper, *Evolution Strategies as a Scalable Alternative to Reinforcement Learning* [1], published in March 2017.

The underlying idea of ES methods is simple: on every iteration, we perform random perturbation of our current policy parameters and evaluate the resulting policy fitness function. Then we adjust the policy weights proportional to the relative fitness function value.

The concrete method used in the paper above is called **Covariance Matrix Adaptation Evolution Strategy (CMA-ES)** in which the perturbation performed is the random noise sampled from the zero-mean, identity variance normal distribution. Then we calculate the fitness function of the policy with weights equal to the weights of the original policy plus the scaled noise. Next, according to the obtained value, we adjust the original policy weights by adding the noise multiplied by the fitness function value, which moves our policy toward weights with a higher value of the fitness function. To improve the stability, the update of the weights is performed by averaging the batch of such steps with different random noise.

More formally, the method above could be expressed as this sequence of steps:

1. Initialize learning rate α, noise standard deviation σ, and initial policy parameters θ_0.

2. For t = 0, 1, 2, ... perform:

    1. The sample batch of noise with a shape of the weights $\epsilon_1, \ldots, \epsilon_n \sim \mathcal{N}(0, I)$.

    2. Compute returns $F_i = F(\theta_t + \sigma \epsilon_i)$ for $i = 1, \ldots, n$.

    3. $\theta_{t+1} \leftarrow \theta_t + \alpha \frac{1}{n\sigma} \sum_{i=1}^n F_i \epsilon_i$ to update weights.

The algorithm above is the core of the method presented in the paper, but, as usual, in the RL domain, the core method is not enough to obtain good results, so the paper includes several tweaks to improve the method, although the core is the same. Let's implement and test it on our *"fruit fly"* environment: CartPole.

ES on CartPole

The complete example is in `Chapter16/01_cartpole_es.py`. In this example, we use the single environment to check the fitness of the perturbed network weights. Our fitness function will be the undiscounted total reward for the episode:

```python
#!/usr/bin/env python3
import gym
import time
import numpy as np

import torch
import torch.nn as nn

from tensorboardX import SummaryWriter
```

From the `import` statements, you can notice how self-contained our example is. We're not using PyTorch optimizers, as we do not perform backpropagation at all. In fact, we could avoid using PyTorch completely and work only with NumPy, as the only thing we use PyTorch for is to perform a forward pass and calculate the network's output.

```
MAX_BATCH_EPISODES = 100
MAX_BATCH_STEPS = 10000
NOISE_STD = 0.01
LEARNING_RATE = 0.001
```

The amount of hyperparameters is also small and includes the following values:

- `MAX_BATCH_EPISODES` and `MAX_BATCH_STEPS`: The limit of episodes and steps we use for training

- `NOISE_STD`: The standard deviation σ of the noise used for weight perturbation

- `LEARNING_RATE`: The coefficient used to adjust the weights on the training step

```
class Net(nn.Module):
    def __init__(self, obs_size, action_size):
        super(Net, self).__init__()
        self.net = nn.Sequential(
            nn.Linear(obs_size, 32),
            nn.ReLU(),
            nn.Linear(32, action_size),
            nn.Softmax(dim=1)
        )

    def forward(self, x):
        return self.net(x)
```

The model we're using is a simple one-hidden layer NN, which gives us the action to take from the observation. We use PyTorch NN machinery here only for convenience, as we need only the forward pass, but it could be replaced by a bunch of matrices multiplications and nonlinearities.

```
def evaluate(env, net):
    obs = env.reset()
    reward = 0.0
    steps = 0
    while True:
        obs_v = torch.FloatTensor([obs])
        act_prob = net(obs_v)
```

```
        acts = act_prob.max(dim=1)[1]
        obs, r, done, _ = env.step(acts.data.numpy()[0])
        reward += r
        steps += 1
        if done:
            break
    return reward, steps
```

The function above plays a full episode using the given policy and returns the total reward and the number of steps. The reward will be used as a fitness value, while the count of steps is needed to limit the amount of time we spend on forming the batch. The action selection is performed deterministically by calculating argmax from the network output. In principle, we could do the random sampling from the distribution, but we've already performed the exploration by adding noise to the network parameters, so the deterministic action selection is fine here.

```
def sample_noise(net):
    pos = []
    neg = []
    for p in net.parameters():
        noise_t = torch.tensor(np.random.normal(size=p.data.size()).
astype(np.float32))
        pos.append(noise_t)
        neg.append(-noise_t)
    return pos, neg
```

In the `sample_noise` function, we create random noise with zero mean and unit variance equal to the shape of our network parameters. The function returns two sets of noise tensors: one with positive noise and another with the same random values taken with a negative sign. These two samples are later used in a batch as independent samples. This technique is known as *mirrored sampling* and is used to improve the stability of the convergence. In fact, without the negative noise, the convergence becomes very unstable.

```
def eval_with_noise(env, net, noise):
    old_params = net.state_dict()
    for p, p_n in zip(net.parameters(), noise):
        p.data += NOISE_STD * p_n
    r, s = evaluate(env, net)
    net.load_state_dict(old_params)
    return r, s
```

The preceding function takes the noise array created by the function we've just seen and evaluates the network with noise added. To achieve this, we add the noise to the network's parameters and call the evaluate function to obtain the reward and number of steps taken. After this, we need to restore the network weights to their original state, which is completed by loading the state dictionary of the network.

The last and the central function of the method is `train_step`, which takes the batch with noise and respective rewards and calculates the update to the network parameters by applying the formula, $\theta_{t+1} \leftarrow \theta_t + \alpha \frac{1}{n\sigma} \sum_{i=1}^{n} F_i \epsilon_i$.

```
def train_step(net, batch_noise, batch_reward, writer, step_idx):
    norm_reward = np.array(batch_reward)
    norm_reward -= np.mean(norm_reward)
    s = np.std(norm_reward)
    if abs(s) > 1e-6:
        norm_reward /= s
```

In the beginning, we normalize rewards to have zero mean and unit variance, which improves the stability of the method.

```
    weighted_noise = None
    for noise, reward in zip(batch_noise, norm_reward):
        if weighted_noise is None:
            weighted_noise = [reward * p_n for p_n in noise]
        else:
            for w_n, p_n in zip(weighted_noise, noise):
                w_n += reward * p_n
```

Then we iterate every pair (noise, reward) in our batch and multiply the noise values with the normalized reward, summing together the respective noise for every parameter in our policy.

```
    m_updates = []
    for p, p_update in zip(net.parameters(), weighted_noise):
        update = p_update / (len(batch_reward) * NOISE_STD)
        p.data += LEARNING_RATE * update
        m_updates.append(torch.norm(update))
    writer.add_scalar("update_l2", np.mean(m_updates), step_idx)
```

As a final step, we use the accumulated scaled noise to adjust the network parameters. Technically, what we do here is a gradient ascent, but the gradient was not obtained from the backpropagation, but from the Monte-Carlo sampling method. This fact was also demonstrated in the above-mentioned paper [1], where the authors showed that CMA-ES is very similar to the PG method, differing in just the way that we get the gradients' estimation.

```
if __name__ == "__main__":
    writer = SummaryWriter(comment="-cartpole-es")
    env = gym.make("CartPole-v0")

    net = Net(env.observation_space.shape[0], env.action_space.n)
    print(net)
```

The preparation before the training loop is simple: we create the environment and the network.

```
step_idx = 0
while True:
    t_start = time.time()
    batch_noise = []
    batch_reward = []
    batch_steps = 0
    for _ in range(MAX_BATCH_EPISODES):
        noise, neg_noise = sample_noise(net)
        batch_noise.append(noise)
        batch_noise.append(neg_noise)
        reward, steps = eval_with_noise(env, net, noise)
        batch_reward.append(reward)
        batch_steps += steps
        reward, steps = eval_with_noise(env, net, neg_noise)
        batch_reward.append(reward)
        batch_steps += steps
        if batch_steps > MAX_BATCH_STEPS:
            break
```

Every iteration of the training loop starts with batch creation, where we sample the noise and obtain rewards for both positive and negated noise. When we reach the limit of episodes in the batch, or the limit of the total steps, we stop gathering the data and do a training update.

```
        step_idx += 1
        m_reward = np.mean(batch_reward)
        if m_reward > 199:
            print("Solved in %d steps" % step_idx)
            break

        train_step(net, batch_noise, batch_reward, writer, step_idx)
```

To perform the update of the network, we call the function that we've already seen. Its goal is to scale the noise according the total reward and then adjust the policy weights in the direction of the averaged noise.

```
writer.add_scalar("reward_mean", m_reward, step_idx)
writer.add_scalar("reward_std", np.std(batch_reward), step_idx)
writer.add_scalar("reward_max", np.max(batch_reward), step_idx)
writer.add_scalar("batch_episodes", len(batch_reward), step_idx)
writer.add_scalar("batch_steps", batch_steps, step_idx)
speed = batch_steps / (time.time() - t_start)
writer.add_scalar("speed", speed, step_idx)
print("%d: reward=%.2f, speed=%.2f f/s" % (step_idx,
m_reward, speed))
```

The final steps in the training loop write metrics into TensorBoard and show the training progress on the console.

Results

Training can be started by just running the program without the arguments:

```
rl_book_samples/Chapter16$ ./01_cartpole_es.py
Net (
    (net): Sequential (
        (0): Linear (4 -> 32)
        (1): ReLU ()
        (2): Linear (32 -> 2)
        (3): Softmax ()
    )
)
1: reward=9.54, speed=6471.63 f/s
2: reward=9.93, speed=7308.94 f/s
3: reward=11.12, speed=7362.68 f/s
4: reward=18.34, speed=7116.69 f/s
...
20: reward=141.51, speed=8285.36 f/s
21: reward=136.32, speed=8397.67 f/s
22: reward=197.98, speed=8570.06 f/s
23: reward=198.13, speed=8402.74 f/s
Solved in 24 steps
```

From my experiments, it usually takes ES about 40-60 batches to solve CartPole. The convergence dynamics for the above run are shown on the following charts, with quite a steady result:

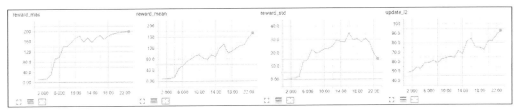

Figure 1: Convergence of the ES method on the CartPole environment

ES on HalfCheetah

In the next example, we'll go beyond the simplest ES implementation and look at how this method can be parallelized efficiently using the *shared seed* strategy proposed by the paper [1]. To show this approach, we'll use the environment from the roboschool library that we already experimented with in *Chapter 15, Trust Regions – TRPO, PPO, and ACKTR*, **HalfCheetah**, which is a continuous action problem where a weird two-legged creature gains reward by running forward without injuring itself.

First, let's discuss the idea of shared seeds. The performance of the ES algorithm is mostly determined by the speed that we can gather our training batch, which consists of sampling the noise and checking the total reward of the perturbed noise. As our training batch items are independent, we can easily parallelize this step to a large number of workers sitting on remote machines (that's a bit similar to the example from *Chapter 11, Asynchronous Advantage Actor-Critic* when we gathered gradients from A3C workers). However, naive implementation of this parallelization will require a large amount of data to be transferred from the worker machine to the central *master*, which is supposed to combine the noise checked by the workers and perform the policy update. Most of this data is the noise vectors, the size of which is equal to the size of our policy parameters.

To avoid this overhead, quite an elegant solution was proposed by the paper's authors. As noise sampled on a worker is produced by a pseudo-random number generator, which allows us to set the random seed and reproduce the random sequence generated, the worker can transfer to the master only the seed that was used to generate the noise. Then, the master can generate the same noise vector again using the seed. Of course, the seed on every worker needs to be generated randomly, to still have random optimization process. This allows for dramatically decreasing the amount of data needed to be transferred from workers to the master, improving the scalability of the method. For example, the authors reported linear speed up in optimizations involving 1440 CPUs in the cloud.

In our example, we'll check local parallelization using the same approach. The code is placed in Chapter16/02_cheetah_es.py. As the code significantly overlaps with the CartPole version, we'll focus here only on the differences.

We will begin with the worker, which is started as a separated process using the PyTorch multiprocessing wrapper. The worker's responsibilities are simple: for? every iteration it obtains the network parameters from the master process, then it performs the fixed amount of iterations where it samples the noise and evaluates the reward. The result with the random seed is sent to the master using the queue.

```
RewardsItem = collections.namedtuple('RewardsItem',
    field_names=['seed', 'pos_reward', 'neg_reward', 'steps'])
```

The namedtuple above is used by the worker to send the results of the perturbed policy evaluation, and it includes the random seed, reward obtained with the noise, reward obtained with the negated noise, and the total amount of steps we performed in both tests.

```
def worker_func(worker_id, params_queue, rewards_queue, device,
noise_std):
    env = make_env()
    net = Net(env.observation_space.shape[0], env.action_space.
shape[0]).to(device
    net.eval()

    while True:
        params = params_queue.get()
        if params is None:
            break
        net.load_state_dict(params)
```

On every training iteration, the worker waits for the network parameters to be broadcasted from the master. The value of None means that the master wants to stop the worker.

```
        for _ in range(ITERS_PER_UPDATE):
            seed = np.random.randint(low=0, high=65535)
            np.random.seed(seed)
            noise, neg_noise = sample_noise(net, device=device)
            pos_reward, pos_steps = eval_with_noise(env, net, noise,
noise_std, device=device)
            neg_reward, neg_steps = eval_with_noise(env, net,
neg_noise, noise_std, device=device)
            rewards_queue.put(RewardsItem(seed=seed,
pos_reward=pos_reward,
                                          neg_reward=neg_reward,
steps=pos_steps+neg_steps))
```

The rest is almost the same as the previous example, with the only difference being in the random seed generated and assigned before the noise generation. This will allow the master to regenerate the same noise only from the seed. Another difference lies in the function used by the master to perform the training step.

```
def train_step(optimizer, net, batch_noise, batch_reward, writer,
step_idx, noise_std):
    weighted_noise = None
    norm_reward = compute_centered_ranks(np.array(batch_reward))
```

In the previous example, we normalized the batch of rewards by subtracting the mean and dividing by the standard deviation. According to the ES paper, better results could be obtained using ranks instead of actual rewards. As ES has no assumptions about the fitness function (which is a reward in our case), we can make any rearrangements in the reward that we want, which wasn't possible in the case of DQN, for example. Here, **rank transformation** of the array means replacing the array with indices of the sorted array. For example, array [0.1, 10, 0.5] will have rank array [0, 3, 2]. The compute_centered_ranks function takes the array with the total rewards of the batch, calculates the rank for every item in the array and then normalizes those ranks. For example, an input array of [21.0. 5.8. 7.0] will have ranks [2, 0, 1] and the final centered ranks will be [0.5, -0.5, 0.0].

```
    for noise, reward in zip(batch_noise, norm_reward):
        if weighted_noise is None:
            weighted_noise = [reward * p_n for p_n in noise]
        else:
            for w_n, p_n in zip(weighted_noise, noise):
                w_n += reward * p_n
    m_updates = []
    optimizer.zero_grad()
    for p, p_update in zip(net.parameters(), weighted_noise):
        update = p_update / (len(batch_reward) * noise_std)
        p.grad = -update
        m_updates.append(torch.norm(update))
    writer.add_scalar("update_l2", np.mean(m_updates), step_idx)
    optimizer.step()
```

Another major difference in the training function is the usage of PyTorch optimizers. To understand why they are used and how it was possible without doing backpropagation, some explanations are required. First of all, in the ES paper it was shown that the optimization method used by the ES algorithm is very similar to gradient ascent on the fitness function, with the difference being how the gradient was calculated. The way the **Stochastic Gradient Descent (SGD)** method is usually applied, the gradient is obtained from the loss function by calculating the derivative of the network parameters with respect to the loss value. This imposes the limitation on the network and loss function to be differentiable, which is not always the case, for example, the rank transformation performed by the ES method is not differentiable. On the other hand, optimization performed by ES works differently. We randomly sample the neighborhood of our current parameters by adding the noise to them and calculating the fitness function. According to the fitness function change, we adjust the parameters, which pushes our parameters in the direction of a higher fitness function. The result of this is very similar to gradient-based methods, but the requirements imposed on our fitness function are much looser: the only requirement is our ability to calculate it.

However, if we're estimating some kind of gradient by randomly sampling the fitness function, we can use standard optimizers from PyTorch. Normally, optimizers adjust parameters of the network using gradients accumulated in the parameter's grad field. Those gradients are accumulated after the backpropagation step, but due to PyTorch's flexibility, the optimizer doesn't care about the source of the gradients. So, the only thing we need to do is to copy the estimated parameters' update in the grad field and ask the optimizer to update them. Note that the update is copied with a negative sign, as optimizers normally perform the gradient descent (as in a normal operation, we're **minimizing** the loss function), but in this case, we want to do the gradient ascent. It is very similar to the **Actor-Critic method (A2C)**, when the estimated PG was taken with the negative sign, as it shows the direction to **improve** the policy.

The last chunk of different code is taken from the training loop performed by the master process. Its responsibility is to wait for data from worker processes, perform the training update of parameters, and broadcast the result to the workers. The communication between the master and workers is performed by two sets of queues. The first queue is per-worker and used by the master to send the current policy parameters to use. The second queue is shared by the workers and used to send the already mentioned RewardItem structure with the random seed and rewards:

```
params_queues = [mp.Queue(maxsize=1) for _ in range
(PROCESSES_COUNT)]
rewards_queue = mp.Queue(maxsize=ITERS_PER_UPDATE)
workers = []
```

```
for idx, params_queue in enumerate(params_queues):
    proc = mp.Process(target=worker_func, args=(idx, params_queue,
rewards_queue, device, args.noise_std))
    proc.start()
    workers.append(proc)

print("All started!")
optimizer = optim.Adam(net.parameters(), lr=args.lr)
```

In the beginning of the master, we create all those queues, start worker processes, and the optimizer.

```
for step_idx in range(args.iters):
    # broadcasting network params
    params = net.state_dict()
    for q in params_queues:
        q.put(params)
```

Every training iteration starts with network parameters being broadcast to the workers.

```
t_start = time.time()
batch_noise = []
batch_reward = []
results = 0
batch_steps = 0
batch_steps_data = []
while True:
    while not rewards_queue.empty():
        reward = rewards_queue.get_nowait()
        np.random.seed(reward.seed)
        noise, neg_noise = sample_noise(net)
        batch_noise.append(noise)
        batch_reward.append(reward.pos_reward)
        batch_noise.append(neg_noise)
        batch_reward.append(reward.neg_reward)
        results += 1
        batch_steps += reward.steps
        batch_steps_data.append(reward.steps)

    if results == PROCESSES_COUNT * ITERS_PER_UPDATE:
        break
    time.sleep(0.01)
```

Then, in the loop, the master waits for enough data to be obtained from the workers. Every time a new result arrives, we reproduce the noise using the random seed.

```
train_step(optimizer, net, batch_noise, batch_reward, writer,
step_idx, args.noise_std)
```

As the last step in the training loop, we call the function we've already seen, which calculates the update from the noise and rewards and calls the optimizer to adjust the weights.

Results

The code supports the optional --cuda flag, but, from my experiments, I get zero speeding up from the GPU, as the network is too shallow and the batch size is only one for every parameter's evaluation. This also suggests potential speed improvements by increasing the batch size that we use during the evaluation, which can be done using multiple environments in every worker and carefully working with noise data inside the network. Values shown for every iteration are mean reward obtained, speed of training (in observations per second) two timing values, showing how long (in seconds) it took to gather data and perform the training step, and then three values about the episode lengths: mean, min, and max number of steps during the episodes:

```
rl_book_samples/Chapter16$ ./02_cheetah_es.py
Net (
   (mu): Sequential (
      (0): Linear (26 -> 64)
      (1): Tanh ()
      (2): Linear (64 -> 64)
      (3): Tanh ()
      (4): Linear (64 -> 6)
      (5): Tanh ()
   )
)
All started!
0: reward=10.86, speed=1486.01 f/s, data_gather=0.903, train=0.008,
steps_mean=45.10, min=32.00, max=133.00, steps_std=17.62
1: reward=11.39, speed=4648.11 f/s, data_gather=0.269, train=0.005,
steps_mean=42.53, min=33.00, max=65.00, steps_std=8.15
2: reward=14.25, speed=4662.10 f/s, data_gather=0.270, train=0.006,
steps_mean=42.90, min=36.00, max=59.00, steps_std=5.65
3: reward=14.33, speed=4901.02 f/s, data_gather=0.257, train=0.006,
steps_mean=43.00, min=35.00, max=56.00, steps_std=5.01
4: reward=14.95, speed=4566.68 f/s, data_gather=0.281, train=0.005,
steps_mean=43.60, min=37.00, max=54.00, steps_std=4.41
...
```

The dynamics of the training show very quickly a policy improvement in the beginning (in just 100 updates, which is seven minutes of training, the agent was able to reach the score of 700-800), but afterwards, it got stuck and wasn't able to switch from keeping the balance (when Cheetah can reach up to 900-1000 total reward) to the running mode with much higher reward of 2.5k and more:

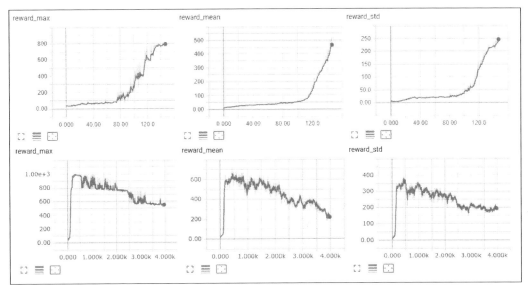

Figure 2: HalfCheetah convergence using the ES method

Genetic algorithms

Another class of black-box methods that has recently become a popular alternative to the value-based and PG methods is genetic algorithms or GA. It is a large family of optimization methods with more than two decades of history behind it and a simple core idea of generating the population of N individuals, each of which is evaluated with the fitness function. Every individual means some combination of model parameters. Then some subset of top performers is used to produce (which is called mutation) the next generation of the population. This process is repeated until we're satisfied with the performance of our population.

There are lots of different methods in the GA family, for example, how to complete the mutation of the individuals for the next generation or how to rank the performers. Here we'll consider the simple GA method with some extensions, published in the paper by *Felipe Petroski Such, Vashisht Madhavan, and others,* called *Deep Neuroevolution: Genetic Algorithms are a Competitive Alternative for Training Deep Neural Networks for Reinforcement Learning* [2].

In this paper, the authors analyzed the simple GA method, which performs Gaussian noise perturbation of the parent's weights to perform mutation. On every iteration, the top-performer was copied without modification. In an algorithm form, the steps of a simple GA method can be written as follows:

1. Initialize mutation power σ, population size N, number of the selected individuals T, initial population P^0 with N randomly-initialized policies and their fitness $F^0 = \{F(P_i^0)|i = 1\dots N\}$.

2. For generation $g = 1\dots G$:

    1. Sort generation P^{g-1} in the descending order of fitness function value F^{g-1}.

    2. Copy elite $P_1^g = P_1^{g-1}, F_1^g = F_1^{g-1}$.

    3. For individual $i = 2\dots N$:

        - k = randomly select parent from $1\dots T$.

        - Sample $\epsilon \sim \mathcal{N}(0, I)$.

        - Mutate parent $P_i^g = P_k^{g-1} + \sigma\varepsilon$.

        - Get its fitness $F_i^g = F(P_i^g)$.

There have been several improvements to this basic method proposed in the paper, which we'll discuss later. For now, let's check the implementation of the core algorithm.

GA on CartPole

The source code is in `Chapter16/03_cartpole_ga.py` and it has lots in common with our ES example. The difference is in the lack of the gradient ascent code, which was replaced by the network mutation function as follows:

```
def mutate_parent(net):
    new_net = copy.deepcopy(net)
    for p in new_net.parameters():
        noise_t = torch.from_numpy(np.random.normal(size=p.data.
size()).astype(np.float32))
        p.data += NOISE_STD * noise_t
    return new_net
```

The goal of the function is to create a mutated copy of the given policy by adding a random noise to all weights. The parent's weights are kept untouched, as a random selection of the parent is performed with replacement, so this network could be used again later.

```
NOISE_STD = 0.01
POPULATION_SIZE = 50
PARENTS_COUNT = 10
```

The count of hyperparameters is even smaller than with ES and includes the standard deviation of the noise added-on mutation, the population size, and the number of top performers used to produce the subsequent generation.

```
if __name__ == "__main__":
    writer = SummaryWriter(comment="-cartpole-ga")
    env = gym.make("CartPole-v0")

    gen_idx = 0
    nets = [
        Net(env.observation_space.shape[0], env.action_space.n)
        for _ in range(POPULATION_SIZE)
    ]
    population = [
        (net, evaluate(env, net))
        for net in nets
    ]
```

Before the training loop, we create the population of randomly initialized networks and obtain their fitness.

```
    while True:
        population.sort(key=lambda p: p[1], reverse=True)
        rewards = [p[1] for p in population[:PARENTS_COUNT]]
        reward_mean = np.mean(rewards)
        reward_max = np.max(rewards)
        reward_std = np.std(rewards)

        writer.add_scalar("reward_mean", reward_mean, gen_idx)
        writer.add_scalar("reward_std", reward_std, gen_idx)
        writer.add_scalar("reward_max", reward_max, gen_idx)
        print("%d: reward_mean=%.2f, reward_max=%.2f,
reward_std=%.2f" % (
            gen_idx, reward_mean, reward_max, reward_std))
        if reward_mean > 199:
            print("Solved in %d steps" % gen_idx)
            break
```

In the beginning of every generation, we sort the previous generation according to their fitness and record statistics about future parents.

```
prev_population = population
population = [population[0]]
for _ in range(POPULATION_SIZE-1):
    parent_idx = np.random.randint(0, PARENTS_COUNT)
    parent = prev_population[parent_idx][0]
    net = mutate_parent(parent)
    fitness = evaluate(env, net)
    population.append((net, fitness))
gen_idx += 1
```

In a separate loop, over new individuals to be generated, we randomly sample a parent, mutate it, and evaluate its fitness score.

Results

Despite the simplicity of the method, it works even better than ES, solving the CartPole environment in just several generations. In my experiments with the code above, it takes five to ten generations to solve the environment:

```
rl_book_samples/Chapter16$ ./03_cartpole_ga.py
0: reward_mean=20.60, reward_max=25.00, reward_std=2.76
1: reward_mean=44.40, reward_max=55.00, reward_std=6.70
2: reward_mean=73.30, reward_max=105.00, reward_std=16.66
3: reward_mean=100.40, reward_max=167.00, reward_std=30.75
4: reward_mean=140.20, reward_max=172.00, reward_std=21.99
5: reward_mean=137.50, reward_max=172.00, reward_std=14.63
6: reward_mean=157.70, reward_max=200.00, reward_std=22.07
7: reward_mean=198.20, reward_max=200.00, reward_std=4.24
8: reward_mean=200.00, reward_max=200.00, reward_std=0.00
Solved in 8 steps
```

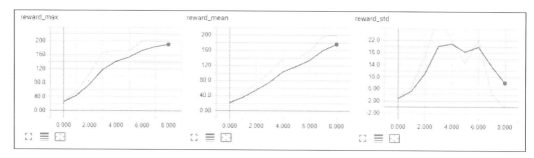

Figure 3: GA convergence on CartPole

GA tweaks

In the Deep Neuroevolution paper [2], the authors checked two tweaks to the basic GA algorithm. The first, with the name **deep GA**, aimed to increase the scalability of the implementation and the second, called **novelty search**, was an attempt to replace the reward objective with a different metric of the episode. In the following example, we'll implement the first improvement, while the second one is left as an optional exercise.

Deep GA

Being a gradient-free method, GA is potentially even more scalable than ES methods in terms of speed, with more CPUs involved in the optimization. However, the simple GA algorithm that we've seen has the similar bottleneck as ES methods: policy parameters have to be exchanged between the workers. In the above-mentioned paper, the authors proposed a trick similar to the shared seed approach but taken to an extreme. They called it deep GA, and at its core, the policy parameters are represented as a list of random seeds used to create this particular policy's weights.

In fact, the initial network's weights were generated randomly on the first population, so the first seed in the list defines this initialization. On every population, mutations are also fully specified by the random seed for every mutation. So, the only thing we need to be able to reconstruct the weights is the seeds themselves. In this approach, we need to reconstruct the weights on every worker, but usually this overhead is much less than the overhead of transferring full weights over the network.

Novelty search

Another modification to the basic GA method, also checked in the Deep Neuroevolution paper, was novelty search (NS), proposed by *Lehman and Stanley* in their paper, *Abandoning Objectives: Evolution Through the Search for Novelty Alone*, published in 2011 [3].

The idea of NS is in stopping following the reward being the primary objective driving the optimization process, replacing it with a different target and rewarding the agent for exploring the behavior that it has never checked before (that is, novel). According to their experiments on the maze navigation problem, with lots of traps for the agent, NS works much better than other, reward-driven approaches.

To implement NS, we define the so-called behavior characteristic (BC) (π), which describes the behavior of the policy and a distance between two BCs. Then, the k-nearest neighbor approach is used to check the novelty of the new policy and drive the GA according to this distance. In the Deep Neuroevolution paper, sufficient exploration by the agent was needed. The approach of NS significantly outperformed the ES, GA, and other, more traditional approaches to RL problems.

GA on Cheetah

In our final example in this chapter, we'll implement the parallelized deep GA on the HalfCheetah environment. The complete code is in `Chapter16/04_cheetah_ga.py`. The architecture is very close to the parallel ES version, with one master process and several workers. The goal of every worker is to evaluate the batch of networks and return the result to the master, which merges partial results into the complete population, ranks the individuals according to the obtained reward and generates the next population to be evaluated by the workers.

Every individual is encoded by a list of random seeds used to initialize the initial network weights and all subsequent mutations. This representation allows very compact encoding of the network, even when the number of parameters in the policy is not very large. For example, in our network with two hidden layers of 64 neurons, we have 6278 float values (the input is 26 values and the action is six floats). Every float occupies 4 bytes, which is the same size used by the random seed. So, the deep GA representation proposed by the paper will be smaller up to 6278 generations in the optimization.

In our example, we perform parallelization on local CPUs, so the amount of data transferred back and forth doesn't matter much, but if you have a couple of hundred cores to utilize, the representation might become a significant issue.

```
NOISE_STD = 0.01
POPULATION_SIZE = 2000
PARENTS_COUNT = 10
WORKERS_COUNT = 6
SEEDS_PER_WORKER = POPULATION_SIZE // WORKERS_COUNT
MAX_SEED = 2**32 - 1
```

The set of hyperparameters is the same as in the CartPole example, with the difference of a larger population size.

```
def mutate_net(net, seed, copy_net=True):
    new_net = copy.deepcopy(net) if copy_net else net
    np.random.seed(seed)
    for p in new_net.parameters():
```

```
        noise_t = torch.from_numpy(np.random.normal(size=p.data.
size()).astype(np.float32))
        p.data += NOISE_STD * noise_t
    return new_net
```

There are two functions used to build the networks based on the seeds given. The first one performs one mutation on the already created policy network and it can perform mutation in place or by copying the target network based on arguments (copying is needed for the first generation).

```
def build_net(env, seeds):
    torch.manual_seed(seeds[0])
    net = Net(env.observation_space.shape[0], env.action_space.
shape[0])
    for seed in seeds[1:]:
        net = mutate_net(net, seed, copy_net=False)
    return net
```

The second function creates the network from scratch using the list of seeds. The first seed is passed to PyTorch, to influence the network initialization, and subsequent seeds are used to apply network mutations.

The worker function obtains the list of seeds to evaluate and outputs individual OutputItem tuples for every result obtained. The function maintains the cache of networks to minimize the amount of time spent recreating the parameters from the list of seeds. This cache is cleared for? every generation, as every new generation is created from the current generation winners, so there is only a tiny chance that old networks could be reused from the cache.

```
OutputItem = collections.namedtuple('OutputItem', field_
names=['seeds', 'reward', 'steps'])


def worker_func(input_queue, output_queue):
    env = gym.make("RoboschoolHalfCheetah-v1")
    cache = {}

    while True:
        parents = input_queue.get()
        if parents is None:
            break
        new_cache = {}
        for net_seeds in parents:
            if len(net_seeds) > 1:
                net = cache.get(net_seeds[:-1])
                if net is not None:
                    net = mutate_net(net, net_seeds[-1])
```

```
                    else:
                        net = build_net(env, net_seeds)
                else:
                    net = build_net(env, net_seeds)
                new_cache[net_seeds] = net
                reward, steps = evaluate(env, net)
                output_queue.put(OutputItem(seeds=net_seeds,
  reward=reward, steps=steps))
            cache = new_cache
```

The code of the master process is also straightforward. For every generation, we send the current population's seeds to workers for evaluation and wait for the results. Then we sort the results and generate the next population based on the top performers. On the master's side, the mutation is just a seed number generated randomly and appended to the list of seeds of the parent.

```
            batch_steps = 0
            population = []
            while len(population) < SEEDS_PER_WORKER * WORKERS_COUNT:
                out_item = output_queue.get()
                population.append((out_item.seeds, out_item.reward))
                batch_steps += out_item.steps
            if elite is not None:
                population.append(elite)
            population.sort(key=lambda p: p[1], reverse=True)

            elite = population[0]
            for worker_queue in input_queues:
                seeds = []
                for _ in range(SEEDS_PER_WORKER):
                    parent = np.random.randint(PARENTS_COUNT)
                    next_seed = np.random.randint(MAX_SEED)
                    seeds.append(tuple(list(population[parent][0]) +
  [next_seed]))
                worker_queue.put(seeds)
```

Results

To start the training, just launch the source code file. For every generation, it shows the result on the console:

```
rl_book_samples/Chapter16$ ./04_cheetah_ga.py
0: reward_mean=31.28, reward_max=34.37, reward_std=1.46,
speed=5495.65 f/s
1: reward_mean=45.41, reward_max=54.74, reward_std=3.86,
speed=6748.35 f/s
```

```
2: reward_mean=60.74, reward_max=69.25, reward_std=5.33, speed=6749.70
f/s
3: reward_mean=67.70, reward_max=84.29, reward_std=8.21, speed=6070.31
f/s
4: reward_mean=69.85, reward_max=86.38, reward_std=9.37, speed=6612.48
f/s
5: reward_mean=65.59, reward_max=86.38, reward_std=7.95, speed=6542.46
f/s
6: reward_mean=77.29, reward_max=98.53, reward_std=11.13,
speed=6949.59 f/s
```

The overall dynamics are similar to ES experiments on the same environment, with the same problems getting out of the local optima of 1010 reward. After four hours of training and 250 generations, the agent was able to learn how to stand perfectly but wasn't able to figure out that running could bring more reward. Possibly, the NS method could overcome this issue:

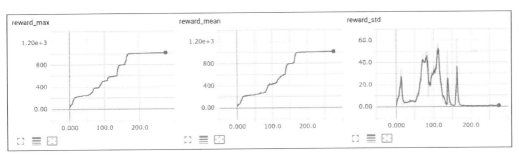

Figure 4: GA convergence on HalfCheetah

Summary

In this chapter, we saw two examples of black-box optimization methods: evolution strategies and genetic algorithms, which make less assumptions about the reward system, but nevertheless can provide competition for other analytical gradient methods. Their strength lies in good parallelization on a large amount of resources and the smaller amount of assumptions that they have on the reward function.

In the next chapter, we'll take a look at a different sphere of modern RL development: model-based methods.

References

1. Tim Salimans, Jonathan Ho, Xi Chen, Szymon Sidor, Ilya Sutskever, Evolution Strategies as a Scalable Alternative to Reinforcement Learning, arXiv:1703.03864

2. Felipe Petroski Such, Vashisht Madhavan, and others, Deep Neuroevolution: Genetic Algorithms are a Competitive Alternative for Training Deep Neural Networks for Reinforcement Learning arXiv:1712.06567

3. Lehman and Stanley, Abandoning Objectives: Evolution Through the Search for Novelty Alone, Journal Evolutionary Computation archive Volume 19 Issue 2, Summer 2011 Pages 189-223

17
Beyond Model-Free – Imagination

In this chapter, we'll take a brief look at the model-based methods in **Reinforcement Learning** (**RL**) and reimplement the DeepMind model, which adds imagination to agents. Model-based methods allow us to decrease the amount of communications with the environment, by building a model of the environment and using it during the training.

Model-based versus model-free

In the *Taxonomy of RL methods* section in *Chapter 4*, *The Cross-Entropy Method*, we saw several different angles we can classify RL methods from. We distinguished three main aspects:

- Value-based and policy-based
- On-policy and off-policy
- Model-free and model-based

There were enough examples of methods on both sides of the first and the second categories, but all the methods we've seen so far were 100% model-free. This doesn't mean that model-free methods are more important or better than their model-based antagonists. Historically, due to their sample-efficiency, the model-based methods have been used in the robotics field and other industrial controls. That is happened due to the cost of the hardware and the physical limitations of samples that could be obtained from a real robot. Robots with a large amount of degrees of freedom are not widely accessible, so RL researchers are more focused on computer games and other environments where samples are relatively cheap. However, the ideas from robotics are infiltrating, so, who knows, maybe the model-based methods will enter the focus quite soon. For now, let's start from the beginning and understand where the difference lies.

In the names of both classes, "model" means the model of the environment, which could have various forms, for example, providing us with a new state and reward from the current state and action. All the methods that we've seen so far put zero effort into predicting, understanding, or simulating the environment. What we were interested in was proper behavior (in terms of the final reward), specified directly (a policy) or indirectly (a value), given the observation. The source of observations and reward was the environment itself, which in some cases could be very slow and inefficient.

In a model-based approach, we're trying to learn the model of the environment to reduce this "real environment" dependency. If we have an accurate environment model, our agent can produce any number of trajectories that it needs, simply by using this model instead of executing the actions in the real world. To some degree, the common playground of RL research is also just models of the real world, for example, Mujoco or PyBullet are simulators of physics used to avoid building real robots with real actuators, sensors, and cameras to train our agents. The story is the same with Atari games or the TORCS car racing simulator: we use computer programs that model some processes, and these models can be executed quickly and cheaply. Even our CartPole example is an over-simplified approximation of the real cart with the stick attached (by the way, in PyBullet and Mujoco there are more realistic CartPole versions with 3D actions and more accurate simulation).

There are two motivations for using the model-based approach in respect to model-free. The first and the most important one is sample-efficiency caused by less dependency on the real environment. Ideally, by having an accurate model, we can avoid touching the real world and use only the trained model. In real applications, it is almost never possible to have the precise model of the environment, but even an imperfect model can significantly reduce the number of samples needed. For example, in real life, you don't need an absolutely precise mental picture of some action (such as tying shoelaces or crossing the road), but this picture helps you in planning and predicting the outcome. The second reason for a model-based approach is the transferability of the environment model across the goals. If you have a good model for a robot manipulator, you can use it in a wide variety of goals, without retraining everything from scratch.

There are lots of details in this class of methods, but the goal of this chapter is to give you an overview and take a closer look at one particular research paper, which has tried to combine both the model-free and model-based approaches in a sophisticated way.

Model imperfections

There is a serious issue with the model-based approach: when our model makes mistakes or is just inaccurate in some regimes of the environment, the policy learned from this model could be totally wrong in real-life situations. To deal with this, we have several options. The most obvious option is to "make the model better." Unfortunately, this can just mean that we'll need more observations from the environment, which is what we've tried to avoid. The more complicated and nonlinear the behavior that the environment has, the worse the situation will be for modelling it properly.

Several ways have been discovered to tackle this issue, for example, the *local models* family of methods, when we replace one large environment model with a small regime-based set of models and train them using trust-region tricks in the same way that **Trust Region Policy Optimization (TRPO)** does. Another interesting way of looking at environment models is to augment model-free policy with model-based paths. In that case, we're not trying to build the best possible model of the environment, but just giving our agent extra information and letting it decide by itself whether the information will be useful during the training or not.

One of the first steps in that direction was carried out by DeepMind in their system, UNREAL, described in the paper by *Max Jaderberg, Volodymyr Mnih, and others,* called *Reinforcement Learning with Unsupervised Auxiliary Tasks*, published in 2016 (arXiv:1611.05397) [1]. In this paper, the authors augmented the **Asynchronous Advantage Actor-Critic (A3C)** agent with extra tasks learned in an unsupervised way during the normal training. The main tests of the agent were performed in a partially observable first-person view maze navigation problem, when the agent needs to navigate the Doom-like maze obtaining the reward for gathering things or executing other actions. The novel approach of the paper was in artificially injecting extra auxiliary tasks not related to the usual RL methods' objectives of value or discounted reward. Those tasks were trained in an unsupervised way from observations and include the following:

- **An immediate reward prediction**: From the history of observations, the agent was asked to predict the immediate reward of the current step

- **Pixel control**: The agent was asked to communicate with the environment to maximize the change in its view

- **Feature control**: The agent was learning how to change specific features in its internal representation

Those tasks were not directly related to the main agent's objective of maximizing the total reward, but they allowed the agent to get a better representation of low-level features and allowed UNREAL to get better results. The first task of immediate reward prediction could be seen as a tiny environment model, aiming to predict the reward. I'm not going to cover the UNREAL architecture in detail, but recommend that you read the original paper.

The paper that we'll cover in detail in this chapter was also published by DeepMind researchers: *Theophane Weber, Sebastien Racantiere, and others,* called *Imagination-Augmented Agents for Deep Reinforcement Learning* (arXiv:1707.06203) [2]. In the paper, the authors augmented the model-free path of the standard A3C agent with the so-called "imagination module," which provides extra help for the agent to make decisions about the actions.

Imagination-augmented agent

The overall idea of the new architecture called **imagination-augmented agent (I2A)** is to allow the agent to imagine future trajectories by the current observations and incorporate these imagined paths into its decision process. The high-level architecture is shown in the following diagram:

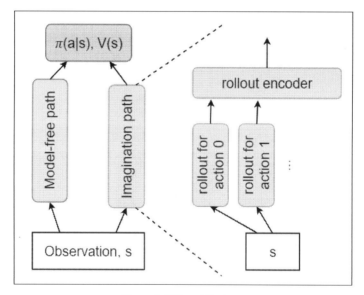

Figure 1: I2A architecture

The agent consists of two different paths used to transform the input observation: model-free and imagination. Model-free is a standard set of convolution layers transforming the input image in high-level features. Another path is called **imagination** and consists of a set of trajectories "imagined" from the current observation. The trajectories are called rollouts and are produced for every available action in the environment. Every rollout consists of a fixed number of steps into the future and on every step a special model, called the **Environment Model (EM)**, (but not to be confused with the expectation maximization method), produces the next observation and predicted immediate reward from the current observation and the action to be taken.

Every rollout for every action is produced by taking the current observation into the EM and then feeding the predicted observation to the EM again N times. On the first step of the rollout, we know the action (as this is the action for which the rollout is generated), but on the subsequent steps, the action is chosen using the small "rollout policy network," which is trained in conjunction to the main agent. The output from the rollout is N steps of imagined trajectory starting from the given action and continuing into the future according to the learned rollout policy. Every step of the rollout is imagined observation and predicted immediate reward. All the steps from the single rollout are passed to another network, called "rollout encoder," which encodes them into the fixed-size vector.

For every rollout, we get those vectors, concatenate them together, and feed them to the head of the agent, which produces the usual policy and value estimations for the A2C algorithm. As you can see, there are some moving parts here, so I've tried to visualize all of them in the following diagram for the case of two rollout steps and two actions in the environment. In the upcoming subsections, we will describe every network and steps performed by the method in detail.

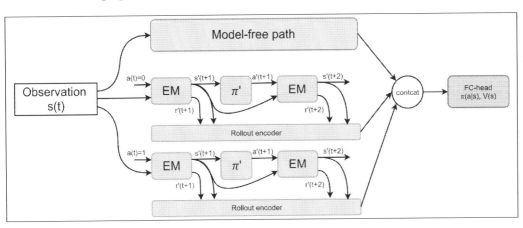

Figure 2: Imagination path architecture

The environment model

The goal of the environment model is to convert the current observation and the action into the next observation and the immediate reward. In the paper [2], the authors tested the I2A model on two environments: the Sokoban puzzle and MiniPacman arcade game. In both cases, the observations were pixels, so the environment model returned the pixels as well, plus the float value for the reward. To incorporate the action into the convolution layers, the action was one-hot encoded and broadcasted to match the observation pixels, one color plane per action. This transformation is illustrated in the following diagram:

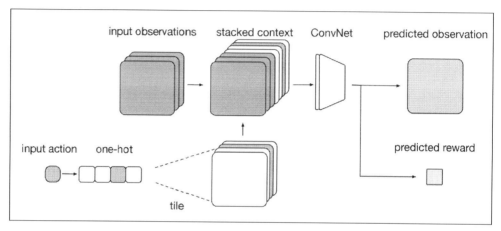

Figure 3: The EM structure

There are several possible ways that this environment model could be trained. The authors discovered that the fastest convergence is obtained by pre-training the environment model using another, partially trained baseline agent as a source of environment samples.

The rollout policy

During the rollout steps, we need to make decisions about the action to be taken during our imagined trajectory. The action for the first step is set explicitly, as we produce individual rollout trajectory for every action we have, but the subsequent steps require somebody to make this decision. Ideally, we would like those actions to be similar to our agent's policy, but we cannot just ask our agent to produce the probabilities, as it will require rollouts to be created in the imagination path. To break this tie, a separate "rollout policy" network is trained to produce similar output to our main agent's policy. The rollout policy is a small network, with similar architecture to A3C, which is trained in parallel to the main I2A network using a cross-entropy loss between the rollout policy network output and the output of the main network. In the paper, this training process is called "policy distillation."

The rollout encoder

The final component of the I2A model is the rollout encoder, which takes rollout steps (observation and reward pairs) as an input and produces the fixed-sized vector, which embeds the information about the rollout. In this network, every rollout step was preprocessed with a small convolution network to extract the features from the observation and these features were converted into a vector of fixed size by the LSTM network.

The outputs from every rollout were concatenated together with features from the model-free path and used to produce the policy and the value estimation in the same way as in the A2C method.

Paper results

As mentioned above, to check the effect of imagination in RL problems, the authors used two environments that require planning and taking decisions about the future: randomly generated Sokoban puzzles and the MiniPacman game. In both environments, the imagination architecture showed better results over the baseline A2C agent.

In the rest of this chapter, we'll apply the model to the Atari Breakout game and check the effect ourselves.

I2A on Atari Breakout

The code and training path of I2A is a bit complicated and includes lots of code and several steps. To understand it better, let's start with a brief overview. In this example, we'll implement the I2A architecture described in the paper, adopted to the Atari environments, and test it on the Breakout game. The overall goal is to check the training dynamics and the effect of imagination augmentation on the final policy.

Our example consists of three parts, which correspond to different steps in the training:

1. Baseline A2C agent in `Chapter17/01_a2c.py`. The resulting policy is used for obtaining observations of the environment model.

2. Environment model training in `Chapter17/02_imag.py`. It uses the model obtained on the previous step to train EM in an unsupervised way. The result is EM weights.

3. The final I2A agent training in `Chapter17/03_i2a.py`. In this step, we use the EM from step 2 to train a full I2A agent, which combines the model-free and rollouts paths.

Due to size of the code, we are not going to describe the whole code here, rather focusing instead on the important parts.

The baseline A2C agent

The first step in the training has two goals: to establish the baseline, which will be used to evaluate the I2A agent and obtain the policy for the EM step. The EM is trained in an unsupervised way from the tuples (s, a, s', r) obtained from the environment. So, the final quality of the EM is heavily dependent on the data it has been trained on. The closer the observations to the data experienced by the agent during the real action, the better the final result will be.

The code is in `Chapter17/01_a2c.py` and `Chapter17/lib/common.py` and is the standard A2C algorithm we've already seen several times. To make the training data generation process reusable in I2A agent training, I haven't used PTAN library classes and reimplemented data generation from scratch, which is in the `common.iterate_batches()` function and responsible for gathering observations from environments and calculating discounted rewards for the experienced trajectories. This agent also has all hyperparameters set very close to the OpenAI Baseline A2C implementation, which I've used during debugging and the implementation of the agent. The only difference is the initialization of the initial weights (I rely on standard PyTorch initialization of weights) and the learning rate decreased from 7e-4 to 1e-4 to improve the stability of the training process.

For every 1000 batches of training, a test of the current policy was performed, which consisted of three full episodes and five lives each to be played by the agent. The mean reward and the number of steps were recorded and the model was saved every time that a new best training reward had been achieved. The configuration of the testing environment is different in two ways from environments used during the training: first of all, the test environment plays full episodes, instead of per-life episodes, so the final reward on the test episodes is higher than the reward during the training. The second difference is that the test environment uses unclipped reward to make the test numbers interpretable. Clipping is a standard way to improve the stability of Atari training, as in some games, the raw score could have large magnitude, which negatively influences the estimated advantage variance.

Another difference from the classical Atari A2C agent is the number of frames given as an observation. Usually, four consequent frames are given, but from my experiments, I found out that the Breakout game has a very similar convergence on just two frames. Working with two frames is faster, so everywhere in this example the observation tensor has the dimensionality of (2, 84, 84).

To make trainings repeatable, the fixed random seed is used in the baseline agent. This is done by the `common.set_seed`, function which sets the random seed for NumPy, Torch (both CPU and CUDA) and every environment in the pool.

EM training

The EM is trained on data produced by the baseline agent and you can specify any weight file saved on the previous step. It does not necessarily have to be the best model, as it just needs to be "good enough" to produce relevant observations.

The EM definition is in `Chapter17/lib/i2a.py`, the `EnvironmentModel` class, and has an architecture that mostly follows the model present in the paper [2], for the Sokoban environment. The input to the model is an observation tensor accompanying the action to be taken, passed as integer value. The action is one-hot encoded and broadcasted to the observation tensor dimensionality. Then both the broadcasted action and observation are concatenated along the "channels" dimension, giving the input tensor of (6, 84, 84), as Breakout has four actions.

This tensor is processed with two convolution layers of 4 × 4 and 3 × 3, then the residual layer is used when the output is processed by a 3 × 3 convolution, the result of which is added to the input. The resulting tensor has been fed into two paths: one is deconvolution, producing the output observation and another is a reward predicting path, consisting of two convolution layers and two fully connected layers.

The EM has two outputs: immediate reward value, which is a single float, and next observation. To reduce the dimensionality of the observation, the difference with the last observation is predicted. So, the output is a tensor ($1, 84, 84$). Besides the decrease in the amount of values we need to predict, the difference has the benefit of being zero-centered and zero-valued for frames when nothing has changed, which will be dominating during the Breakout gameplay, when only a few pixels usually change from frame to frame (the ball, the paddle, and the brick being hit). The architecture and code for EM is shown in the below diagram:

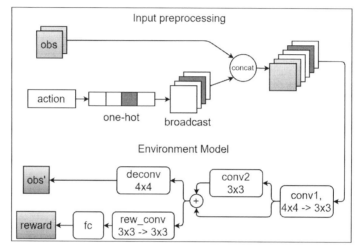

Figure 4: EM architecture and its input preprocessing

```
EM_OUT_SHAPE = (1, ) + common.IMG_SHAPE[1:]

class EnvironmentModel(nn.Module):
    def __init__(self, input_shape, n_actions):
        super(EnvironmentModel, self).__init__()

        self.input_shape = input_shape
        self.n_actions = n_actions

        # input color planes will be equal to frames plus one-hot
encoded actions
        n_planes = input_shape[0] + n_actions
        self.conv1 = nn.Sequential(
            nn.Conv2d(n_planes, 64, kernel_size=4, stride=4,
padding=1),
            nn.ReLU(),
            nn.Conv2d(64, 64, kernel_size=3, padding=1),
            nn.ReLU(),
        )
```

```
        self.conv2 = nn.Sequential(
            nn.Conv2d(64, 64, kernel_size=3, padding=1),
            nn.ReLU()
        )
        # output is one single frame with delta from the current
frame
        self.deconv = nn.ConvTranspose2d(64, 1, kernel_size=4,
stride=4, padding=0)

        self.reward_conv = nn.Sequential(
            nn.Conv2d(64, 64, kernel_size=3),
            nn.MaxPool2d(2),
            nn.ReLU(),
            nn.Conv2d(64, 64, kernel_size=3),
            nn.MaxPool2d(2),
            nn.ReLU()
        )

        rw_conv_out = self._get_reward_conv_out((n_planes, ) +
input_shape[1:])
        self.reward_fc = nn.Sequential(
            nn.Linear(rw_conv_out, 128),
            nn.ReLU(),
            nn.Linear(128, 1)
        )

    def _get_reward_conv_out(self, shape):
        o = self.conv1(torch.zeros(1, *shape))
        o = self.reward_conv(o)
        return int(np.prod(o.size()))

    def forward(self, imgs, actions):
        batch_size = actions.size()[0]
        act_planes_v = torch.FloatTensor(batch_size,
self.n_actions, *self.input_shape[1:]).zero_()
        act_planes_v = act_planes_v.to(actions.device)
        act_planes_v[range(batch_size), actions] = 1.0
        comb_input_v = torch.cat((imgs, act_planes_v), dim=1)
        c1_out = self.conv1(comb_input_v)
        c2_out = self.conv2(c1_out)
        c2_out += c1_out
        img_out = self.deconv(c2_out)
        rew_conv = self.reward_conv(c2_out).view(batch_size, -1)
        rew_out = self.reward_fc(rew_conv)
        return img_out, rew_out
```

The training process of EM is simple and straightforward. The pool of 16 parallel environments is used to populate the batch of 64 samples. Every entry in a batch consists of the current observation, the next immediate observation, the action taken, and the immediate reward obtained. The final loss being optimized is a sum of the observation loss and the reward loss. The observation loss is the **Mean Squared Error (MSE)** loss between the predicted delta for the next observation and the real delta between the current and the next observation. The reward loss is again the MSE between rewards. To emphasize the importance of observation, the observation loss has a scale factor of 10.

The imagination agent

The final step in the training process is the I2A agent, which combines the model-free path with rollouts produced by the EM, trained on the previous step.

The I2A model

The agent is implemented in the `I2A` class in the `Chapter17/lib/i2a.py` module:

```
class I2A(nn.Module):
    def __init__(self, input_shape, n_actions, net_em, net_policy,
rollout_steps):
        super(I2A, self).__init__()
```

The arguments of the constructor provide the shape of observations, the amount of actions in the environment, and the two networks used during rollout: EM and rollout policy and, finally, the count of steps to perform during rollouts. Both EM and rollout policy networks are stored in a special way to prevent their weights from being included in I2A network parameters.

```
        self.n_actions = n_actions
        self.rollout_steps = rollout_steps

        self.conv = nn.Sequential(
            nn.Conv2d(input_shape[0], 32, kernel_size=8,
stride=4),
            nn.ReLU(),
            nn.Conv2d(32, 64, kernel_size=4, stride=2),
            nn.ReLU(),
            nn.Conv2d(64, 64, kernel_size=3, stride=1),
            nn.ReLU(),
        )
```

The preceding code specifies the model-free path, which produces the features from the observation. The architecture is a familiar Atari convolution.

```
conv_out_size = self._get_conv_out(input_shape)
fc_input = conv_out_size + ROLLOUT_HIDDEN * n_actions
self.fc = nn.Sequential(
    nn.Linear(fc_input, 512),
    nn.ReLU()
)
self.policy = nn.Linear(512, n_actions)
self.value = nn.Linear(512, 1)
```

The input of the layers that will produce the policy and the value of the agent is combined from the features obtained from the model-free path and encoded rollouts. Every rollout is represented with the ROLLOUT_HIDDEN constant (equals to 256), which is a dimensionality of the LSTM layer inside the RolloutEncoder class.

```
self.encoder = RolloutEncoder(EM_OUT_SHAPE)
self.action_selector =
ptan.actions.ProbabilityActionSelector()
        object.__setattr__(self, "net_em", net_em)
        object.__setattr__(self, "net_policy", net_policy)
```

The rest of the constructor creates the RolloutEncoder class (which will be described later in this section) and stores the EM and rollout policy networks. Both of these networks are not supposed to be trained together with the I2A agent, as the EM is not trained at all (it is pretrained on the previous step and remains fixed) and the rollout policy is trained with a separate policy distillation process. However, PyTorch 's Module class automatically registers and joins all fields assigned to the class. To prevent the EM and rollout policy networks from being merged into the I2A agent, we save their references via the __setattr__ call, which is a bit hacky, but does exactly what we need.

```
def _get_conv_out(self, shape):
    o = self.conv(torch.zeros(1, *shape))
    return int(np.prod(o.size()))

def forward(self, x):
    fx = x.float() / 255
    enc_rollouts = self.rollouts_batch(fx)
    conv_out = self.conv(fx).view(fx.size()[0], -1)
    fc_in = torch.cat((conv_out, enc_rollouts), dim=1)
    fc_out = self.fc(fc_in)
    return self.policy(fc_out), self.value(fc_out)
```

The `forward()` function looks simple, as most of the work here is inside the `rollouts_batch()` method. The next and last method of the I2A class is a bit more complicated. Originally, it was written to perform all rollouts sequentially, but that version was painfully slow. The new version of the code performs all rollouts at once, step-by-step, which increases the speed almost five times, but makes the code slightly more complicated:

```
def rollouts_batch(self, batch):
    batch_size = batch.size()[0]
    batch_rest = batch.size()[1:]
    if batch_size == 1:
        obs_batch_v = batch.expand(batch_size *
self.n_actions, *batch_rest)
    else:
        obs_batch_v = batch.unsqueeze(1)
        obs_batch_v = obs_batch_v.expand(batch_size,
self.n_actions, *batch_rest)
        obs_batch_v = obs_batch_v.contiguous().view(-1,

*batch_rest)
```

In the beginning of the function, we take the batch of observations and we want to perform `n_actions` rollouts for every observation of the batch. So, we need to expand the batch of observations, repeating every observation `n_actions` times. The most efficient way of doing this is to use the PyTorch `expand()` method, which can repeat any tensor with 1 dimensionality and repeat it along this dimension any amount of times. In case our batch consists of one single example, we just use this batch dimension, otherwise we need to inject the extra unit dimension right after the batch dimension and then expand along it. Regardless of this, the resulting dimensionality of the `obs_batch_v` tensor is (`batch_size * n_actions, 2, 84, 84`).

```
        actions = np.tile(np.arange(0, self.n_actions,
dtype=np.int64), batch_size)
        step_obs, step_rewards = [], []
```

After that, we need to prepare the array with the actions that we want EM to take for every observation. As we repeated every observation `n_actions` times, our actions array will also have the form `[0, 1, 2, 3, 0, 1, 2, 3, ...]` (Breakout has four actions in total). In the `step_obs` and `step_rewards` lists, we'll save observations and immediate rewards produced for every rollout step by the EM model. This data will be passed to `RolloutEncoder` to be embedded into fixed-vector form.

```
for step_idx in range(self.rollout_steps):
    actions_t = torch.tensor(actions).to(batch.device)
    obs_next_v, reward_v = self.net_em(obs_batch_v,
actions_t)
```

Then we start the loop for every rollout step. For every step, we ask the EM network to predict the next observation (returned as delta to the current observation) and immediate reward. Subsequent steps will have actions selected using the rollout policy network.

```
step_obs.append(obs_next_v.detach())
step_rewards.append(reward_v.detach())
# don't need actions for the last step
if step_idx == self.rollout_steps-1:
    break
```

We store observation delta and immediate reward in lists for `RolloutEncoder` and stop the loop if we're at the final rollout step. The early stop is possible, as the rest of code in the loop is supposed to select the actions, but for the last step we don't need actions at all.

```
# combine the delta from EM into new observation
cur_plane_v = obs_batch_v[:, 1:2]
new_plane_v = cur_plane_v + obs_next_v
obs_batch_v = torch.cat((cur_plane_v, new_plane_v),
dim=1)
```

To be able to use the rollout policy network, we need to create a normal observation tensor from the delta returned by the EM network. To do this, we take the last channel from the current observation, add the delta from EM to it, creating a predicted frame, and then combine them into the normal observation tensor of shape, `(batch_size * n_actions, 2, 84, 84)`.

```
# select actions
logits_v, _ = self.net_policy(obs_batch_v)
probs_v = F.softmax(logits_v, dim=1)
probs = probs_v.data.cpu().numpy()
actions = self.action_selector(probs)
```

In the rest of the loop, we use the created observations batch to select the actions using the rollout policy network and convert the returned probability distribution into the action indices. Then the loop continues to predict the next rollout step.

```
step_obs_v = torch.stack(step_obs)
step_rewards_v = torch.stack(step_rewards)
flat_enc_v = self.encoder(step_obs_v, step_rewards_v)
return flat_enc_v.view(batch_size, -1)
```

When we are done with all the steps, two lists `step_obs` and `step_rewards` will contain tensors for every step. Using the `torch.stack()` function, we join them on the new dimension. The resulting tensors will have rollout steps as the first dimension and `batch_size * n_actions` as the second dimension. These two tensors are passed to `RolloutEncoder`, which produces an encoded vector for every entry in the second dimension. The output from the encoder is a tensor of `(batch_size*n_actions, encoded_len)` and we want to concatenate encodings for different actions of the same batch sample together. To do this, we just reshape the output tensor to have `batch_size` as the first dimension, so the output from the function will have a `(batch_size, encoded_len*n_actions)` shape.

The Rollout encoder

The `RolloutEncoder` class accepts two tensors: observations of `(rollout_steps, batch_size, 1, 84, 84)` and rewards of `(rollout_steps, batch_size)` and applies a **Recurrent Neural Network (RNN)** along the rollout steps to convert every batch series into the encoded vector. Before the RNN, we have a preprocessor which extracts features from the observation delta given by the EM, then the reward value is just appended to the features vector.

```
class RolloutEncoder(nn.Module):
    def __init__(self, input_shape, hidden_size=ROLLOUT_HIDDEN):
        super(RolloutEncoder, self).__init__()

        self.conv = nn.Sequential(
            nn.Conv2d(input_shape[0], 32, kernel_size=8,
stride=4),
            nn.ReLU(),
            nn.Conv2d(32, 64, kernel_size=4, stride=2),
            nn.ReLU(),
            nn.Conv2d(64, 64, kernel_size=3, stride=1),
            nn.ReLU(),
        )
```

The observation preprocessor has the same Atari convolution layers, except that the input tensor has a single channel, which is a delta between consecutive observations, produced by the EM.

```
        conv_out_size = self._get_conv_out(input_shape)

        self.rnn = nn.LSTM(input_size=conv_out_size+1,
hidden_size=hidden_size, batch_first=False)
```

The RNN of the encoder is an LSTM layer. The `batch_first=False` argument is a bit redundant (as the default value for the argument is also `False`), but left here to remind us about the input tensor order, which is a `(rollout_steps, batch_size, conv_features+1)`, so the time dimension has zero index.

```
def _get_conv_out(self, shape):
    o = self.conv(torch.zeros(1, *shape))
    return int(np.prod(o.size()))

def forward(self, obs_v, reward_v):
    """
    Input is in (time, batch, *) order
    """
    n_time = obs_v.size()[0]
    n_batch = obs_v.size()[1]
    n_items = n_time * n_batch
    obs_flat_v = obs_v.view(n_items, *obs_v.size()[2:])
    conv_out = self.conv(obs_flat_v)
    conv_out = conv_out.view(n_time, n_batch, -1)
    rnn_in = torch.cat((conv_out, reward_v), dim=2)
    _, (rnn_hid, _) = self.rnn(rnn_in)
    return rnn_hid.view(-1)
```

The `forward()` function is obvious from the encoder architecture and first extracts the features from all `rollout_steps*batch_size` observations and then applies LSTM to the sequence. As an encoded vector of the rollout, we take the hidden state returned by the last step of the RNN.

Training of I2A

The training process has two steps: we train the I2A model in the usual A2C manner and we do a distillation of the rollout policy using a separate loss. The distillation training is needed to approximate the I2A behavior by a smaller policy used during rollout steps to select actions. The actions chosen in imagined trajectories should be similar to the actions that the agent will choose in real situations. However, during the rollouts, we cannot just use our main I2A model to make action selection, as the main I2A model will need to do rollouts again. To break this contradiction, distillation is used, which is a very simple cross-entropy loss between the policy of the main I2A model during the training and the policy returned by the rollout policy network. This training step has a separate optimizer responsible only for rollouts policy parameters.

The piece of the training loop which is responsible for distillation is given below. Array `mb_probs` contains the probabilities of actions chosen by the I2A model for observations, `obs_v`.

```
        probs_v = torch.FloatTensor(mb_probs)).to(device)
        policy_opt.zero_grad()
        logits_v, _ = net_policy(obs_v)
        policy_loss_v = -F.log_softmax(logits_v, dim=1) *
probs_v.view_as(logits_v)
        policy_loss_v = policy_loss_v.sum(dim=1).mean()
        policy_loss_v.backward()
        policy_opt.step()
```

Another step in the training that is supposed to train the I2A model is performed exactly the same way as we train the usual A2C, ignoring all the internals of the I2A model: the value loss is the MSE between the predicted and discounted reward approximated by the Bellman equation, while the **Policy Gradient** (**PG**) is approximated by the advantage multiplied by log-probability of the chosen action. This is nothing new.

Experiment results

In this section, we'll take a look at the results of our multi-step training process

The baseline agent

To train the agent, run `Chapter17/01_a2c.py` with the optional `--cuda` flag to enable GPU and required `-n` option with the experiment name used in TensorBoard and in a directory name to save models.

```
Chapter17$ ./01_a2c.py --cuda -n tt
AtariA2C (
  (conv): Sequential (
    (0): Conv2d(2, 32, kernel_size=(8, 8), stride=(4, 4))
    (1): ReLU ()
    (2): Conv2d(32, 64, kernel_size=(4, 4), stride=(2, 2))
    (3): ReLU ()
    (4): Conv2d(64, 64, kernel_size=(3, 3), stride=(1, 1))
    (5): ReLU ()
  )
  (fc): Sequential (
    (0): Linear (3136 -> 512)
    (1): ReLU ()
  )
  (policy): Linear (512 -> 4)
```

```
   (value): Linear (512 -> 1)
)
4: done 13 episodes, mean_reward=0.00, best_reward=0.00,
speed=99.96
9: done 11 episodes, mean_reward=0.00, best_reward=0.00,
speed=133.25
10: done 1 episodes, mean_reward=1.00, best_reward=1.00,
speed=136.62
13: done 9 episodes, mean_reward=0.00, best_reward=1.00,
speed=153.99
...
```

In 500k training iterations, the A2C was able to reach the mean reward of 450 on test episodes with five lives and unclipped reward. The maximum test reward on three full episodes was 650.

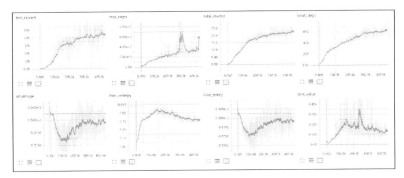

Figure 5: Baseline convergence

Training EM weights

To train the EM, you need to specify the policy produced during the baseline agent training. In my experiments, I've taken the policy from the partially-trained agent to increase the potential diversity of the EM training data.

```
Chapter17$ ./02_imag.py --cuda -m
res/best/01_a2c_clip/best_0342.333_119000.dat -n tt
EnvironmentModel (
  (conv1): Sequential (
    (0): Conv2d(6, 64, kernel_size=(4, 4), stride=(4, 4),
padding=(1, 1))
    (1): ReLU ()
    (2): Conv2d(64, 64, kernel_size=(3, 3), stride=(1, 1),
padding=(1, 1))
    (3): ReLU ()
  )
```

```
  (conv2): Sequential (
    (0): Conv2d(64, 64, kernel_size=(3, 3), stride=(1, 1),
padding=(1, 1))
    (1): ReLU ()
  )
  (deconv): ConvTranspose2d(64, 1, kernel_size=(4, 4), stride=(4, 4))
  (reward_conv): Sequential (
    (0): Conv2d(64, 64, kernel_size=(3, 3), stride=(1, 1))
    (1): MaxPool2d (size=(2, 2), stride=(2, 2), dilation=(1, 1))
    (2): ReLU ()
    (3): Conv2d(64, 64, kernel_size=(3, 3), stride=(1, 1))
    (4): MaxPool2d (size=(2, 2), stride=(2, 2), dilation=(1, 1))
    (5): ReLU ()
  )
  (reward_fc): Sequential (
    (0): Linear (576 -> 128)
    (1): ReLU ()
    (2): Linear (128 -> 1)
  )
)
Best loss updated: inf -> 1.7988e-02
Best loss updated: 1.7988e-02 -> 1.1621e-02
Best loss updated: 1.1621e-02 -> 9.8923e-03
Best loss updated: 9.8923e-03 -> 8.6424e-03
...
```

In 100k training iterations, the loss stopped decreasing and the EM model with the smallest loss could be used for final training of the I2A model.

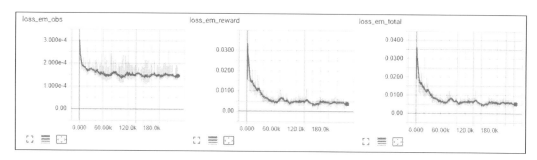

Figure 6: EM training

Training with the I2A model

The imagination path comes with significant computation cost, which is proportional
to the amount of rollout steps performed. I've experimented with several values for
this hyperparameter and for Breakout there is not much difference between five and
three steps, but the speed is almost two-times faster.

```
Chapter17$ ./03_i2a.py --cuda --em res/best/02_env_larger-
batch\=64/best_6.9029e-04_106904.dat -n tt
I2A (
  (conv): Sequential (
    (0): Conv2d(2, 32, kernel_size=(8, 8), stride=(4, 4))
    (1): ReLU ()
    (2): Conv2d(32, 64, kernel_size=(4, 4), stride=(2, 2))
    (3): ReLU ()
    (4): Conv2d(64, 64, kernel_size=(3, 3), stride=(1, 1))
    (5): ReLU ()
  )
  (fc): Sequential (
    (0): Linear (4160 -> 512)
    (1): ReLU ()
  )
  (policy): Linear (512 -> 4)
  (value): Linear (512 -> 1)
  (encoder): RolloutEncoder (
    (conv): Sequential (
      (0): Conv2d(1, 32, kernel_size=(8, 8), stride=(4, 4))
      (1): ReLU ()
      (2): Conv2d(32, 64, kernel_size=(4, 4), stride=(2, 2))
      (3): ReLU ()
      (4): Conv2d(64, 64, kernel_size=(3, 3), stride=(1, 1))
      (5): ReLU ()
    )
    (rnn): LSTM(3137, 256)
  )
)
2: done 1 episodes, mean_reward=0.00, best_reward=0.00, speed=6.41 f/s
4: done 12 episodes, mean_reward=0.00, best_reward=0.00, speed=90.84 f/s
7: done 1 episodes, mean_reward=0.00, best_reward=0.00, speed=69.94 f/s
...
```

In 200k training steps, I2A was able to reach the mean reward of 400 on test, which shows better dynamics than the baseline. The maximum test reward on three full episodes was 750, which is also better than the 650 obtained by the baseline.

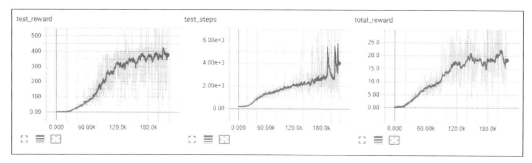

Figure 7: I2A convergence (rewards and steps)

The chart with test reward for both I2A (blue) and baseline A2C (orange) is shown in the following diagram:

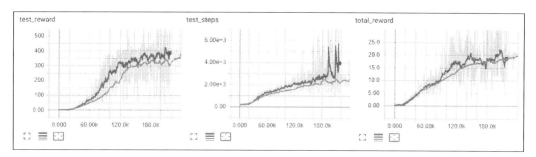

Figure 8: I2A compared with the baseline A2C

I also ran an experiment with a single step in the rollout and, surprisingly, the training dynamics between one step and three steps weren't much different, which may be a sign that in Breakout, the agent doesn't need to imagine the trajectory for too long to get the benefits from the EM. This is appealing, as with a single step we don't need rollout policy at all (as the first step is always performed on all actions) and an RNN is also not needed, which can significantly speed up the agent, pushing its performance close to the baseline A2C.

Summary

In this chapter, we discussed the model-based approach to RL and implemented one of the recent research architectures from DeepMind, which augments the model of the environment into the model-free agents. This model tries to join both model-free and model-based paths into one, to allow the agent to decide which knowledge to use.

In the upcoming chapter (which will be the last in the book), we'll take a look at a recent DeepMind breakthrough in the area of full-information games: the AlphaGo Zero algorithm.

References

1. *Reinforcement Learning with Unsupervised Auxiliary Tasks* by *Max Jaderberg, Volodymyr Mnih*, and others, (arXiv:1611.05397)

2. *Imagination-Augmented Agents for Deep Reinforcement Learning* by *Theophane Weber, Sebastien Racantiere*, and others, (arXiv:1707.06203)

18

AlphaGo Zero

In the last chapter of the book, we'll continue our discussion about the model-based methods and check the cases when we have a model of the environment, but this environment is being used by two competing parties. This situation is very familiar in board games, where the rules of the game are fixed and the full position is observable, but we have an opponent who has a primary goal of preventing us from winning the game.

Recently, DeepMind proposed a very elegant approach to such problems, when no prior domain knowledge is required, but the agent improves its policy only via self-play. This method is called **AlphaGo Zero,** and it will be the main focus of the chapter, as we implement the method for playing the game, *Connect4*.

Board games

Most board games provide a setup that is different from an arcade scenario. The Atari game suite assumes that one player is making decisions in some environment with complex dynamics. By generalizing and learning from the outcome of their actions, the player improves their skills, increasing the final score.

In a board games setup, the rules of the game are usually quite simple and compact. What makes the game complicated is the amount of different positions on the board and the presence of an opponent with an unknown strategy, who tries to beat us in the game. The ability to observe the game state and explicit rules opens up the possibility to analyze the current position, which wasn't the case for Atari. The analysis means taking the current state of the game and evaluating all the possible moves that we can take, then choosing the best move as our action.

The simplest approach to evaluation is to iterate over the possible actions and recursively evaluate the position after the action is taken. Eventually, this process will lead us to the final position, when no more moves are possible. By propagating the game result back, we can estimate the expected value of any action in any position. One possible variation of this method is called **minimax**, which is when we are trying to make the strongest move, but our opponent is trying to take the worst move for us, so we are iteratively minimizing and maximizing the final game objective of walking down the tree of game states (which will be described in detail later).

If the amount of different positions is small enough to be analyzed entirely, like in the *TicTacToe* game (which has only 138 terminal states), it's not a problem to walk down this game tree from any state that we have and figure out what's the best move to take.

Unfortunately, this brute-force approach doesn't work even for medium-complexity games, as the number of configurations grows exponentially. For example, in the game of *draughts* (also known as *checkers*), the total game tree has $5*10^{20}$ nodes, which is quite a challenge even for modern hardware. In the case of more complex games, like *chess* or *Go*, this number is much larger, so it's just not possible to analyze all the positions reachable from every state. To handle this, usually some kind of approximation is used, when we analyze the tree up to some depth. With a combination of careful search stop criteria, called **tree pruning**, and the smart predefined evaluation of positions, we can make a computer program that plays complex games at a fairly good level.

In late 2017, DeepMind published an article in the journal *Nature*, presenting the novel approach called AlphaGo Zero, which was able to achieve a superhuman level of play in complex games, like *Go* and *chess*, without any prior knowledge except the game rules. The agent was able to improve its policy by constantly playing against itself and reflecting on the outcomes. No large game databases, handmade features, or pretrained models were needed. Another nice property of the method is its simplicity and elegance.

In the example of this chapter, we'll try to understand and implement this approach for the game *Connect4* (also known as *four in a row* or *four in a line*), to evaluate it ourselves.

The AlphaGo Zero method

Overview

At a high level, the method consists of three components, all of which will be explained in detail later, so don't worry if something is not completely clear from this section:

- We traverse constantly the game tree, using the **Monte-Carlo Tree Search (MCTS)** algorithm, the core idea of which is to semi-randomly walk down the game states, expanding them and gathering statistics about the frequency of moves and underlying game outcomes. As the game tree is huge, both in terms of the depth and width, we're not trying to build the full tree, just randomly sampling the most promising paths of it (that's the source of the method's name).

- At every moment, we have a *best player*, which is the model used to generate the data via the self-play. Initially, this model has random weights, so it makes the moves randomly, like a four-year-old just learning how *chess* pieces move. However, over time, we'll replace this best player with better variations of it, which will generate more and more meaningful and sophisticated game scenarios. Self-play means that the same *current best* model is being used on both sides of the board. This might look not very useful, as having the same model play against itself has an approximately 50% chance outcome, but that's actually what we need: samples of the games where our best model can demonstrate its best skills. The analogy is simple: it's usually not very interesting to watch the match between the outsider and the leader. The leader will win easily. What is much more fun and intriguing to see is when players of roughly equal level are competing. That's why the final in any championship attracts much more attention than the preceding matches: both teams or players in the final usually excel in the game, so they will need to play their best game to win.

- The third component in the method is the training process of the other *apprenticeship* model, which is being trained on the data gathered by the best model during the self-play. It could be compared to a kid sitting and constantly analyzing the *chess* parties played by two grown-ups. Periodically, we play several matches between this trained model and our current best model, and in case the trainee is able to beat the best model in a significant amount of games, we announce the trained model as the new best and the process continues.

Despite the simplicity and even naivety of this, AlphaGo Zero was able to beat all the previous AlphaGo versions and became the best Go player in the world, without any prior knowledge except the game rules. After the paper called *Mastering the Game of Go Without Human Knowledge* [1] was published, DeepMind adapted the same method to fit *chess* and published the paper called *Mastering Chess and Shogi by Self-Play with a General Reinforcement Learning Algorithm* [2], where the model trained from scratch beat the Stockfish, which was the best *chess* program and took more than a decade of human experts to develop.

Now let's check all three components of the method in detail.

Monte-Carlo Tree Search

To understand what MCTS does, let's consider a simple subtree of the *TicTacToe* game, as shown in the following diagram. In the beginning, the game field is empty and the cross needs to choose where to move. There are nine different options for the first move, so our root state has nine different branches leading to the corresponding states.

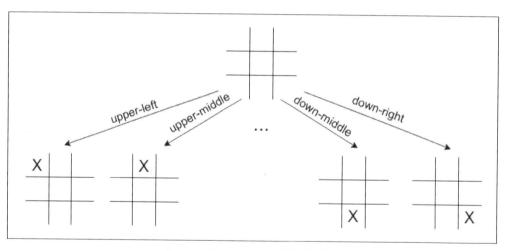

Figure 1: The game tree of TicTacToe

The amount of possible actions at some particular game state is called the **branching factor**, showing the bushiness of the game tree. Of course, this is not constant and may vary, as some moves are not always doable. In the case of *TicTacToe*, the amount of available actions could vary from nine at the beginning of the game, to zero at the leaf nodes. The branching factor allows us to estimate how quickly the game tree grows, as every available action leads to another set of actions that could be taken.

For our example, after the cross has made their move, the nought has eight alternatives at every nine positions, which makes 9*8 total positions at the second level of the tree. The total amount of nodes in the tree can be up to 9! = 362880, but the actual number is less, as not all the games could be played to the maximum depth.

TicTacToe is tiny, but if we consider larger games, and think about the count of the first moves that the white could make at the beginning of a *chess* game (which is 20) or the number of spots that the white stone could be placed at in *Go* (361 in total for a 19 × 19 game field), the amount of game positions in the complete tree quickly becomes enormous, as with every new level, the amount of states gets multiplied by an average amount of actions that we can perform on the previous level.

To deal with this combinatorial explosion, random sampling comes into play. In general MCTS, we're performing many iterations of depth-first search, starting at the current game state and either selecting the actions randomly or with some strategy, which should include enough randomness in its decisions. Every search is continued until the end state of the game, then it is followed by updating the weights of the visited tree branches according to the game's outcome. This process is similar to the value iteration method, when we played the episodes and the final step of the episode influenced the value estimation of all the previous steps. This is a general MCTS and there are lots of variants of this method, related to expansion strategy, branch selection policy, and other details.

In AlphaGo Zero, a variant of the MCTS is used. For every edge (representing the move from some position), this set of statistics is being stored: a prior probability $P(s, a)$ of the edge, a visit count $N(s, a)$, and an action-value $Q(s, a)$. Each search starts from the root state following the most promising actions, selected using the utility value $U(s, a)$, proportional to $Q(s,a) + \frac{P(s,a)}{1+N(s,a)}$. Randomness is added to the selection process to ensure enough exploration of the game tree. Every search could end up with two outcomes: the end state of the game is reached or we've faced the state that hasn't been explored yet (in other words, has no statistics for values). In the latter case, the policy **Neural Network (NN)** is used to obtain the prior probabilities and the value of state estimation and the new tree node with $N(s, a) = 0$, $P(s, a) = p_{net}$ (which is a probability of the move returned by the network) and $Q(s, a) = 0$ is created. Besides the prior probability of the actions, the network returns the estimation of the game's outcome (or value of the state) as seen from the current player.

As we've obtained the value (by reaching the final game state or by expanding the node using the NN), the process called the *backup of value* is performed. During the process, we traverse the game path from bottom to the root and update statistics of every visited intermediate node, in particular, the visit count $N(s, a)$ is incremented by one and $Q(s, a)$ is updated to include the game outcome from the current state perspective. As two players are exchanging moves, the final game outcome is changing the sign in every backup step.

This search process is performed several times (in AlphaGo's case, one-to-two thousand searches are performed), gathering enough statistics about the action to use the $N(s, a)$ counter as an action probability to be taken in the root node.

Self-play

In AlphaGo Zero, the NN is used to approximate the prior probabilities of the actions and evaluate the position, which is very similar to the **Actor-Critic (A2C)** two-headed setup. On the input of the network, we pass the current game position (augmented with several previous positions) and return two values. The policy head returns the probability distribution over the actions and the value head estimates the game outcome as seen from the player's perspective. This value is undiscounted, as moves in *Go* are deterministic. Of course, if you have stochasticity in the game, like in backgammon, some discounting should be used.

As has already been described, we're maintaining the *current best* network, which constantly self-plays to gather the training data for our *apprentice network*. Every step in each self-play game starts with several MCTS from the current position, to gather enough statistics about the game subtree, which are used to select the best action. The concrete selection depends on the move and our settings. For self-play games, which are supposed to produce enough variance in the training data, the first moves are selected in a stochastic way. However, after some amount of steps (which is a hyperparameter in the method), action selection becomes deterministic and we select the action with the largest visit counter $N(s, a)$. In evaluation games (when we're checking the network being trained versus the current best model), all steps are deterministic and selected solely on the largest visit counter.

Once the self-play game has been finished and the final outcome has become known, every step of the game is added to the training dataset, which is a list of tuples (s_t, π_t, r_t), where s_t is the game state, π_t is the action probabilities calculated from MCTS sampling, and r_t is the game's outcome from the perspective of the player at step t.

Training and evaluation

The self-play process between two clones of the current best network provides us with the stream of the training data, consisting of states, action probabilities, and position values obtained from the self-play games. With this at hand, our training is simple: we sample minibatches from the replay buffer of training examples and minimize the **Mean Squared Error (MSE)** between the value head prediction and actual position value, as well as cross-entropy loss between predicted probabilities and sampled probabilities π.

As mentioned earlier, once in several training steps, the evaluation of the trained network is performed, which consists of playing several games between the current best and trained networks. Once the trained network become significantly better than the current best network, we copy the trained network into the best network and continue the process.

Connect4 bot

To see the method in action, let's implement AlphaGo Zero for *Connect4*. The game is for two players with fields 6 × 7. Players have disks of two different colors, which they drop in turn to any of the seven columns. Disks fall to the bottom, stacking vertically. The game objective is to be the first to form a horizontal, vertical or diagonal group of four disks of the same color. Two game situations are shown in the diagram. On the first, the red player has just won, while on the second, the blue player is going to form a group.

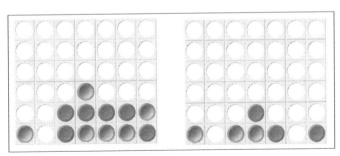

Figure 2: Two game positions in Connect4

Despite the simplicity, this game has $4.5*10^{12}$ different game states, which is challenging for computers to solve with brute force. This example consists of several tools and library modules:

- `Chapter18/lib/game.py`: Low-level game representation, which contains functions to make moves, encode and decode the game state, and other game-related utilities.

- `Chapter18/lib/mcts.py`: MCTS implementation that allows GPU-expansion of leaves and node backup. The central class here is also responsible for keeping the game node statistics, which are reused between the searches.

- `Chapter18/lib/model.py`: The NN and other model-related functions, such as the conversion between game states and model's input and the playing of a single game.

- `Chapter18/train.py`: The main training utility that glues everything together and produces the model checkpoints of the new best networks.

- `Chapter18/play.py`: The tool to organize the automated tournament between the model checkpoints. This accepts several model files and plays the given amount of games against each other to form a leaderboard

- `Chapter18/telegram-bot.py`: The bot for the Telegram chat platform that allows the user to play against any model file keeping the statistics. This bot was used for human verification of the example's results.

Game model

The whole approach is based on our ability to predict the outcome of our actions, so in other words we need to be able to get the resulting game state after we execute some particular game move. This is a much stronger requirement than we've had in Atari environments and Gym in general, where you cannot specify any current state that you want to act from. So, we need a model of the game that encapsulates the game's rules and dynamics. Luckily, most board games have a simple and compact set of rules, which makes the model implementation a straightforward task.

In our case, the full game state of *Connect4* is represented by the state of the 6 × 7 game field cells and the indicator of who is going to move. What is important for our example is to make the game state representation occupy as little memory as possible, but still allow it to work efficiently. The memory requirement is dictated by the necessity of storing large amounts of game states during the MCTS. As our game tree is huge, the more nodes we are able to keep during MCTS, the better our final approximation of move probabilities will be, so, potentially, we'd like to be able to keep millions, or maybe even billions of game states in the memory.

With this in hand, the compactness of the game state representation could have a huge impact on memory requirements and the performance of our training process. However, the game state representation has to be convenient to work with, for example, checking the board for a winning position, making a move and finding all the valid moves from some state.

To keep this balance, in `Chapter18/lib/game.py`, two representations of the game field were implemented. The first *encoded* form is very memory-efficient and takes only 63 bits to encode the full field, which makes it extremely fast and lightweight as it fits in a machine world on 64-bit architectures. Another *decoded* game field representation has the form of a list, with length seven, where every entry is a list of integers and keeps the disks in a particular column. This form takes much more memory, but is more convenient to work with.

I'm not going show the full code of `Chapter18/lib/game.py`, but if you need it, it's available in the repo. Here, let's just take a look at the list of the constants and functions that it provides:

```
GAME_ROWS = 6
GAME_COLS = 7
BITS_IN_LEN = 3
PLAYER_BLACK = 1
PLAYER_WHITE = 0
COUNT_TO_WIN = 4
INITIAL_STATE = encode_lists([[]] * GAME_COLS)
```

The first two constants in the preceding code define the dimensionality of the game field and are used everywhere in the code, so you can try to change them and experiment with a larger or smaller game. The `BITS_IN_LEN` value is used in state encoding functions and specifies how many bits are used to encode the height of the column (amount of disks present). In the 6 × 7 game, we could have up to six disks in every column, so three bits is enough to keep values from zero to seven. If you change the number of rows, you will need to adjust `BITS_IN_LEN` accordingly.

The `PLAYER_BLACK` and `PLAYER_WHITE` values define the values used in the *decoded* game representation and, finally, `COUNT_TO_WIN` sets the length of the group that needs to be formed to win the game. So, in theory, you can try to experiment with the code and train the agent for, say, five-in-a-row on a 20 × 40 field by just changing four numbers in `game.py`.

The INITIAL_STATE value contains the *encoded* representation for an initial game state, which has GAME_COLS empty lists. The rest of the code is functions. Some of them are used internally, but some make an interface of the game used everywhere in the example. Let's list them quickly:

- encode_lists(state_lists): Converts from *decoded* to *encoded* representation of the game state. The argument has to be a list of GAME_COLS lists, with the contents of the column specified in the bottom-to-top order. In other words, to drop a new disk on the top of the stack, we just need to append it to the corresponding list. The result of the function is an integer with 63 bits representing the game state.

- decode_binary(state_int): Converts from the integer representation of the field back into the list form.

- possible_moves(state_int): Returns the list with indices of columns which could be moved from the given encoded game state. The columns are numbered from zero to six, left to right.

- move(state_int, col, player): The central function of the file, which provides game dynamics combined with a win/lose check. In arguments, it accepts the game state in the encoded form, the column to place the disk in and the index of the player which moves. The column index has to be valid (be present in the result of possible_moves(state_int)), otherwise the exception will be raised. The function returns a tuple with two elements: a new game state in the encoded form after the move has been performed and a Boolean indicating the move leading to the win of the player. As a player can win only after their move, a single Boolean is enough. Of course, there is a chance of getting a draw state (when nobody won, but there are no possible moves remaining). Such situations have to be checked by calling the possible_moves function after the move() function.

- render(state_int): Returns a list of strings, representing the field's state. This function is used in the Telegram bot to send the field state to the user.

Implementing MCTS

MCTS is implemented in Chapter18/lib/mcts.py and represented by a single class MCTS, which is responsible for performing a batch of MCTS search and keeping the statistics gathered during it. The code is not very large, but still has several tricky pieces, so let's check it in detail.

```
class MCTS:
    def __init__(self, c_puct=1.0):
        self.c_puct = c_puct
        # count of visits, state_int -> [N(s, a)]
```

```
        self.visit_count = {}
        # total value of the state's action,
        # state_int -> [W(s, a)]
        self.value = {}
        # average value of actions, state_int -> [Q(s, a)]
        self.value_avg = {}
        # prior probability of actions, state_int -> [P(s,a)]
        self.probs = {}
```

The constructor has no arguments except the `c_puct` constant, which is used in the node selection process and mentioned in the original AlphaGo Zero paper [1] as *could be tweaked to increase exploration*, but I'm not redefining it anywhere and haven't experimented with it. The body of the constructor creates an empty container to keep statistics about the states. The key in all of those dicts is the encoded game state (an integer) and values are lists, keeping the various parameters of actions that we have. The comments above every container have the same notations of values as in the AlphaGo Zero paper.

```
    def clear(self):
        self.visit_count.clear()
        self.value.clear()
        self.value_avg.clear()
        self.probs.clear()
```

The preceding method clears the state without destroying the MCTS object, which happens when we switch *the current best* model to the new one and the gathered statistics become obsolete.

```
    def find_leaf(self, state_int, player):
        """
        Traverse the tree until the end of game or leaf node
        :param state_int: root node state
        :param player: player to move
        :return: tuple of (value, leaf_state,
        player, states, actions)
        1. value: None if leaf node, otherwise equals
        to the game outcome for the player at leaf
        2. leaf_state: state_int of the last state
        3. player: player at the leaf node
        4. states: list of states traversed
        5. actions: list of actions taken
        """
        states = []
        actions = []
        cur_state = state_int
        cur_player = player
        value = None
```

This method is used during the search to perform one single traversal of the game tree, starting from the root node given by the `state_int` argument and keeping walking down until one of these two situations has been faced: we reach the final game state or a yet unexplored leaf has been found. During the search, we keep track of the visited states and the executed actions to be able to update the nodes' statistics later.

```
while not self.is_leaf(cur_state):
    states.append(cur_state)

    counts = self.visit_count[cur_state]
    total_sqrt = m.sqrt(sum(counts))
    probs = self.probs[cur_state]
    values_avg = self.value_avg[cur_state]
```

Every iteration of the loop processes the game state that we're currently at. For this state, we extract the statistics that we need to make the decision about the action.

```
if cur_state == state_int:
    noises = np.random.dirichlet([0.03] *
                                 game.GAME_COLS)
    probs = [0.75 * prob + 0.25 * noise for prob,
             noise in zip(probs, noises)]
score = [value + self.c_puct * prob * total_sqrt /
         (1 + count)
         for value, prob, count in zip(values_avg,
                                       probs, counts)]
```

The decision about the action is taken based on the `action` utility, which is a sum between $Q(s, a)$ and the prior probabilities scaled to the visit count. The root node of the search process has an extra noise added to the probabilities to improve the exploration of the search process. As we perform MCTS from different game states along the self-play trajectories, this extra noise ensures that we've tried different actions along the path.

```
invalid_actions = set(range(game.GAME_COLS)) -
                      set(game.possible_moves(cur_state))
for invalid in invalid_actions:
    score[invalid] = -np.inf
action = int(np.argmax(score))
actions.append(action)
```

As we have calculated the score for the actions, we need to mask out invalid actions for the state (for example, when the column is full, we cannot place another disk on the top). After that, the action with the maximum score is selected and recorded.

```
cur_state, won = game.move(cur_state, action,
                           cur_player)
if won:
    # if somebody won the game, the value of the final
    # state is -1 (as it is on opponent's turn)
    value = -1.0
cur_player = 1-cur_player
# check for the draw
if value is None and len(game.possible_moves(cur_state))
== 0:
    value = 0.0

return value, cur_state, cur_player, states, actions
```

To finish the loop, we ask our game engine to make the move, returning the new state and the indication of whether the player won the game. The final game states (win, lose, or draw) are never added to the MCTS statistics, so they will always be leaf nodes. The function returns the game's value for the leaf player (or None if the final state hasn't been reached), the current player at the leaf state, the list of states we've visited during the search, and the list of the actions taken.

```
def is_leaf(self, state_int):
    return state_int not in self.probs

def search_batch(self, count, batch_size, state_int, player,
            net, device="cpu"):
    for _ in range(count):
        self.search_minibatch(batch_size, state_int, player,
                    net, device)
```

The main entry point to the MCTS class is the search_batch() function, which performs several batches of searches. Every search consists of finding the leaf of the tree, optionally expanding the leaf and doing backup. The main bottleneck here is the expand operation, which requires the NN to be used to get the prior probabilities of the actions and the estimated game value. To make this expansion more efficient, we use minibatches, when we search for several leaves, but then perform expansion in one single NN execution. This approach has one disadvantage: as several MCTS searches are performed in one batch, we don't get the same outcome as the execution of them serially.

Indeed, initially, when we have no nodes stored in the MCTS class, our first search expands the root node, the second will expand some of its child nodes, and so on. However, one single batch of searches can expand only one root node in the beginning. Of course, later, individual searches in the batch could follow the different game paths and expand more, but in the beginning, minibatch expansion is much less efficient in terms of exploration than sequential MCTS.

To compensate for this, I still use minibatches, but perform several of them.

```
def search_minibatch(self, count, state_int, player, net,
                     device="cpu"):
    backup_queue = []
    expand_states = []
    expand_players = []
    expand_queue = []
    planned = set()
    for _ in range(count):
        value, leaf_state, leaf_player, states, actions =
        self.find_leaf(state_int, player)
        if value is not None:
            backup_queue.append((value, states, actions))
        else:
            if leaf_state not in planned:
                planned.add(leaf_state)
                leaf_state_lists =
                game.decode_binary(leaf_state)
                expand_states.append(leaf_state_lists)
                expand_players.append(leaf_player)
                expand_queue.append((leaf_state, states,
                                     actions))
```

In minibatch search, we first perform the leaf search starting from the same state. If the search has found a final game state (in that case, the returned value will not be equal to None), no expansion is required and we save the result for a backup operation. Otherwise, we store the leaf for later expansion.

```
    if expand_queue:
        batch_v = model.state_lists_to_batch(expand_states,
                expand_players, device)
        logits_v, values_v = net(batch_v)
        probs_v = F.softmax(logits_v, dim=1)
        values = values_v.data.cpu().numpy()[:, 0]
        probs = probs_v.data.cpu().numpy()
```

To expand, we convert the states into the form required by the model (there is a special function in the `model.py` library) and ask our network to return prior probabilities and values for the batch of states. We'll use those probabilities to create nodes, and the values will be backed up on a final statistics update.

```
# create the nodes
for (leaf_state, states, actions), value, prob in
        zip(expand_queue, values, probs):
    self.visit_count[leaf_state] = [0] *
                                game.GAME_COLS
    self.value[leaf_state] = [0.0] * game.GAME_COLS
    self.value_avg[leaf_state] = [0.0] *
                                game.GAME_COLS
    self.probs[leaf_state] = prob
    backup_queue.append((value, states, actions))
```

Node creation is just storing zeros for every action in the visit count and action values (total and average). In prior probabilities, we store values obtained from the network.

```
for value, states, actions in backup_queue:
    # leaf state is not stored in states and
    # actions, so the value of the leaf will be
    # the value of the opponent
    cur_value = -value
    for state_int, action in zip(states[::-1],
                                actions[::-1]):
        self.visit_count[state_int][action] += 1
        self.value[state_int][action] += cur_value
        self.value_avg[state_int][action] =
            self.value[state_int][action] /
            self.visit_count[state_int][action]
        cur_value = -cur_value
```

The backup operation is the core process in MCTS, which updates the statistics for a state visited during the search. The visit count of the taken actions is incremented, the total values are just summed, and the average values are normalized using visit counts. It's very important to properly track the value of the game during the backup, as we have two opponents, and at every turn, the value changes the sign (as a winning position for the current player is a losing game state for the opponent).

```
def get_policy_value(self, state_int, tau=1):
    """
    Extract policy and action-values by the state
    :param state_int: state of the board
    :return: (probs, values)
```

```
    """
    counts = self.visit_count[state_int]
    if tau == 0:
        probs = [0.0] * game.GAME_COLS
        probs[np.argmax(counts)] = 1.0
    else:
        counts = [count ** (1.0 / tau) for count in counts]
        total = sum(counts)
        probs = [count / total for count in counts]
    values = self.value_avg[state_int]
    return probs, values
```

The final function in the class returns the probability of actions and the action values for the game state, using the statistics gathered during MCTS. There are two modes of probability calculation, specified by the τ parameter. If it equals to zero, the selection becomes deterministic, as we select the most frequently visited action. In other cases, the distribution given by $\frac{N(s,a)^{\frac{1}{\tau}}}{\sum_k N(s,k)^{\frac{1}{\tau}}}$ is used, which, again, improves exploration.

Model

The NN used is a residual convolution net with six layers, which is a simplified version of the network used in the original AlphaGo Zero method. On the input, we pass the encoded game state, which consists of two 6 × 7 channels. The first has 1.0 places with the current player's disks and the second channel has 1.0, where the opponent has their disks. This representation allows us to make the network player invariant and analyze the position from the perspective of the current player.

The network consists of the common body with residual convolution filters. The features produced by them are passed to the policy and the value heads, which are the combination of a convolution layer and a fully connected layer. The policy head returns the logits for every possible action (which are the column to drop the disk) and a single-value float. The details are available in the `Chapter18/lib/model.py` file.

Besides the model, this file contains two functions: the first, with the `state_lists_to_batch` name, converts the batch of game states represented in lists into the model's input form. The second method has the `play_game` name and is very important for both the training and testing processes. Its purpose is to simulate the game between two NNs, performing MCTS and optionally storing the taken moves in a replay buffer.

```
def play_game(mcts_stores, replay_buffer, net1, net2,
              steps_before_tau_0, mcts_searches, mcts_batch_size,
              net1_plays_first=None, device="cpu"):
    if mcts_stores is None:
```

```
    mcts_stores = [mcts.MCTS(), mcts.MCTS()]
elif isinstance(mcts_stores, mcts.MCTS):
    mcts_stores = [mcts_stores, mcts_stores]
```

The function accepts lots of parameters:

- The MCTS class instance, which could be a single instance or the list of two instances or None. We need to be flexible there to cover different usages of this function.

- An optional replay buffer.

- NNs to be used during the game.

- The amount of game steps needed to be taken before the τ parameter used for the action probability calculation will be changed from 1 to 0.

- The amount of MCTS to perform.

- The MCTS batch size.

- Who plays first.

```
state = game.INITIAL_STATE
nets = [net1, net2]
if net1_plays_first is None:
    cur_player = np.random.choice(2)
else:
    cur_player = 0 if net1_plays_first else 1
step = 0
tau = 1 if steps_before_tau_0 > 0 else 0
game_history = []
```

Before the game loop, we initialize the game state and make a selection of the first player. If there was no information given about who will make the first move, it is chosen randomly.

```
result = None
net1_result = None

while result is None:
    mcts_stores[cur_player].search_batch(mcts_searches,
                                         mcts_batch_size,
                                         state, cur_player,
                                         nets[cur_player],
                                         device=device)
    probs, _ = mcts_stores[cur_player].get_policy_value(
                                                    state,
                                                    tau=tau)
    game_history.append((state, cur_player, probs))
    action = np.random.choice(game.GAME_COLS, p=probs)
```

At every turn, we perform MCTS to populate the statistics and then obtain the probability of actions, which will be sampled to get the action.

```
state, won = game.move(state, action, cur_player)
if won:
    result = 1
    net1_result = 1 if cur_player == 0 else -1
    break
cur_player = 1-cur_player
# check the draw case
if len(game.possible_moves(state)) == 0:
    result = 0
    net1_result = 0
    break
step += 1
if step >= steps_before_tau_0:
    tau = 0
```

Then, the game state is updated using the function in the game engine module and the handling of end-of-game situations is performed.

```
if replay_buffer is not None:
    for state, cur_player, probs in reversed(game_history):
        replay_buffer.append((state, cur_player, probs,
                              result))
        result = -result

    return net1_result, step
```

At the end of the function, we populate the replay buffer with probabilities for the action and the game result from the perspective of the current player. This data will be used to train the network.

Training

With all those functions in hand, the training process is a simple combination of them in the correct order. The training program is available in `Chapter18/train.py`, and it has logic which has already been described: in the loop, our current best model constantly plays against itself, saving the steps in the replay buffer. Another network is being trained on this data, minimizing the cross entropy between the probabilities of actions sampled from MCTS and the result of the policy head. MSE between the value head predictions, about the game and the actual game result, is also added to the total loss.

Periodically, the network being trained and the current best network play 100 matches, and if the current network is able to win in more than 60% of them, the network's weights are synced. This process continues infinitely, hopefully, finding models that are more and more proficient in the game.

Testing and comparison

During the training process, the model's weights are saved every time the current best model is replaced with the trained model. As a result, we get multiple agents of various strength. In theory, the skills of the later models should be better than preceding ones, but we'd like to check it ourselves.

To do this, there is a tool, `Chapter18/play.py`, which takes several model files and plays a tournament when every model plays a specified number of rounds with all others. The result table, with the number of wins achieved by every model, will represent the relative model's strength.

Another way of checking the performance of resulting agents is by playing them against humans. This has been done by me, my kids (thanks Julia and Fedor!), and my friends, who played several matches against the selected models of various strength. This has been done using the bot written for Telegram messenger, which allows the user to select the model to play against and keeps the global score table for all plays. The bot is available in `Chapter18/telegram-bot.py` and has the same requirements and installation process as the bot from *Chapter 12, Chatbots Training with RL* (to get it up and running, you need a Telegram bot token to be created and placed in the config file).

Connect4 results

To make the training fast, the hyperparameters of the training process were intentionally chosen to be small. For example, at every step of the self-play process, only 10 MCTS were performed, each with a minibatch size of eight. This, in combination with efficient minibatch MCTS and the fast game engine, made training very fast. Basically, after just one hour of training and 2,500 games played in the self-play mode, the produced model was sophisticated enough to be enjoyable to play against. Of course, the level of its play was well below even a kid's level, but it showed some rudimentary strategies and made mistakes in only every other move, which was good progress.

The training was left running for a day, which resulted in 55k games played by a best model and, in total, 102 best model rotations. The training dynamics are shown in the following charts:

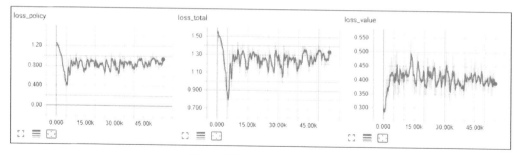

Figure 3: Training convergence

The tournament verification was complicated by the number of different models, as several games needed to be played by each pair to estimate their strength. To handle this, all 102 models where separated in 10 groups (sorted by time), next 100 games were played between all pairs in each group, and then two favorites from each group were selected for a final round. The chart with the scores obtained by the systems in the final is shown here. The x axis is the model's index, while the y axis is the amount of wins that the system achieved:

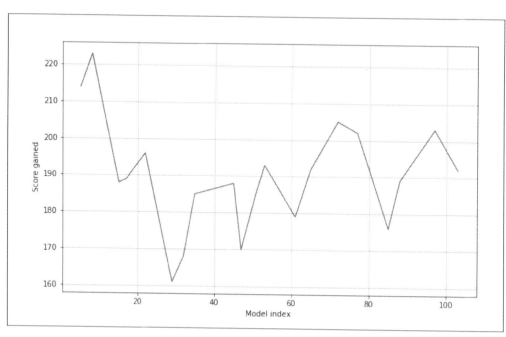

Figure 4: Results of the tournament between the trained agents

From the preceding chart, it is obvious that the system found the best strategy very early, but later, for some reason, degraded significantly. The system slowly started to recover, but the process was too slow. Probably, the hyperparameters (especially the amount of MCTS and size of the replay buffer) could be tuned to improve the result. Also, the fact that subsequent models have a worse gameplay might be a sign that more games are required during the evaluation of the trained network.

The top-10 final leaderboard is shown here:

1. best_008_02500.dat: w=223, l=157, d=0

2. best_005_01900.dat: w=214, l=166, d=0

3. best_072_40500.dat: w=205, l=174, d=1

4. best_097_52100.dat: w=203, l=177, d=0

5. best_077_42600.dat: w=202, l=178, d=0

6. best_022_12200.dat: w=196, l=184, d=0

7. best_053_31000.dat: w=193, l=187, d=0

8. best_065_36600.dat: w=192, l=188, d=0

9. best_103_55700.dat: w=192, l=188, d=0

10. best_017_09800.dat: w=189, l=191, d=0

Similar results were obtained from the human verification, when the best results were shown by the best_008_02500.dat model, which was able to win 50% of the played games.

Figure 5: The leaderboard of human verification; my daughter is dominating

Summary

In this chapter, we implemented the AlphaGo Zero method, created by DeepMind to solve board games with perfect information. The primary point of this method is to allow agents to improve their strength via self-play, only without any prior knowledge from human games or other data sources.

References

1. *Mastering the Game of Go Without Human Knowledge*, David Silver, Julian Schrittwieser, Karen Simonyan, and others, *doi:10.1038/nature24270*

2. *Mastering Chess and Shogi by Self-Play with a General Reinforcement Learning Algorithm*, David Silver, Thomas Hubert, Julian Schrittwieser, and others, *arXiv:1712.01815*

Book summary

My congratulations on reaching the end of the book! I hope that the book was useful and you enjoyed reading it as much as I enjoyed gathering material and writing all the chapters. As a final word, I'd like to wish you good luck in this exciting and dynamic area of RL. The domain is developing very rapidly, but with an understanding of the basics, it becomes much simpler for you to keep track of the new developments and research in this field.

There are lots of very interesting topics left uncovered, such as partially observable MDPs (where environment observations don't fulfill the Markov property) or recent approaches to exploration, such as the count-based methods. There is a lot of recent activity around multi-agent methods, where many agents need to learn how to coordinate to solve a common problem. We also haven't mentioned the memory-based RL approach, where your agent can maintain some sort of a memory to keep its knowledge and experience. Lots of efforts are put into increasing the RL sample efficiency, which will ideally be close to human learning performance, which is still a far-reaching goal at the moment. Of course, it is not possible to cover the full domain in a small book, because new ideas appear almost every day. However, the goal of the book was to give you a practical foundation in the field, simplifying your own learning of the common methods.

Finally, I'd like to quote Volodymir Mnih's words from his talk, *Recent Advances and Frontiers in Deep RL*, on the Deep RL Bootcamp 2017: "The field of deep RL is very new and everything is still exciting. Literally, nothing is solved yet!"

Other Books You May Enjoy

If you enjoyed this book, you may be interested in these other books by Packt:

Python Machine Learning - Second Edition

Sebastian Raschka, Vahid Mirjalili

ISBN: 978-1-78712-593-3

- ▶ Understand the key frameworks in data science, machine learning, and deep learning
- ▶ Harness the power of the latest Python open source libraries in machine learning
- ▶ Master machine learning techniques using challenging real-world data
- ▶ Master deep neural network implementation using the TensorFlow library
- ▶ Ask new questions of your data through machine learning models and neural networks
- ▶ Learn the mechanics of classification algorithms to implement the best tool for the job
- ▶ Predict continuous target outcomes using regression analysis
- ▶ Uncover hidden patterns and structures in data with clustering
- ▶ Delve deeper into textual and social media data using sentiment analysis

Deep Learning with TensorFlow - Second Edition

Giancarlo Zaccone, Md. Rezaul Karim

ISBN: 978-1-78883-110-9

- ▸ Apply deep machine intelligence and GPU computing with TensorFlow

- ▸ Access public datasets and use TensorFlow to load, process, and transform the data

- ▸ Discover how to use the high-level TensorFlow API to build more powerful applications

- ▸ Use deep learning for scalable object detection and mobile computing

- ▸ Train machines quickly to learn from data by exploring reinforcement learning techniques

- ▸ Explore active areas of deep learning research and applications

Python Interviews

Mike Driscoll

ISBN: 978-1-78839-908-1

- How successful programmers think
- The history of Python
- Insights into the minds of the Python core team
- Trends in Python programming

Leave a review - let other readers know what you think

Please share your thoughts on this book with others by leaving a review on the site that you bought it from. If you purchased the book from Amazon, please leave us an honest review on this book's Amazon page. This is vital so that other potential readers can see and use your unbiased opinion to make purchasing decisions, we can understand what our customers think about our products, and our authors can see your feedback on the title that they have worked with Packt to create. It will only take a few minutes of your time, but is valuable to other potential customers, our authors, and Packt. Thank you!

Index

C

candlestick chart 219
CartPole variance 265-267
categorical DQN
  about 195-197
  implementing 197-205
  results 205-207
chatbot example
  about 316
  BLEU score 318
  cornell.py file 317
  cross-entropy method 326-330
  data, checking 332-334
  data.py file 318
  model 319-326
  results 344
  SCST training 336-343
  SCST training, running 343
  structure 316-317
  Telegram bot 345-348
  trained model 334-336
  training code 330-332
  utils.py module 319
chatbots
  entertainment human-mimicking 316
  goal-oriented 316
  overview 303-305
Connect4 bot
  about 497, 498
  comparison 509
  game model 498-500
  MCTS implementation 500-506
  model 506-507
  results 509-511
  testing 509
  training process 508
continuous space
  need for 399
convolution model 237-239
Cornell Movie-Dialogs Corpus
  reference 316
correlation 283-284
**Covariance Matrix Adaptation Evolution
    Strategy (CMA-ES) 445**

cross-entropy
  on CartPole 81-89
  on FrozenLake 90-94
  theoretical background 95, 96
curriculum learning 312
custom layers 60-63

D

data 218
decoder 309
**deep deterministic policy gradients
    (DDPG) 411**
deep GA 461
Deep Learning (DL) 28
DeepMind Control Suite 426
deep NLP basics
  about 305
  embeddings 307-308
  Encoder-Decoder 309
  RNNs 306
deep Q-learning
  about 125-126
  correlation, between steps 128
  interaction, with environment 127
  Markov property 129
  SGD optimization 128
deep Q-network (DQN) method 399
deterministic policy gradients
  about 410-411
  exploration 411-412
  implementation 412-417
  results 417
  videos, recording 418
Dilbert Reward Process (DRP) 17
distributional policy gradients
  about 419
  architecture 419
  implementation 420-424
  results 425
Docker
  reference 357
double DQN
  about 172
  implementing 173-176
  results 176, 177

I

I2A model
training with 487, 488
I2A, on Atari Breakout
about 473
baseline A2C agent 474
EM training 475-478
imagination agent 478
implementing 478-481
rollout encoder 482, 483
training process 483
imagination-augmented agent
about 470, 471
environment model 472
paper results 473
rollout encoder 473
rollout policy 472
imagination path 471
independent Gaussian noise 178

K

KaiTai binary parser language
reference 383
key decisions 219, 220
Kullback-Leibler (KL) divergence 256, 314

L

loss functions
about 63
nn.BCELoss 63
nn.CrossEntropyLoss 64
nn.MSELoss 63
nn.NLLLoss 64

M

machine learning (ML) 304
Markov chain 12
Markov decision process (MDP) 19, 22
Markov process 12-15
Markov property 12, 129
Markov reward process 16-19
mean squared error (MSE) 478, 497
minimax 492

Mini World of Bits (MiniWoB)
benchmark 353, 354
model-based approach
model imperfections 469
versus, model-free approach 467, 468
models
about 229
convolutional model 230
Monitor 43-46
Monte-Carlo Tree Search (MCTS) 493
MuJoCo
about 401
URL 401
multiprocessing
in Python 288

N

natural language 303, 304
neural network (NN)
about 221, 495
building blocks 59
noisy networks
about 178
implementing 179-181
results 182-184
notebook gradients 56
novelty search
about 461
implementing 462
N-step DQN
about 168-170
implementing 170-172
NumPy 28

O

OpenAI
reference 30
OpenAI Gym API
about 30
action space 30
CartPole session 36-38
environment 33, 34
environment, creating 34-36
observation space 31-32

W

X

84659547R00304

Made in the USA
San Bernardino, CA
10 August 2018